# Why Congress

# Why Congress

PHILIP A. WALLACH

# OXFORD
## UNIVERSITY PRESS

Oxford University Press is a department of the University of Oxford. It furthers
the University's objective of excellence in research, scholarship, and education
by publishing worldwide. Oxford is a registered trade mark of Oxford University
Press in the UK and certain other countries.

Published in the United States of America by Oxford University Press
198 Madison Avenue, New York, NY 10016, United States of America.

Library of Congress Cataloging-in-Publication Data
Names: Wallach, Philip A., author.
Title: Why Congress / Philip A. Wallach.
Description: First Edition. | New York : Oxford University Press, [2023] |
Includes bibliographical references and index.
Identifiers: LCCN 2022053732 (print) | LCCN 2022053733 (ebook) |
ISBN 9780197657874 (Hardback) | ISBN 9780197657898 (epub) | ISBN 9780197657904
Subjects: LCSH: United States. Congress. | United States—Politics and government.
Classification: LCC JK1021 .W34 2023 (print) | LCC JK1021 (ebook) |
DDC 328.73—dc23/eng/20230123
LC record available at https://lccn.loc.gov/2022053732
LC ebook record available at https://lccn.loc.gov/2022053733

DOI: 10.1093/oso/9780197657874.001.0001

Printed by Sheridan Books, Inc., United States of America

*For my daughters, Bina, Ettie, and Fanya*

Boredom with established truths is a great enemy of free men. So there is some excuse in troubled times not to be clever and inventive in redefining things, or to pretend to academic unconcern or scientific detachment, but simply to try to make some old platitudes pregnant. . . . Politics, like Antaeus in the Greek myth, can remain perpetually young, strong, and lively so long as it can keep its feet firmly on the ground of Mother Earth.

—Bernard Crick, *In Defense of Politics* (1962)

# Contents

# Introduction

This book makes a simple argument: Americans disagree with each other. We have disparate interests, conflicting visions of the good, and divergent judgments about prudent policy. Nevertheless, we must find ways to accommodate each other in addressing the biggest problems of the day, and Congress is the place we must do it. Accordingly, Congress must be a place where many voices find ways to harmonize. Today, unfortunately, it is too often a place where exactly two discordant notes sound, over and over, with little concern for anything except which the American people will hate less at the next election. Our legislature's diminishment impairs our ability to make good policy. Even more importantly, it threatens the vitality of our politics, contributing to the pervasive sense that our nation is coming apart at the seams.

Many people seem to believe that Congress could not really be any different in our current political environment: America is polarized, so Congress is polarized. A few even talk themselves into believing that, given the state of our country, we have the best of all possible congresses, with legislators fairly reflecting widespread acrimony while still finding a way to keep things going. More common are those who want to meet congressional dysfunction by minimizing its harms or, better yet, mounting a major constitutional overhaul.

The long-running, well-documented trend of Americans sorting themselves into red and blue tribes has certainly played a role in Congress' transformation into an acrimonious, thin institution. But typical accounts drastically underestimate the importance of *ideas* about Congress and especially how our lawmakers conceive of their own roles in our constitutional system. Congress has not always been as it is now; indeed, as the first part of this book shows, it flourished in some of the last century's most difficult moments. Even today, if legislators want to make their institution more than a venue for the two parties to insult each other, they can reorganize it to make it so.

That is admittedly a big "if." Most of our most famous legislators today sought their offices precisely because they wanted to wage partisan combat on a bigger stage, and their idea of the institution arguably fits the reality today. An old distinction between "show horses" and "work horses" in Congress was no doubt meant to value the latter more highly, but the decline of committee work and regular order in the contemporary Congress makes it harder for the workers to accomplish much on behalf of their constituents or the nation as a whole. In part, this book is addressed to those frustrated work horses as a message of hope and a prod to action. Armed with the ambition to take hold of our problems and a willingness to disrupt stale political arrangements, they can make their chambers into the organs of self-government that our framers envisioned. Doing so would have the happy side effect of making their jobs much more meaningful and satisfying. Members of Congress should bridle at being reduced to "glorified telemarketers."[1]

Our dysfunctional politics invites many different explanations and prescriptions. Indeed, a cottage industry of academics and professional reformers spends its days trying to play physician to the American body politic. Some argue that our electoral institutions must change; some that our parties must be transformed; some that our nation's leaders must rise above the grubby realm of special interest politics and the perpetual chase after campaign dollars before anything can be fixed.

This book assumes, with James Madison, that while transcending a politics of interests may make for an enchanting vision, it is an unreliable and ultimately dangerous way to approach politics. Interests ought not to be villainized as "vested" or "special"—as "wicked demiurges" bent on frustrating the pure impulses of our democracy.[2] Nor should they be regarded as necessarily wholesome. *Nemo iudex in causa sua*, "No one should be a judge in his own case," endures as one of the most ancient and hallowed maxims of free societies for good reason.

Factions—whether they be interest based or tribal, ideological or religious—divide our society, and their divisiveness can seem noxious and intolerable. Yet our constitutional order demands that we actively and faithfully represent them in our politics. Why? As Madison says in Federalist No. 10, to suppress faction we might abolish liberty, but to do so would be as wrongheaded as wishing for the "annihilation of air . . . because it imparts to fire its destructive agency." To be a free, self-governing people is to commit to a political system that copes with our differences rather than seeking to suppress them. This work will not often be pretty, nor will it generally yield policies that economists or other specialists would design. But by representing and accommodating our factions, pluralistic politics gives us the means to work through problems peacefully.

Given our system's historical success, we often take for granted its preservation of social peace and free politics. We are tempted by seemingly loftier goals. But if our politics comes to be dominated by devotees of a few different "isms," it runs the risk of becoming disconnected from people's real interests, and we may misjudge what our fellow citizens require to remain committed to our shared national project. We should realize what a precarious achievement our constitutional order is, and how indispensable congressional representation is to maintaining it.

When Congress fails in its representative function, our constitutional system does not give us many other resources for keeping people together—presidential elections, which have come to dominate our political scene, are abominable for this purpose. When Congress works, its fluctuating coalitions act as engines of national cohesion, and our representatives are able to make regular adjustments to the demands of a changing world. A viable and functional politics is far more valuable to our social well-being than a few technocratically optimal policy choices ever could be.

This book takes no position on whether other nations' political systems can balance their societies' interests using mechanisms other than a powerful, thriving legislature. They may—though anxieties about "democratic deficits" across the developed world suggest that failures of representation are taking their toll on plenty of countries beyond our own. But the vitality of our own liberal, pluralist Constitution depends on Congress—which means that, whether we like it or not, much about our country's future depends on members of Congress.

Members should not imagine they will make their institution well loved. Asked in 1925 to reflect on his two decades in the House, Speaker of the House Nicholas Longworth (R-OH) replied:

> During the whole of that time we have been attacked, denounced, despised, hunted, harried, blamed, looked down upon, excoriated, and flayed. I refuse to take it personally. . . . From the beginning of the republic, it has been the duty of every free-born voter to look down upon us, and the duty of every free-born humorist to make jokes at us.

He went on to say that in the eyes of the press and the public Congress could do no right: legislate actively, it would be called "meddlesome"; fail to legislate, it would be called "incompetent" or "do-nothing." He concluded: "The only way for a Congressman to be happy is to realize he has no chance."[3]

Criticism of—and even contempt for—Congress is an entirely ordinary feature of American political life. Many people speak ill of our legislature today, but that is no special cause for concern. It is, indeed, a reliable feature of a free society.

More concerning is the extent to which the educated public, the chattering classes, and even legislators themselves have lost the ability to mount an affirmative defense of Congress as an indispensable pillar of our constitutional order. Ask a thoughtful citizen today what role our Congress plays in our public life, and you are likely to receive a witheringly cynical answer— something to the effect of, "Foul things up." One of the wisest people I know gave only a marginally more charitable answer: "Maybe Congress is optimally weak," such that for all of its problems it can't cause serious trouble. The title of one of the most widely read books about Congress written in the past decade, by my esteemed colleagues Tom Mann and Norm Ornstein, seems to say it all about the current state of the institution: *It's Even Worse Than It Looks.*

## Plan of the Book

To squarely confront this advanced state of doubt about our Constitution's first branch, this book answers the question "Why Congress?" from several directions. Most fundamentally: Why is a representative legislature important in the first place? When we face difficult problems, why should we turn for answers to nonspecialist legislators whose main talent is vote getting, instead of to experts? Why should we allow the president, who is elected by the whole country, to be thwarted so often by coalitions in Congress representing a minority of citizens?

Chapter 1 provides high-level answers to these questions by describing representation's critical role in our political order, which is quite distinct from the role of democracy. Following Madison's famous Federalist No. 10, it explains the promise of taming interests through structured competition and dialogue with each other. Congress is not perfect, nor does it solve problems with great efficiency. It is all too human. But Congress' shortcomings do not render it a constitutional liability. Rather, Congress' plural, representative nature makes it the only body in our system capable of setting our national priorities while respecting the diversity of our vast citizenry. Only congressional deliberation is capable of tackling the thorniest challenges in a way that the whole nation will accept as legitimate. In other words, while experts clearly surpass generalist legislators in solving well-defined problems, only through robust (and sometimes ugly) debates among legislators can we settle *which* problems our government will address and how we will approach our most intractable conflicts.

The chapter goes on to consider how the legislature's practical operations affect its ability to act as a genuinely representative assembly. Following the partisan career of Representative Madison in the House, it attends to the difficulties of organizing interest group competition without offering up the *res publica* to opportunistic predators or installing a permanent ruling clique. The chapter also charts the development of a rival school of American thought, articulated most influentially by Woodrow Wilson in his professorial days, which called for stronger political parties to tame factional competition and offer American voters a clear choice at the polls. It explains that Wilson, like Representative Madison before him, had good reason to worry that a chaotic legislative process could not maintain a reasonable balance of interests. However, his reform program, once generalized and yoked to the idea of a president as the nation's ideal, singular representative, opened the door to an era of stifling partisan orthodoxy. Stepping back, I offer a framework for thinking about the importance of legislative organization to the success of representative government, in which legislators must guard against the dangers of disorganized chaos on one side and overbearing centralized leadership on the other.

## The Wonders of a Working Congress

With this groundwork established, Part I of the book shows the value of congressional representation in action, turning its attention to two of the country's most difficult tests. In each, our collective historical imagination gives pride of place to presidential leadership, almost entirely missing out on our legislature's critical contributions.

Chapter 2 examines the little-considered role that Congress played during World War II. Congress did not devise America's winning military strategies nor closely manage the massive civilian operations that made the wartime production boom possible. It did not even bring the American people around to supporting the war—biased against American involvement in overseas conflict, its resolve solidified only after bombs fell on Pearl Harbor and ended the country's hopes of avoiding bloodshed.

What legislators did do, admirably, was distribute the massive burdens entailed by transforming the nation into a world-bestriding superpower, possessed of the mightiest navy and air force the world had ever known and providing much of its allies' war materiel. Whereas Britons were inspired to give their utmost by the specter of the London Blitz, and the Soviet people were fighting to eject a marauding invader from their homeland, the American people were insulated by two oceans from the worst of the carnage. Because they were "fighting this war on imagination alone," Americans, never an uncritical lot, did not quietly accept the rationing, price inflation, and massive tax increases imposed on them during the war. Nor, for all the admiration that many felt for their commander-in-chief, did they simply want Franklin D. Roosevelt to sort out these matters as he saw fit.

Instead, healthy wartime debates in Congress yielded reasonable and politically legitimate arrangements. Legislators also blocked the executive branch from becoming an unaccountable controller of the American economy after the war. Roosevelt is rightly remembered as the dominant presence in American politics during this time, but his influence over the home front was limited—precisely because he could not, as a single person, hope to fairly represent the multiplicity of interests struggling with the disruptions of war. The president sometimes leaned on Congress to balance these interests because of his keen sense of his own limitations. Other times, Congress, the presidency, and the burgeoning administrative state were antagonists, and the nation ultimately profited from the legislature's stubborn resistance against some of FDR's most ambitious plans for organizing the American economy.

Chapter 3 takes up Congress' role in the struggle for civil rights in the 1960s. To many 21st-century observers, Southern senators' use of the filibuster to frustrate progress on civil rights epitomizes our legislators' unwillingness to do the right thing even when a solid majority is united behind a righteous cause. President Lyndon Johnson's triumph over the segregationists seems an example to be emulated, proof that our country's narrow-minded bigots can be beaten if only a president musters courage, fortitude, and Machiavellian ruthlessness to transcend the limitations that Congress ordinarily imposes.

I argue that this conventional understanding completely misunderstands the role that Congress played in securing an effective and enduring change in federal law. Congress' structure, including but not limited to the tradition of the filibuster in the Senate, did allow segregationists to slow progress on civil rights, but it also promoted a virtuous competition between the two parties to see which could harness the momentum of the civil rights movement. Supermajority requirements ultimately called forth an irresistibly broad and bipartisan coalition that left the Southerners an isolated rump. Far from transcending the system that Congress imposed, civil rights advocates conformed their efforts to that system, and in doing so won over the hearts of many more of their fellow citizens than they originally thought possible.

Most importantly, by allowing Southerners the chance to use every parliamentary maneuver in the book in defense of their lost cause, congressional leaders enabled Southern representatives to accept the inevitability of their defeat and then tell their constituents to obey the new law of the land, however much they despised it. Southerners resented the Supreme Court's *Brown v. Board of Education* decision as an illegitimate imposition and rendered it effectively impotent. But their involvement in a functional, if painful and drawn-out, political process led them to react quite differently to the passage of the Civil Rights Act. Desegregation came off with surprisingly little social strife or violence. Southern racists were not run out of American politics; Congress' structure did not allow the victorious advocates of racial equality to erase the stain of racism from the nation's governing system, a great disappointment to those who believe the aim of politics should be moral purity. But Congress did secure a political compromise that has endured remarkably well over the past half century, through many cycles of partisan control. A lasting settlement on civil rights was won not by steamrolling or circumventing the congressional process, but by working through it.

## Congressional Transformation

The case for Congress established, Part II of the book grapples with the question of why our contemporary Congress became such a disappointment. The story is somewhat winding; several decades of institutional developments led up to the modern era of partisan enmity. Ideas about how Congress fit into the constitutional system were in flux, as were the practical techniques used to organize activity in both the House and Senate.

Notwithstanding their triumphs on civil rights and many other land-mark statutes in the second half of the 1960s, liberal reformers believed that Southern conservatives still held too much power by virtue of their seniority-guaranteed committee chairmanships. They set out to overhaul the organization of Congress, especially the House of Representatives. Chapter 4 chronicles the reforms they implemented in the 1970s, including the fragmentation of power into subcommittees and the radical expansion of legislative staff. It follows these developments into the post-Watergate pe-riod, when Congress determined to make itself more capable of checking the "imperial presidency" through measures including the War Powers Resolution, the Congressional Budget Act of 1974, scores of legislative vetoes, and the placement of new inspectors general embedded within ex-ecutive agencies.

While these reforms expanded legislative capacities and opened Congress to the public more directly than ever before, I argue that they neverthe-less failed to put Congress in a position to fulfill its core constitutional role. Instead of improving the institution's ability to grapple with the major issues of the day, congressional reforms drove Congress to an extreme of decentral-ization that spread members' attention thin. Subcommittees dedicated them-selves to oversight and meddled in the minutiae of administration, and they frequently ended up as the tools of well-organized interest groups. Congress had overcome the shortcomings of the clubby system that prevailed around 1960, but it was becoming a place that rewarded scandal mongering and posturing, in part because of new transparency rules that made backroom operating more difficult. Reform reinvigorated Congress but left it struggling for a sense of itself. A countervailing reform impulse toward centralization mostly failed to take root in the 1970s but laid the groundwork for later con-solidation of leadership power.

The Democratic reformers of the 1970s disagreed among themselves about many things, but they were nearly united in seeking to shut minority Republicans out of power. Conservatives during the Nixon and Ford years therefore turned toward the executive branch, abandoning an earlier tradi-tion that had emphasized a vital legislature as the bulwark of self-government and liberty. Despite Republicans' recapture of the Senate in 1980, this trend accelerated during the Reagan and Bush years. The Speakership of Jim Wright (D-TX), which began in 1987, featured intensification of partisan struggles and a loss of faith in bipartisan cooperation, and ended in scandal in 1989, represented a fateful inflection point for Congress.

Chapter 5 follows these developments and explains why Republicans, after decades in the minority, ended up nearly united in their hostility toward Congress, which they denounced as corrupted and preoccupied with harassing the president. Their resulting vision of Congress' place in the Constitution owed much to the Wilsonian strain of thinking, in which the most important thing legislators could do was offer Americans a clear choice between parties.

In 1994, Republicans' critical message helped them secure control of both chambers of Congress. They proceeded to overhaul the workings of the legislature, especially the House, implementing a vision of a more business-like institution run hierarchically by its central leadership. Such a Wilsonian model was not well suited to Congress' constitutional position, however, and the 104th Congress lacked both the votes and the legislative finesse to pass most of its ambitious agenda to shrink America's welfare state. Speaker of the House Newt Gingrich believed he had a sweeping mandate and attempted to shape his role into a kind of shadow presidency, with disastrous political consequences.

Chapter 6 considers Congress' ensuing development in the 21st century. Although Gingrich was rebuffed, his vision of a leader-dominated Congress geared toward partisan confrontation largely prevailed. Even the Senate belatedly followed this centralizing turn, with leaders of both parties working to shut down amendments and tightly control the agenda. In both chambers, free-flowing debate has been virtually banished, to the detriment of America's ability to deliberately resolve its most difficult problems.

The second half of the chapter offers a portrait of federal policymaking in the current protracted moment of intense partisan conflict. Our polarized Congress is often an impossibly gridlocked body, with filibustering having transformed from an attention-focusing, oratorical ordeal to a routine obstacle bereft of actual debate. When legislators fail to address important questions, policymaking migrates into the executive branch and judiciary, generally with serious limitations. But other dynamics exist in the current legislature too. Partisan majorities sometimes push legislation through, only to face legitimacy problems afterward.

Bipartisan majorities have not disappeared from the scene entirely. Indeed, in responding to the serious crises of the 21st century, erstwhile adversaries have shown an ability to pass ambitious legislation quickly. But, in contrast to the state-building period of the 1960s and '70s, Congress has not set the agenda or provided a forum for serious deliberation about these changes.

Instead, congressional leaders brokered deals and then demanded quick ratification from members, often creating a sense that policies with huge distri-
butional consequences were undertaken haphazardly or without taking the
public interest to heart.

## The Costs of Dysfunction

Part III of the book looks at two of the most daunting policy challenges of the
21st century, one a slow burn and the other a serious emergency, in each case
examining the costs entailed when Congress fails to work through difficult
problems.

Chapter 7 examines Congress' many failed attempts to arrange a grand
compromise on immigration and border control. Legislators have hardly
shrunk from the issue, making serious pushes for ambitious legislation in
four different congresses in the 21st century. In two of those instances, their
attempts at compromise had strong backing from congressional leaders. And
yet, despite clear indications that majorities of legislators favored some kind
of reform, Congress came up short each time. Skeptics of immigration, who
felt that the last big compromise on the issue in 1986 had played them for
fools, intransigently opposed any deal not centered around legal enforcement. Proponents of reform never found a way to win this group's trust.

Nor did they succeed in working around them. While the civil rights
movement broadened its coalition to win in the 1960s, champions of immigration reform instead turned their energies toward securing policy changes
through executive action. They had considerable success, with President
Barack Obama adopting two ambitious policies meant to enable millions of
illegal immigrants to study and work in the United States. But the difficulties
of those policies illustrate the shortcomings of circumventing Congress.
Acting by executive fiat may bring quick victories but only exacerbates political tensions. Festering political and legal opposition is likely to seriously
diminish the value of the policy gains. That does not remove the temptation,
however, which appeals to political actors on both ends of the political spectrum. Chapter 7 concludes with a brief examination of President Trump's
attempts to fund construction of the southern border wall without Congress'
cooperation.

If the struggle with immigration shows the ills flowing from a gridlocked
Congress, Congress' coronavirus response, considered in Chapter 8, shows

that congressional action without deliberation does not necessarily promote national cohesion. Surprising those who imagined it was completely moribund, Congress acted boldly at the outset of the coronavirus pandemic. Passing a flurry of bipartisan economic relief bills, legislators unleashed massive deficit spending unprecedented in peacetime. Americans' material standard of living remained steady through 2020, thanks primarily to Congress' bipartisan resolve.

But whereas the World War II–era Congress examined in Chapter 2 helped legitimate and democratize the nation's great struggle, the COVID Congress almost exclusively provided cash. The historic legislation they passed in March and April 2020 was accompanied by little meaningful public deliberation about the difficult tradeoffs that COVID-19 forced onto American society. As the acute phase of crisis response abated, lawmakers never seriously pursued broadly acceptable compromises on crucial issues such as lockdowns, testing, and vaccine regulations. Although Congress provided a second round of spending, COVID-19 mostly disappeared from the legislature's agenda even as it killed hundreds of thousands more Americans.

Expectations for Congress today are very low, and a widespread belief that public health experts were best suited to handle pandemic policy questions has led some to question whether legislators could have really done anything more. But legislators' deference to agencies such as the Centers for Disease Control and Prevention and the Food and Drug Administration was often unwarranted, as bureaucrats refused to depart from familiar routines to confront the fast-moving crisis. A more active legislature that took into account all manner of considerations, not only public health concerns, would have been better equipped to broker compromises backed by broad coalitions. Such work could have secured better policies and a less rancorous politics.

## Where Congress Goes from Here

Part IV turns to the question of where Congress goes from here, laying out three plausible paths in the decades to come. Three short chapters each begin with a dispatch from the future, in which a commentator from 2039— Congress' 250th birthday—reflects on the institution's place in American politics.

Chapter 9 lays out the first scenario, "Decrepitude," in which Congress' current dysfunctions worsen and reforms only marginally affect the system.

Simply keeping the government's lights on becomes a constant struggle, and the expectation that Congress will be a major player in the policymaking process (further) decays. American government develops new ways of working around its broken legislature, which is reduced to a peanut gallery of angry onlookers.

Chapter 10 lays out a second scenario, "Rubber Stamp," in which reformers frustrated with congressional inaction break through and make major changes, eliminating the filibuster, restricting amendments, and providing for automatic continuing resolutions whenever Congress fails to pass spending laws. Remote participation is embraced, allowing members to cast their votes from afar. Congress would, in this scenario of Wilsonian reform, become less of a nuisance to those who resent its ability to obstruct the president's program. But it would become little more than a venue for cheap talk, much like the legislature of an authoritarian country. Such chambers are not without their purposes, but they are in no way responsible for making their countries' most important decisions. Where, then, will meaningful deliberation about those central questions migrate? I suggest that the disquieting answer might be "social media" and explore what that would entail for America's already explosive political culture.

Chapter 11 lays out a final scenario, "Renewal," in which Congress rediscovers and recommits to its constitutional role as a pluralist, decentralized representative body responsible for deciding the major questions facing the country. Committees are restored to primacy through rule changes that ensure they can set the agenda, members put their constituents' policy needs ahead of their party leaders' calls for lockstep unity (perhaps in response to changes in candidate selection procedures), and floor debate is recovered as a means of actual persuasion. Congress offloads ministerial duties so it can focus on the weightiest issues—and by doing so, our representative legislature helps our country come to some meaningful accommodations on difficult issues such as immigration. This chapter includes a skeptical, though not dismissive, discussion of whether major structural changes, such as a significant expansion of the House of Representatives or a move toward different electoral rules, might restore Congress' vigor.

Most books about public policy conclude with a chapter suggesting reforms, and of course I favor those included in the "Renewal" scenario. But this book instead concludes with an open letter to members of Congress, entreating them to be their own deliverers. While some combination of the "Decrepitude" and "Rubber Stamp" scenarios currently looks likely, real change could come if factions of legislators decide that their policy ambitions are important enough to warrant disrupting the institutional status quo. Individual members of Congress will have to decide that being reduced to voting on command is beneath their constitutional dignity. In short, America's legislators, whose ambitions are supposed to make our system of separated powers function, will need to arm themselves with a confident answer to the book's title question. Congress' future is ultimately up to them.

# 1

# What Congress Alone Can Do

The more power is divided the more irresponsible it becomes.
—Woodrow Wilson, *Congressional Government* (1885)[1]

Nothing is more deceptive or more dangerous than the pretence of a desire to simplify government. The simplest governments are despotisms; the next simplest, limited monarchies; but all republics, all governments of law, must impose numerous limitations and qualifications of authority, and give many positive and many qualified rights. In other words, they must be subject to rule and regulation. This is the very essence of free political institutions. The spirit of liberty is, indeed, a bold and fearless spirit; but it is also a sharp-sighted spirit; it is a cautious, sagacious, discriminating, far-seeing intelligence; it is jealous of encroachment, jealous of power, jealous of man.... Neither does it satisfy itself with flashy and temporary resistance to illegal authority. Far otherwise. It seeks for duration and permanence. It looks before and after; and, building on the experience of ages which are past, it labors diligently for the benefit of ages to come. This is the nature of constitutional liberty; and this is *our* liberty, if we will rightly understand and preserve it.
—Sen. Daniel Webster, May 7, 1834[2]

Who should rule: one, few, or many? Ancient political philosophers were preoccupied by that question, fascinated by states' tendency to cycle from one answer to another. They were convinced that any of the forms could serve the common good, or abuse it.

For those of us living in modern democracies, the question would seem to be settled—"we the people" are sovereign, rejecting domination by any small group or single leader. The many will rule; that is the essence of our political order.

But unlike the citizens of an ancient Greek city-state, "we the people" cannot all fit into an arena or a town square. We cannot all deliberate together, let alone choose in some enormous collective act. To realize democracy in practice, we have to employ institutions in which relatively few people actively wield power on behalf of the whole country's common good. In short, we must rely on some system of representation to proceed with the work of government.

In constructing our representative institutions, we must make some momentous choices about how exactly the manyness of our democracy will be brought to life. Our first, naïve instinct might be to seek a representation that precisely corresponds to the full diversity of our society. But if we indulged that impulse, we would find ourselves in the position of the Cartographers' Guild in Borges' miniature story, who "struck a Map of the Empire whose size was that of the Empire, and which coincided point for point with it."[3] The opposite temptation is also potent. Perhaps all of that complexity can be somehow synthesized; perhaps we will find, at bottom, that we are not many but one. But as Aristotle said of Plato's *Republic*, "There is a point at which a *polis*, by advancing in unity, will cease to be a *polis*; there is another point, short of that, at which it may still remain a *polis*, but will none the less come near to losing its essence, and will thus be a worse *polis*. It is as if you were to turn harmony into mere unison, or to reduce a theme to a single beat. The truth is that the *polis* is an aggregate of many members."[4]

Once we realize the impossibility of one-to-one representation and the danger of all-to-one simplification, we have to decide where in our political system manyness and complexity will be allowed to enter and where they will be suppressed for the sake of tractability.

This chapter argues that in the American constitutional system, Congress is the place where our nation's diversity must be represented, where our many factions must be given the chance to bump against and accommodate each other. Our legislative chambers—the House of Representatives and the Senate—must each find a way to organize themselves to corral our nation's dizzying diversity of interests rather than be stampeded by them. At the same time, they must resist the urge to achieve consensus by means of suppressing or excluding dissenting voices. If they cannot do so, the very republican character of our government—the choice to have the many rule instead of the few—will be at risk.

In Federalist No. 10, James Madison famously argued that a pure democracy "can admit of no cure for the mischiefs of faction" but that an extended republic would enjoy "the greater security afforded by a greater variety of parties, against the event of any one party being able to outnumber and oppress the rest." In a well-formed Madisonian legislature, faction flourishes, but there is enough plurality of interests to prevent the dominance of any of them. Members faithfully represent the important interests of their constituents, without confusing their own self-interest with the common good.

And yet Madison acknowledged that there could be too many representatives, who would then be "unduly attached" to "local circumstances and lesser interests" and "too little fit to comprehend and pursue great and national objects."

Since at least the late 19th century, a line of critics has charged that this is precisely Congress' problem: it is dominated by little men, preoccupied by parochial interests because of their electoral bases and rarely able to work through their differences well enough to govern sensibly. The critics' proposed solutions generally seek to make Congress speak in a more unified voice, the better to streamline government. As Woodrow Wilson expressed in this chapter's epigraph, allowing too much multiplicity in Congress makes a muddle of American government, where no actor can ever be held accountable for the actions of the whole. In this way of thinking, society's complexity can and must be given its due during election campaigns, which, if well framed, can yield clear-cut political choices flowing into clear-cut governmental actions.

This critique of Congress—which I refer to as Wilsonian—has undeniable rhetorical force. Its preference for clean lines and simplicity seems logical, tidy, modern. Its charge that Congress in its current form is irredeemably flawed sometimes seems to be conventional wisdom today.

The messier Madisonian tradition it opposes, however, is better suited to coping with the complexity of life in our extended republic. Juxtaposed with Wilson's punchy slogan, Daniel Webster's winding defense of a more complicated political system may seem unwieldy. And yet Webster better captures the essence of our constitutional order and our American way of dealing with the problem of faction. Our representative system boasts many contrivances to make it more difficult for a bare majority to work its will cleanly. In the judgment of Wilsonians from the 1880s to the present, that leaves us out of step with the modern world. Perhaps the preference for polyphony was appropriate for the nation's early days, some Wilsonians concede, but those simpler times are gone, and we face too many challenges to put up with an inefficient government today.

If we consider Congress just one institution among many for policymaking, the Wilsonian question as to which is most efficient seems unavoidable—and we cannot deny that Congress comes out looking downright stupid. Legislators are selected by popularity contests, and many make fools of themselves. The laws they pass are byzantine and complicated, designed to take in "political" concerns rather than "practical" ones. And worst of all, as the title of a famous article puts it, "Congress Is a 'They,' Not an 'It.'"[5] *They* frequently fail to come to any agreement at all, even on matters of universally acknowledged importance. If what we want is good policy, what are we doing relying on these characters?!

Then too, if what we want is *democratic* direction of policymaking, is Congress really the best way of getting it? As contemporary commentators are very fond of reminding us, the manipulation of House district boundaries and small states' disproportionate influence in the Senate guarantee that neither of these bodies will exactly reflect the overall opinion of the electorate. Even worse, when our legislators spend many years in Washington, away from the constituents they represent, the experience almost invariably changes them, enlarging the gap between the representative and the people. Especially in the age of instantaneous communications, shouldn't we consider making more decisions by asking the people directly, through referenda or continuous opinion polling or some other means of online democracy? Can't we cut out all the middlemen?

These challenges should not be taken lightly. If Congress excels at neither efficiency nor democracy, why bother with it at all?

We can't hope to offer a persuasive answer without reference to the way representation uniquely binds a country together. Long before modern democratic ideas won acceptance, representation emerged as a force capable of legitimizing government. A brief digression into the beginnings of the English Parliament will help us to understand why representation is so fundamental to building a nation and making it capable of collective deliberation. From there, we can turn to the beginnings of Parliament's lineal descendant, Congress, and consider its distinctive virtues for building trust in a factious nation.

## The Origins of Our Representative Government

For a legislature to bring a nation together, its citizens must believe it is genuinely *representative*. What does that mean, exactly? The great political theorist

Hanna Fenichel Pitkin defined representation as "the making present *in some sense* of something which is nevertheless *not* present literally or in fact." She observed: "Now, to say that something is simultaneously both present and not present is to utter a paradox, and thus a fundamental dualism is built into the meaning of representation."[6] Representation is not a simple concept that can be boiled down to being a faithful messenger of known information; nor is it just about one person "being like" a group of others (what theorists call "descriptive representation"). "Representatives should be articulate rather than just typical," as Pitkin puts it.[7] To successfully represent a constituency, a member must be accepted as a legitimate spokesperson for the community. To successfully represent a whole nation, the assembly of members must find a way to transform the concerns of all their constituencies into a meaningful and authoritative proceeding.

Our modern perspective gives us a particular idea of how this will operate. Nearly all of us share certain democratic ideas about how elections should work, believe that our actual election procedures instantiate those principles tolerably well, and are prepared to abide by the results of elections, whatever they may be. But we should not think that representative government and democracy are the same thing. They are not. Indeed, representation and democracy are ideas somewhat in tension with each other, and historically it was representative government that emerged first in our nation's prehistory.[8]

The English Parliament, the ancestor of our Congress, was not established by a charter document like the US Constitution; it did not come to possess its legitimacy by an act of democratic ratification or even through obedience to a clear set of procedures. Magna Carta in 1215 did not create it, and in fact there is no decisive founding moment to single out as the institution evolved in the 13th and 14th centuries. It emerged not because of any principled commitment to representative government, let alone political empowerment of regular people, but because an institutionalized body provided a practical way of working through tensions between the king and his barons, whose consent and cooperation he needed to levy taxes.

In a writ summoning a parliament in 1295, Edward I wrote: "What touches all, should be approved of all, and it is also clear that common dangers should be met by measures agreed upon in common."[9] Was the king, known as "Longshanks," a proto-democrat seeking to understand and channel the will of his subjects? No, in his understanding, he was the sovereign and the men assembled in his parliament were there to aid him in governing wisely.[10] He and his nobles—all of whom spoke French as their first language at this point in English history—would "*parlez*," and a "parliament" was simply their discussion. Before consenting to the king's requests for funds (which they could, and sometimes did, refuse to do), this group could air all manner of grievances and effectively enter into negotiations with the monarch.

Edward found that he could turn these discussions to his advantage by bringing in a somewhat broader, more representative group of men including knights of the shire from counties. He also included burgesses from the towns, whose power came from expanding commerce and who made natural allies for a king offering them what amounted to a rudimentary rule of law and protection from the arbitrary predation of the barons—whom Edward rightly saw as rivals. In turn, since they were the ones with the money, the burgesses could support the monetization of feudal obligations as a way of increasing their own influence.

Eventually, the practice of including these "commoners" brought about the House of Commons—but, as the English historian A. F. Pollard explained a century ago, it is a mistake to imagine the House of Commons beginning as a self-aware mover of the English state. Instead, it arose as the knights and burgesses routinized the functions of countering the king's requests for funds (which came ever more frequently during the Hundred Years' War) with petitions for redress of grievances. "The common petition," Pollard observed, "required common deliberation, common action, and perhaps even a common clerk; the common action became a habit, the habit an institution, and the institution a house."[11] Physically convening the country's disparate factions and putting them into conversation with each other began development of a functional politics, something more than just an attempt to bend the king's ear.

This evolution, which accelerated during the 14th century, did not immediately produce a reliable system of government. Even as parliaments came to be the venue in which power struggles between the crown and magnates played out their final chapters, it was not a decisive force. As Winston Churchill put it, "Parliament was not the author, or even the powerful agent, in these changes, but only the apprehensive registrar of these results of martial and baronial struggles. . . . Parliament was but the tool and seal of any successful party in the State."[12]

The institutionalization of representation nevertheless had a profound effect. Pollard offered a searching analysis of what the emergence of Parliament—now becoming something properly worthy of a capital "P"— had accomplished:

The great service which parliaments rendered in the middle ages was not, in fact, to make England a constitutional state, but to foster its growth into a national state based on something broader and deeper than monarchical centralization, to make national unity a thing of the spirit rather than a territorial expression or a mechanical matter of administration, to evoke a common political consciousness at Westminster and then to propagate it in the constituencies. The value of parliaments consisted not so much in what members brought with them as what they took away.[13]

This began as an almost formulaic transaction in which the important thing was the representatives' legal power to confer the consent of their communities ("*plena potestas,*" as with the modern power of attorney). But as Parliament matured, the substance and weight of its deliberations came to elevate the representative body into an embodiment of the nation and its interests. In the 15th century, representatives were first referred to as "members" of Parliament—a word that before had meant a "limb" (usually, yes, that one) of a body.[14] The membership of Parliament reflected elements from all around the country; but just as importantly, representatives returned to their communities as full *members of the central body*, thereby forging a sense of centralized identity. Pollard put a rather fine point on it: "It is grotesque to speak of 'England' doing anything at all before parliaments appeared, because there was no 'England' capable of doing it."[15]

The body drew its legitimacy from its plurality, but as it flourished, it rendered the nation one. That equation may be nearly as inscrutable as the mystery of the trinity, and its sustainability depends on not pushing too hard on either side of it. As historian Edmund Morgan observed, there is a permanent tension between the idea that, once assembled, "the people" are fully embodied as a singular whole and the idea that the body is an assemblage of geographically anchored representatives. If representatives merely convey the parochial interests of their districts as messengers, the body is likely to lose its ability to bind together the whole. But if the body leans too heavily on its "national authoritarian" character, as the revolutionary Long Parliament did in the 17th century, it is likely to lose its credibility as an assemblage.

Contrary to our instincts about representative government, very little of this had anything to do with election by majorities of "voters." Some burgesses and knights of the shire were elected, but just as often they were selected by other local officeholders. When there were contested elections, they were decided by voice votes or shows of hands that bore little resemblance to modern balloting.[16] Representative government is an achievement distinct from democracy, and in our mother country's history, it was the representative system that played a decisive nation-building role. Representatives came together and argued as a single body, without discarding their communities' interests or distinctive views. In doing so, they forged a national sensibility—something kings could not achieve on their own.

Not until the 19th century would Britain seek to make a broad franchise and democratic elections the clear basis of Parliament's legitimacy. Even as Parliament's strength came to match and then surpass that of the monarch, its system of representation remained highly idiosyncratic. It nevertheless was widely accepted as a legitimate part of the English Constitution for centuries. But one group of Englishmen came to find their own representation in the system profoundly inadequate in the mid-18th century: Britain's American colonists.

## Representing Americans

For most of the 18th century, the powers-that-be in London treated their North American colonies with what Edmund Burke would later call "a wise and salutary neglect." By doing little to enforce British controls on trade over the colonists, the mother country allowed them to range widely and prosper, ultimately redounding to the benefit of English merchants who enjoyed a rapidly growing and increasingly prosperous market. After fighting the French and Indian War on American soil, however, Britain decided to reimpose itself and extract a reliable stream of revenues from its colonies, starting with the Stamp Act of 1765. The project was a colossal miscalculation and generated a backlash so massive that it led most of the colonies' leading lights to question the viability of their relationship with Britain. War broke out within a decade, and American independence was accomplished by 1783.

British policymakers' misjudgment of what the colonists would bear was a failure, first and foremost, of representation. "The American Revolution took place . . . not because people suddenly became super-sensitive to their rights, or—an even more unlikely theory—because they suddenly became nationalistic, but because the existing government broke down," wrote the (British) political theorist Bernard Crick. The central government did not *actually* represent what the colonists believed or cared about; and the "virtual" representation it was supposed to enjoy, with English members of Parliament meant to take up American concerns because of their common fundamental interests, was much too attenuated to properly register their growing alarm at the costs being imposed on them. Even Burke, who defended the idea of virtual representation against those who advocated for a tight electoral connection, thought that Americans' situation left them effectively unrepresented in London.[17] This failure left the government blind to what taxes Americans would tolerate. "Political representation is, then, a device of government before ever it can be sensibly viewed as a 'right' of the governed," Crick explained. "If it is not made use of, a government may not be able to govern at all."[18]

By the Americans' lights, the failure of representation had deep moral as well as practical importance. Deeply influenced by John Locke's rendition of natural rights and his emphasis on consent, North American political thinkers were deeply skeptical of all of the British Parliament's claims to sovereignty. Indeed, although they believed there were clear indications of a consensual relationship between colonial subjects and the king, they were skeptical that the representation enjoyed by Britons themselves was really legitimate given its reliance on implicit fictions rather than explicit consent.[19]

In a 1774 pamphlet, founding father James Wilson argued that the single most important protection of liberty in the British Constitution was the presence of representatives drawn from the body of the people: "The interest of the Representatives is the same with that of their constituents. Every measure, that is prejudicial to the nation, must be prejudicial to *them*, and their posterity. They cannot betray their electors, without, at the same time, injuring themselves."[20] The absence of American representatives at Westminster, and the fact that members of Parliament were not themselves subject to the laws made for the American colonies, deprived Americans of this crucial protection. Claims of "virtual representation" in Parliament were simply misdirection, concealing the lack not only of historical consent but also of *rational* consent, consistent with the protection of citizens' natural rights. Without real representation, Americans' rights and happiness were not effectively guaranteed; and since these were the proper end of government, Parliament was utterly without legitimate authority over them.

When Americans finally declared their independence, they pointedly declined to refer to Parliament at all. But again, their objections to "a long train of abuses and usurpations" revolved as much around their insufficient protection through representation as around their objections to particular policies. After all, they charged that the pattern of British actions "evinces a design to reduce them under absolute Despotism," which should have been impossible if their concerns were really represented.

To form a new national union capable of breaking away from the old empire, Americans' first instinct was to bring their representatives into congress with each other. Colonial assemblies had become the dominant force in American government over the course of the 18th century as they came to be understood as legitimate representations of colonists' full range of interests, in contrast to the royal governors and councils suspected of working on behalf of alien and oppressive elements. To create a new national sensibility would require a Continental Congress, the first of which was convened in 1774, the second from 1775 to 1781. (These assemblies' legitimacy did not depend on a standardized system of elections, as members were sometimes elected by the public, sometimes by colonial legislatures, and sometimes by the Committees of Correspondence that had organized opposition to the British.) When they deliberately designed a more elaborate constitution in the Articles of Confederation, its Congress, in which each state would cast one vote, was its central element.

These bodies were severely limited and ultimately inadequate for a durable national government—the Articles' unanimity requirements, in particular, compounded some of the problems of manyness. Still, their nation-building accomplishments, including setting the terms of settlement in the West, were considerable. Forrest McDonald's classic history of the 1780s, *E Pluribus Unum*, explains that as Americans went to war, the colonies became the United States by virtue of their cooperation in arms, their accumulation of a national debt to pay for the war, and their common representation in the Congress.[21] The colonies might easily have fallen to infighting during this difficult period, but they hung together—barely.

There were moments when dissolution looked immanent. When the Confederation Congress failed to find a way to pay soldiers' overdue wages, its members were more or less chased out of Philadelphia in June 1783. The frequent inability to produce a quorum in Congress as it met in Princeton, Annapolis, and Trenton from late 1783 until January 1785 symbolized the disunited condition of the states. The Confederation Congress sometimes seemed to be more a gathering of ambassadors from mutually suspicious allies than a representative, deliberative body capable of working through differences. Many observers thought that Shays' Rebellion in August 1786 portended disunion.

At this point, twelve of the thirteen states decided to send delegates to the Constitutional Convention in Philadelphia. They hoped to create a genuinely sovereign national government, powerful enough to make and enforce policy in service of the national good but representative enough to avoid the errors of the Parliament of the 1760s. Working out the operative representative principle was one of their central challenges, and in the Constitution they devised a necessarily complicated answer, adopting representation by population in the lower house and equal representation for states in the upper house to bridge the divide between large and small states. Just as importantly, this scheme divided "the people into various aspects or capacities of themselves," as McDonald put it. The representative government they devised was "of (that is, from) the people; hopefully, it would be for the people; but by no means would it be by the people."[22] Representative government, in which the manyness of America was represented in two different ways, would be the binding force of the new nation. "We the people," speaking in one voice, would ordain the Constitution as the foundational law, but, with the president elected through the elaborate mediating mechanism of the Electoral College, the people would not be directly instantiated anywhere in the new government.[23]

## The Challenges of Representation in Action—The Early Days of Party

The Constitution's defenders believed that its reliance on representation was not a second-best substitute for democracy but was actually a superior way of dealing with the country's problems and holding the new nation together. Noah Webster observed that when ancient democracies sought to give every one of their citizens a voice in legislating, that practice was "the cause of innumerable evils." For the Roman republic the assembly of the whole people was "a circumstance that exposed their government to frequent convulsions and to capricious measures." By providing a mediating body capable of containing interests and situating them in the context of a search for the common good, the modern invention of representation "seems to be the perfection of human government."[24] Writing as Publius, James Madison, too, emphasized the novelty of the American system. If Europeans could claim the discovery of representation as one element of government, "America can claim the merit of making the discovery the basis of unmixed and extensive republics."[25]

Madison's famous Federalist No. 10 explains the particular advantages of representative politics in an extended republic, where the sheer variety of interests would ensure no one group could dominate. America may only have had about four million people, but their economic and geographic concerns were incredibly diverse. Nor were they pulled together by any national transportation and communication infrastructure. In addition to geographically rooted concerns, Madison envisioned creditors and debtors, "the landed and the manufacturing classes," and different classes of potential taxpayers as factions likely to be set against each other. This was a complicated political scene, and Madison expected that only the free interplay of factions could hope to produce end results consonant with the public good. Wishing for "enlightened statesmen" to simply "adjust these clashing interests" was vain. The representatives of the different sections would have to have it out with each other.[26]

Madison was careful to caution that not every scheme of representing the extended republic's manifold factions could succeed. In Federalist No. 58, he warned that making representatives too numerous would, counterintuitively, reduce the number of "men who will in fact direct their proceedings." With too many representatives on hand, the assembly would begin to take on some of the characteristics of an unruly people, more likely to include "members of limited information and of weak capacities" who could be more easily swayed by "passion over reason." He went on:

> The people can never err more than in supposing that by multiplying their representatives beyond a certain limit, they strengthen the barrier against the government of a few. Experience will forever admonish them that, on the contrary, AFTER SECURING A SUFFICIENT NUMBER FOR THE PURPOSES OF SAFETY, OF LOCAL INFORMATION, AND OF DIFFUSIVE SYMPATHY WITH THE WHOLE SOCIETY, they will counteract their own views by every addition to their representatives. The countenance of the government may become more democratic, but the soul that animates it will be more oligarchic. The machine will be enlarged, but the fewer, and often the more secret, will be the springs by which its motions are directed.[27]

Beyond just the number of representatives, Madison's admonition may be applied to the character of representation more broadly. Not every kind of interface between the public and their representatives is conducive to the common good; manyness in representation must be carefully calibrated if it is to avoid becoming a veneer for the control of the self-interested few.

To the Constitution's critics, its system of representation was no worthy substitute for the kind of close-knit democratic deliberation possible in small communities. Instead, the far-flung federal system was almost certain to collapse into some form of oligarchy, with the central government a creature used to oppress the true people. The Anti-Federalist Richard Henry Lee, writing as Federal Farmer, argued that the scheme of representation it set out would necessarily privilege the views of the already powerful. To be truly representative, its members would need to be much more numerous and mirror the full range of the public, having "the same interests, feelings, opinions, and views the people themselves would were they all assembled." Meanwhile, as a result of convening representatives in a capital, "wealth, offices, and the benefits of government would collect in the centre."[28] George Mason, another opponent of the Constitution, insisted that in the new "House of Representatives there is not the substance, but the shadow only of representation; which can never produce proper information in the legislature, or inspire confidence in the people.—The laws will, therefore, be generally made by men little concerned in, and unacquainted with their effects and consequences." In other words, the very deficiency of representation that doomed British government in America would soon plague the new nation's home-grown legislature, and in fact Mason charged that what would start as a "moderate aristocracy" would quickly transform into "a monarchy, or a corrupt oppressive aristocracy."[29]

Such criticisms could, ultimately, only be answered in practice. When the First Congress began its work in the temporary capital city of New York on March 4, 1789, its legislators felt the weight of their responsibility; only they could give concrete forms to the generalities of the Constitution and show that it was capable of supporting an enlightened politics. As James Madison, now a representative of Virginia's Fifth District, cautioned his fellow members of the House, they would need to take special care since decisions "at this time made, will become the permanent exposition of the constitution."[30]

Congress' first days were not auspicious, as both chambers lacked quorums. But by April, once members from across the country had overcome the harsh winter and pitiful roads, enough assembled to do business, and these original 59 representatives and 22 senators agreed upon rules of procedure and administered their oaths of office. In the Senate, they decisively rejected a proposed amendment that would have guaranteed "the people" the right "to instruct their representatives," with many legislators insisting that "binding instructions were inconsistent with the very idea of a deliberative body."[31] Although their most famous work was the Bill of Rights, many legislators saw the "amendment problem" as a distraction. As Rep. John Vining of Delaware put it, "The people are waiting with anxiety for the operation of the Government. Have they passed a revenue law? Is not the daily revenue escaping us? Let us not perplex ourselves by introducing one weighty and important question after another, till some decisions are made."[32]

On a remarkable range of such concrete matters, the legislators got to work hashing out compromises. They instituted a tariff and created a system of customs collectors and port officials to enforce it, thereby creating a reliable source of revenue for the national government that the Congress of the Articles of Confederation never managed. Before long, they would add a tax on whiskey. They addressed the nation's war debts, structured the executive departments and federal courts, and established the first federal crimes and copyright laws. They worked through a thorny debate over the future location of the nation's capital, with the House's initial vote for a location on the Susquehanna abandoned in favor of the Senate's choice of one on the Potomac.[33]

If the First Congress showed the promise of the politics of the extended republic in action, the Second Congress began to show the challenges more clearly. Factions that had easily worked through their differences in the interest of successfully launching constitutional government were more inclined to develop deeper suspicions once underway. The most explosive fight was over the Bank of the United States, chartered by a February 1791 Act of Congress at the urging of Secretary of the Treasury Alexander Hamilton. The bank was to be Hamilton's tool for consolidating and rendering manageable the nation's debts, but before it even opened for business many began to worry that it would mostly function as a tool to enrich Northern debt speculators. Madison wrote to his friend and ally, Secretary of State Thomas Jefferson, that "stockjobbers" were becoming "the praetorian band of the government—at once its tool and its tyrant; bribed by its largesses, and overawing it, by clamors and combinations."[34] In other words, an organized and powerful faction was subverting the kind of open play of interests that Madison, in Federalist No. 10, had said would safeguard American self-government, and using federal power to pursue its own self-interest.

Madison and Jefferson believed that they needed to organize an opposition party—a Republican Party—capable of combating the pernicious influence of this small, predatory elite to preserve the genuine representativeness of Congress. In the words of Madison biographer Jay Cost, they "did not see their party as a faction, but rather the avatar of a broad majority, anchored on the general principles of self-government in pursuit of the common interest."[35] In his writings for the new party's newspaper of record, the *National Gazette*, Madison mounted a defense of a party built specifically to repel predation by the faction of Federalist financiers. The Federalists, he warned, were few in number but wily in action, and they would work "by corrupt influence, substituting the motive of private interest in place of public duty, converting its pecuniary dispensations into bounties to favorites, or bribes to opponents, accommodating its measures to the avidity of a part of the nation instead of the benefit of the whole." The Republicans, on the other hand, would bring together the rest of the country to overcome distinctions and, through shared reason, promote "a general harmony" on behalf of freedom and the broader public good.[36] Representative Madison had discovered the need for internal organization and even the beginnings of party institutions to organize the interplay of factions.

The drive to better organize congressional opposition to the executive branch sometimes led to institutional innovations that would endure beyond partisan conflict. In 1795, for example, the House permanently established its Ways and Means Committee as a counterweight against the Treasury Department's expertise, and other standing committees would soon follow.[37]

But partisan organization did not simply lift America's legislature into some happy realm of political moderation. Instead, partisan warfare between Federalists and Republicans intensified, and the 1790s became one of the nastiest periods of American political history. As the French Revolution's violence threw the perils of unrepresentative government into harsh relief, the two nascent parties, now further divided between Franco and Anglophiles, savaged and slandered each other in the most personal terms in competing partisan newspapers. Republicans characterized Federalists as "corrupt monarchists."[38] Federalists returned fire by charging the Republicans with inviting anarchy through reckless, vulgar demagoguery.[39] Each loudly proclaimed that the other was a dangerous faction threatening constitutional government.

By the time George Washington completed his second term as president in 1796, he believed this partisan competition might be deadly to American politics. In his widely published Farewell Address, he told his fellow countrymen they needed to treasure their representative system: "The independence and liberty you possess are the work of joint councils and joint efforts—of common dangers, sufferings, and successes." He then warned of efforts to

> organize faction, to give it an artificial and extraordinary force—to put in the place of the delegated will of the nation the will of a party; often a small but artful and enterprising minority of the community; and, according to the alternate triumphs of different parties, to make the public administration the mirror of the ill concerted and incongruous projects of faction, rather than the organ of consistent and wholesome plans digested by common councils and modified by mutual interests.[40]

Things got worse before they got better; the Federalist-dominated Fifth Congress would pass the Sedition Act of 1798, giving it the ability to criminally prosecute its opponents for their criticisms. Voters partially resolved the conflict through their widespread rejection of Federalists in the election of 1800, but when Madison was elected president in 1808, an explosive partisan environment again made governing difficult.[41]

My purpose here is not to enter into an extended discussion of legislative organization in the early republic. Instead, brief acquaintance with the experience of the early congresses can lead us to a generalizable point: too little organization can leave a representative body adrift, easy prey for opportunists; too much party organization, on the other hand, may serve to squelch the very give-and-take between factions that makes the whole arrangement fertile. Before building that insight out more systematically, let us consider another moment of congressional history in which dissatisfaction with the role of factions led to changes in organization.

## The Wilsonian Critique—Responsible Representation

Nearly a century after Madison aired his concerns about disorganization enabling factional predation, another observer of American government would charge Congress as beholden to avaricious interests. Woodrow Wilson, a doctoral student at the new Johns Hopkins University, offered up a cutting critique of the Congress of his day. But his argument would transcend the historical moment that had produced it, coming to be seen as a universal prescription for good government and ultimately a justification for profoundly rebalancing the American constitutional system away from Congress.

Wilson, born in Virginia and raised in Georgia, grew up in the shadow of his father, a minister who became a founder of the Presbyterian Church in the Confederate States of America. The son took from his father a famous moralistic streak, and when he looked out over the Congress of the 1880s, he did not like what he saw.

Henry Adams' novel *Democracy*, published anonymously in 1880, gives a sense of what Wilson encountered. The book, a smash hit, portrays a young society widow trying to find her way in a thoroughly corrupt capital dominated by Sen. Silas P. Ratcliffe, loosely based on Sen. James G. Blaine. Adams described his leadership:

> Ratcliffe was a great statesman. The smoothness of his manipulation was marvelous. No other man in politics, indeed no other man who had ever been in politics in this country, could—his admirers said—have brought together so many hostile interests and made so fantastic a combination. . . . The beauty of his work consisted in the skill with which he evaded questions of principle. As he wisely said, the issue now involved was not one of principle but of power. The fate of that noble party to which they all belonged, and which had a record that could never be forgotten, depended on their letting principle alone. Their principle must be the want of principles.[42]

Above all else, Ratcliffe and his retinue are concerned with federal positions, the glue that keeps their coalition together; they are aghast at the possibility of a new president coming in and taking from them "their honestly earned harvest of foreign missions and consulates, department-bureaus, customhouse and revenue offices, postmasterships, Indian agencies, and army and navy contracts."[43]

Wilson's more sober but equally successful analysis, *Congressional Government*, first published in 1885, touched on many of the same themes. Of American parties, he lamented, "They are like armies without officers, engaged upon a campaign which has no great cause at its back. Their names and traditions, not their hopes and policy, keep them together."[44]

His concern about the diffuseness of party coalitions was given tangible form in his concern about the predominance of committees, whose bills frequently received almost no scrutiny from the larger chambers before being passed into law. The most famous pronouncement in *Congressional Government*, still faithfully quoted as an accurate description in textbooks today, is: "It is not far from the truth to say that Congress in session is Congress on public exhibition, whilst Congress in its committee-rooms is Congress at work."[45] But Wilson's discussion here is not merely descriptive. He was seriously concerned that by moving the body's work to committee rooms, which were then totally closed off from the public, Congress effectively delegated "its deliberative functions to the Standing Committees."[46] He eloquently states his deepest worry:

> The practices of debate which prevail in its legislative assembly are manifestly of the utmost importance to a self-governing people; for that legislation which is not thoroughly discussed by the legislating body is practically done in a corner. It is impossible for Congress itself to do wisely what it does so hurriedly; and the constituencies cannot understand what Congress does not itself stop to consider.

Wilson's concerns here recall Madison's of the 1790s. Without the test of public debate and scrutiny, Congress was free to make policies that served factions rather than the common good, while neglecting the great issues of the day. Such an organization leads to low-quality policymaking and also serious legitimacy problems. Ordinary citizens will have little sense of how their own representatives fit into this swampy affair and little hope of calling them to account for anything that Congress does. Any group of citizens seeking reforms will be utterly disoriented. The sense of representativeness that the legislature depends on will be jeopardized.

In searching for a solution to this illegibility, Wilson looked enviously across the Atlantic at the energetic Liberal government of William Gladstone in the United Kingdom, which he saw as incomparably better able to formulate and then implement a coherent program. If America, too, had "responsible parties" headed by "a few authoritative leaders," then it, too, could have a structured political conflict that the majority of citizens could readily understand, even "those persons who can make something out of men but very little out of intangible generalizations."[47] This "responsible party government" would become the idée fixe of Wilsonian reformers down to the present.

What would happen to the "mischiefs of faction," Madison's central challenge for republican political life, in the system Wilson envisioned? In essence, parties would be responsible for taming factions on their own terms before offering up their syntheses for adjudication by voters.

Wilson was far from clear on how parties themselves could overcome factions, but he did fasten on party caucuses as one mechanism working to organize and clarify the politics of his day. By convening and seeking to work out some agenda acceptable to all, the caucus "is meant as an antidote to the Committees. It is designed to supply the cohesive principle which the multiplicity and mutual independence of the Committees so powerfully tend to destroy."[48] But, since the caucuses met entirely out of public view, they could not serve to make parties truly responsible to citizens. As Wilson saw it in the mid-1880s, the only real answer was much stronger congressional leadership working hand in glove with a copartisan president (even though divided government had prevailed as Wilson wrote his book). The fewness of leaders would then serve as corrective to the disorienting manyness of the people and their venal representatives.

In the years following *Congressional Government*'s first publication, the House of Representatives transformed itself in ways that were, to a remarkable degree, consistent with Wilson's wishes. Speaker of the House Thomas Brackett Reed (R-ME), first elected to that post in 1889, believed that "the best system is to have one party govern and the other party watch"—and he intended to keep the governing party united.[49] Reed ended the House minority's ability to obstruct the majority's business through the practice of the "disappearing quorum," in which members would refuse to register their presence and thereby render the body without a sufficient number to do its business. At Reed's instruction, in January 1890 the House clerk began to record members' presence whether they acknowledged a roll call or not; when members sought to leave the House chamber, Reed dramatically barred the doors.[50] Under "Czar Reed's" leadership, Republicans began to facilitate something very much like Wilson's responsible party government. Committees worked under the Speaker, not independently of him.

In the preface to the fifteenth printing of his book (probably the single most successful work of American political science ever) in 1900, Wilson approvingly noted how the House had changed over the past decade. "The country is beginning to know that the Speaker and the Committee on Rules must be held responsible in all ordinary seasons for the success or failure of the session, so far as the House is concerned," he observed. But, with the

Senate unreformed, this was not nearly enough to satisfy Wilson.[51] During his academic career as a professor at Wesleyan University and then Princeton University, he would forthrightly argue that the Constitution would have to be amended if Americans were to have any hope of truly responsible parties. Down to the present day, some Wilsonians have maintained that line.

Wilson's own arguments, however, evolved as the years went on. He came to advocate "responsible government under the Constitution," which would treat the existing constitutional order as malleable enough to be made workable, at least if strong leaders would make it so.[52] No longer focused on congressional leaders, Wilson came to think that the president was the only figure with sufficient stature to provide an organizing influence. To Wilson, the president's status as the only official elected by the whole body of the people would elevate his concerns over the parochial interests of legislators, forcing him to take responsibility for providing a coherent agenda.

In his 1908 *Constitutional Government in the United States*, Wilson proclaimed that the president's election by the whole nation made him the natural spokesperson for the general good. As he summed up:

> The President is at liberty, both in law and conscience, to be as big a man as he can. His capacity will set the limit; and if Congress be overborne by him, it will be no fault of the Constitution,—it will be from no lack of constitutional powers on its part, but only because the President has the nation behind him, and Congress has not.[53]

The change in Wilson's thinking is portentous. While his early critique of Congress focused on the inadequacy of the legislature's public deliberations and looked within the institution for the solution, his later president-centered writing seems to suppose that all the meaningful deliberation can and should happen away from Congress, in the great public sphere of party conventions and election campaigns. It was in the simple, grand choices of presidents that the American people could give direction to their political leaders; after that, it would be up to those leaders to preside over an energetic and efficient administration capable of delivering on the promises they had made. The extended republic's manyness could be tamed and transcended, with its faithful representation now seeming to confuse and complicate things rather than being crucial to the successful functioning of government. Congressional opposition to executive initiative would jeopardize the survival of the whole political organism, whose "life is dependent upon [its organs'] quick cooperation, their ready response to the commands of instinct or intelligence, their amicable community of purpose."[54]

Wilson had hardly invented the idea of the president as the nation's singular representative; the Constitution's structure creates obvious opportunities for the chief executive to present himself in this way, and presidents going back to Thomas Jefferson have done so.[55] But his and other progressives' suggestion that a singular president would better represent the nation's interests than a plural Congress would be particularly influential. As we shall see, the goal of unifying Congress in service of the president's agenda has recurred again and again in recent times.

*Change of circumstance*

## The Challenges of Representation in Action—The Vicissitudes of Congressional Organization

Speaker Reed's dominance may not have been strong enough for Wilson, but it came to distress many participants in American politics. One of Reed's successors as Speaker, Joseph Gurney "Boss" Cannon (R-IL) (depicted in Figure 1.1), personally chaired the Rules Committee and used its powers to shape the congressional agenda, ruthlessly shutting his rivals out of the legislative process. That included not only Democrats in the minority but also members of his own party who failed to support his version of party orthodoxy with sufficient zeal. "Inevitably, members knew they would be pleading on bended knee before the Speaker for favors to perpetuate themselves in office," complained Rep. George Norris (R-NE). "We are no less Republicans because we would be free members of Congress. We do not need to be kept on leading strings," said another member of Cannon's majority.[56]

Dissatisfaction with Cannon's tight control led to one of the seminal moments in congressional history: the 1910 overthrow of Cannon, in which Norris and 41 other progressive members of the majority joined with opposition Democrats to expel the Speaker from the Rules Committee and instead require the whole House to choose its membership. So ended Cannon's stranglehold on the congressional agenda.

This sequence of events here is worth dwelling on. Wilson formulated his desire for responsible party government during a time of extensive decentralization in Congress. Many others shared his concerns about a directionless institution at the mercy of special interests, and members of Congress themselves soon imposed order by consolidating power in the congressional

**Figure 1.1**  A 1908 political cartoon dramatizes Speaker Joseph Cannon's (R-IL) control of the House by depicting the body's members as his clones.
*Source:* Berryman Political Cartoon Collection, National Archives.

leadership. That arrangement, in turn, led some members to feel that their institution had become too dominated by a single way of thinking, which itself served a single set of interests to the exclusion of others. Republican orthodoxy circa 1910 was not broad or nimble enough to address all of the people's concerns during a time of rapid industrialization and urbanization; adherence to one man's conception of his party's program was a recipe for tyranny rather than "responsible" government. Addressing new problems would require a devolution of power back to the committee system that Wilson so resented. After Cannon's demotion, committee chairmen would be selected strictly by the longevity of their tenure, with the Speaker powerless to depose them.

Let us now abstract away from particulars to think about the ways in which congressional organization seeks to enable a system of representation that can discipline and benefit from factional conflict rather than becoming the tool of it.

To understand the vicissitudes of congressional organization, envision a pendulum, shown in Figure 1.2, with openness on one side and tight control on the other.[57] At either extreme, pathological conditions and factions become threatening. On the side of openness, too much manyness leads to an ineffectual scrum. In the ensuing cacophony, interests can opportunistically push policies that benefit themselves but are contrary to the public good. On the side of control, too much suppression of manyness leads to a stranglehold by one faction or alliance of factions. One voice predominates, which can facilitate the programmatic coherence for which Wilson pined but risks losing its genuinely representative character, fixing itself in pursuit of a crystallized ideology increasingly disconnected from facts on the ground. Attempts to

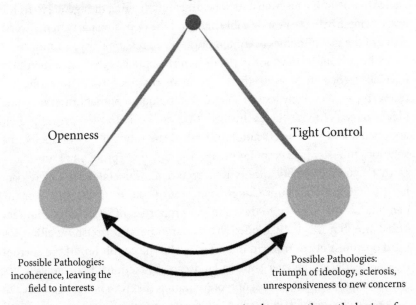

### The Pendulum of Congressional Organization

Openness

Tight Control

Possible Pathologies: incoherence, leaving the field to interests

Possible Pathologies: triumph of ideology, sclerosis, unresponsiveness to new concerns

**Figure 1.2** Congressional organization can swing between the pathologies of manyness and too much control.

alert the ruling clique of neglected concerns are treated as distractions, and the rule of the many begins to shade into the rule of the few.

These twin pathologies ought to be familiar to anyone who has sat through many meetings. If a meeting's presiding officer is determined to hear from all comers on every question, the session can stretch on interminably without ever reaching any decisions. On the other hand, if the leader has a preconceived agenda that he or she is determined to march through, the other participants may rightly feel that their presence was superfluous, even if from time to time they are expected to vote "aye."

Legislators themselves are likely to be keenly aware of the shortcomings of each extreme, and as a result they will push things toward some kind of balance. Attractive normative and practical arguments come easily to hand, since both openness and orderliness are appealing values. In pushing for openness, representatives can point to the importance of many-sided deliberation and connection with the complexity of the citizenry; they can criticize the neglect of an important concern; or they can simply point to the adverse effects of the dominant regime's politics and policies. In pushing for greater control, representatives can point to the dangers of incoherence, the importance of banding together in support of (their own party's) programmatic agenda to overcome obstruction, and the benefits of offering voters a clear choice in upcoming elections. As we will see, controlling the agenda to frame one's own party in the best possible light and the opposing party in the worst is one of the major themes of contemporary congressional organization.

An important feature of the pendulum metaphor is that once members have succeeded in pushing their legislative chamber away from one extreme, they are unlikely to find a natural stopping point that preserves some ideal balance of these values. Instead, they are likely to keep pressing their arguments and push the pendulum toward the other side. Eventually, the solutions to yesterday's pathology become tomorrow's problem to solve.

That dynamic quality means that arguments for congressional reform need to take into account Congress' current position in the swing of the pendulum—one can try to describe the properties of a desirable moment of balance, but it is folly to offer abstract arguments for pushing either toward openness or control without reference to the conditions of the current legislature. Given the ever-shifting landscape of factions in a changing society and the changing modes of representation (likely to be very sensitive to changes in communications technologies, among other factors), a functional organizational system will always be a moving target.

For some political observers, the efforts required in this Sisyphean quest to see faction adequately represented, but not overrepresented, seem exhausting and wasteful. Like the later Woodrow Wilson, they may begin to think that congressional parochialism—the plurality of representation that Congress embodies—is the foremost obstacle to sound government in America. Two of the most articulate and self-conscious modern Wilsonians, William Howell and Terry Moe, declare: "The path to effective government requires moving Congress from the front seat of legislative policymaking to the back seat, where its pathologies can do less damage."[58] To their way of thinking, presidents with big ideas are the only political actors with the chance to represent the real, transcendent interests of the American people. Congressional reform should make our legislature less burdensome, which (they implicitly suggest) will also free us from the constraints of factional politics. If we embrace singular leadership corrected by episodic and clarifying national elections, we will reap the benefits of clear vision; if we stubbornly persist in adhering to our decentralized and minority-protecting Constitution as we have known it, we will reap the whirlwind of chaotic politics, bad government, and perhaps a populist backlash that endangers our whole way of life.[59]

Can we banish the many daunting challenges that America's diversity imposes on our nation by simply sending unruly legislators to the backseat of our national vessel? There are reasons to wonder whether, made officially *ir*responsible, legislators would make such a ruckus as to make it impossible for the driver to proceed safely. There are also plenty of reasons to doubt that a president so empowered would really rise above interest group competition; contemporary political scientists have consistently shown that presidents practice their own forms of parochialism, strategically directing their administrative resources to curry favor with particular sets of voters.[60] More to the point, this metaphor should make us wonder: Should we really be putting our faith in a single national driver? Can one person contain a vision sufficient for the whole nation?

## Congress' Distinctive Strengths

Having pondered the promise and challenge of representation at some length, we are now in a position to return to the question of what makes Congress indispensable in our system—and why we still desperately need our representative legislature to live up to the Madisonian vision of factional deliberation.

There is much more to politics than rendering policy decisions. Engineers confront clear, well-formulated problems susceptible to better and worse answers. But political work is not just policy engineering; it is much harder because the basic dimensions not only of the solutions but also of the problems themselves are contested. Finding answers is hard; finding answers that account for an entire political community, even as it changes over time, and even as parts vehemently disagree with each other, is much harder.

The very characteristics of our representative legislature that would-be reformers find most exasperating—its messiness, balkiness, multiplicity—are those that render it capable, in ways the other branches are not, of maintaining the bonds that hold together our sprawling republic. Congress is many, not one; plural, not singular. But so, of course, is our vast and varied country. An assemblage of representatives drawn from the whole of our diverse, factious country can forge a sense of national identity in a way the acts of a singular head of state or a centralized bureaucracy cannot.

Critics of Congress are right to say the legislature is often a poor champion of efficient government relative to the executive branch—there is no sense in pretending that legislators are something they are not. But those who think that seals the case against Congress fail to realize the deeper goods and goals that representative government serves: building coalitions, generating trust, and creating real political accountability. In a deeply divided nation, such as ours today, we need to rely on a system of government that allows provisional cooperation between seemingly opposed factions. In our system, that means giving a prominent place to a Congress where many voices can play off of each other rather than simply sort themselves into irreconcilable warring camps.

An approach that depends on provisional coalition building has several notable benefits. First, it creates room for the "strange bedfellows" that distinguish the political realm. In a legislature, unexpected issues can cause political opponents to find common cause, building trust between factions even without resolving deeper differences. As political theorist Nadia Urbinati observes, "Representative politics has the power of unifying and connecting (through friction or concurrence) the 'fluctuating' 'atomic units' of civil society by projecting citizens into a future-oriented perspective."[61]

Second, the continuous nature of a representative assembly—in which "generations" of members overlap and expect to negotiate with each other indefinitely—creates room for a complicated favor economy. Mutual give-and-take across the whole range of issues allows accommodation of different groups' most intense preferences, while also allowing the "losers" in one round of bargaining to keep faith with a larger process they trust will serve them in another round. As David Mayhew, one of the most astute contemporary observers of Congress, puts it, "Assemblies can excel at weighing voter intensities and blending them into packages. These various services . . . unlovely as they may loom in day-to-day performance, can be a help to legitimizing a system across a heterogeneous public."[62]

Third, and perhaps most important, mutual seeking of workable compromise generates policies that don't conform to any side's "right" answer. Whereas a search for consensus limits possibilities, the frisson implicit in compromise creates them: the need to act in ways that are not ideal to fend off worse possibilities, including systemic breakdown, calls forth solutions not present in any of the contending schools of thought.

Cultivating a sense among citizens that they are represented is especially crucial in a low-trust political environment. If we lived in a world in which trust was strong and stable, much of what goes on in a legislature might well be regarded as wasteful, but, at least for 21st-century America, this is not a realistic possibility. Instead, as John Dunn writes, the *hopeful* scenario for political life is to find ourselves forever grappling with "the construction, reproduction, and repair of structures of well-founded mutual trust."[63] Because a diverse and free society is unlikely to be able to long sustain a deeply felt trust, much of politics is always a matter of cultivating trust sufficient for some purpose.

Trust exists between particular persons, not in abstraction, and so it is difficult to predict what people will be distrustful about. A well-functioning legislature will extend lots of *provisional* trust to many people but can adjust its levels of trust very quickly in response to changing public sentiment. When we learn that trust was extended wrongly, underlying trust in representatives can make that failure bearable—or voters can readily get themselves new representatives at the next election.

The sense of trustworthiness and accountability, as achieved by our political actors, does not entail getting "right answers" or performing at maximum efficiency. Instead, it is based on the ability to give persuasive reasons when called to account. The executive branch must manage to persuade the Congress (and often courts) of the nonarbitrariness, legality, and usefulness of its activities, lest the legislature deprive it of resources or cancel its initiatives. Legislators must work to persuade each other of the merits of their proposals in order to form working majority coalitions. And legislators must present accounts of themselves that sufficiently preserve their constituents' trust in order to get re-elected.

In each of these cases, offering an account is more than just the uttering of certain formulaic justifications, whether legal, logical, or moralistic; the listeners must be addressed on terms that *they* will find acceptable. As Thucydides had it, "One who forms a judgment on any point, but cannot explain himself clearly to the people, might as well have never thought at all on the subject."[64] Bryan Garsten puts it another way: "The effort to persuade requires us to engage with others wherever they stand and to begin our argument there, as opposed to simply asserting that they would adopt our opinion if they were more reasonable."[65] Meaningful equality between citizens means taking their concerns seriously, whatever their credentialing or expertise.

The kind of accountability that a diverse group of representatives will demand is thus an antidote to the sins of insularity and groupthink that so often plague bureaucracies. Experts may well find it burdensome to explain themselves to elected representatives—after all, it is *they* who are capable of assessing which kind of accounting is sufficient, not generalist legislators. The wisdom of our Madisonian Constitution lies in rejecting that thinking, ensuring that no branch can assume a mindset in which the judgment of only one kind of anointed people matters.

So much for the abstract framing. Much more convincing will be to see what our healthy Congress accomplished in action.

# PART I
# WHEN CONGRESS WORKED

Presidents dominate our understanding of American political history. They are easily countable, and perhaps we can even rattle off their names without much trouble. Each can be centered in a single frame and featured in biographical books and movies. They make ready protagonists, their travails and triumphs coming alive to us naturally.

Congress is much harder to pin down. More than 12,000 men and women have served in the body. Their activity is a complicated whirl, visible in whole to nobody, not even the most senior and powerful members of the institution. The most talented storyteller will have difficulty writing a page-turner about Congress, and a movie with the House or Senate as its subject, rather than just its setting, would be faintly absurd. Legislators do not lend themselves to epic retellings of their finest moments or darkest hours.

Because of its disadvantage in our collective imagination, we tend to undervalue Congress and its contributions.

Chapters 2 and 3 offer modest correctives, telling the stories of two of our country's most severe trials through the lens of Congress' contributions. During World War II and in the push to end racial segregation that culminated in the Civil Rights Act of 1964, legislators embraced their manyness and managed to guide the nation through sacrifice and tumult. The Madisonian balancing acts that they performed were not always lovely—faithfully representing all of America's factions seldom is. But they nevertheless succeeded in holding America together when immense strains might have pulled the nation apart.

Throughout the years narrated in these chapters, the pendulum had swung far toward decentralization, with committee chairmen selected by seniority wielding immense power. Each party's central leadership acted as coordinators rather than commanders—or, at least, this is how they acted when they were most successful. That, too, is hard to turn into a compelling story, but it is worth a serious try.

# 2

# Congress and World War II

> We call this a people's war, and it is well to remember that the Congress is the people's Congress. It is in the Congress that out of the clash of contending opinions is forged the democratic unity of a democratic people.
>
> —Speaker of the House Sam Rayburn, 1943[1]

Representative democracy did not seem to have a bright future in the 1930s. Fascism and communism were on the rise, surging behind charismatic leaders who claimed to directly embody the wills of their nations. The perceived success of these regimes' economic and military expansion caused many in America to wonder if our antique Madisonian system, with a slow, deliberative Congress at its center, had been rendered obsolete by autocratic efficiency. "If this country ever needed a Mussolini, it needs one now," declared Sen. David Reed (R-PA) ahead of the 1932 election. "Leave it to Congress, we will fiddle around here all summer trying to satisfy every lobbyist, and we will get nowhere. The country wants stern action, and action taken quickly."[2] Sounding a more sober note in 1940, Harvard political scientist Pendleton Herring worried that America's government "was originally designed for no such complex necessities" as those that dominated the contemporary world.

> What can we do with what we have? Can our government meet the challenge of totalitarianism and remain democratic? Is the separation of powers between the legislative and executive branches compatible with the need for authority? In seeking firm leadership do we open ourselves to the danger of dictatorship?[3]

We know that America's democracy rose to these challenges in the years that followed. But our popular narratives about how that happened are almost completely silent when it comes to the distinctive contributions of our representative legislature. What did Congress do during World War II? Even history buffs may draw a blank. Our images of America at war are dominated by the rousing speeches and shrewd diplomacy of Franklin Roosevelt; the military leadership embodied by George Marshall, Dwight Eisenhower, George Patton, and Douglas MacArthur; the brave deeds of American soldiers, sailors, and airmen; and the steely determination of Americans laboring on the home front.

Those who do address Congress' wartime record often portray legislators as isolationists who hampered Roosevelt's neo-Wilsonian efforts to support Allied resistance to Axis aggression before Pearl Harbor, only to rather abjectly empower his administration after the Japanese attack on Hawaii. In other words: before America was attacked, Congress succeeded in making a nuisance of itself, and after, the best that can be said of it is that it got itself out of the way. In this telling, America triumphed not because of our distinctive constitutional system, but in spite of it; we beat the Axis at their own game with the singular leadership and efficiency of a transcendent president and brilliant military commanders.

There is truth in such claims. Until Pearl Harbor, anti-war sentiment was much stronger in Congress than in the Roosevelt administration. And once Congress declared war on December 8, 1941, the legislature did indeed confer immense administrative powers on the executive branch, largely for the purposes of transforming the nation's economy to support the war effort.

But this is far from the whole story. As we saw in Chapter 1, Congress, in its distinctive Madisonian role, creates space for the messy representation of and deliberation between American society's diverse factions, and thus mediates between society and government. This ordinary constitutional function, far from being an inconvenience in wartime, was essential to building a legitimate and effective war effort without compromising the Constitution. Congress played to its institutional strengths before and during the war, representing the concerns of Americans who were not terribly eager to see their lives turned upside down for the sake of repelling aggression in distant lands. Legislators, more than the president or his advisors, were responsible for figuring out how to distribute the immense burdens imposed by the war. In doing so, they often made choices contrary to Roosevelt's desires, overriding his veto on several consequential occasions—including in a dramatic confrontation over taxation. For many of the difficult balancing acts faced by the nation, such as the effort to control prices, Congress moved the decision-making into new administrative agencies. But its delegations were bounded, both in scope and in time, and legislators did not merely recede into the background once they empowered executive branch officials. Instead, they pursued a defensible (if imperfect) path of constructive involvement without interfering so much as to grind things to a halt. Their efforts were indispensable in generating the trust in the executive branch's activities (including secretive ones) that was necessary to marshal the nation's resources effectively.

Finally, Congress generally resisted the president's efforts to use the crisis of wartime as an opportunity to effect social change. Though many historians have regretted Congress' posture, legislators' insistence that factional concerns, even seemingly petty ones, be taken seriously even during an emergency was crucial to cementing the broadest possible public support for the war effort. Far from deferring to their commander-in-chief, American voters delivered big gains to Republicans in the 1942 midterm elections. That empowered a conservative coalition to stand against overreach by Roosevelt and ensured that America's economy would not remain under central direction after the war ended. By incubating anti-communism through the duration of America's alliance with the Soviet Union, legislators also prepared the United States to draw a sharp contrast between freedom and totalitarianism in the postwar world.

Across the Atlantic, Winston Churchill led a wartime unity government in Britain, which included both Tories and Labourites. But the only Republicans in Roosevelt's cabinet were Secretary of War Henry Stimson and Secretary of the Navy Frank Knox. As a matter of constitutional necessity, the full range of Americans' concerns could only be represented in a Congress that did not entirely suppress its plural character in the name of patriotic solidarity. That meant embracing debates that occasionally became bitterly partisan, and it meant accepting that coalitions in Congress would sometimes succeed in promoting parochial interests above what seemed to be a more sober apprehension of the national interest. But accepting these modest downsides, and allowing for a flourishing opposition even in wartime, did not undermine America's war effort. Instead, America preserved the political freedom for which it was fighting, throughout the war and beyond it. As Ira Katznelson puts it, "It was, in short, the central operative role of Congress that most distinguished the United States from the forces of brutality and the absence of political competition that characterized dictatorships."[4]

Congress' role during the war deserves to be appreciated and celebrated, even if its achievements were more mundane than glorious.

## Sharing the Load

The war put a massive burden on Americans, one they were not always eager to carry. Americans most often looked back on their country's involvement in the First World War with disgust rather than pride. Although American doughboys' entrance into the war was decisive in bringing the war to a close, victory had cost the United States 117,000 dead and another 200,000 wounded with little to show for it. At home, the economic benefits seemed to flow to war profiteers and the largest corporations, while in Europe the Treaty of Versailles had failed to stabilize the continent. Instead, with its punitive reparations imposed on Germany, it had planted the seeds of a new conflict.

As Europe descended into war in 1939, most Americans were dead set against repeating that earlier experience. Midwestern isolationists who had opposed entrance into World War I were the loudest opponents of war, but even coastal elites shrank from entanglement in Europe's problems. As historian Geoffrey Kabaservice describes in his chronicle of America's liberal establishment, the America First Committee began as a student movement, founded by "young anti-interventionist students . . . convinced that they were smarter and more sophisticated than the members of their fathers' generation had been." It attracted advisors as unconservative as Chester Bowles and John L. Lewis, and counted among its young members many future leaders, including Sargent Shriver, Potter Stewart, and Gerald Ford.[5] When Roosevelt sought to bolster America's ability to supply the Allied cause through his Neutrality Act of 1939, even staunch New Deal supporters such as Rep. Caroline O'Day (D-NY) expressed reservations at "our country [furnishing] arms or implements of war and slaughter to other nations."[6]

Thus, Congress' resistance to American involvement early in the war channeled sentiments shared broadly by Americans. Nevertheless, Congress did not stand in the way of a significant preparedness push beginning in 1940. That year, with only intermittent support from Roosevelt's administration, legislators conducted a prolonged and vigorous debate over the institution of the nation's first peacetime draft, culminating in passage of the Selective Service Act in September.[7] In March 1941, Congress joined with the administration to push through the Lend-Lease Act, thereby fulfilling Roosevelt's promise to turn the United States into the "arsenal of democracy." Congress took pains to ensure that the country's production of armaments would avoid the war profiteering that marked World War I's mobilization. In 1940, Congress passed an excess profits tax—the first step of a war-long effort to ensure there would not arise "new war millionaires out of dead sons," as one constituent worried.[8]

Congressional foot-dragging may have kept Roosevelt from getting the nation into the war earlier. Nevertheless, legislators' reluctance had not stopped the country from making enormous changes that readied it for war. And once bombs had fallen on their country's soil, Americans understood themselves as conducting "a patriotic war of defense."[9] Yet they were still not particularly enthusiastic. As Pearl Harbor receded and no new attacks on America's shores materialized (notwithstanding a few scares), Americans began to feel that the Allies' cause was distant from their own lives. As the historian John Morton Blum put it, "Europe had been occupied, Russia and China invaded, Britain bombed; only the United States among the great powers was 'fighting this war on imagination alone.'"[10]

The massive reorientation of the American economy toward war production brought many opportunities, and many Americans on the home front saw their incomes soar after the decade of the Depression. Yet the vertiginous changes the war brought were as often disruptive as liberating: marriages suffered and the divorce rate soared; milk, meat, and housing were in short supply; the psychological toll of combat drove many servicemen (and their family members) to drink; and high school enrollment fell while juvenile delinquency skyrocketed.[11] Americans knew they were supposed to bear these burdens in the name of shared sacrifice, but in practice they were likely to rationalize their own failures to put the nation's needs first. They worried that some other group was free-riding or that "some blockheaded bureaucrat was bungling the whole thing," wasting any sacrifices they and their families might make.[12]

What the federal government needed most was money. Huge sums were required to transform the US Army, only the 18th largest in the world in 1940, into a world-class fighting force.[13] But funds were also urgently needed to produce and deliver war materiel for America's hard-pressed allies, who, especially early in the war, were losing incredible amounts of supplies to German U-boat attacks. By the end of the war, American industry would produce nearly two-thirds of Allied equipment: "297,000 aircraft, 193,000

artillery pieces, 86,000 tanks, 2 million army trucks." What had already been
the largest industrial sector in the world doubled in size by 1945.[14] America's
ability to deliver supplies helped keep together the fragile alliance between
the United States, Britain, and the Soviet Union; Russian soldiers called their
cans of Lend-Lease-provided Spam "Second Fronts" through the years of
waiting for the opening of a second front in Western Europe.[15]

Paying for all of this required overhauling America's tax system, including
imposing burdens on middle- and working-class citizens who had rarely
before paid any income taxes. High taxes imposed during World War I had
been quickly repealed by 1920, and the New Deal had proceeded rather gin-
gerly in imposing significant taxes on anyone but the wealthy. But Roosevelt
understood that the war made a wide tax base unavoidable. In 1940, the
president simply left it to Congress to figure out how to impose the burdens
of a growing military, instructing the legislature (by means of a letter from
Secretary of the Treasury Henry Morgenthau) to raise $500 million "to be
obtained by devices Congress defined."[16] Congress delivered by lowering
the exemption for income taxes. In 1941, Roosevelt worked closely with
Congress to add five million taxpayers to the income tax rolls, a 30 percent
increase expected to add another $3.5 billion in revenue—a figure unprece-
dented at the time but soon to be surpassed.[17]

Once the war was on, however, Congress and FDR clashed over tax policy.
In one flashy episode, the president insisted Congress impose an after-tax
cap of $25,000 on wartime salaries. His ostensible rationale was that this
would help fight inflation, but legislators balked, seeing it as a symbolic sop
to left-wing allies rather than an effective policy measure (especially since
it exempted capital gains). Undeterred, Roosevelt implemented the measure
through executive action pursuant to the inflation-fighting powers he had
been granted in late 1942. After Republicans' gains in the 1942 midterms,
Congress repudiated his move, attaching a repeal of his action to a debt
ceiling increase passed with overwhelming bipartisan support in March
1943.[18] By Congress' lights, tax policy was not to be used as a vehicle for social signaling just then.

Instead, it needed to focus squarely on raising revenue. The White House
preferred to make the income tax far more steeply progressive and close
loopholes, while Congress preferred to broaden the base and raise excise
taxes. They compromised without much difficulty in 1942 on a bill that
raised the number of regular income tax filers from 13 million to 28 million
and imposed a further Victory Tax (to be partially rebated once the war was

won) with a low exemption that applied to 50 million Americans (out of a working-age population of around 85 million).

To ensure that the large share of Americans who had just joined the ranks of income tax filers would meet their obligations, some mechanism was needed to make the system more workable for ordinary people. Withholding taxes from wage payments was the apparent solution, but it created a new challenge: if 1942 taxes were collected in early 1943, and 1943 taxes were collected continuously throughout that year, Americans would find themselves hit with two years' worth of taxes simultaneously. That was both economically and politically unacceptable, but there was no obvious solution given the panoply of interests at stake. Twenty-five witnesses testifying before the House Ways and Means Committee offered 25 different plans.

The most influential came from Beardsley Ruml, treasurer of R. H. Macy and Company and chairman of the Federal Reserve Bank of New York, who championed a withholding proposal coupled with full forgiveness of 1942 taxes (illustrated in Figure 2.1). From a cash flow perspective, one Democratic lawmaker urged the president, Treasury "will lose nothing until the day of Judgment, and at that date no one will give a damn."[19] Nevertheless, the administration furiously opposed full forgiveness, saying that it favored the wealthy (who owed a larger share of taxes for 1942). Plenty of legislators, including Southern Democrats who often clashed with the president, took the president's side. Others, including most Republicans, felt that the administration's position would punish ordinary taxpayers for no fault of their own; as Rep. Harold Knutson (R-MN) put it, "In short, the New Deal majority were giving a stone to the great masses of the people, when they asked for bread."[20]

Although the impasse seemed serious, this is the sort of quandary that legislative bargaining excels at solving. Factional horse trading and lively floor debates produced very different bills in each chamber, setting up a conference committee to work out a compromise acceptable to a broad majority. After days of deliberating, the parties reached an agreement: the Current Tax Payment Act of 1943 forgave 75 percent of 1942 obligations but offered complete forgiveness for anyone owing less than $50 to relieve the burden on low-income taxpayers. By effectively giving many interests a seat at the table, Congress deftly and definitively settled the transition to modern income taxation.[21]

With the fight over withholding's implementation concluded, a major showdown over wartime taxes followed. In late 1943, Roosevelt asked Congress to come up with $10.4 billion in revenue increases, including

**Figure 2.1**   1943 political cartoon by Clifford Berryman depicting Treasury General Counsel Randolph Paul and Secretary of the Treasury Henry Morgenthau Jr. while a crowd at the Capitol supports the Ruml Plan.
Source: Cartoon Drawings Collection, Library of Congress Prints and Photographs Division.

$6.5 billion from individuals. Aghast at these numbers, Congress did not even begin negotiations, instead choosing to entirely ignore the president's request. Under the leadership of Ways and Means Committee Chairman Rep. Robert Doughton (D-NC), the House fashioned a bill that would raise just $2 billion in new revenue, infuriating the administration. When the Senate went along with the House proposal, Roosevelt vetoed it, declaiming that it was "not a tax bill but a tax relief bill, providing relief not for the needy, but for the greedy."[22] He also harped on disagreements already worked through in the Current Tax Payment Act, leading journalist Allen Drury to compare the veto message to a "mad dog snarling at the postman."[23]

Congress responded ferociously. Members of the House decried the veto message as evidence "that the executive department of the government has declared open warfare upon the legislative department," thereby jeopardizing the very freedom for which America fought.[24] They also warned that elements of the administration "think the American way of life is out of date" and were seeking to replace it with rule by "a group of wizards located in Washington."[25]

Doughton and Knutson, who was the ranking member on the Ways and Means Committee, issued an extraordinary bipartisan joint statement. At stake, they declared, was

> the question whether the taxing power shall continue to be exercised by the duly elected Representatives of the American people, or whether such power is to be surrendered and turned over to, or be dictated by, a small group of irresponsible theorists in the Treasury Department. . . . The President's proposal . . . would threaten the solvency of all business and undermine its ability to provide jobs when the war ends.[26]

Senate Majority Leader Alben Barkley (D-KY) (pictured in Figure 2.2) reacted even more dramatically. The moderate Kentuckian (who would later be Truman's vice president) owed his position to Roosevelt's support and had been a reliable New Dealer and supporter of the administration. But he felt, he said in a later off-the-record interview, "that things had reached a point where the President was taking every opportunity and going out of his way to belittle and slap Congress around. . . . How could I face the Senate thereafter, having failed to protest against such an assault?"[27] Barkley delivered a 45-minute denunciation of Roosevelt's message. He was especially offended by the president's suggestion that the complexity of the tax system was Congress' fault; the truth, Barkley said, was that it was Treasury Department experts who had pushed confusing rules, and if Congress was to blame it was only for accepting their advice.[28]

Near the end, Barkley declared: "This statement, Mr. President, is a calculated and deliberate assault upon the legislative integrity of every Member of Congress." Because the administration thought so little of a Congress that had so often accommodated it, Barkley said he had no choice but to resign his leadership position. Senators of both parties were beside themselves with enthusiasm at Barkley's resistance, and before long Democrats voted to re-elect Barkley as majority leader. FDR conciliated Barkley, but Congress

**Figure 2.2** Speaker of the House Sam Rayburn (D-TX) with Senate Majority Leader Alben Barkley (D-KY) in July 1939.

*Source:* Harris & Ewing Collection, Library of Congress Prints and Photographs Division.

nevertheless decisively overrode the veto, 299–95 in the House and 72–14 in the Senate. The administration was chastened by this episode, after which the Treasury Department no longer sought to use tax policy for ambitious purposes.

With three-quarters of a century of hindsight, it may be easy to regard these fights over taxation as somehow unimportant. Would it really have been so bad if the president had gotten his way and extracted a larger share of national income during that time of national testing? But we should not be so quick to dismiss the political concerns of such a massive majority coalition. Questions of taxation and representation have always been fundamentally linked in English and American history; time and again, decoupling taxation and representation destroyed the government's legitimacy. Far better than the president, legislators were attuned to just how much sacrifice their constituents could be asked to make—and, as reflected in limited polling data available at the time, Americans were generally against higher income taxes.[29] Responding to this sentiment, more than three-quarters of legislators decided it was important to take a stand against another historic expansion of the nation's tax burden. The executive branch looked at the nation's war needs and derived revenue targets; the legislative branch looked to the nation's people and understood that, whatever the numbers said, they were exhausted by the government's demands.

The failure to meet the administration's revenue target did not, of course, prove ruinous. Congress was just as determined to win the war as the president and made the choices needed to set the nation up for victory, even if that meant refusing some of what the administration declared necessary. Lawmakers' faithful representation of the people's interests strengthened the link between the people and the wartime government and was thus a major factor in the successful war effort.

## Taking Political, Not Managerial, Responsibility

Legislators' desire for America to win the war led them to extend an extraordinary amount of trust to both the civilian and military arms of Roosevelt's administration. At some level, they had no choice: they understood that the legislature is totally unsuited to the work of military logistics. Ahead of the 1942 midterms, Speaker Sam Rayburn commented, "Congress cannot run the war and knows it. The war must be run by experienced people who have made a life study of it."[30]

But we can acknowledge that Congress was obliged to endow the executive with unprecedented power without supposing that the questions of *how* it should do so were obvious or trivial. Congress needed to fashion a regime that was potent but still accountable, capable of beating back hostile empires without itself becoming imperious. It needed to ensure that America's war governance was consistent with the nation's founding principles and sense of fair play. At stake was the very survival of the American constitutional regime of separated powers in a world increasingly inclined to regard it as antiquated. Even before the war began, experts called for Congress to get out of the way and grant to the president "sweeping and complete control" of the economy and media if war broke out.[31] Congress refused such a complete abdication and instead struck an effective balance in constructing America's wartime regime. Its successes, some of which were only partial, built the trust that the executive then relied on. Without that trust, the United States could not have orchestrated many of its most difficult wartime feats, including the nation's very expensive but top-secret push to build atomic weapons.

Sen. Arthur Vandenberg (R-MI), a leading isolationist turned administration ally after Pearl Harbor, encouraged members of his own party to stand with the president, asserting in 1943 that "partisan politics as such should stop at the water's edge."[32] Indeed, curtailing partisan point scoring for the duration of a conflict is generally imagined as a regulative ideal for legislators. But during World War II, the principle had as much bite in the opposite direction: Republicans and some conservative Democrats feared that Roosevelt might use his wartime power to brand his political opponents as inherently unpatriotic and ensconce his liberal faction as a permanent majority.

One noteworthy episode in this vein involves America's official propaganda organs. The Office of Facts and Figures, created in 1941, began by furnishing official statistics but soon found that approach ineffective at shaping the public narrative. By 1942, the office was following a suggestion by the political scientist Harold Lasswell: "The *Strategy* of Truth in communication" required "the tactics of clarity and vividness," rather than literalness.[33] As such, it began utilizing a wider variety of media, including short movies, to expound the virtues of American society relative to those of the Axis powers. One such movie, *The White House*, struck many Republicans as propaganda meant to give the president the upper hand in domestic affairs. Similarly, after having been rebranded as the Office of War Information (OWI), the office produced a comic book in 1943 illustrating *The Life of Franklin D. Roosevelt*.

After their gains in the 1942 midterm elections, Republicans and conservative Democrats could combine their numbers for a majority in the House. They were determined to nip Roosevelt's aggrandizing tendency in the bud. Rep. John Taber (R-NY), the ranking member of the Appropriations Committee, thundered against using taxpayer funds in service of publications that were "partly drivel, partly insidious propaganda against Congress and for a fourth term."[34] The House followed Taber's lead, voting in June 1943 to entirely defund the OWI's domestic operations, although a small amount of funding would be salvaged in the conference with the Senate.

While Congress in the instance of the OWI blatantly repudiated the administration's politicization of a war agency, legislators took many more subtle steps to prevent things from coming to such a pass for other policies. During the war, Congress pioneered new uses of the legislative veto, usually in the form of provisions that provided for the termination of an authority either on a particular date or upon a presidential proclamation or a congressional concurrent resolution.[35] In providing funds to the military, Congress had to strike a delicate balance: it did not want to hamstring any efforts through constantly "stop[ping] to count the cost," but it also did not want to issue blank checks. As a result, it created new procedures enabling the executive branch to transfer funds between programs without further congressional authorization.[36] More generally, Congress knit close relations between its committees and corresponding administrative agencies. As one political scientist and veteran of the War Production Board put it after the war, "Reliance solely on external controls, however, may prove as empty and illusory as a Maginot line in a mechanized age."[37] Close cooperation, rather than inflexible bureaucratic requirements, would be the way forward.[38]

Congress would trust—but also verify, notably through the use of several special committees dedicated to overseeing various aspects of the administration's and the military's practices. While steering clear of questions of military strategy and operations, legislators called hearings to focus attention on other possible abuses. In February 1943, the House created the Select Committee to Investigate Acts of Executive Agencies beyond the Scope of Their Authority, chaired by Rep. Howard Smith (D-VA). Republicans and conservative Democrats used this committee to sniff out any attempts to use wartime programs as extensions of the New Deal policies of the 1930s and put Roosevelt on the defensive. In December 1943, the president told reporters that "'Dr. New Deal,' a specialist in internal medicine, had been succeeded by an orthopedic surgeon, 'Dr. Win-the-War.'"[39] The Select Committee made a significant institutional contribution too, by warning against legislators' tendency to take dictation from wartime agencies. It highlighted the need to reform Congress' committee system and expand its professional staff to make it capable of understanding the executive branch's activities, themes that would be taken up by the Joint Committee on the Organization of Congress in 1945 and incorporated into the consequential Legislative Reorganization Act of 1946.[40]

Most important was the Senate Special Committee to Investigate the National Defense Program, better known as the Truman Committee. The committee made Harry Truman (D-MO) famous, and not vice versa. The future president was a fairly low-profile senator until he conceived of the committee in response to a high volume of constituent letters complaining of waste and favoritism in the construction of Fort Leonard Wood in Missouri.[41]

By the end of 1941, the committee had 10 members, all relatively junior with few other important responsibilities, and a growing staff.

The Truman Committee demonstrated how congressional oversight can contribute to trust in the work of the executive branch, rather than simply offering up misdeeds as the fodder for scandal. Its members possessed a strong sense of moral righteousness in rooting out corporate greed and waste, but from the start they also were guided by a negative historical example, the Civil War Committee on the Conduct of War, which had at times seriously impaired the Union's war effort. With the executive branch generally preoccupied with overseas operations, the Truman Committee found an important role to play by policing the industrial mobilization of the home front. At first, it initiated its own investigations of people being paid to stand around on cost-plus contracts, or dollar-a-year men diverting spending to their companies at unfavorable rates. Once the committee had established its reputation, it was inundated with letters containing leads to follow. Its investigations made it a formidable force in shaping first the Office of War Production and then the Office of War Mobilization, which were the agencies most responsible for setting procurement policy.

Some level of fraud was surely inevitable in the midst of the outpouring of dollars needed to fuel America's wartime economic transformation. Given the positive effects of spending on America's economy, some may have been tempted to simply treat fraud and self-dealing as inevitable costs of doing business. Surely there were bigger fish to fry than contractors padding their margins by hiring some extra do-nothing workers. But the American people, then as now, were keenly attuned to questions of fairness. As a top mobilization official put it, "Each of us will be looking for the moat [sic] in the other fellow's eye."[42] By curtailing and deterring fraud and by conspicuously showing that fairness was prized by Congress, the Truman Committee helped to build trust in the war effort, allowing Americans of every political stripe to unite on its behalf.

That trust paid enormous dividends in an episode that deserves to be remembered as one of Congress' finest moments, despite being totally unknown to the American public at the time. The Truman Committee had received a large number of letters from workers involved in a mysterious enterprise. Because these workers understood nothing about the nature of their work, many of them worried that they might be involved in somehow defrauding the government. Truman took these queries and consulted with Secretary of War Henry Stimson, who told him "that it was an undertaking paralleling a German project and that the first country to succeed would probably win the war."[43] For Truman, that explanation was enough.

Given that it was Congress that had to provide the funding for the Manhattan Project, legislative knowledge of the top-secret project actually extended a bit further. When committees inquired after the anomalous use of some funding streams, they were generally put off with assurances similar to the one that satisfied Truman. But five members of the House Appropriations Committee toured Oak Ridge Laboratory, and five leading senators were fully briefed. They were expected to secure their colleagues' assistance without further spreading the true nature of the project. Described Sen. Styles Bridges (R-NH):

> These Senators were asked to take the leadership in providing appropriations by not identifying the various sums which went into this project by including the amounts under various headings and to vouch for the necessity of doing this to our colleagues in our respective parties without disclosing to them in any way whatsoever the purpose for which they were to be used except to say they were for a very vital matter. . . . I think the development of the Manhattan Project in which the money was provided by Congress in such complete confidence was one of the best examples of the functioning of our democratic processes in an emergency.[44]

Congress did not attempt to manage the details, or even the broad shape, of the quest to develop a new super-weapon. But its leaders nevertheless ensured that the project was grounded in congressional consent, if an unusually clandestine sort.

It is easy to dismiss Congress' accomplishments during the war as somehow ancillary or disconnected from the painstaking, painful work of securing victory. Investigating abuses in industrial practices, after all, did not gain any territory or repel any enemy advances. But it was only through the critical probing of the administration's activities that the diverse nation, still as full of contending factions as ever, could build the trust necessary to undertake many of the actions that would turn the tide of war. At least in the United States, the necessary solidarity could not be induced through propaganda but had to be wrought through legislative give-and-take.

## Return to Normalcy

As Congress monitored and jousted with the executive branch and military during the war, many particulars undoubtedly eluded its grasp. It achieved political, not managerial, accountability. And the political question to which it was most keenly attuned was: What would become of the American economy once the war was over? Here was a conflict that directly pitted the president's claims to personally embody and direct the national interest against a Madisonian vision of American plurality.

When it came to the economy, Congress was much more effective at representing and accommodating the disparate interests of business, labor, and consumers than FDR. Congress stood on the side of what might be called a return to normalcy, including restoring the primacy of free enterprise as soon as practicable and dismantling some of the most imposing bureaucracies ever created in the nation's history. The president stood on the side of some degree of continued centralized control, lest the nation fall prey to out-of-control inflation and perhaps social unrest. During the last years of the war and the first years of the peace, Congress emerged largely victorious on these issues, much to the nation's benefit.

One emblematic victory would elevate Harry Truman, symbol of wartime fairness and economy, to the vice presidency. He replaced Henry Wallace of Iowa, who had one of the stranger resumes in American presidential history. Wallace took over his family's agricultural newspaper when Warren Harding appointed his father secretary of agriculture. He became a leading expert on hog pricing and a prominent advocate of government support of farmers. He was also a great admirer of the Soviet Union and its agricultural efforts in the far north, which he hoped could be emulated in Alaska.[45]

FDR appointed Wallace as secretary of agriculture in 1933, a dozen years after his father. In 1940, the president championed the outspoken progressive as his choice for vice president. Upon taking that office in 1941, Wallace was unusually active in shaping the administration's policy. In just two years, Roosevelt made him chairman of the Board of Economic Warfare (BEW) and the Supply Priorities and Allocation Board and then a member of the War Production Board. Throughout this time, the vice president was the administration's most insistent advocate of postwar economic planning, both at home and abroad. Through its contracts with exporters of raw materials in the developing world, Wallace sought to empower poor laborers and thereby promote social equality.[46]

Sen. Robert Taft (R-OH) challenged the wisdom of "setting up an international W.P.A." and rallied congressional conservatives to oppose Wallace's ambitions. Accusing the BEW of harboring communists and of introducing inefficiency into the vital procurement process, these legislators mounted a vigorous assault on Wallace's position. Roosevelt put an end to this confrontation by terminating the operations of the BEW in July 1943, transferring its responsibilities to a newly created Office of Economic Warfare.[47]

By the 1944 election season, Roosevelt's political advisors urged him to drop Wallace from the ticket entirely. FDR remained enamored of Wallace, but he eventually relented, accepting Truman as a reasonable substitute who would not antagonize the party's conservatives. Roosevelt made Wallace commerce secretary in consolation, but not before congressional conservatives successfully stripped that office of control over federal lending activities.[48] Given Wallace's open admiration for the agricultural and industrial policies of the Soviet Union—he marveled that "the Russians could do so much in such a short time" after a 1944 visit to collective farms that were actually dressed-up gulags—America's representatives did the country a service by marginalizing his potentially disastrous influence.

More generally, especially after the midterm elections of 1942, Congress stood against attempts to use the war to reorder American society. After the rise of government-owned industry, legislators worried that there would be no going back. Taft said that industrial plants' return to "private industry, may well be doubted, unless Congress is constantly on guard, and determined to restore a system of privately owned and operated enterprise."[49] Describing the victorious challengers of the 1942 elections, *Fortune* magazine wrote that they "were almost entirely normalcy men, quiet, churchgoing, family men, not quite prohibitionists, men whose outlook was limited to their states and their regions. They may be relied upon to investigate Washington thoroughly. Many of them think they have a mandate to repeal all New Deal reforms."[50] The 78th Congress, convened in 1943, terminated New Deal agencies they believed had outlived their usefulness, including the Civilian Conservation Corps, Works Progress Administration, National Youth Administration, and Rural Electrification Administration. But they also targeted the National Resources Planning Board, a wartime creation of Roosevelt's that had proposed postwar expansions of the nation's social security system along with continued state ownership of key industries.[51] Rep. Hugh Peterson (D-GA) captured Congress' mood when he chided the board's ambition of a "world-planned economy." He continued: "We should first win the war. I learned long ago that 'one thing at a time and that done well is a very good rule as many can tell.' "[52]

Congress also spent the duration of the war grappling with what may have been the most powerful agency on the home front, the Office of Price Administration (OPA). Americans' incomes were up while consumption opportunities declined, which naturally created inflation. To control it, Roosevelt established a precursor to the OPA by executive order in August 1941, and Congress spent the remainder of the year trying to figure out how to set it up on a permanent basis. With the government gearing up to determine the relative value of commodities and living space and farm and industrial labor, the conflict of interests involved was head-spinning. People's livelihoods were at stake, and so was their ability to put food on the table. No legislator wanted to be party to an arrangement that would deprive his constituents of their "share of the nation's prosperity."[53] Lacking any obvious way forward, the House began its deliberations under an open rule and ended up with a hash of a bill. Said Rayburn, "Hell, with the House in this frame of mind, we've got to take what we can get, then hope the Senate will do better. This thing is horribly messed up."[54] The Senate bill privileged agricultural interests, but legislators staggered forward to put the agency on independent footing by January 1942. Though they had made nobody particularly happy, they had managed to achieve a tolerable balance between consumer and producer interests in difficult circumstances.

The OPA's central regulation, known as "General Max," was vague enough to leave plenty of room for interpretation, which empowered the agency to affect the size and shape of American consumer markets throughout the wartime economy. It built up a huge, decentralized workforce that rose to 60,000 by the end of 1943 and employed an army of some 300,000 volunteers who worked as the agency's eyes and ears, alerting it to violations by merchants who raised their prices above permitted levels.[55]

Congress struggled to control this behemoth, whose work the president believed was of the utmost importance to maintaining order on the home front. During the course of the war, the president pushed to lower food prices and legislators representing rural America pushed back. Agricultural interests prevented the OPA's original statute from fixing many agricultural prices at less than 110 percent of prewar levels, but Roosevelt demanded that the agency be empowered to set stricter standards. Indeed, in September 1942 he issued a rather startling ultimatum to Congress: "In the event that the Congress should fail to act, and act adequately, I shall accept the responsibility, and I will act."[56] Members were aghast at this treatment, with Sen. Robert LaFollete Jr. (Progressive-WI) saying that the president had "placed a pistol at the head of Congress" and Senator Taft gravely warning that "the doctrine that is asserted leaves Congress as a mere shell of a legislative body."[57] Still, although Congress did not give him exactly what he wanted by his October 1 deadline, they gave him nearly what he wanted on October 2. The battle over the agency raged on in 1943, with FDR successfully vetoing a reauthorization that would have reduced the OPA's authority. Through the end of the war, the OPA received reauthorizations that kept it powerful, and indeed its ability to combat inflation improved in 1944 and 1945.

Finally, with the war over, Congress channeled producerist interests to bring down the OPA. In 1946, Truman and Congress engaged in a fierce back-and-forth over renewal, with the agency surviving in a weakened form after a temporary expiration. But the politics changed entirely that autumn when meat producers, frustrated with low price caps, withheld their goods in protest, leading meat production to fall 80 percent in September and then almost to zero in October. Meat shortages became a media sensation, and the OPA quickly lost its grassroots support. Congressional Republicans campaigned that year on the slogan: "Had enough?"[58] They won decisive victories, regaining control of the House and Senate for the first time since before Roosevelt's election, and they saw the OPA to its extinction in 1947, dismantling the most far-reaching surveillance bureaucracy in American history.

Congress also quietly rebuffed an idea with bipartisan backing that might well have altered the trajectory of our society: a civilian manpower draft. Throughout the war, the government had actively sought to ensure that war industries could get the employees they needed to meet production goals. The War Manpower Commission, created by the president in April 1942, coordinated the work of many government agencies. Yet the labor market remained free, with worker churn creating all sorts of problems for industrial and agricultural interests alike. Congress was acutely sensitive to these problems and periodically intervened to change draft exemptions to help industries, and especially farms, retain the manpower they needed.

But from the outset of the war, many supported a more sweeping solution: national service legislation empowering the federal government to assign people to particular jobs. Champions of the policy argued, with seemingly unassailable logic, that if the nation could draft men to send into combat, why should it not have the equivalent power to draft men to send into factories producing war materiel? In the executive branch, the idea was consistently championed by the cabinet's lone Republican, Secretary of War Stimson, who eventually convinced Roosevelt to propose the idea in his 1944 State of the Union address. Roosevelt's call to "make available for war production or for any other essential services every able-bodied adult in this Nation" met a cool reception in Congress.[59] In his 1945 State of the Union, Roosevelt renewed his push with greater urgency, insisting that national service legislation was "the most efficient and democratic way of insuring full production for our war requirements."[60]

This time, Congress seriously took up the question. Some members in both chambers, including Sen. Joseph O'Mahoney (D-WY), worried that applying military sanctions "to individuals working for other individuals or organizations which may profit from their labor, is altogether out of harmony with our system of government."[61] The House nevertheless passed a bill that would have given the Selective Service System coercive power to assign men between 18 and 45 to particular jobs. The Senate too passed a bill, although it empowered the Office of War Mobilization to act more like a traffic director and stopped short of conferring coercive power. A conference committee incorporated elements from both bills, and while it removed the power to jail a man for refusing his assignment, the final bill nevertheless referred to "an obligation" to work when called, making it unclear just what coercive power was being conferred. The House narrowly adopted the conference report. But opponents in the Senate made an impassioned case. O'Mahoney warned that it would amount to "the adoption of the principles upon which Hitler regimented the workers of Germany . . . [and] Joseph Stalin and his predecessor, Lenin, regimented the people of Russia."[62] The Senate decisively rejected the report, 29–46, on April 3, 1945. Civilian employment would remain a matter of free choice, whatever inefficiencies that entailed.

It would be hard to overstate the importance of this choice: America's representatives had steered the nation away from centralized direction of the economy, preserving civilian liberty even when this decidedly inconvenienced the war effort.

Throughout the war, legislators also pushed against a system in which organized labor would dominate. With workers in high demand during the war, union membership soared, from 10.5 million in 1941 to nearly 15 million in 1945. Members saw their wages rise and benefits expand, especially pensions.[63] But unions' willingness to strike in the midst of war often alienated the public, and even President Roosevelt was determined to curtail their ability to disrupt war industries.[64] After fraught negotiations produced several abandoned bills, Congress followed FDR's seizure of mines in 1943 by passing the Smith-Connally Act. The law prevented unions from directly contributing to political campaigns, gave the War Labor Board new enforcement powers, and required prestrike plebiscites to be supervised by the federal government. The president, dissatisfied with various particulars, issued a veto, but both chambers of Congress passed overrides quickly, delivering to FDR what *Time* magazine called the "most stinging rebuke of his entire career."[65] Legislators of both parties were determined to ensure that organized labor would not have undue influence in charting America's political course.

They had reason to be concerned about the Roosevelt administration's relationship to labor. To give one illustrative example, the *New York Times'* Arthur Krock reported that when FDR was on the cusp of dropping Wallace in favor of Truman as his 1944 running mate, he asked one of his associates to "clear it with Sidney."[66] He was referring to Sidney Hillman, head of the Amalgamated Clothing Workers of America and, at that point, also of the Congress of Industrial Organizations Political Action Committee (CIO-PAC).

Republicans certainly worried about the political threat posed by the rise of CIO-PAC and other labor-affiliated groups. More generally, though, members of both parties feared that labor leaders like Hillman were radicals opposed to America's free enterprise system and representative government itself. For instance, in June 1942 the House Un-American Activities Committee (HUAC) issued a "Special Report on Subversive Activities Aimed at Destroying Our Representative Form of Government," with much of its criticism directed at the Union for Democratic Action, a lobbying group chaired by then-socialist Reinhold Niebuhr. When this interest group set out to "purge" members it saw as "obstructionist," the HUAC report asserted, it was effectively advancing the belief "that the sole remaining function of Congress is to ratify by unanimous vote whatever wish is born anywhere at any time in the whole vast structure of the executive branch of Government down to the last whim of any and every administrative official."[67] In 1944, HUAC targeted Hillman's CIO-PAC. The committee's chairman, Rep. Martin Dies (D-TX), argued that the CIO-PAC had violated the Smith-Connally Act's prohibition on labor organizations directly contributing to political campaigns and that it, too, had the ultimate goal of "destroying parliamentary government" by backing "men who will serve as their stooges in the

Congress of the United States." It noted that men with established ties to the Communist Party were well represented on the CIO-PAC's leadership.[68]

At the time and ever since, HUAC's work has been dismissed as an ugly manifestation of the American public's reactionary instincts and "paranoid style," a precursor of the McCarthyism that respectable opinion would decisively repudiate in the early 1950s. HUAC certainly tended toward the bombastic and inflammatory. But when it challenged the president's judgment on this matter of grave importance, the committee faithfully represented the concerns of constituents. Its warnings of communist and Soviet infiltration of the labor movement's organizations, and even of the Roosevelt administration itself, turned out to contain a great deal of truth.[69] Their warnings that Joseph Stalin would put Eastern Europe under his thumb and become America's enemy after the war likewise were prescient.

From our vantage point today, it is nevertheless easy to pooh-pooh congressional concerns about organized labor as overheated. With private sector unions so weakened in the 21st century, it is easy to romanticize the labor movement and wish that it could have done more to advance the lot of ordinary working Americans. But most Americans of the 1940s did not think of things in that way. To them, union leaders sometimes came close to resembling racketeers, exploiting favorable New Deal statutes to line their own pockets without regard for ordinary laborers' welfare.[70] Invoking these sorts of images, bipartisan supermajorities in Congress would pass the Taft-Hartley Act (which restricted permissible actions and structures for unions) over Truman's veto in June 1947.

Scholars with fond hopes of a fairer economy managed by a powerful federal bureaucracy have often cast aspersions on Congress' wartime role in rejecting centralized economic planning, national service legislation, and organized labor's overweening power.[71] As they see it, the crisis of the war ought to have been an opportunity to instantiate Roosevelt's Second Bill of Rights, which included guarantees of employment, housing, and medical care for all. Judged on its willingness to make good on the president's promises, Congress was a major disappointment.

But that is the wrong standard by which to judge our representative body. Americans were not eager to return to the ravages of the Depression that had immediately preceded the war, but they continued to believe in a return to liberty and free opportunity, rather than a managed economy. Their representatives in Congress championed that vision by obviating the executive-driven pressures toward state-managed, labor-dominated corporatism.

America would continue to rely on pluralistic deliberation, not technocratic direction, to resolve basic questions of economic order and distribution. Legislators did not win the war, but they did ensure that American victory would perpetuate a recognizably American way of life.

## The Path Not Taken

There was another way forward in victory, vividly demonstrated by America's Soviet allies. The war was far more personal for the Soviet people than for Americans: merciless invaders pillaged their homeland and they responded with a kind of raw, passionate hatred rarely seen across the Atlantic. Alexei Surkov's poem, "I Hate," published in 1942, captured their resolve: "My heart is hard as stone. / I hate them deeply. / My house has been defiled by Prussians, / Their drunken laughter dims my reason. / And with these hands of mine, / I want to strangle every one of them."[72] Soviet citizenry was mobilized for war far more thoroughly than America's, manning historically large armies and working grueling schedules to produce weapons. The losses they proved able to bear were staggering. Historian Richard Overy notes: "The rest of Europe was conquered for less than the losses [the Soviets] suffered in December 1942 and January 1943."[73]

Russians bore this trial with extraordinary resolve, managing to evacuate and rebuild their country's war manufacturing capacity farther east from the front in 1942. Unlike in America, where the allocation of industrial tasks had an ad hoc, informal character, the Soviets accomplished their task through top-down central planning that emphasized simple goals and massive scale. With the Soviet people motivated by pursuit of socialist glory, hatred of the enemy, and fear of the gulag, this method of production by brute force succeeded, which in turn allowed the Red Army to turn the tide against the Nazis. Overy remarks: "How Soviet workers kept going, month after month, exhausted, hungry, terrified that any slip or dereliction might be classified as sabotage, defies belief. No other population was asked to make this level of sacrifice; it is unlikely that any western workforce would have tolerated conditions so debilitating."[74]

We in the West should probably acknowledge and appreciate our wartime ally's remarkable resilience more than we do. Without the Soviet people's sacrifice, there is no guarantee that the Axis powers could have been defeated. And yet, in hindsight, we would not wish for this kind of resolve for ourselves. We know the terrible cost of Stalin's domination of his own people, both in lives lost and in freedoms surrendered. We know that the brute-force methods that succeeded during the war could not be sustained over decades, nor could they produce a modern economy.

Americans fought to victory—in both World War II and the Cold War—because of a different sort of confidence. In a 1947 speech, Sen. Richard Russell (D-GA) reflected on what gave Americans, whose "civilization and system of government" were "denounced as decadent," the courage to fight. He concluded: "It was the working of the American heritage. It was the knowledge that our institutions of government had brought us more freedom, more happiness, and more material blessings than any other people have ever enjoyed. We did not propose to see them destroyed."[75]

Our willingness to countenance free encounters between diverse and competing factions, even in the midst of total war, had much to do with our ability to soldier on to victory. Our willingness to let obstinate legislators openly oppose our president and his administration, even in the depths of war, ultimately gave us a sounder basis for trust and real cooperation than the Soviet Union's willingness to crush those who stood in its leaders' way. Aaron Friedberg convincingly argues that the persistence of anti-statist ideologies in American politics paradoxically helped the nation achieve decisive material superiority in its struggle with communism.[76] It was in Congress that the champions of these ideologies acted effectively as the yang to the executive branch's yin.

America was never in danger of imitating the Soviet way—but that was precisely because our Congress continued to practice free, adversarial politics even in the middle of a national crisis. Far from tearing the country apart, the struggles of our nation's representatives bound it together and legitimized the necessarily burdensome actions of the executive branch.

# 3

# The Achievement of Civil Rights

Great public issues are not subject to our personal timetables; they do not accommodate themselves to our individual preference or convenience. They emerge in their own way and in their own time. We do not compel them; they compel us. We look in vain if we look backward to past achievements which might spare this Senate the necessity of reaching difficult decisions on the civil rights question. We hope in vain if we hope that this issue can be put over safely to another tomorrow, to be dealt with by another generation of Senators. The time is now. The crossroads is here in the Senate.

—Senate Majority Leader Mike Mansfield, 1964[1]

America's Southern states enacted Jim Crow laws that enforced segregation between whites and blacks in the last decades of the 19th century. By the 1960s, the rigid racial hierarchy they created had endured for generations, and many white Southerners insisted that their region's way of life depended on resisting the mounting demands for racial equality that came from around the country. Rallying that intense opposition, in January 1963 the newly elected governor of Alabama, George Wallace, famously proclaimed his dedication to "segregation now . . . segregation tomorrow . . . segregation forever!"

In June that year, Wallace stood at an auditorium doorway at the University of Alabama, declaring his defiance of a federal court order admitting three black students. He relented only after President John F. Kennedy federalized the Alabama National Guard and ordered them to remove the governor by force if necessary. In July, Wallace made his way to Capitol Hill to testify before the Senate Commerce Committee then considering civil rights legislation. He struck a threatening tone: "If you intend to pass this bill, you should make preparations to withdraw all our troops from Berlin, Vietnam, and the rest of the world because they will be needed to police America."[2]

When contemporary historians reflect on the trajectory of racial relations in America, they often focus on the overwhelming power of white backlash, in which reactionaries mobilize and turn back social progress.[3] Readers of such commentary might be forgiven for thinking that white Southerners made good on Wallace's threat—that, to the extent that desegregation succeeded in the South, it was only because white Southerners succumbed to the imposition of overwhelming physical force.

But that simply wasn't so. There was no military occupation of the South in the 1960s to rival that of a century earlier. Instead, after the passage of the Civil Rights Act of 1964, desegregation—the 20th century's most momentous, foundational change in social relations—took place with remarkably little social strife or violence. Less than a year after Wallace's threat, the new law ensured that schools and public accommodations, such as restaurants and hotels, were open to all races. Although they had bitterly fought the legislation, the vast majority of white Southern political leaders urged their constituents to comply with it. Compliance did not come instantly or completely peacefully, especially in more rural areas. But the overwhelming majority of Southerners heeded their leaders' calls to respect the new law, despite their own reservations and resentments.

What enabled this remarkable feat?

In the public imagination, credit is often divided between two great men: Martin Luther King Jr. and Lyndon Baines Johnson. Popular historian Jon Meacham, for example, marvels at LBJ's resolve and clarity of vision in the hours after he was sworn in following John F. Kennedy's assassination in November 1963. Thinking ahead to how he could deliver the civil rights victory that Kennedy had not secured, Johnson told aides: "Well, I'm going to tell you, I'm going to pass the civil rights bill and not change one word of it. I'm not going to cavil and I'm not going to compromise." Meacham comments: "Fate had given him the ultimate power, and he intended to use it."[4] In this telling, Johnson's ability to channel social pressure generated by King and his followers through their nonviolent direct action made the triumph of 1964 possible. The law's final passage is best understood as "the result of incredibly intense work by the president to force the triumph of hope and history over political calculation and fear."[5]

We must reject the easy satisfaction this framing of the civil rights story offers. As much as we yearn for tales of big-hearted heroes triumphing over hate-filled enemies, we do ourselves and our forebears a grave disservice by imagining that our nation coped with the enormous challenges of integration because of the greatness of a president and a civil rights leader.

Instead, if we closely examine the real origins of the Civil Rights Act of 1964, we see that Congress was the institution that drove the cause forward and made it possible for desegregation to happen so relatively peacefully. Far from being dragged along by a bold-thinking executive, it was members of Congress who reacted most urgently to the groundswell of energy generated by the civil rights movement. Both Democrats and Republicans felt intense pressure to establish themselves as the party of civil rights, leading to virtuous competition between them. Working closely with the NAACP's legendary lobbyist, Clarence Mitchell—a too-often-neglected civil rights leader known as the "101st senator," who understood the value of the inside game— members of Congress maneuvered within the political environment that activists had created by assembling a bill capable of securing passage.[6]

Southern senators' filibusters undoubtedly delayed the moment of civil rights' triumph. But the struggle to overcome their obstruction was completely necessary to changing the *politics* of the issue such that the *policy* change would be accepted and endure. The contrast to an earlier attempt to dismantle one form of segregation by court order, following the famous *Brown v. Board of Education* Supreme Court ruling in 1954, is striking. That bid to dictate change with reference to high constitutional principle was a nearly complete failure. White segregationists' power in the South was morally noxious and constitutionally suspect—but it was, for all that, no less politically overwhelming.

The legislative process nevertheless provided the means of beating them. The filibuster as it was then practiced—which was quite different from the routine maneuver we are familiar with today—halted all other Senate business and therefore focused the nation's attention on the issue at stake. In previous years, Southerners' willingness to employ the parliamentary tactic of endless debate had forced the watering down of ambitious bills. But the filibuster was ultimately a blessing in disguise for the movement's champions. Being forced to muster a two-thirds supermajority capable of breaking the filibuster made them reach beyond their core supporters and build a remarkably broad coalition for change. To persuade conservative Midwesterners, especially, proponents of civil rights developed new organizing strategies, conscripted America's churches to their cause, and ensured that civil rights would be understood as a bipartisan triumph. In both the House and Senate,

Southern Democrats ended up almost entirely isolated in their defense of segregation.

The most underappreciated aspect of the civil rights story is how these irreconcilable opponents of social change came to be reconciled to the new law and, indeed, to defend its legitimacy to their disappointed and angry constituents. Achieving this feat required the majority to demonstrate two virtues in short supply in our own political moment: forbearance and magnanimity. The champions of civil rights were, understandably, frustrated by Southerners' willingness to use every procedural trick in the book to block their progress. But the civil rights coalition mostly suffered through those difficulties rather than changing the rules to ease the path to legislation. Although President Johnson urged the Senate's Democratic leadership to beat the Southerners into submission as quickly as possible, Senate Majority Leader Mike Mansfield resolutely resisted that course. He believed in the importance of the Senate's manyness and preferred to let every perspective receive its zealous representation. He consulted closely with Richard Russell of Georgia—the Southerners' leader and the bill's most formidable opponent— in devising the procedures that controlled the Senate's consideration of the bill. By giving Russell and his team of 19 filibustering senators their chance to demonstrate their intense opposition to civil rights, Mansfield ensured that these political leaders would retain the trust of their voting constituents. He embraced the spirit of compromise and entertained huge numbers of amendments to avoid making Southerners feel the law had been jammed down their throats. These decisions ensured that, much as they resented the imposition of the "Federal Force bill," Southerners accepted Congress' act as a legitimate manifestation of the rule of law.

Far from being ostracized, Southern Democrats remained members in good standing, both in their party and in Congress. For those 21st-century readers who regard racism as the worst sin imaginable, this forbearance may seem like something to be ashamed of. Such an absolutist position is fundamentally anti-democratic and insensitive to the value of social peace. We should be thankful that the racists' defense of segregation ended in defeat and sorry it took so long. At the same time, keeping them in the building discouraged them from pursuing extralegal extremism. The Senate's 1972 decision to rename the Old Senate Office Building as the Richard B. Russell Jr. Senate Office Building—a name it retains today—reflects this wisdom. Part of the genius of Congress is that a man who was on the wrong side of history in one of the great political struggles of the age could nevertheless be regarded as one of the great champions of the Senate's institutional values and therefore of the endurance of the American republic.

## Taking Up Civil Rights

Civil rights had made halting progress in the mid-20th century. Harry Truman desegregated the US military in 1948, just two weeks after soon-to-be-Sen. Hubert Humphrey (D-MN) sent his party's convention into a furor by declaring that it was time for "the Democratic party to get out of the shadow of states' rights and walk forthrightly into the bright sunshine of human rights."[7] But including civil rights in the party's platform led Southern delegates to walk out of the convention and organize the States' Rights Democratic Party, also known as the Dixiecrats. Their candidate, Strom Thurmond of South Carolina, carried four states and 39 electoral votes that fall.

Democrats were determined to avoid such a rift in the next presidential election. Nominee Adlai Stevenson of Illinois insisted that racial progress must be allowed to proceed at its own pace throughout the country. His running mate in 1952 was Sen. John Sparkman of Alabama, a staunch segregationist. Their opponent, Dwight Eisenhower, opposed segregation but thought that the federal government was not empowered to dismantle it. The candidates' positions changed little in their 1956 rematch.[8]

The Supreme Court's landmark 1954 decision, *Brown v. Board of Education*, in which the justices unanimously ruled that the doctrine of "separate but equal" treatment for blacks and whites was incompatible with the Constitution, created pressure for change. In a second decision in 1955, they ordered that schools desegregate "with all deliberate speed." Far from resolving the issue, however, these cases sparked an intense legal struggle in which Southern state and local governments engaged in "massive resistance" to nullify the force of the court's declaration.[9] In Congress, 82 representatives and 19 senators issued the so-called Southern Manifesto, a March 1956 document that denounced judicial overreach and the "chaos and confusion" that it was causing in their states' educational systems.

Liberals in Congress were determined to build on *Brown* and push civil rights issues past the resistance of Southerners. They had the support of Senate Majority Leader Lyndon Baines Johnson (D-TX), who was determined to prove his mettle as a national, and not merely regional, leader by securing a victory on civil rights. Though he had not signed onto the Southern Manifesto, he hoped to find some compromise acceptable to his fellow Southerners.

Johnson continued to work closely with Richard Russell, his mentor in the Senate from the time of his election in 1948. Russell, whose life was politics, became governor of Georgia when he was 35 years old. Two years later, he won election to the US Senate, where he would represent his state for the next 38 years. His stature in military affairs was unmatched; congratulated for "serving under" six presidents, he insisted that he "served with" them. Johnson kept Russell's desk on the Senate floor next to his and relied heavily on the Georgian's parliamentary expertise.[10]

Far from wanting to steamroll Russell in 1957, Johnson worked closely with him to figure out just how watered down the Civil Rights Act of that year needed to be to avoid a serious filibuster. They reached a compromise, and Russell was able to prevent most Southerners from mounting a filibuster. Strom Thurmond alone took the floor to block the bill's progress, keeping it for 24 hours and 18 minutes before he relented. The rather weak law then passed easily, creating the Commission on Civil Rights and the Civil Rights Division at the Department of Justice. But their feeble enforcement powers sorely disappointed liberals of both parties.

After making enormous gains in the 1958 midterm elections, liberal Democrats pushed again for a strong federal civil rights bill. Although their bill, which focused on federal enforcement of voting rights in the South, was significantly pared back from liberals' ideal, Johnson and Russell could not reach an accord this time. As the Southerners launched a filibuster, Johnson pressured them by putting the Senate into round-the-clock sessions. With the exception of a single 15-minute recess, the Southerners managed to continue their filibuster continuously for 125 hours. Newspapers overflowed with photographs of senators demonstrating their steadfastness by sleeping on cots arrayed in the Senate chamber, the better to take up denunciations of federal overreach at a moment's notice. Finally, after several amendments further weakened the bill, the Southerners relented and allowed the meager bill to become the little-remembered Civil Rights Act of 1960. Conceding substantive defeat as the bill headed to passage, liberal Democrat Joseph Clark (D-PA) offered his imaginary sword to Richard Russell to symbolize his side's Appomattox-like surrender.[11]

Sen. John F. Kennedy (D-MA) spoke forcefully in favor of civil rights during his victorious 1960 campaign for president, which created great expectations for his administration. But once inaugurated, he looked back upon the frustrating experience of the previous year and concluded he would be wise to turn his energies elsewhere.[12] In truth, Kennedy remained of two minds on civil rights. Although he sympathized with blacks in their struggles for dignity, he had also been deeply affected by the Southern "lost cause" version of American history, which depicted Reconstruction as an atrocity perpetrated by the North.[13] In May 1961, as civil rights advocates expected the administration to back a liberal bill then gathering momentum, Kennedy's press secretary announced, "The president does not consider it necessary at this time to enact new civil rights legislation."[14] The executive branch would push various changes on behalf of civil rights, but the president would not try to work through Congress. Instead, Kennedy sought to develop good working relationships with the Southerners who, as the chairmen of so many of Congress' most important committees, dominated Congress and could help him move other parts of his agenda.

The civil rights movement, though, ensured that its cause could not be ignored. Beginning in 1961, Freedom Riders hoped to expose the brutality of segregation by provoking aggression against interracial groups on interstate buses. They succeeded, suffering attacks in Alabama, including mob violence in Birmingham on May 21 that had to be dispersed by the Alabama National Guard. For months the Freedom Riders' efforts continued to generate pressure for action, to Kennedy's consternation.

Congress responded in several ways. In 1962, the Senate and then the House passed what would become the 24th Amendment to the Constitution, which prohibits states from imposing poll taxes for federal elections. Since only five states still imposed such taxes, this victory had a limited impact. Senate Majority Leader Mike Mansfield and Senate Minority Leader Everett Dirksen (R-IL) proposed a more effective law, which would have forced states to waive literacy tests in federal elections for all citizens possessing at least a sixth-grade education. But Southerners effectively mobilized against that proposal, and a failed cloture vote led to a quick abandonment of the bill.[15]

## Competing to Be the Champion

In the new Congress that began in 1963, members of Congress began to treat civil rights as a top priority. In 1963, a remarkable 89 civil rights bills were referred to the House Judiciary Committee, about half from each party. Liberal Republicans, led by Rep. John Lindsay (R-NY), were especially keen to cast themselves as the true champions of civil rights, in contrast to the Democratic president's failure to live up to his own rhetoric. They rallied around a strong bill introduced January 31, 1963, which proposed empowering the Civil Rights Commission to investigate election fraud, creating a federal commission for equal opportunity of employment, and authorizing the Justice Department to initiate school desegregation litigation.[16]

In June 1963, Attorney General Robert Kennedy, the administration's point man on civil rights, testified before a subcommittee of House Judiciary and found himself harshly attacked by Lindsay, who took him to task for his ignorance of pending Republican bills. Lindsay also accused the administration of merely giving lip service to the goal of desegregating public accommodations. After that encounter, notwithstanding RFK's personal animosity toward the New York representative, the administration began to see Lindsay as someone it needed to court, lest he rally liberals of both parties behind a radical bill, which might make it difficult for the administration to work with its party's Southern wing on any issue.[17]

Even not-so-liberal Republicans sought to position their "Party of Lincoln" as the leader on civil rights. Since their congressional delegation almost entirely lacked Southerners, they could take up the banner of racial progress with little fear of backlash in their home districts—especially if they focused entirely on de jure segregation, largely confined to the South, and left alone the de facto segregation prevalent throughout the country. Rep. William McCulloch (R-OH), ranking member of the House Judiciary Committee, proved to be an especially important champion of civil rights. A few years practicing law in Jacksonville, Florida, early in his career had turned him against Jim Crow. As a result, since his first election to Congress in 1946, he pushed the issue, notwithstanding its limited relevance to his largely rural, overwhelmingly white district.[18] Given the Ohio representative's ability to bring along dozens of other Midwestern conservatives, McCulloch would become one of the key players in negotiations as the push for a law became more serious.[19]

It hardly seems remarkable that partisan competition should lead to a virtuous struggle to champion a reform of great national importance. Still, a focus on presidential competition has often obscured the importance of this dynamic for civil rights. Since Sen. Barry Goldwater (R-AZ) famously ran against the Civil Rights Act during his 1964 campaign, many people have wrongly come to think that the politics of civil rights featured Democrats transforming themselves into the party of racial progress and Republicans responding by taking up the cause of Southern whites in the name of individual liberty. If those are decent descriptions of Johnson and Goldwater's evolutions, they do not at all reflect the action that led to the law's passage. In fact, the more complicated competition facilitated by legislative maneuvering pushed civil rights forward in 1963. Moderate Democrats, including President Kennedy, were forced into action by the civil rights movement, but also by the threat that Republicans might make inroads with civil rights constituencies.

## Building an Overwhelming Coalition

Ultimately, this competition gave rise to cooperation, as civil rights leaders and their congressional allies in both parties came to terms with just how difficult it would be to overcome Southern opposition in Congress. To achieve the requisite supermajority support, a single, united coalition would need to come together out of the fractious variety of supporters. Having to clear such a high bar would prove fortuitous. By the time of the March on Washington, on August 28, 1963, United Auto Workers (UAW) President Walter Reuther could say: "We've put together the broadest working legislative coalition we've ever had. And we're going to work, not only on the Hill, but we're going to be able to mobilize the grassroots support back home in critical congressional districts where a fellow has to be persuaded."[20]

Getting to that point would not be easy. Although civil rights groups were winning some important victories, such as James Meredith's admission to the University of Mississippi on October 1, 1962, their support for a bill was still unfocused and fragmented. Significant tensions persisted between more "establishment" groups such as the NAACP and Urban League, newer groups such as King's Southern Christian Leadership Conference (SCLC), and more radical elements who thought that white-dominated organs of power would never deliver meaningful change. Only in 1963 would the Leadership Conference on Civil Rights, established in 1950 as a coordinating body, come into its own as an effective organizer of civil rights lobbying activity. Soon the group began to strategize closely with the administration and turned its efforts toward convincing the Midwestern Republicans who could provide the pivotal votes to break a filibuster in the Senate.[21] The March on Washington, in August 1963, further helped bring civil rights activists together as a unified coalition.[22]

June 1963 was the key month for the Kennedy administration, though. First, on June 5, the president met with Dirksen and House Republican leaders Charles Halleck (R-IN) and Leslie Arends (R-IL). He was surprised to find them all generally supportive of a strong civil rights bill, opening a realistic path in both chambers.[23] Next, on June 11, the University of Alabama was desegregated despite Governor George Wallace's infamous "stand in the schoolhouse door." Kennedy issued an executive order asserting federal control of the Alabama National Guard and then gave a televised speech in which he echoed the movement's themes and vowed to act. "We are confronted primarily with a moral issue. It is as old as the scriptures and is as clear as the American Constitution," Kennedy declared.[24] Just hours after his speech, civil rights leader Medgar Evers was brutally murdered outside of his Mississippi home, further steeling Kennedy's resolve. A day after Evers, a veteran, was buried in Arlington National Cemetery, the administration introduced its bill on June 20 in cooperation with House Judiciary Committee Chairman Emanuel Celler (D-NY).

Celler had been a member of the House since 1923 and was one of Congress' most ardent champions of civil rights. The liberal New Yorker had taken over leadership of the Judiciary Committee in 1949 and would not relinquish it until he left Congress in 1973 (with the exception of two Republican-controlled years). He had been instrumental in moving the Civil Rights Acts of 1957 and 1960. But in 1963, he wanted a more ambitious bill to pass, a conviction only strengthened by the bombing of the 16th Street Baptist Church in Birmingham, Alabama, in September 1963.

In the bill being drafted in his subcommittee, Celler took up civil rights groups' strongest demands, including voting rights provisions that would bind both federal and state elections, desegregation of all kinds of public accommodations, and establishment of a powerful Equal Employment Opportunity Commission with nearly limitless jurisdiction. He believed these provisions could be traded away in negotiations, still leaving a strong bill. But the committee's ranking Republican, the aforementioned McCulloch, and the Kennedy administration were horrified at moves they believed jeopardized the bill's chances. Southerners actually sought to help along the more ambitious version of the bill, believing it would be defeated on the House floor. Kennedy's administration reluctantly decided to push for a weaker bill. Confronting the full Judiciary Committee, Robert Kennedy put the point succinctly: "What I want is a bill, not an issue."[25]

After some delicate negotiating, Celler allowed his bill to be defeated in the full committee, which instead reported out a bipartisan bill negotiated by McCulloch and the White House on October 29, by a vote of 23–11. Civil rights leaders were disappointed by this weaker alternative, but the administration was committed to working closely with Republicans to build as broad a coalition as possible.

The bill still had an unclear path forward, however. In the Senate, the bill would inevitably have to overcome a Southern filibuster. In the House, the Rules Committee and its chairman, Howard W. Smith (D-VA), posed the greatest challenge. Smith, whose Virginia district was not far from Washington but whose commitment to segregation was as ardent as any Mississippian's, had been a member of the House since 1931 and chairman of the Rules Committee since 1955. A significant House bill is usually taken up on the floor according to a "special rule" dictating the parameters of debate, which means that the Rules Committee acts as gatekeeper for the House's agenda. Smith's ability as chairman to bottle up legislation, using any number of stalling tactics, was the consistent bane of liberals, who were beginning to plot an overthrow of his authority, perhaps even by ending the hallowed seniority system for committee leadership. The most direct way to take the matter out of Smith's hands would be a discharge petition, but getting a majority of members to support such an extraordinary circumvention of regular procedure would be quite difficult; traditionally, a party's members in the House vote in lockstep on the rules that structure debate.

Once again, the need to demonstrate overwhelming support led to a broadening and solidifying of the coalition for civil rights. In November, as the bill's backers sought a way past Smith, advocates from the Leadership Conference on Civil Rights swarmed the House office buildings, followed by members of the United Steel Workers of America and hundreds of college students coordinated through a joint effort of campus religious organizations.[26]

Then, on November 22, President Kennedy was assassinated in Dallas. Although his killing had nothing to do with civil rights, the movement's leaders and now-President Johnson understood that they could push the civil rights bill as a way to honor the dead president's legacy. Coordinating through the Leadership Conference on Civil Rights, activists fanned out across the country to districts of undecided representatives, pressuring them to sign their names to the discharge petition. Protests, which had briefly stopped after the president's death, resumed and made clear demands on Congress. In Louisiana, 400 protesters of mixed races attended a memorial for JFK, then marched to their local post office to send letters to their members of Congress demanding support for the Civil Rights Act. At Johnson's urging, national media portrayed Smith as the "Tyrant in the House" who was thwarting the will of the people.[27]

By mid-December, the discharge petition had 165 supporters, and Smith believed it was only a matter of time until a majority effectively overthrew him. To forestall that eventuality, he scheduled a hearing on the bill for January. On January 30, the Rules Committee finally reported the bill out on an open rule, 11–4, allowing for just over a week of debate and amendments.

In a memorable and momentous twist, during these hearings Smith pressured liberals on the bill's exclusion of sex as a protected characteristic. As a friend of Alice Paul, the leader of the National Women's Party, and a longtime supporter of an Equal Rights Amendment (as many Southern Democrats were), he argued it would be perverse for black women to be protected against discrimination but not white women, who would suddenly find themselves a legally disadvantaged class. Because liberal advocates of civil rights assumed that Smith's advocacy of women's rights was meant as a poison pill to make the bill less palatable to conservatives, they found themselves opposing sex equality. On this front, however, Smith and his ally Rep. Martha Griffiths (D-MI) prevailed. The House voted to approve his amendment, 168–133.[28]

Finally, on February 10, 1964, the House passed the Civil Rights Act by the imposing margin of 290–130. Sixty-nine percent of the voting members of the House had backed the law. A nearly equivalent margin would be required in the Senate, where 67 votes were required to invoke cloture and put a stop to Southerners' inevitable filibuster. As in the House, that meant that Midwestern and Western conservatives would be pivotal.

Johnson thought the best way forward would be to steamroll the opposition. He imagined whipping civil rights groups and unions into a frenzy, putting overwhelming pressure on wavering senators. He also wanted around-the-clock sessions of the Senate, which would physically wear the filibusterers out. But it would not be the president's strategies that would ultimately get the Civil Rights Act across the line.

Indeed, the bill's champions worried that an all-out push from black protestors and union members would simply raise the hackles of the conservatives whose votes were needed to overcome a filibuster. The NAACP's Mitchell, in particular, counseled the opposite tack. By the time of the push for the 1964 act, he was already a fixture on Capitol Hill, where he had been championing racial justice since 1950. "His ability to find support where others thought none existed," his biographer notes, "was a source of wonderment among supporters and opponents alike." The Constitution-revering Mitchell assiduously built personal relationships with Republican senators and winked at (not entirely implausible) rumors that he himself might be a Republican; he sought always "to deal with people on the basis of one human relating to another."[29]

To build the broadest coalition possible, the civil rights advocates' main strategy was to work through the nation's churches.[30] Already in the House, church-organized pressure had been brought to bear. According to Clay Risen, "Republican representatives returned from their Christmas vacations complaining of the near-constant visits, letters, and phone calls from their ministers and fellow congregants urging them to support the bill." Of the 67 Midwestern representatives targeted by these efforts, 62 voted yes on the final bill.[31]

In their efforts to win support, America's churches achieved a remarkable degree of ecumenism. The National Council of Churches, inspired to action by King's Letter from a Birmingham Jail and the sense of urgency that his direct-action strategy had inspired, organized a Commission on Religion and Race in 1963. This body made passing the Civil Rights Act its top priority, mobilizing church members of all denominations to lobby their representatives and senators, both in Washington and in their home states. From the outset, they targeted the Midwest. In 1964, they developed their own vote-counting system staffed by volunteers. As the Senate deliberated, they recruited volunteers with personal connections to senators to bend their ears in private.[32] They also mounted impressive public-facing efforts. For example, as the filibuster in the Senate dragged on, a Theology Students' Vigil for Civil Rights created an effective counter-visual to the endless debate at the Capitol. Day and night, shifts of three students—one Jewish, one Protestant, and one Catholic—stood silently before the Lincoln Memorial.[33] Said Richard Russell: "Washington has not seen such a gigantic and well-organized lobby since the legislative days of the Volstead Act and the Prohibition amendment."[34]

An April 28 speech at Georgetown University delivered by Eugene Blake Carson shows just how self-consciously church leaders worked to broaden the civil rights coalition. Carson, a leading Presbyterian minister who had championed civil rights since the mid-1950s, conceded to an audience of religious leaders and three US senators that winning over die-hard segregationists would be impossible. Yet, he believed advocates of the law could win those

> who are confused and fearful, some selfishly indifferent, content to sit on the sidelines, who see no clear moral or spiritual issue before the nation, who allow consideration of order, peace, or private profit, to neutralize their too general moral commitment to justice or freedom. These are the Americans we must win to our side of the contest.[35]

Among the persuadable were many of the Illinois constituents of Senator Dirksen, whose leadership position and ability to speak for Midwestern conservatives made him the pivotal actor in the Senate. With Dirksen's support, there would be a good chance to achieve cloture; without it, almost none. And so the majority leader, Mansfield, put his trust in Dirksen to push the bill and gave him ample opportunity to claim credit for its progress.[36] Many civil rights advocates were dismayed by this state of affairs, believing that Dirksen would water down the crucial Title VII, dealing with employment discrimination, as the price of his support. Though Dirksen did extract a few modest concessions, he left the core of the bill intact.[37] More generally, as historian Julian Zelizer notes, many liberal groups were frustrated that Dirksen was getting so much attention. "Demands expressed by brave African Americans and white college youth were now to be answered by a white, antigovernment Midwestern conservative. Conservatives who blocked legislation for years were then allowed to take credit for bills they were finally forced to accept."[38] But if this irked liberals, it nevertheless represented the genius of the system at work. The need for this broad cooperation had, of course, made passing the Civil Rights Act more difficult, but it also set it up to endure. (By making it a truly bipartisan effort, Mansfield also thwarted any plan that Southern Democrats might have had to stop the progress of civil rights by dramatically switching parties.[39]) Through Mansfield, Humphrey, and Dirksen, shown together in Figure 3.1, practically the whole of the Senate was drawn into strategizing about how to move the bill forward, past the filibuster. Of the 16 conservative Midwestern and Western Republicans, 11 would eventually support cloture.

Southerners were left to take their lonely stand.

**Figure 3.1** Sens. Everett Dirksen (R-IL), Hubert Humphrey (D-MN), and Mike Mansfield (D-MT) pictured together in 1965.
*Source:* Archives & Special Collections, Mansfield Library, University of Montana.

## Beating the Irreconcilables, and Then Reconciling Them

In charting the bill's path to become law, Mansfield shunned Johnson's preferred strategy of round-the-clock sessions meant to exhaust the Southerners. "This is not a circus sideshow," he said. "We are not operating a pit with spectators coming into the galleries at night to see senators of the Republic come out in bedroom slippers without neckties, with their hair uncombed, and pajama tops sticking out of their necks."[40]

Mansfield's path to the Senate's top job, unusual for his time and completely unheard of in ours, contributed to his faith in working through difficult colleagues, rather than running over them. Born in New York City in 1903 to Irish immigrants, when he was seven his mother died and his father suffered a serious construction accident. He was sent with his siblings to live with his aunt and uncle, who ran a store in Great Falls, Montana. After clashing with them, he spent some months in a home for orphaned children. In 1917, just 14 years old, he falsified his birth records and joined the Navy, working to escort convoys across the Atlantic during World War I. When the conclusion of the war brought his discharge, he signed up for a year in the Army; when that proved unsatisfying, he joined the Marines, which sent him to the Philippines and China during two years of service. Discharged again at the age of 22, Mansfield then spent the next decade of his life working in the copper mines of Butte. After he married his wife, Maureen, she convinced him to return to his long-abandoned education. At the University of Montana, he studied and then taught East Asian history until Maureen pushed him to enter politics. Unsuccessful in 1940, he was elected to the House in 1942 and served there for a decade. Throughout his tenure in Congress, he stayed unusually attentive to his constituents, reading every letter and refusing to use an auto-pen to sign responses. On Capitol Hill, his quiet, dependable manner impressed his colleagues, who came to appreciate his integrity and equanimity. He was included in the Democratic leadership as chief assistant whip in 1948. To a professor who wrote him to inquire about his governing philosophy, he described himself as "a conservative-liberal" who believed "in slow evolutionary changes and in some instances, would vote as a conservative in the hope that in so doing, the desired changes, once achieved, would be more acceptable, and as a result would be of a more durable nature."[41] That approach would come to define Mansfield's pivotal role in the struggle for civil rights.

Mansfield won election to the Senate in 1952 and immediately hitched his wagon to Johnson's, supporting the Texan for minority leader rather than his own Montana colleague. Johnson rewarded him with a spot on the Foreign Relations Committee, where he pursued his abiding interest in the Far East. In 1956 he won a promotion to majority whip. Johnson found Mansfield dependable and manipulable, and so when he left to become vice president after the election of 1960, he pushed for the Montanan to become majority leader.[42]

Once out of Johnson's shadow, however, Mansfield proved to be full of his own ideas about how the Senate should function. Although he had functioned in Johnson's hard-drinking, bullying regime, Mansfield detested his predecessor's imperious style of leadership. Mansfield saw his job as promoting the equality of senators within the institution and safeguarding the health and role of the institution within the larger political system.[43] As Kennedy's agenda struggled, Mansfield's restrained style led many to regard him as dull and ineffectual. But his preference for a regularized calendar and respectful treatment of his colleagues put him in an excellent position to chart a path forward for the Civil Rights Act.

After the House passed its bill, Mansfield sat down with Richard Russell to lay out how things would go. Mansfield told Russell that he would use his power to ensure that the bill was not referred to the Senate Judiciary Committee, where Sen. James Eastland (D-MS) would surely bury it.[44] That much of a deviation from normal procedure was needed. On the other hand, he would maintain nightly recesses, meaning that the filibusterers would not need to hold the floor around the clock. And he would not strictly enforce the Senate rule that limited each senator to two speeches per legislative day, which meant that Southerners could rotate their speakers more easily. Russell had to concede that the majority leader was treating his team of Southern intransigents with the utmost comity and consideration. Throughout what was to become one of the most intense legislative conflicts in American history, the two men continued entirely cordial personal relations.

Southerners knew that national opinion had decisively turned against them, but they did not seriously consider yielding without a fight. They believed in the wisdom of segregation and the dignity of the South's hierarchical social system. As importantly, they felt they would be breaking a sacred trust with their (white) constituents if they failed to defend segregation. By drawing out the debate for as long as possible, they hoped that new developments, such as summer riots, might swing opinion back in their favor at least for another season.[45] As the main filibuster began on March 30, 1964, Russell told reporters, "We intend to fight this bill with all the vigor at our command."[46]

The basic outlines of the competition were as follows. As long as the Senate was in session, the 20 filibustering Southerners needed to hold the floor with continuous speeches; failing to do so at any time would bring debate to an end and allow the Senate to vote. To occupy their time, the group split into three platoons (with Russell acting as organizing leader). Each platoon member needed to hold the floor for four hours without a break. But they could, at any time, note the absence of a quorum, which would force 51 senators to turn up in the chamber. If they did not, the Senate would adjourn for the day, relieving the filibusterers. Much of the burden therefore fell on senators in the majority, who needed to stay close to meet these quorum calls. Both Democrats and Republicans supporting the bill created duty rosters to keep senators on hand. After a failure to produce a quorum on April 4, Humphrey and Mansfield furiously chewed out their side's lack of dedication. The filibuster was thus a test of the intensity of each side's commitment.

At any time, the Senate could cut off debate if 67 senators voted for cloture. But there was a strong sense of tradition weighing against this maneuver. The Senate's sense of itself as "the greatest deliberative body on earth" was based in part on the idea that as long as a senator had something to add to a debate, he or she would be allowed to do so. Russell and his allies referred to cloture as a "gag rule," suggesting that their opponents might try to silence them because they could not manage to meet their arguments head on. The filibuster was nearly sacrosanct, then—but not quite, as an important 1962 episode showed. Faced with a rapidly evolving, chaotic market in communications satellites, legislators sought to create a regulatory system. A contingent of Senate liberals found the bill advanced by the Senate Commerce Committee too friendly to business, and they decided to talk it to death, notwithstanding the fact that many of these same members had previously denounced Southerners' use of the filibuster. The Southerners were prepared to defend their colleagues' prerogative, but Republicans eventually joined with the bill's Democratic supporters to invoke cloture on a 73–27 vote.[47] A 1965 Senate report noted that this was "the first time since 1927, and only the fifth time in Senate history, that the Senate voted to close debate on a bill."[48] As the confrontation over civil rights came into view, it seemed likely that cloture was in play, even if it offended some senators' institutional sensibilities.

When we think of famous filibusters, we often remember instances in which the speaker departs entirely from the substance of the issue at hand in order to continue speaking. In his 24-hour one-man filibuster of the Civil Rights Act of 1957, Thurmond read a succession of historic documents, including the Declaration of Independence and Washington's Farewell address. When Sen. Alfonse D'Amato (R-NY) held the floor for some 15 hours in 1986, he filled some of the time by reading from the Washington, DC, phone book. In 2013, in the midst of holding the floor for 13 hours, Sen. Ted Cruz (R-TX) read Dr. Seuss' *Green Eggs and Ham* at his daughters' bedtime. By contrast, the 1964 filibuster included a great deal of real substance. Both the Southerners and the bill's supporters were eager to debate each other's points.

Much of the debate sounded in great constitutional questions. Southerners knew that old-fashioned racial fearmongering would make it easier to villainize them in the press, so they presented themselves as defenders of America's constitutional order—and as "educators" of American citizens, who needed to be alerted to the danger the bill posed. For the federal government to insert itself into people's most basic commercial relations seriously threatened the future of freedom of association, the Southerners argued. States were on the road to becoming powerless bodies, and before long Washington would become a totalitarian menace no less threatening than Nazism or communism. The bill's supporters were ready with defenses, explaining why the Civil Rights Act was necessary to realize the 14th Amendment's guarantee of equal protection of the law and the 15th Amendment's guarantee of an effective vote. But their primary justification for the law was the terrible burdens that segregation imposed on black Americans seeking work and simply trying to travel the country. At an abstract level, their impaired life possibilities created a serious detriment to interstate commerce, giving the federal government every right to regulate it out of existence on the way to a more perfect union.

At some point, the substantive debate lost steam, and what could once be defended as educational deliberation transitioned into pure obstruction. In May, liberals negotiated with Dirksen to resolve several issues before pushing for cloture. Conservative Republicans then threw their plans into question by announcing that Dirksen had cut them out of the process. Mansfield deftly took their leader aside and found that their support could be purchased with floor votes on a few small amendments, one of which passed.[49]

Finally, after Robert Byrd (D-WV) gave a 14-hour speech to cap off the filibuster, cloture was invoked on June 10, 1964. The relentless pressure campaign to win over Midwesterners left little doubt about what the outcome would be. Still, no filibuster against civil rights legislation had ever before been ended with cloture, so the moment was filled with high drama. Russell, speaking for the filibusterers, framed the question as one of political freedom. "Within the hour, the Senate will decide whether it will abandon its proud position as a forum of free debate by imposing cloture or gag rule upon its members," he said, while warning again that the law's means of operation would put the nation on the road to totalitarianism.[50] The bill's champions, on the other hand, were in high spirits. Humphrey quoted the St. Crispin's Day speech of Shakespeare's Henry V.[51] To justify cloture, Dirksen adapted words from Victor Hugo: "Stronger than all the armies is an idea whose time has come." He also sought to strike a note of magnanimity for the South, quoting Henry W. Grady of Georgia, who in an 1888 address had declared: "There was a South of slavery and secession—that South is dead. There is a South of union and freedom—that South thank God is living, breathing, growing every hour."[52]

As the speeches came to an end, all 100 senators gathered together in the chamber and the roll call began. Sen. Clair Engle (D-CA), dying of a brain tumor, had to be wheeled in by a Navy corpsman, at which point he indicated his "aye" vote by pointing to his eye. The final vote was 71–29 in favor of ending debate; Democrats voted 44–23 and Republicans 27–6. Johnson's contribution to this victory was securing the commitment of exactly one senator, Carl Hayden (D-AZ), who was relieved that his vote was not ultimately needed and voted no. As cheers filled the chamber, the filibuster ended after 75 days, including 534 hours of debate.[53] Passing the bill itself had to wait for the disposal of hundreds of amendments offered, but Southerners were fairly desultory in their efforts by then. Anguished in defeat, Russell offered a bizarre amendment to submit the bill to a national referendum, which was easily defeated on June 12.[54] On June 19, the bill passed 73–27.

At the first recess after the cloture vote, Russell had been graciously walked to his office by none other than Clarence Mitchell, the NAACP's chief lobbyist who had, at long last, defeated his Southern adversaries. Despite their fierce opposition, Mitchell and Russell had always maintained a cordial relationship. With victory having been secured, Mitchell felt compassion for his defeated foe, whom he thought had "seemed almost to be feeling the pain of the pressure." Mitchell was struck by Russell's willingness to forego any truly incendiary tactics.[55] As they walked, Russell regained his gentlemanly composure and congratulated Mitchell on his victory. He told him that the Southerners' resistance had ultimately helped the cause of civil rights. "If the opponents had not put up the fight they had, the bill would never have been enforceable in the South," Russell said.

Whereas Southerners had regarded the Supreme Court's *Brown v. Board of Education* decision as an undemocratic imposition, no one could deny that Southerners had been given their chances against the Civil Rights Act.[56] Russell credited Humphrey with letting Southerners have their say; another opponent of the bill said it was largely Mansfield's calming presence that helped the fight happen "without leaving large schisms."[57]

It is worth considering how Southern legislators behaved at this point, once the bill was certain to become law. We are all too familiar today with legislators who, having been decisively defeated in some policy debate, nevertheless assure their constituents that they have not really lost and must continue fighting as if nothing has changed. A few Southerners did strike that kind of defiant note in 1964, including Thurmond and Wallace. But they made up a tiny minority of elected leaders. Instead, most Southern legislators were impressed by the decisiveness of their defeat—precisely because their filibuster had focused the nation's attention, and the breaking of it had revealed the overwhelming strength and determination of their opposition.

As the Senate's amended version of the bill went to the House for approval, one Southern representative changed his vote to support the new order (bringing the total number of "yea" votes from Southern Democrats to 9 out of 118).[58] Charles Weltner (D-GA) said, "Change, swift and certain, is upon us. And we in the South face some difficult decisions. We can offer resistance and defiance, with their harvest of strife and tumult . . . or we can acknowledge this measure as the law of the land." It was time to look ahead to a New South, Weltner argued.[59]

Most Southern legislators did not manage that degree of equanimity, but they still told their constituents to accept the law of the land. Russell, as the leader of the filibuster, was especially important in this regard. In a speech at Berry College in Rome, Georgia, on July 15, 1964, he, like Dirksen, cited Henry Grady's vision of a renewed South. Turning to the Civil Rights Act, he said:

> It is the understatement of the year to say that I do not like these statutes. There are hundreds of thousands of people who feel as I do about them. However, they are now on the books and it becomes our duty as good citizens to learn to live with them for as long as they are there. The constitutionality of some of the provisions will be tested immediately in the courts. While it is being adjudicated, all good citizens will learn to live with the statute and abide by its final adjudication, even though we reserve the right to advocate by legal means its repeal or modification.[60]

Selective compliance with laws based on one's own personal beliefs would be incompatible with the rule of law, Russell argued, taking the chance to cast aspersions on the civil rights movement. And "good and patriotic citizens" should avoid all violence, however tense the months ahead might be. He concluded:

> I still have faith in the soundness of our free institutions and in the inherent good judgment of the American people. I can but believe that in time the people of this nation will turn back the trend toward statism and enforced conformity in every activity of life.

Violence and defiance are no substitute for the long campaign of reason and logic we must wage to overcome the prejudices and misconceptions which now influence the majority of the American people in this field.

The response of Georgia's *Macon Telegraph* to this speech spoke volumes: "If Senator Russell . . . argues obedience and condemns defiance, who in this country has standing to suggest otherwise?"[61] President Johnson thanked Russell for his statement, calling it "as significant as any I have heard made by a public official in this country."[62] Some of Russell's fellow filibusterers sounded similar themes, including Allen Ellender (D-LA), Herman Talmadge (D-GA), and William Fulbright (D-AR).[63]

Once the law passed, it was implemented quickly and with remarkably little resistance. Some commercial establishments did close their doors rather than admit black customers; restaurant owner Lester Maddox chased potential black customers away with a gun, before later closing his establishment, and in 1966 was elected governor of Georgia. But such cases were rare enough that they made national news. Especially in the cities of the South, compliance was overwhelming and rapid, confirmed by civil rights groups' deliberate testing. The law was slower to penetrate rural areas, yet even there violent resistance was rare.[64] Enforcement began by the end of July. By December, the Supreme Court unanimously upheld the public accommodations requirements of the law in two cases.[65] At no time did an organized campaign of opposition gain traction.[66]

Passage of the Civil Rights Act of 1964 hardly solved America's race relations problems. The law's voting sections proved to be largely ineffectual during the 1964 election season, with 57 percent of Southern blacks still not registered—94 percent in Mississippi. After Democrats' landslide victories in that election, Congress quickly turned its attention to passing another voting bill. After the horrific violence against black protesters on the Edmund Pettus Bridge on Bloody Sunday, March 7, 1965, a broad bipartisan coalition once again mobilized in support of the law, making its passage inevitable. Southerners were allowed a 24-day filibuster, but their effort was obviously doomed. As Zelizer puts it, Mansfield thought it important to give his Democratic colleagues "their dramatic last stand, so they could demonstrate to their constituents that they understood and shared their opposition to the bill. He didn't want to destroy the Southerners; he knew that when Congress moved beyond civil rights issues, their votes could be useful to the Democratic Party."[67] Like the Civil Rights Act the year before, the Voting

Rights Act passed with overwhelming bipartisan support, with Southern Democrats isolated in their opposition. Specific parts of the regime imposed by the Voting Rights Act would become controversial, but once again the core of the act has maintained overwhelming bipartisan support over the last half century.[68]

In the second half of the 1960s, the Civil Rights Act also desegregated Southern public schools as the Supreme Court's *Brown v. Board of Education* decision, delivered a decade earlier, had been unable to do. As political scientist Gerald Rosenberg demonstrated, progress after *Brown* was painfully slow, with just 1.2 percent of Southern black children attending schools with white classmates in 1964. By the 1965–66 school year, that figure rose to 6.1 percent, and by 1972–73 it was 91.3 percent.[69] The new statutory regime changed Southern officials' mindset with a combination of effective carrots and sticks in a way the Supreme Court's command could not. While so-called segregation academies sprung up as a way for some white Southerners to avoid integrated schools, these never included more than a small fraction of Southern students.[70] Again, the Civil Rights Act wrought massive change with an impressively modest level of backlash.

The path that the civil rights laws, born of legislative struggle, have taken in our politics can be profitably contrasted with another policy that emerged from the racial turmoil of the 1960s: affirmative action. Sociologist John David Skrentny has chronicled the policy's haphazard beginnings. The framers of the Civil Rights Act thought they were making preferential hiring of minorities flatly illegal; on the Senate floor, Hubert Humphrey called claims that the act would lead to quotas a "bugaboo" and said, "In fact the very opposite is true."[71] However, in the wake of race riots and widespread black anger, the Johnson administration's desire to "do something" led to presidential directives adopting race-conscious contracting policies for federal construction projects and encouraging private corporations to adopt similar policies. Johnson starkly told business leaders in July 1967, "You can put these people to work and you won't have a revolution because they've been left out. If they're working, they won't be throwing bombs in your homes and plants. Keep them busy and they won't have time to burn your cars."[72] Race-conscious hiring programs also offered a way to confront America's racial inequities without large federal expenditures, which were hard to come by in the cash-strapped Vietnam War years. At no point did a majority of the public support these policies; nor were they championed by civil rights advocates.

In spite of its inauspicious beginnings, affirmative action was not targeted for reversal by the Nixon administration. In part because of his administration's liberal elements and in part because he was eager to create difficulties for organized labor, Nixon embraced the policy and institution-alized it in 1969.[73] That drew the ire of many in Congress, including Everett Dirksen. A rather arcane battle ensued, hinging on the comptroller general's overruled finding that the program was illegal. While the Senate effectively voted to defund the program, the House sided with the administration; al-though it seems hard for us to imagine, most Democrats voted to end affirm-ative action, and most Republicans to preserve it. The politics of the issue shifted drastically in the early 1970s, as Nixon decided to woo the "hard hat" vote and repudiated his administration's earlier policies. But by that time, the policy had taken on a life of its own in the executive branch and in the courts, soon moving from private employment to school admissions.[74]

Affirmative action would survive, then, and indeed become part of the fabric of late 20th-century American life. However, unlike the desegregation of public accommodations and the outlawing of employment discrimination, both of which became political nonissues as they achieved widespread ac-ceptance, affirmative action has remained bitterly controversial throughout its history. Because it was never properly contested in the legislative arena, its opponents have always been able to question its basic legitimacy, seek its overthrow in the Supreme Court, and denounce it as a pernicious form of reverse racism.[75]

## Why 1964 Was Unlike 1861 or 2021

Many political observers take a process-neutral view of government; that is, they believe *what* the government does is all that matters, while questions of *how* the government proceeds are fundamentally inconsequential. From that perspective, if we believe that the Civil Rights Act and Voting Rights Act made positive social changes, then the years of delays imposed by Southern Democrats must be regarded in a purely negative light. If the laws were good, then passing them later rather than sooner was bad.

Those who make their lives in the world of politics do not think this way. For them, and especially for those who were most important in shaping the push for civil rights in Congress in the early 1960s, respecting the distinctive traditions of the House and the Senate was an important good—not only in its own right, but because it provided an unparalleled means for dealing with social conflict. Legislators of the time did not agree on exactly what those traditions required; at some points, Russell's rhetoric made it seem like any set of parliamentary procedures that ended in congressionally imposed desegregation ought to be regarded as tyrannical. But his actions spoke louder than his words. Once he had lost, he was obliged to admit that the majority had acted with graciousness and respect for him and his colleagues. He did not denounce Congress, but continued to revere it. He did not try to convince his constituents that the Senate's leaders were traitors, but continued to work closely with them on matters of national importance.

When we think about the struggle for civil rights, we most often focus on the terrible sacrifices it required from the brave men, women, and even children who were willing to put themselves in harm's way to call America to justice. It is altogether fitting and proper that we should do this.

But we should also ask: Why did this turn out to be one of the defining triumphs of our democratic process, rather than the cause of a second civil war? Why was this nation, so full of racial animosity, able to digest such a radical social change?

A well-functioning Congress had a great deal to do with this success. Southern representatives were able to mount an effective defense of their intense segregationist beliefs for years. Yet that very defense pushed the fierce advocates on the other side of the question to broaden their coalition, ultimately leaving the Southerners isolated. At the same time, by giving them opportunities to keep fighting in Congress, the system itself discouraged any incipient desire for secessionism. There was never any serious talk of Southerners leaving the union or mounting an armed insurrection as they suffered their defeat in 1964.[76] The contrast with 1861, and even 2021, could hardly be sharper.

American politics has degenerated into civil war only once since the nation won its independence almost a quarter millennium ago. Those of us who focus on this country and its institutions sometimes take this record for granted, presuming that conflicts will be dealt with through political maneuvering in the short term and through electoral majorities working their will in the long run. But maintaining the civil peace in a country as diverse and factious as ours is far from automatic. A well-functioning legislature is indispensable to ensuring that in the process of navigating social changes, no group is driven to desperation.

To achieve these peaceful resolutions, the *how* is as important as the *what*. Russell asserted, "The tempo of change is the crux of the whole matter," and pushed for more delay. Mansfield believed that the moment had come for a reckoning. History has vindicated Mansfield (who would later go on to be the US ambassador to Japan under both Carter and Reagan, and who was awarded the Presidential Medal of Freedom in 1989). Despite their substantive disagreement, both men understood themselves as engaged in a cooperative enterprise of handling social conflict and change. The two men continued to work closely in the years following the passage of the Civil Rights Act.

Russell died in 1971, having continued to serve in the Senate until the very end. He was immediately honored as a statesman of the first rank. In 1972, the Senate decided to rename its two historic office buildings; the "Old S.O.B." would become the Russell building, and the "New S.O.B." would be named for Dirksen, who had died in 1969.

At a 1996 dedication of a statue of Russell in the rotunda of his eponymous building, Vice President Al Gore praised the senator's many policymaking contributions; on national security, "Senator Russell had no peer," and the Georgian had done a great deal to combat poverty in the rural South. But Gore concluded by appreciating "that reverence to his life, his spartan apartment, his utter devotion to the Senate as an institution, his enduring selflessness that inspired even those with whom he disagreed."[77]

The statue remains standing today. But can we still appreciate the qualities that Russell possessed, a half century after his death? Given well-grounded contemporary revulsion for his earnest racism, it seems hard to imagine. He was a man of another age, and we are understandably eager to leave behind his most famous commitment; there are certainly strong arguments to be made that a segregationist should no longer be honored by having his name on one of Congress' most important buildings. Even then, however, we should endeavor to remember and appreciate Russell's qualities. He was, even more importantly than a defender of segregation, a champion of the Senate and its deliberative tradition. He was a representative of his region, but he demonstrated how acting as a representative can serve the national good, even in defeat. Without an appreciation of that spirit, it is difficult to know how the nation is supposed to work its way through the thorniest problems.

How and why did we lose track of that deep respect for process? To those questions we now turn.

# PART II
# CONGRESS TRANSFORMED

Having considered Congress at its best in Part I, we now turn to examine our legislature's evolution over the last half century. The House and Senate saw dramatic reversals during that time. The dominant hold of Southern conservative committee chairmen was already breaking by the late 1960s, opening the door to new forms of organization.

As we will see in Chapter 4, congressional reformers in the 1970s were divided on which way they wanted the organizational pendulum to swing. Some sought centralized leadership, but for the time being they mostly lost out. Instead, Congress experimented with radically decentralized power structures that opened the legislature to the messy plurality of American society. Legislators soon judged that system to be unworkable and, over the ensuing decades, pushed the institution toward obedience to strong leaders.

Chapter 5 focuses on conservatives' role in effecting this change. Long shut out of congressional power, Republicans took control of the Senate from 1981 to 1986. Even so, with the House still in Democratic hands and Ronald Reagan in the White House, conservatives developed a considered critique of the legislative branch and its inappropriate encroachments on the executive. They proselytized a vision of Congress as hopelessly corrupted. Taking on a distinctly Wilsonian reform sensibility, they organized around a coherent policy vision and went on to landslide victories in the 1994 midterm elections. Once in power, they achieved a further consolidation of leadership power, but their determination to spite the institution they now controlled detracted from their ambitious policymaking efforts.

Chapter 6 chronicles the partisan struggles of the first two decades of the 21st century. Although the two parties have frequently traded off control of Congress, both have adhered to a model of leaders exercising tight control of the agenda. Deliberation has suffered, and today's Congress flattens America's diversity rather than allowing its complex representation. The triumph of polarization has not brought us more responsible government either. Instead, much of our policymaking bypasses the legislative branch entirely, leaving the executive branch and courts to sort things out. This leaves our country less able to reach a sense of resolution on any important matter and creates disorienting policy uncertainty in the shadow of perpetual litigation.

Each of these chapters dives into matters of legislative organization, many of which ordinary readers may regard as forbidding—the word "arcane" is often used to describe parliamentary procedures for a reason. But we must attend alike to formal rules and informal pathways of legislative power if we are to understand what kind of representation Congress is supporting. As we will see, different organizational choices entail very different capabilities for our legislature, with fateful consequences for our nation.

# 4

# Cacophony

## The Reforms of the 1970s

The Congress must regain the will to govern. . . . We must be willing
to take the political heat involved in making hard choices between
competing public needs.

—Rep. Barbara Jordan (D-TX), April 18, 1973[1]

No matter how assertive [Congress] is, or how creative and qualified
for leadership individual members are, maybe the institution is not
really equipped to act as a strong leader.

—Sen. Edmund Muskie (D-ME), September 1978[2]

Having passed the Civil Rights Act, Voting Rights Act, and President
Johnson's Great Society legislation, members of Congress might well
have regarded their institution with some pride. Theirs was a body that
had successfully navigated a series of major social and governmental
transformations, holding together in the midst of national turmoil.

Instead, many members of Congress joined outside reformers in thinking
America's legislature needed disruption. Like Woodrow Wilson in the 1880s,
they were frustrated by imperious committees that failed to join their work
to any coherent party program. House liberals' understanding of their institution was based, in the words of Nelson Polsby, on "folklore that built
up . . . after 1937 about lost opportunities, bills withdrawn or modified, watered down or defeated on account of insuperable obstacles somewhere in
the organizational structure of the House."[3] As reformers saw things, the
Congress of the mid-1960s had done much to transform the federal government, but old-fashioned political structures had stopped it from doing so
much more.

Many who took this view were influenced by an influential 1950 report of the American Political Science Association (APSA), "Toward a More Responsible Two-Party System," which argued that America's loose, ideologically unfocused parties made sound government impossible in the nuclear age. It recommended that each party create a 50-member national Party Council that would be charged with ensuring that all members of the party worked cooperatively.[4] The resulting differentiation between two programmatic parties would create meaningful "responsibility" to voters.

Recall that Madison had worried about faction not only in the sense of "special interests," each comprising a small fraction of society, but also about a "majority faction" in which the larger part of the citizenry unjustly preys on the smaller. The pluralistic system he envisioned for the extended republic, as manifested in Congress, would minimize this problem by the heterogeneity of representatives. But the APSA committee, in one perceptive critic's words, "apparently hopes that all factions in the party will argue themselves into agreement and that the problem of the relative rights of majorities and minorities seldom need arise."[5] Factional struggle in the legislature would be contained by powerful parties, which would—somehow—dissolve factional struggle among the lawmakers within their ranks as they fashioned clearly differentiated policy programs.

As we will see in Chapters 5 and 6, American politics would come to realize the APSA committee's hopes for partisan separation, roughly from the mid-1980s to the present day. Although neither party succeeded in building party machinery capable of imposing programmatic coherence, congressional leaders did manage to stifle lawmakers whose ambitions did not neatly coincide with the national party's political objectives. To put it mildly, the greater differentiation between the two parties achieved has not had happy consequences for American politics. But to understand this later dynamic, we must first attend to developments in the 1970s, a tumultuous era in Congress in which nearly the opposite reform impulse won out. As neo-Wilsonian reformers sought to swing the pendulum of congressional organization toward centralized control, a separate group of members opportunistically sought to decentralize power out to subcommittees. Both of these groups were dominated by ideological liberals—indeed, confusingly, sometimes a single member was attracted by both reform impulses simultaneously.

The decentralizers made their mark most clearly in the 1970s. Arguing that only a more democratized legislature could respond to the voices of all Americans and meet their ever-expanding demands, they overhauled

Congress' organization. By 1980, both the House and the Senate were transformed. The power of committee chairmen was smashed, and the clubby environment that reformers believed had kept important issues from receiving consideration was a thing of the past. Agenda control was decentralized and secrecy diminished.

This was no longer a Congress closed off to the American people. A shift away from powerful committee chairmen toward subcommittee government multiplied access points for citizens hoping to gain a foothold in the legislative process. A huge expansion of congressional staff gave legislators much greater capacity to interface with their constituents. But, contrary to the hopes of those who thought openness would make Congress more responsive to popular concerns, the pendulum had swung too far toward openness, leaving congressional affairs a muddle. In practice, it was the growing ranks of well-organized interest groups who were best able to take advantage of the multiplied access points.

And so by the end of the 1970s, Congress was increasingly viewed as a playground for special interests—especially by Republicans. Although a number of GOP members had at first joined with Democrats pursuing institutional change, hoping to increase their own opportunities for real influence, reform in the 1970s was mostly a Democratic project often implemented through decisions of the Democratic Caucus. As their majorities in Congress swelled, Democrats showed little compunction about systematically minimizing the influence of their partisan opponents, so Republicans and conservatives began to see Congress as an institution inimical to their interests. Chapter 5 takes up this theme at length.

Even for the reformers on Capitol Hill, who were glad to have vanquished the imperious "barons" of the old committee system, the decade ended with concerns that subcommittees had "taken on trappings of feudal domains whose leaders have adopted a policy of mutual noninterference in the affairs of their peers."[6] Having sought openness, Congress had made itself unmanageable and cacophonous. Having sought a stronger presence in oversight, Congress had made itself scandal hungry and reactive.

This chapter proceeds by offering two parallel stories of reform in the 1970s. First, it focuses on the power struggles within the legislature and the many experiments with agenda setting that Democrats tried. Second, it looks at reform efforts meant to secure "good government" in a variety of ways, including by building up a more capable Congress that would more energetically oversee and police the executive branch. Unfortunately, even as Watergate gave Congress a chance to regain stature in the eyes of the American public, a series of scandals damaged its reputation.

The chapter concludes by taking stock of Congress during the presidency of Jimmy Carter, himself a vocal proponent of government reform. With huge majorities during Carter's term, Democrats seemed poised to transform the federal government, and perhaps the nation. Instead, Congress struggled, unfocused and unpopular. Ethics reforms seemed only to bring further embarrassing scandals into the public eye. After a few promising developments early in 1977, Carter's legislative vision dissipated over the course of his term. Congressional approval fell to all-time lows and Democrats struck many as irredeemably beholden to various special interest groups, a case that their increasingly restive Republican opponents would take to the public with great zeal. Before long, the pendulum would be swinging again.

## Changing Process, Shifting Power—The Rise of Subcommittee Government

The process of reform that culminated in the early 1970s began earlier. In the Senate, a seniority-privileging system of "apprenticeship" had reigned through most of the 1950s. If a younger member wanted to make his way into the exercise of power, he was instructed to "Keep your mouth shut and your eyes open."[7] For a large new cohort of Northern liberal Democrats elected in 1958, however, this long game seemed rigged against them. They sought to break the dominance of the conservative coalition and soon found that the intense media scrutiny on their institution (heightened by the presence of five presidential aspirants) gave them the means to bypass apprenticeship. Even freshman senators, such as Eugene McCarthy (D-MN), found opportunities to command attention on the national stage. As we saw in Chapter 3, Majority Leader Mansfield's new style was accommodating and allowed a full airing of senators' views. By the early 1960s, then, the Senate was experiencing "a flood of individual self-expression," a trend that would only intensify later.[8]

The House was not far behind. The Democratic Study Group (DSG), founded in 1959, organized the efforts of Midwestern and Northern liberals who won seats in former Republican strongholds. Beyond providing mutual support in fundraising and production of campaign materials, these members set out to alter the balance of power within the Democratic Party, challenging the grip of the entrenched "Boston-Austin Connection." They progressed by creating an independent source of policy information for liberals, developing an independent whipping operation, and eventually overhauling the mechanisms of decision-making in the House.[9] In 1969, the DSG helped resuscitate the Democratic Caucus as a functioning institution after many years in abeyance—it had been of limited use to a big tent party that expected members' views to frequently conflict. Monthly meetings of all of the party's House members soon gave liberal reformers (who continued to coordinate through the DSG) a venue to press their case for new internal party rules.[10]

Two reformers with outsized personalities and opposing visions of how the House should operate drove many of the changes in the people's chamber in the 1970s. Rep. Richard Bolling (D-MO), first elected to the House in 1948, was brilliant, steeped in congressional history, and often arrogantly pedantic with his colleagues. In his 1964 book, *House Out of Order*, he declared the House "a shambles," railing against "power divided among a few autocrats and unrepresentative groups" and a centralized leadership too weak to overcome them. To reorient the chamber to the public good, reformers would need to dismantle seniority rules and implement a jurisdictional reorganization of committees.[11] Most of all, Bolling wanted to see a stronger Speaker who would act as "the actual operating head of the party's legislative apparatus." That would allow the vision of "responsible party government" advocated by the APSA report to flourish, as Democrats would coordinate around a clear agenda and the Speaker would be held accountable not only to his party colleagues but also to the voting public.[12] As we saw in Chapter 3, in the course of pursuing civil rights, liberal reformers already made a good start on this path, first diluting conservatives' control of the Rules Committee in 1961 and then bringing it to heel in late 1963 on the way to passage of the Civil Rights Act.

Bolling's counterpart was Rep. Phillip Burton (D-CA) of San Francisco, a progressive ally of union bosses and a champion of an enlarged welfare state. A man of prodigious appetites and undisguised ambition, Burton made his mark in the House from the time of his first election in 1964. Whereas Bolling drew his power from his relatively senior position on the House Rules Committee (which he would chair from 1979 to 1982) and was a connoisseur of process, Burton established his reputation on Capitol Hill by picking fights on behalf of liberal causes. In 1967, for example, he took a stand against a scheduled freeze of federal welfare payments, getting a *New York Times* columnist to gush, "Around here, it sometimes requires browbeating, black-mail, mixed metaphors and guts to feed poor children."[13] Burton's mode of politics anticipated the rise of entrepreneurial politicians in Congress, each empowered to steer the federal government's largesse and regulatory heft on behalf of their constituents and their vision of the public good.

The two men—both liberal Democrats—had some common enemies, in-cluding the conservative chairmen who posed a continuing threat to liberal legislation. Although the seniority principle for chairmen had been honored as sacrosanct ever since the "Revolt of 1910" overthrew the power of Speaker Cannon, reform-minded members insisted that seniority was "crippling effective leadership and making it impossible to present and pursue a co-herent legislative program," in the words of an influential 1970 DSG report.[14] A Democratic Caucus group chaired by Julia Butler Hansen (D-WA), which included Burton, devised a procedure by which 10 members could force a whole-caucus vote on a chairmanship. That mechanism's first use in 1971 failed but sent a strong message that chairmen would be accountable. In 1973, votes were forced on every chairman, and a further rule change instituted secret ballots if 20 percent of the caucus requested them. Although no chairman was voted out, momentum was building.[15] Finally, after the historic wave election of 1974, liberals ousted three of five chairmen targeted by the DSG. In a telling sign of a new order, the huge and feisty class of Democratic freshmen demanded that "prospective" chairmen present their agendas for their perusal. With these ousters and a spate of retirements, by 1977 half of all House chairmen had not held their positions in 1974; not coincidentally, new chairmen were much more liberal than their predecessors.[16] By helping to decide who would be chairmen, younger members of the House majority now shared in power in a way that had been completely beyond them in the heyday of committee barons.

But if Burton, Bolling, and other liberals could cooperate in struggling against Southern conservatives' power, they were deeply suspicious of each other on other fronts. Bolling reflected: "Burton was just like Lyndon Johnson. He had the damn fool idea that getting something done was more important than making the process of democracy real to people. It's a leg-islative trick. If you do that, you destroy process and faith in process and government of laws." Burton, for his part, dismissed Bolling as a "white collar liberal" whose interest in rules blinded him to the importance of winning policy victories that would improve poor Americans' lives.[17] The two men and their allies often worked at cross-purposes, with Bolling's more senior group pursuing greater agenda control for top leaders and Burton's more ideological group seeking to *further* diffuse power to members of middling seniority (like Burton himself) and to increase members' abilities to push policy to the left of what the caucus might otherwise support.[18]

Burton used subcommittee government as the vehicle for his ambitions. Subcommittees had been proliferating ever since the Legislative Reorganization Act of 1946 reduced the number of standing committees from 43 to 19. But they mostly operated as tame subsidiaries of full committees, hand-picked by chairmen and, unsurprisingly, operated as tools for realizing their agendas. If a subcommittee undertook activities at odds with the chairman's priorities, in the next Congress it might simply disappear. But new rules pushed through the Democratic Caucus, again through the Hansen Committee, transformed subcommittees into independent bastions of power by limiting the number of subcommittee chairmanships any member (including full chairmen) could hold and giving subcommittee chairmen the ability to hire their own staffer. In 1973, a "Subcommittee Bill of Rights" fixed jurisdictions, gave the caucus responsibility for appointing chairmen, and directed more staff and budgetary resources to the previously subordinate bodies.[19] Liberals were the major champions of these reforms, and they expected, correctly, that they would be the major beneficiaries in the long run. Even in the 92nd Congress (1971–72), the 16 members becoming new subcommittee chairmen were disproportionately liberal and non-Southern.[20]

The House's 132 subcommittees in 1973 quickly became the engines of activity in the chamber, with full committees acting as their supervisors and coordinators, a clear devolution of power that empowered many members of the majority. Rep. Mo Udall (D-AZ) advised Democratic members that if you didn't know a colleague's name, addressing him as "Mr. Chairman" was generally safe enough.[21] But the decentralized regime came with immediate challenges. Members had difficulty attending all of their meetings. At a deeper level, there was reason to worry that the fragmentation of power had created more access points for special interests, who could target just a few staffers in several different subcommittees to move their agenda or stop troublesome legislation that in past years would have been unassailable with the support of powerful committee chairmen.[22] The Speaker of the House, Carl Albert (D-OK), had been an energetic coalition builder earlier in his career but now struck many of his colleagues as a spent force, incapable of

keeping up with this complexifying scene that was quickly becoming an un-
gainly mess.

In one significant attempt to regain some order, in 1973 Bolling convinced House leaders to create a Select Committee on Committees, with him
as chair (pictured in Figure 4.1). The committee recognized policymaking
had become "fragmented and split"—observing that "As the Members' committee responsibilities increase . . . other important functions and services
must suffer."[23] Against this, Bolling hoped to restructure jumbled committee jurisdictions to better correspond to executive branch functions and
empower Democratic leaders in an effort to tidy things up. Staffed by political scientists, the committee's proposals embodied their hope that strong,
centralized party leadership would energize Congress against growing executive branch power. But, for all the clarity of his vision and mastery of the
House's parliamentary arcana, Bolling proved inept at navigating the delicate power politics entailed by a jurisdictional shake-up. For his part, Burton
said the effort "isn't really reform" and actively worked against it, reasoning

**Figure 4.1**  Rep. Richard Bolling (D-MO) chairing a meeting of the Select
Committee on Committees in June 1973.
*Source:* LaBudde Special Collections, UMKC University Libraries.

that liberal reformers should bide their time until after the 1974 mi
elections, when they expected to make significant gains.[24] Joining forces w
turf-protecting chairmen, they sunk Bolling's plan with a 111–95 secret vo
of the Democratic Caucus, referring the committee's recommendations to
the Hansen Committee, which responded by devising an extremely diluted
substitute. The proposals were pitted against each other, along with another
substitute amendment offered by Republicans, in a complicated floor debate
in October 1974. The Hansen substitute won out, 203–165, mostly on the
strength of Democratic support.[25] It did very little to reverse the trend toward fragmentation; indeed, its doubling of committee staffing only accelerated the process.[26] Two later bodies organized on behalf of centralizing
reforms accomplished basically nothing.[27] Bolling had lost.

House Democrats did make two important changes on behalf of their
leadership in 1975. The first came in the wake of the self-destruction of
Wilbur Mills (D-AR), the legendary chairman of the Ways and Means
Committee whose substance abuse problems spiraled out of control until he
was pulled over near Washington's Tidal Basin, drunk and accompanied by
his mistress, a former stripper, who had two black eyes. Two months later,
the duo appeared together on stage at a club in Boston and the congressman
declared he would make her a star; Mills' proud career was all but over.[28]
Immediately following these incidents, House Democrats reassigned the
power to make committee assignments, which had for decades belonged
to Ways and Means, to the Steering and Policy Committee, a more liberal
body closer to leadership. The second change gave the Speaker the ability to
choose all of the majority's members of the Rules Committee, ensuring that it
would never again become the bill killer it had been under Howard Smith.[29]
Nevertheless, powerful subcommittees would endure as the major engine of
legislative work in the House all the way until Newt Gingrich moved to restore chairmen's power in 1995.[30]

The Senate also saw continued dispersal of power, with two important changes coming in 1975. First came a major change to the operation
of the filibuster. The threshold for invoking cloture was dropped from 67 to
60 votes.[31] At the same time, Mansfield and the majority whip, Sen. Robert
Byrd (D-WV), designed a "track" system that would allow a filibustered bill
to be placed on a parallel agenda rather than blocking other business from
proceeding on the floor. Tracking a filibustered matter could largely satisfy those senators uninvested in it. As a result, the social pressure within
the Senate against filibustering diminished, and the prevalence of filibusters

ore, conservatives and reformers alike deployed new ~~oture~~ filibusters and holds, to bring business to a ' of the cloture threshold.[33] James B. Allen (D-AL) e filibuster in the debate over filibuster reform, ..g incessant amendments and a roll-call vote on л Prayer from St. Francis of Assisi."[34] Mike Gravel (D-AK) ~~...~~ened to extend a personal filibuster by means of introducing a two-volume biography of Gerald Ford into debate via an amendment, which the clerk could then be forced to read in full—though Byrd ultimately ran him off.[35] Unlike the historic filibuster of the Civil Rights Act, these increasingly common obstructive tactics no longer focused the nation's attention on a legislative conflict, however. Instead, they evolved to become a routine, if arcane, part of Senate procedure. Chapter 6 takes up the important question of the filibuster's role in the modern Senate.

Second, as in the House, a reorganization of Senate committees diffused power. Each senator was given three dedicated staffers to handle work on particular committee assignments, which made legislators less dependent on chairmen. Gravel, who championed the change, said that "power is distributed on the basis of knowledge. What we say here in this resolution is that we want the apportionment of knowledge on a more equitable basis."[36] Following the Bolling Committee's example, a bipartisan Senate Select Committee organized in 1977 proposed jurisdictional changes. Unlike in the House, its proposals carried the day, leading to a culling of committees and subcommittees. Still, by imposing limits on how many subcommittees each senator could chair, the main effect was to spread control of subcommittees more broadly, empowering younger members.[37] As in the House, decentralization of power introduced its own challenges, such that in the early 1980s senators were complaining about "chaos" and "quality of life" in an unmanageable chamber.[38]

In both chambers, reformers never did line up behind a single vision or champion. Decentralized power flowed to younger, more liberal members because they had become more numerous and more powerful—but not strong enough to dictate terms to their whole party. Burton had tried when he attempted to make the Democratic Caucus the site of real decision-making for the majority party after becoming chairman in 1975. By party rules, the caucus was only supposed to decide on procedural matters, but on more than one occasion Burton sought to decide substantive matters, once including the decision to cut off military aid to Cambodia. Although the measure carried easily, conservatives cried foul: Why wasn't this a matter for the House International Relations Committee? Rep. Thomas Morgan (D-PA), that committee's chairman, fumed, "If this is the way we're going to operate, let's abolish the committee system, open up the Caucus, and call witnesses."[39] There remained too much diversity within the party to make rallying around whatever the majority of Democrats wanted an appealing strategy, at least in the 1970s.

The contending reform impulses finally had a face-off in 1976 when Albert announced his retirement. Majority Leader Tip O'Neill would become Speaker, but second-in-command was uncertain due to the weakness of the next in line, Majority Whip John McFall (D-CA). Bolling and Burton could have their reckoning. Most observers expected Burton, the more politically adept of the two, to prevail. O'Neill, though, didn't want to see either man win, so he quietly backed another candidate, Deputy Whip Jim Wright (D-TX), keeping alive the so-called Austin-Boston connection. As Bolling and Burton bludgeoned each other in a grueling campaign, Wright picked up backers; he probably also benefited from what might be called "reform fatigue."[40] In one of the most dramatic leadership contests on record, Democrats voted in three ballots. With Burton leading, McFall was eliminated after the first ballot and Bolling, narrowly, on the second. Burton had hoped to face the more moderate Wright on the final ballot, expecting that he could consolidate liberal support. But he had underestimated the resentment of many colleagues who felt he was a tyrant in the making, as well as O'Neill's willingness to work against him. Wright won the third ballot, 148–147.[41] The reform moment was at an end. And, as Chapter 5 details, Wright's eventual ascent to the Speakership would forever alter the House.

## From Legislating to Openness and Oversight

As the different groups jostled for power in the fight over centralization, another strand of reform played out. This one focused, broadly speaking, on the cause of "good government" and making Congress a cleaner, more open institution that would also be capable of reckoning with the excesses and abuses of the executive branch. Especially after Watergate and the cultural shift it engendered, members of Congress wanted to present themselves to the American people as vigilant watchdogs—as overseers of existing power structures as much as framers of new laws. They indeed forced a shift, but the results were decidedly mixed.

Legislators began opening their institution to greater scrutiny in the late 1960s. They were urged on by public interest groups channeling distrust generated largely by the war in Vietnam, the most prominent of which was Common Cause, founded in 1970 by a liberal Republican veteran of the Johnson administration, John Gardner. The new crop of reformers regarded traditional factional politics as profoundly corrupting. By pursuing sunshine laws, ethics reforms, and campaign finance restrictions, they sought to remake Congress as a body that would work on behalf of the common good.[42] Reacting against the stranglehold of reigning interests was hardly new to American politics, of course—as Chapter 1 discussed, such movements have often been responsible for reversing the direction of the organizational pendulum. But the new reformers were unusual in the depth of their disdain for transactional politics of all kinds. They were avid in their desire to disrupt the old ways without having a clear model of how congressional power should operate coherently. As a result, their reforms contributed to the gathering sense of chaos in the 1970s.

One of transparency advocates' major objectives was to make Congress' proceedings more discernible to the general public. Having helped elect many junior members, they broke through with the Legislative Reorganization Act of 1970, which made committee hearings and roll-call votes public (except in extraordinary cases) and ended unrecorded teller votes in its Committee of the Whole. Amendments printed in the *Congressional Record* at least one day in advance of a bill's floor consideration would also be guaranteed at least 10 minutes of debate, making it harder for chairmen to preemptively spike hostile amendments.[43] Liberal reformers hoped that, without "secret votes," conservatives would no longer be able to quietly, and anonymously, stop popular liberal amendments. Other similar changes followed later. In 1973, the House required all kinds of committee meetings to be public, and in 1975 the Senate followed suit. Reformers hoped that more transparency in voting would improve attendance and increase accountability to constituents, thereby improving the legislature's legitimacy. As Rep. Matthew Rinaldo (R-NJ) put it, "Confidence in our government can only come about when the people are able to observe and participate directly in the deliberative process."[44]

These reforms had an immediate impact. Recorded votes did, in fact, deliver higher attendance; an average of 360 members voted on the recorded teller votes of 1971–72, compared with 163 for the unrecorded teller votes of 1969–70. And with the advent of electronic voting in 1973, floor amendment activity exploded. The House had considered around two amendments per day in the 1950s but more than doubled that to four or five per day in the 1970s.[45] The dynamics of congressional life were profoundly altered by these shifts. With more recorded votes, members spent more of their time position-taking and felt they had less room to accommodate their colleagues whenever it might create blowback with their constituents. Opened committee meetings were also, unsurprisingly, more performative and less deliberative. A critic of open hearings, Rep. David Dennis (R-IN), lamented that members could be expected "to make their little speeches for the headlines" rather than focusing on the give-and-take of compromise with their colleagues, which would have to take place elsewhere if at all.[46] When the House began televising its floor sessions in 1977 (a move the Senate would not follow until 1985), it further locked in the idea that a representative's speeches were primarily for those outside of the building. Negotiation, persuasion, and coalition building had become disadvantaged relative to various kinds of grandstanding. More sunshine illuminated legislators' affairs, but the business that took place in shaded nooks and crannies had been more valuable than reformers had realized.

Common Cause and other good government groups also sought to end Congress' informal attitude toward its members' financial arrangements and personal conduct. They successfully won limits on candidate spending ahead of elections with the Federal Election Campaign Act (FECA) of 1971 (a provision the Supreme Court would later strike down in *Buckley v. Valeo*) and established strict reporting requirements for both contributions and expenditures. In response to Watergate, lawmakers passed another FECA in 1974, establishing the Federal Election Commission and a system of public financing for presidential elections, while banning cash donations greater than $100 and capping contributions from both individuals and political committees. These laws assuaged citizens' fears that legislators were being bought with bags of cash, but their unintended effects would open the door to a different kind of special interest influence. The absence of public financing for congressional campaigns, along with the lack of aggregate limits on political action committee (PAC) contributions, incentivized interest groups to spread their influence widely throughout Congress in the years to come. The tendency toward decentralization ensured they would find a plethora of members who could affect policies relevant to them.[47]

Meanwhile, Congress beefed up self-policing of noncampaign behavior, which brought to light all sorts of embarrassing and scandalous behavior. Perhaps the most damaging involved Rep. Wayne Hays (D-OH), chairman of the House Administration Committee since 1971 and an important power broker in the favor economy of Washington. Hays was an anti-reformer par excellence, portraying outside agitators for reform as enemies of the institutional interests of the House. "Do any of you think that John Gardner of Common Cause has any respect for Congress? He has the utmost contempt for all of the Congress," he thundered to the Democratic Caucus as it considered moving to secret votes on committee chairs.[48] In 1975, the caucus narrowly voted to retain him as chairman. That made it all the more embarrassing when, in May 1976, the *Washington Post* published a front-page spread featuring Elizabeth Ray, his former secretary, who alleged she had been on his payroll as his mistress. "I can't type, I can't file, I can't even answer the phone," read the famous caption of her photograph. Hays denied everything, warning his colleagues that they were now "wide open to anyone who wants to make malicious statements about him and who wants to write a book or wants to get in Playboy magazine."[49] But he never effectively rebutted Ray's basic claim of having been kept on the taxpayer's dime and was soon chased from Congress. He was hardly the only member whose sex life became a political liability: another Democratic member was found to have hired his secretary as the result of an affair with her, and two other Democrats were found guilty on prostitution charges.[50]

If such behavior might be dismissed as none of the American people's business, the same could not be said of charges against Rep. Bob Sikes (D-FL), who, as chairman of the Military Construction Appropriations Subcommittee, had apparently favored companies in which he possessed a significant and wrongly undisclosed financial interest. Common Cause and other reformers crusaded against Sikes in 1976, leading to a House censure. When his constituents re-elected him all the same, the Democratic Caucus ultimately voted by a 2–1 margin to strip him of his chairmanship.[51] Legislators may have been making slow and steady progress cleaning their stables, but it came at a great reputational cost in the short term. Nor did it automatically bring about better policymaking. Once Wilbur Mills' scandal (discussed in the previous section) had cost him his job, he was replaced by the far more liberal Al Ullman (D-OR), who struggled to fill the power vacuum left by his departure. Whereas Mills had led a cohesive committee capable of resisting interest group pressure, Ullman failed to find legislative success in the face of newly created subcommittees and an increased roster of 37 fractious representatives.[52]

Notwithstanding its own troubles, Congress in the 1970s was also grappling with an executive branch that appeared to have slipped loose of effective constitutional checks and balances. In foreign affairs, many formerly enthusiastic supporters of presidential leadership found their faith damaged by the war in Vietnam. As Mike Mansfield put it when supporting a prohibition of US military action in Cambodia, over the preceding decades legislators had "handed over to the President on a silver platter" too many of their diplomatic responsibilities.[53] They would orient themselves quite differently in the years to come, organizing numerous investigations into America's covert activities, repealing the Gulf of Tonkin Resolution in 1970, and ultimately cutting off funding for war in Southeast Asia over Nixon's objections.[54] Subsequently, Congress passed the War Powers Resolution over Nixon's veto and created a series of special committees to rein in abuses of American intelligence agencies.

Congress also sought to bulk itself up to punch in the president's weight class on budgeting. Lacking its own green eyeshades, Congress had often been pushed around by the president and his team at the Bureau of the Budget—which Nixon reorganized into the Office of Management and Budget in 1970. Nixon had been aggressive in claiming the right to refuse spending (impound funds) on policies he opposed. To combat this dynamic, Bolling, among others, shepherded the Budget and Impoundment Control Act of 1974 to passage.[55] The law created and procedurally empowered budget committees in each chamber and constrained the president's impoundment power. The Ford and Carter administrations found these new committees forces to be reckoned with.[56] The law also created the Congressional Budget Office (CBO), which quickly became, and remains to this day, something of a modern marvel: a widely respected institution on Capitol Hill that has endured through many changes of political control.[57] As we shall see, though, some of the elements of the budget process would end up working in ways quite unexpected to the reformers who framed the 1974 act—and some would end up not working particularly well at all.

To counter the growth of the executive in other areas, Congress radically expanded its staff. While 19th-century members often operated alone or with a single secretary, legislators had, over time, voted themselves more help. The buildings of today's Hill bear witness to their progress: House office buildings opening in 1908, 1933, and 1965, named for the Speakers at the time of their completion (Cannon, Longworth, and Rayburn), with additional acquisitions in the late 1970s and 2017 (named Ford in 1990 and O'Neill in 2012). Senate Office buildings opened in 1908, 1958, and 1982 (and were eventually named Russell, Dirksen, and Hart). Personal staff, largely devoted to constituency services, had grown significantly since World War II, rising from 1,440 to 4,055 in the House and 590 to 1,749 in the Senate by 1967. But Congress hoped to confront its technical limitations relative to the executive branch in the 1970s, leading it to fill all that office space to the brim.[58] The Bolling Committee had proposed increasing House committee staff from 12 to 30, but the Democratic Caucus did them one better by increasing staff to 42 in early 1975 as part of the buildout of subcommittees.[59] In 1965, standing committees employed 571 staff in the House and 509 in the Senate. By 1974, those figures had shot up to 1,107 and 948, respectively. By 1979, they were 1,909 and 1,269 (see Table 4.1).[60]

Legislators also built up various cadres of nonpartisan professionals who could act as a resource for all legislators and staff members seeking to understand complicated matters. The Congressional Research Service was born out of the Library of Congress' Legislative Reference Service in 1970. Assisting members and committees in every aspect of the policymaking process, it would more than double its personnel to around 900 by 1985.[61] Legislators also created the Office of Technology Assessment in 1972 to give themselves in-house experts who could help them parse complicated technological issues.[62] They experimented with creating watchdogs embedded within agencies, giving them a permanent legal basis with the Inspector General Act of 1978. These inspectors general, while appointed by the president and accountable to agency heads, would nevertheless provide additional eyes and ears for Congress.[63]

Armed with all this new capacity, legislators dramatically expanded their oversight of the executive branch—much to the chagrin of the Nixon and

Table 4.1 Congressional committee staff, 1965–79

| Legislative Chamber | Congressional Committee Staff by Year | | |
|---|---|---|---|
| | 1965 | 1974 | 1979 |
| House | 571 | 1,107 | 1,909 |
| Senate | 509 | 948 | 1,269 |

Source: Brookings Institution, Vital Statistics on Congress, Table 5-5.

Ford administrations, which loudly complained that Congress was trying to usurp properly executive functions. In 1967, congressional committees had 1,797 "days" of hearings, of which 171 were devoted to oversight. By 1973, those figures were 2,513 and 290, respectively; by 1977, they were 3,053 and 537.[64] Some members, such as Rep. John Anderson (R-IL), worried that Congress' oversight boom would lead it to focus on "scandals, corruption a la Watergate, or Executive Branch hanky-panky . . . to bring headlines and turn on the TV klieg lights."[65] Members made some attempts to coordinate the boom of oversight activity, with the House Government Operations Committee made into a kind of clearinghouse after 1974. But oversight is an activity that can thrive in a decentralized, uncoordinated environment. Unlike legislation, which has to draw in a majority of all lawmakers in both houses to ultimately have an effect, oversight seemed attractive to many of the more entrepreneurial young members precisely because it offered a way to affect policy without the burdens entailed by passing a new statute. As Anderson suggested, the problem is that, untethered from legislative ambitions, oversight can become mere spectacle, a form of social commentary no more potent than journalistic exposés.

Three tools used heavily in the 1970s did give oversight some real teeth. First was the legislative veto. Since the 1920s, some statutory provisions had allowed Congress, or sometimes even single chambers or single committees, to override executive actions. As Congress created more regulatory agencies in the 1960s and '70s, it relied ever more heavily on legislative vetoes to give legislators a chance to discipline wayward bureaucrats. Rep. Elliott Levitas (D-GA) sought a "generic veto" for Congress that would apply to all executive branch actions, but that was too radical a rebalancing of power between the branches to gain much traction. Instead, in the 1970s it became standard practice to include multiple vetoes in a single bill, thereby giving committees many opportunities to intervene with agencies' ongoing work without having to pass new legislation.[66]

A second tool was the temporary authorization—sometimes referred to as a "sunset" provision. While most previous agencies and programs had been authorized permanently, allowing them to exist in perpetuity if Congress took no further action, in the 1970s legislators put 30 of 43 new agencies on a shorter leash, with a presumption of expiration without a renewal by Congress. This "sunset movement," championed by both good-government and small-government forces, was meant to ensure congressional committees would retain their leverage to steer the executive branch toward public-spirited outcomes—but, by ensuring that issues would be reopened every few years, it also gave lobbyists more bites at the apple.[67]

The third tool, the appropriations rider, utilized Congress' power of the purse to direct specific aspects of executive branch conduct. Committees had traditionally used their influence informally, through nonstatutory means, in which the relevant appropriators held an ongoing dialogue with the executive branch recipients of their dollars.[68] Riders—provisions forbidding agency officials from using funds to carry out particular policies—put the force of law behind congressional directives. Because lawmakers could count on spending bills being passed each year, attaching their preferences to these bills would come to be a substitute for standalone legislation worked through normal committees.[69]

Together, the buildup of capacity and refinement of strategies for executive branch control allowed Congress to peer over the shoulder of Washington bureaucrats at agencies old and new, giving lawmakers a relatively novel channel of influence. Impressed by these arrangements, political scientists in the 1980s would hypothesize "congressional dominance"—that, given their many ways of tugging on agencies' reins, legislators effectively called all the shots. Those claims were almost certainly overstated, but they nevertheless captured something important about what the 1970s transformation of Congress had accomplished.

That said, there was a clear downside to these developments. As we will see, presidents of both parties would come to decry legislative vetoes as disfiguring Congress' legislative process and infringing on the executive's constitutional domain. The work of reauthorizing turned out to be much more difficult than reformers had envisioned, and authorization rules would come to be observed mostly in the breach; the constant funding of "unauthorized" programs would become a regular, mildly embarrassing feature of Congress that persists to the present day. Appropriations riders, meanwhile, would come to be regarded as a serious threat to regular congressional order by the end of the 1970s, leading to attempts to suppress them.

## Congress in the Carter Administration

Democrats began the 95th Congress in January 1977 with very high hopes. They had a new, more energetic Speaker in O'Neill, and a new Democratic president free and clear of any responsibility for Vietnam, whose outsider's idealism impressed Americans. For a short time prospects looked bright. O'Neill managed to pass Carter's signature energy bill in the House in a matter of months by aggressively using the Speaker's new power of referring important bills to multiple committees, a Bolling reform that had mostly lain dormant under Speaker Albert.

The new Speaker won rhapsodic praise for a new "politics of inclusion" that got buy-in from a remarkably broad swathe of the majority.[70] O'Neill also knew that he had to confront the ethics problem head on. Looking to bolster their reputations for honest dealing, both chambers of Congress passed major ethics reforms, including mandatory disclosure of financial information, strict prohibitions on spending out of office accounts, and limits on outside income.[71]

These hopeful beginnings were short-lived. House Democrats remained divided, with the Bolling and Burton factions still fighting their old war and the (mostly younger) liberals and (mostly older) conservatives still at odds. More damaging still, Congress and Carter worked very poorly together. Carter's team of Georgian imports seemed not to understand the importance of buttering up the old-fashioned Boston politician who presided over the House, putting O'Neill and his guests in the back row of a balcony at the inaugural gala at the Kennedy Center and naming two Republicans as their first Massachusetts appointees.[72] More importantly, Carter had campaigned as an outsider and was not shy in expressing his disdain for the legislature. Like many sunshine reformers, he regarded Washington as a corrupted town in need of uncorrupted leadership. In fine Wilsonian fashion, Carter would write in his memoir, "Members of Congress, buffeted from all sides, are much more vulnerable to [special interest] groups than is the President. One branch of government must stand fast on a particular issue to prevent the triumph of self-interest at the expense of the public."[73]

Meanwhile, the rise of subcommittee government facilitated individual entrepreneurship for the small legion of chairmen but seldom channeled their efforts into viable legislation. A student of these "legislative individualists" saw them as pioneering new ways to garner publicity and build their personal brands, but questioned "whether the generation that burst into national politics in the turbulent 1970s can engineer a new set of arrangements that serves the nation's needs as effectively as it serves their particular desires."[74]

The progress of Carter's energy bill showed the reformed Congress' difficulties. Carter had dubbed the energy crisis "the moral equivalent of war" for a nation dogged by stagflation. He further warned that the world's oil might run out unless dramatic conservation measures were undertaken.[75] Carter's administration staked its reputation on the passage of wildly complex and ambitious regulatory controls and tax measures; the president announced in October 1977 that it would be "legitimate to measure the success of Congress and my own administration . . . on what happens to energy."[76] But while O'Neill had found a way to pass a bill that roughly answered the president's call through his decentralized chamber, in the Senate, 17 subcommittees claimed jurisdiction over energy issues and more than three-quarters of all senators had at least one energy-related assignment—and around half had more than one.[77] Senators were less disposed to impose energy taxes and more inclined to deregulate many facets of the energy and utility industries. Neither Senate leaders nor the president could wrangle such a large and disparate group of members even on the president's top priority. Instead, the bill was adulterated by interests of every variety; popular perception was that oil and gas lobbyists had turned a bill meant to discipline their industry into one that offered them a smorgasbord of benefits and a path toward deregulation, which the House had initially opposed. Finally, after a protracted conference between the two chambers and a liberal application of carrots and sticks by O'Neill, a package narrowly passed in October 1978. But the final laws bore little resemblance to Carter's or the House's original vision. In policy terms, one can make a case that Congress had struck a reasonable balance of the many interests involved—the many tradeoffs entailed in national energy policy are better juggled through Madisonian accommodation than by imposition of a visionary plan. In any case, there was little question that Democrats had lost politically.[78]

Congress' decentralization of power seemed like it would help legislators better represent the nation's remarkable and growing diversity—and there is no question that Congress was paying attention to and acting on a greater variety of the American people's concerns. Reform had solved the problem of a choked-off system, transforming the institution to a degree that might be regarded as almost miraculous. In a regime shift that political scientists Bryan D. Jones, Sean Theriault, and Michelle Whyman have dubbed "the Great Broadening," lasting from roughly 1964 to 1978, the number of topics Congress addressed in introduced bills increased by roughly one-third and the number of topics Congress addressed in roll-call votes roughly doubled.[79] Driven by the increase in staff, congressional activity accelerated and became more intricate during this period. On average, laws got longer and contained more titles.[80] Realizing reformers' ambitions, Congress was definitely doing more.

But "more" is very different from "better." Like many modern-day multitaskers, it seemed that the Congress of the late 1970s noticed much but accomplished little. By the end of the decade many people on and off Capitol Hill were wondering whether, in throwing off the yoke of the imperious chairmen of yesteryear, Congress had made itself unmanageable and cacophonous.[81] *National Journal* noted that once again congressional observers were "[looking] wistfully at the British parliamentary system" as they lamented the "leadership vacuum" where "'responsible activity is not rewarded,'" in the words of a leadership aide.[82] Bolling, whose vision of stronger centralized leadership had mostly been neglected, bemoaned, "Nothing has worked. Our policies are blowing up. We're factionalizing. We're unable to address obvious dilemmas."[83] The old chairmen had exercised too much agenda control, but in the reformed Congress many members wondered whether anyone was capable of keeping Congress focused at all.

The swollen ranks of Hill staffers, which some people hoped would give members the ability to handle the demands of a "modern" agenda, did not seem to solve the problem. They might be able to broaden members' effective fields of vision, but they could not multiply members' own time. Members saw and spoke to each other less than ever. As Michael Malbin noted in an influential critique of the Congress of the late 1970s, the Framers of the Constitution envisioned members of Congress actually deliberating in close contact with each other. Indirect communication through staffers might convey information, but it impaired members' ability to feel each other's responses. "The process no longer forces members to talk to each other to resolve the tough issues," Malbin wrote. Instead, "the agenda keeps them busy with other things," not least of which were the hugely multiplied numbers of oversight hearings held by subcommittees.[84]

Meanwhile, ethics reforms notwithstanding, Congress could not shake the stink of corruption. Press coverage of the 95th Congress fixated on "Koreagate," which involved a South Korean spy who spread his largesse among Washington politicians, including throwing two lavish birthday parties for O'Neill in 1973 and 1974 and entertaining him on junkets in Seoul. Allegations of out-and-out bribery swirled along with harder-to-dispel accusations of influence peddling. A House Ethics Committee investigation never turned up evidence of any quid pro quo with O'Neill, but it did find four Democratic representatives culpable, one of whom would plead guilty to criminal bribery for a scheme manipulating government-financed rice sales to Korea. As that drama wrapped up, the Speaker was roiled by another set of accusations alleging that he had benefited from two sweetheart deals in Massachusetts. Again, O'Neill would be officially cleared, but that hardly made the inquiries less embarrassing to him and to the House.[85] The decade ended with the famous "Abscam" scandal, in which an FBI sting operation secretly filmed a senator and six members of Congress accepting bribes from a man they believed to be an agent of Arab sheiks.[86]

Public perceptions of Congress during this time were abysmal, with approval plummeting from 47 percent in 1974 to an all-time low of 19 percent in fall 1979.[87] The American people thought that their representatives were not up to the task of fighting the disastrous inflation that gripped the country, which reached 18 percent in February 1980. Democrats managed few legislative accomplishments in response to these serious problems. Congress killed off a signature Carter administration proposal to cap rising health care costs, apparently because of legislators' ties to the health care industry. Attempts to focus on oversight backfired; people perceived the buildup of "iron triangles" of influence that included congressional committee staff, bureaucrats, and lobbyists, who collectively milked the status quo and frustrated reform. As it had a generation earlier, the press now clamored against a "do-nothing Congress."[88] In the runup to the 1980 elections, the Republicans ran a famous ad depicting a cigar-chewing O'Neill look-alike driving a big black Lincoln down the highway and eventually running out of gas.[89] Democrats would need to try something very different. As we will see in Chapter 5, in the 1980s they would embrace some of the centralizing proposals and stronger speakership that Richard Bolling had once championed. At the same time, Republicans would significantly turn up the pressure on them, relentlessly criticizing Congress as a way of convincing voters that it was, after decades of Democratic congressional control, time for a new direction.

The 1970s reform experience had wrought remarkable change in Congress. Writing in 1981, political scientist James Sundquist memorably dubbed the 1970s a time of "resurgence" for America's legislature. Sundquist, however, was not bullish on congressional prospects. Traits of distraction, parochialism, and irresponsibility—all of which Sundquist argued were ineradicably linked to Congress' representational role—doomed Congress to fade relative to the executive branch over the longer term, given the demands of modern governance.[90]

But if Sundquist thought Congress was doomed because of tendencies inherent to its nature as a representative legislature, one can also make the converse case: Congress was suffering because it had turned away from many of the virtues distinctive to a legislature. What Sundquist saw as "endemic weaknesses" of the Congress can instead be understood as distinctive virtues, as demonstrated in Chapters 2 and 3. When Congress tried to fashion itself as a shadow executive, involving itself in every aspect of the work of the administrative machinery it had set in motion, it was unable to stand toe to toe with the president or the technocrats and deformed policy as often as improved it. Reformers of the 1970s, however, seldom understood that peril. They reinvigorated Congress but did not put it on a good footing to fulfill its distinctive constitutional responsibilities *as a legislature*. Legislators' increasingly frenzied activity did not make the American people feel better represented or make the Congress better able to address the serious problems of rising crime, high inflation, and stagnating productivity growth. Members of Congress had turned away from a sense of their institution as the place where America's great struggles could be grasped and worked through.

Republicans would grab ahold of part of that critique of what Congress had become in the years to come—but they would convey little sense of the positive possibilities for Congress. Instead, what the great observer of Congress, Dick Fenno, termed "running for Congress by running against Congress" became the dominant political strategy for Republicans in the 1980s and beyond.[91] How they developed that strategy and rode it to majorities in both houses of Congress in 1994—and what it cost them, and us—is the story of the next chapter.

# 5

# Conservatives against Congress

As the separation of powers continues to erode, the present-day Congress has become the most unrepresentative and corrupt of the modern era. It is a Congress that lusts for power but evades responsibility for its actions.... Such an imperial Congress mocks the American precept of self-government that was so carefully crafted by the Founding Fathers.

—Rep. Newt Gingrich (R-GA), 1988[1]

Gerald Ford, first elected to Congress as a young World War II veteran from Michigan's Fifth District in 1948, was known as "a Congressman's Congressman." His quiet skill at facilitating deals between colleagues led fellow House Republicans to choose him as their leader in 1965. A legislative institutionalist, he aspired to become Speaker of the House. Instead, when Vice President Spiro Agnew resigned in scandal in 1973, Democrats indicated they would be happy to confirm Ford as his replacement (which they had to do under the new 25th Amendment to the Constitution). Eight months after Ford moved to the executive branch, Richard Nixon decided he could not continue to fight Congress over Watergate and resigned the presidency. On August 9, 1974, Ford took the oath to become the nation's 38th president—the first (and so far, only) one never elected on a national ticket. He chose as his chief of staff one of his former congressional allies, Donald Rumsfeld, who served four terms as a congressman from Illinois in the 1960s. Rumsfeld had been one of the leaders of a group of reformist House Republicans known as the "Young Turks" who had, for a while, made common cause with liberal Democrats agitating for a more open House.

With so many ties to Congress, Ford's administration seemed an unlikely hotbed of presidentialism. But Ford and his team found themselves in constant conflict with congressional Democrats, who, having won huge majorities in the 1974 midterms (291 House members and 61 senators) were aghast at Ford's pardon of Nixon, sharply at odds with his economic policies, and ever-more critical of the nation's lingering involvement in Vietnam. Ford vetoed a remarkable 66 bills during his two-and-a-half years in office, of which Congress overrode 12. By the time Jimmy Carter narrowly defeated him in 1976, Ford and his allies had come to believe that Congress was out of control, more intent on hounding the executive branch than on constructively legislating. Ford thus took little joy from watching Carter's struggles in office. Immediately after Carter's defeat in the 1980 election, he told *Time* magazine, "We have not an imperial presidency, but an imperiled presidency. Under today's rules . . . the presidency does not operate effectively. . . . That is harmful to our overall national interests."[2]

A Republican freshman in the class of 1978 would take aim at Congress for its transgressions. Newt Gingrich of Georgia, a big-thinking history professor, was one of a new breed of Southern Republicans, who often drew their support from recent migrants from the North (Gingrich himself was born in Pennsylvania). From the time he first ran for Congress in 1974, Gingrich made corruption in the Capitol his major campaign theme—his brochures that year read, "The Politicians Had Their Chance. Now You Can Have Yours."[3] Though he lost twice to incumbent John Flynt (D-GA), in 1978 Flynt retired and Gingrich won his open seat. He would prove to be a relentless innovator in escalating conflict between the two parties, eventually leading Republicans to the almost-forgotten promised land of the majority. Sixteen years after he was first elected, he became Speaker of the House—and, even then, he would remain on the warpath against Congress.

This chapter explores conservatives' views of Congress during the two decades stretching from Watergate through the Republican Revolution. Conservatives were suspicious of the 1970s reforms, which for all of their decentralizing effects had further sidelined Republicans and magnified the power of special interests. Nonetheless, through much of the Reagan administration, with the Senate in Republican hands and the House minority led by Rep. Bob Michel (R-IL), Republicans joined forces with conservative Democrats and found ways to break open the congressional agenda to advance their party's policy goals.

But after Democrats regained control of the Senate after the 1986 midterms and Rep. Jim Wright (D-TX) became Speaker, conservatives' views of Congress hardened into unyielding hostility. Congress, they said, was intent on usurping the executive branch's proper administrative functions.

Republicans became champions of flexibility for the presidency and developed a sharp critique of Congress as a hopelessly corrupted institution. They accused House Democratic leaders of scandalous behavior and tyranny and charged that Congress had become damnably intertwined with the federal bureaucracy, with its oversight function delivering benefits to client groups rather than public-spirited accountability.

Even after taking control of Congress, conservatives (especially in the House) persisted in thinking of the legislature as a source of mischief that needed to be cut down to size, while simultaneously empowering Republican congressional leaders to stand toe to toe with President Bill Clinton. While in the minority, Republicans had sometimes sounded Madisonian reform themes decrying the heavy hand of Democratic Speakers. Once they won the majority, though, conservatives acted like consummate Wilsonians, seeking to maximize the contrast between themselves and the president by confronting him with their own comprehensive agenda, framed as an expression of the American people's will. In part because they expected this strategy to win the presidency in 1996, they continued to pursue reforms that strengthened the president at Congress' expense, the most ambitious being the line-item veto.

Their centralizing efforts were largely successful—but their attempt to dictate a major shrinking of the federal government ended in political disaster. Chastened, Republicans would chart a more modest course in their policy goals and lose their reforming zeal.

Conservatives' policy overreaches have often been featured in analyzing the disappointments of the Republican Revolution. But I argue that there was something more than blind ambition at play: antipathy for Congress seriously constrained Republicans' ability to change the direction of American government in the 1990s. Although they invoked themes of self-government against rule by insulated bureaucrats, they had almost no feel for facilitating a reforming Madisonian politics in which disparate interests made common cause with each other on behalf of the greater good. Conservatives' years of adversarial opposition left them little able to appreciate the unique capacities of a representative legislature or envision it working as a real counterweight to the bureaucracy. In attempting to act as though Republicans in Congress could speak with a single voice—with Gingrich acting as a kind of shadow president—Republicans squandered their best opportunity to reorient America's expanded state and to correct the defects that had so alienated them from Congress in the first place.

## A Last Hurrah for Fluid Coalitions:
## A Divided Congress at Work

Riding Reagan's coattails in 1980, Republicans took 12 Senate seats from Democrats and gained control of the upper chamber for the first time since 1955. The new majority took the opportunity to slash the committee staff that their Democratic predecessors had expanded so quickly, cutting about 10 percent of positions.[4] Since majority staffs were much larger than minority ones, the new levels allowed for Republican hires while requiring large Democratic layoffs. But while Republicans were happy to cut down on bloat, they mostly found that the reshaped committee system served their interests, and so it persisted, "trimmed somewhat but not decimated."[5]

In the House, Democrats' majority was dented but still large, falling from 275 to 242. But O'Neill had a difficult job keeping his membership, which still included a large contingent of conservative Southerners, united against Reagan—especially when the president's popularity soared to around 65 percent in the wake of an assassination attempt. Republicans' newly elected leader, the mild-mannered Bob Michel of Illinois, declared that Republicans would "be making appeals across the aisle" and that "the inherent logic of our arguments, the persuasiveness of our appeal, and the all-around good nature of Republicans will often find success in rallying Democrats to our cause."[6] Michel self-consciously saw himself as a leader in the Rayburn mold, bringing disparate factions together around common ground.[7] He and his whip team would prove the power of "gentle persuasion," conducting "commando raids for votes" among Democrats to assemble a cross-party coalition in support of budget reconciliation bills that cut spending and slashed Americans' personal income tax rates.[8] In spite of Democratic chairmen boxing them out on the Budget and Ways and Means Committees, unified Republicans successfully pressured Democrats to allow votes on their carefully crafted substitute bills, which included dozens of provisions designed to secure particular members' votes, including the indexing of tax brackets.[9] Thanks to Michel's assiduous outreach, coordinated with the White House, both ultimately made it through the Committee of the Whole with bipartisan support. In the Senate, new majority leader Howard Baker (R-TN) kept his party unified in support of the president's top priorities, which was enough because of the budget reconciliation's prohibition of filibusters.[10]

Michel, Baker, and O'Neill worked well enough together to make the early 1980s a fruitful period. Bipartisan coalitions passed an extension of the Voting Rights Act along with deregulations of the savings and loan industry in 1982 and of the cable television industry in 1984. Especially noteworthy was the rescue of the cash-strapped Social Security system in 1983, which saw legislators trudge through the painful work of handing out losses rather than gains. Although regular legislative processes proved unable to generate a solution to an acute funding shortage, an ad hoc and secretive "Gang of Nine" officials from the executive branch and both legislative chambers found a way forward by discovering a provision that both sides could regard as a win—Democrats would see a tax on the benefits of high earners as a tax increase, while Republicans would see it as a benefit reduction. By eschewing credit taking and selling their compromise as the end-product of an in-depth bipartisan study, they managed to arrange a rescue that all sides could hail as a victory—even those whose demands had been overridden in the process. Once again, Congress showed its ability to reconcile the apparently irreconcilable.[11]

The trend of compromise continued after Sen. Bob Dole (R-KS) took over for Baker in 1985, with two enactments in particular showing how disparate factions still found ways of working together. The Gramm-Rudman-Hollings Act of 1985 was described by its sponsors as "a bad idea whose time has come."[12] It represented a bipartisan attempt to get a handle on out-of-control deficits, which contributed to the era's punishingly high interest rates, by subjecting the federal government to indiscriminate budget cuts if preset budget targets weren't hit.[13] Although the budget regime it imposed featured predictable "fudging the numbers and moving the deficit goalposts," it laid the groundwork for later bipartisan budget deals. The famous Tax Reform Act of 1986 was primarily crafted by the Senate Finance Committee and, to a lesser extent, the House Ways and Means Committee. The law showed that in an arena filled with dizzying numbers of interest groups, it was still possible for legislators to pull together and find a way to pursue the general interest.[14]

## Centralization in the House and the Conservative Reaction

In working toward passage of these and other laws, House members were compelled to deal with the hangover of unmanageability left by the fragmenting rise of the subcommittee system in the 1970s. To avoid the cacophony of the decentralized Congress of the Carter years, both parties worked to build greater discipline in their ranks, a process aided by steadily increasing ideological sorting of the electorate and members themselves. House Democrats' whip operation grew from 8 percent of the party's membership in the mid-1970s to 18 percent in 1981 and 40 percent by 1989—a group large enough to act "almost like a mini-Caucus," according to one leader involved.[15] From 1986 to 1988, the Republican Conference imitated many of the rules changes liberals had imposed on the Democratic Caucus in the 1970s, with the goal of binding members to the will of the party's majority.[16]

More controversially, the Democratic majority made many rules changes to empower their leaders to limit debate and control the agenda—belatedly embracing some of Bolling's reform program. Bolling saw through several changes himself as chairman of the Rules Committee from 1979 to 1983. The Missourian worked with Speaker O'Neill to create ever-more restrictive special rules governing floor debates on important legislation. Open rules receded, with three-quarters of important legislation considered under restrictive rules by the mid-1980s.[17] The Rules Committee also went beyond simple restrictions and used more elaborate systems of controlling debate. "King of the Mountain" rules, for example, presented a series of votes on related amendments, stipulating that only the last amendment adopted would be retained. Legislators sometimes regarded this highly structured approach as a fair way to work through a complex issue, but such tools nevertheless had the potential to change the shape of deliberation in the House, driving increasingly partisan voting on amendments.[18] By working closely with the Speaker, the Rules Committee of the 1980s became the leading force for centralized control.[19] During this period, central leaders also used a heavier hand in guiding committees.[20] Once venues for discovering cross-partisan commonalities, committees increasingly became instrumentalities of ideological majorities. Rank-and-file Democrats invited these developments because they judged party unity to be the best counterweight to the Reagan administration, and they were happy to swing the pendulum away from the chaotic arrangements of the late 1970s.

The reduced opportunities for members of the minority to have an impact, both on the floor and in committee, predictably alienated Republican members who felt that their—and their constituents'—concerns were being excluded rather than fairly considered. While Michel's nonconfrontational approach had delivered some impressive results, especially in 1981, many conservatives came to believe that cooperation with the majority was a dead end. Led by the entrepreneurial Gingrich, some younger members organized as the Conservative Opportunity Society in 1983. They hoped to provoke Democrats with a strategy of obstruction and confrontation, which would highlight the stifling rules imposed by Democratic House leaders and call Americans' attention to Republicans' alternative vision for government.[21]

Early on, the group memorably succeeded in rattling Speaker O'Neill, taking advantage of the C-SPAN television cameras that the Speaker had allowed into the House chamber in 1977.[22] Those cameras almost always focused tightly on the member speaking without revealing that the audience included just a few members milling about. Using that perspective to their advantage, in a series of short, incendiary speeches in May 1984 Gingrich and his allies accused Democrats of complicity with communist forces in Latin America. The lack of any rebuttal seemed to imply Democrats had no answer, though in reality they were simply absent from the chamber. O'Neill, infuriated, was baited into retaliating by instructing camera operators to expose the empty chamber when Gingrich and his ally Rep. Bob Walker (R-PA) next spoke. That opportunistic manipulation angered even Michel, who denounced the Speaker's "act of dictatorial retribution." In a floor debate over this fracas, O'Neill violated the chamber's prohibition on "making personalities," or directly insulting another member, by angrily calling out Gingrich.[23] Rep. Trent Lott (R-MS) moved that O'Neill's remarks be stricken from the record. The sitting chair ruled in favor, making O'Neill the first Speaker ever embarrassed in this way.

At stake in this incident was far more than the Speaker's own reputation. Indeed, the fundamental question was what kind of deliberative body the House would be. The Speaker and other Democrats preferred to see the majority pursue its preferences through relatively tightly controlled committee proceedings and structured floor debates. By doing so, they could defend and incrementally build on the relatively popular welfare state their party had created over the last generation, holding ranks against the kind of cross-partisan conservative assault that had struck in 1981. They could also, of course, use their majority to dispense various kinds of federal patronage to allies. To the extent that House Republicans wanted to cooperate in this endeavor—as Michel and others who spent their careers learning how to make a difference on the margins often were—Democrats would include them. If Republicans sought to dictate their own terms of debate, however, they needed to be quashed. This vision of politics hearkened back to

O'Neill's roots in Boston machine politics and emphasized continuity with the (Democrat-dominated) recent past rather than big national debates.

Gingrich and his allies, on the other hand, wanted the House to be the engine of big changes. Like the proponents of responsible party government, they believed the essence of politics was offering voters a clear choice at the polls. They thought that Michel's conciliatory approach amounted to begging for breadcrumbs and deprived Americans of an alternative to the Democrats' status quo. If Americans could be roused to action by high-drama showdowns, they would give Republicans a mandate to replace the "liberal welfare state" with a "conservative opportunity society." As Gingrich would later reflect, "When you give [the media] confrontations, you get attention; when you get attention you can educate." The rising conservative star waxed philosophical about the fit of his style with the current media environment: "It's like the transition from vaudeville to television, like going from being a Broadway actor to being a television star. O'Neill and others are pre-TV, pre-confrontational."[24]

Centralization and conservative reaction would rise to an even more heated pitch under the Speakership of O'Neill's successor, Jim Wright (D-TX). Wright was first elected to Congress in 1954, when party politics in Texas had been coterminous with Democratic politics and Republicans were treated as a superfluous sort of local color. He had come up revering his fellow Texan, Speaker Sam Rayburn, and the cooperative style of the House at that time in which members' "mutual assumption of honor . . . held things together."[25] As we saw in Chapter 4, Wright's ability to straddle intraparty divides helped him beat out Bolling and Burton to become majority leader in 1976, and his succession to the Speakership upon O'Neill's retirement was smooth.

When Wright took up the Speaker's gavel, though, it quickly became evident that his days of consensual politics were long behind him. He thought the Reagan administration was in need of a harsh reality check and that insurgent Republicans were unfit to wield real responsibility. Republicans reciprocated his contempt, but even fellow Democrats found him imperious and easily offended by dissent; as his biographer puts it, "he dictated more than he consulted."[26]

Wright's exercises of agenda control ranged from the petty to the outrageous. Members thought him addicted to arbitrary deadlines and limits to debates. Most dramatically, as Wright sought to push through a revenue-positive reconciliation bill following "Black Monday" in October 1987, his favored rule was voted down. Chamber rules prohibited an identical vote on the same day, but Wright was determined—so he ordered the House adjourned and then immediately reconvened, declaring a new legislative day allowing a new vote. On the brink of losing that revote 207–206, Wright kept the voting open well past its 15-minute limit until he could pressure a wayward Democratic member to switch his vote to "aye."[27] He engineered House passage of a budget resolution using king-of-the-mountain procedures to bypass Republican opposition and enact higher progressive taxes.[28] More generally, Wright wielded the Speaker's power to control committee assignments and rules to the fullest, utilizing tools first made available in the 1970s.[29] There was a widespread sense that House Democrats' program was, more or less, Wright's own program, as the decentralized agenda control of the subcommittee system rapidly receded.

In defending his conduct, Wright sounded Wilsonian notes, insisting that his tighter control of the chamber was needed for efficient policymaking. As he wrote in his memoir, "Instead of autonomous feudal barons each pursuing a leisurely independent course, most members of the hierarchy once described by O'Neill as his 'College of Cardinals' now felt part of a purposeful team."[30] Sounding every bit like Wilson's ideal president, Wright declared that he wanted the Speakership because he "saw things I thought needed doing, and I supposed that I could bring them about."[31]

Notwithstanding their own ambitions to pursue a well-differentiated, coherent agenda, Republicans seethed under Wright's rule. Walker observed: "He is willing to run over us. When he loses battles, instead of gracefully acknowledging defeat, he cheats."[32] Gingrich cast Wright's unwillingness to consider viewpoints beyond his own as emblematic of the sclerotic Democratic majority. In 1988, he wrote: "It is an imperial Congress reigned over by an imperial Speaker enacting special-interest legislation. . . . [It] has become the most unrepresentative and corrupt of the modern era. It is a Congress that lusts for power but evades responsibility for its actions."[33]

## Developing the Conservative Critique of Congress

Gingrich delivered that particular condemnation in a Heritage Foundation edited volume, *The Imperial Congress*. A year later, the American Enterprise Institute would publish *The Fettered Presidency*, another compilation that harshly condemned Congress.[34] These books together offered a statement of a mature anti-Congress ideology, one that the Republican Party took up with enthusiasm after their loss of the Senate in the 1986 midterms.[35] Conservatives charged that the Democratic Congress was more interested in consolidating its own political power and rewarding favored interests through manipulations of governmental power than in honestly debating pressing challenges, especially the failures of the welfare state they built. Several facets of this anti-Congress stance are worth examining.

Conservatives first focused on Democratic abuses of constitutional authority, which they claimed made the executive branch vulnerable to continuous opportunistic exploitation by overreaching lawmakers. Some of their complaints concerned the expanded oversight Congress had begun in the 1970s and continued, with sharper elbows in dealing with the Republicans in the executive branch, in the 1980s. The House Committee on Public Works and Transportation pursued a particularly bruising fight against Reagan's first Environmental Protection Agency administrator, Anne Gorsuch (mother of the Supreme Court justice), holding her in contempt, fighting her in the courts, and finally forcing her resignation in March 1983.[36] Beyond that episode, later scholars would largely agree with conservative concerns that oversight was then becoming more a tool of escalating partisan conflict than a guarantor of administrative competence.[37] The oversight-minded Congress was responsive in some sense, quickly reacting to "many irritants," but it failed to deliver coordinated control, let alone "responsible party governance."[38] The new cadre of inspectors general that Congress had unleashed in the previous decade, meanwhile, forced agencies to focus on producing paperwork rather than completing their missions.[39]

Oversight abuse was only part of a larger pathology of "micromanagement." Conservatives also condemned Congress' more aggressive use of its power of the purse, especially its use of limitation riders,[40] and derided its legislative vetoes as attempts to control quintessentially administrative matters better left to the executive branch. When the Supreme Court struck down legislative vetoes as unconstitutional, they cheered; when Congress sought to keep them as a de facto reality, they complained that legislators once again exceeded their constitutional prerogatives.[41] Finally, conservatives argued that the use of omnibus legislation impermissibly undermined the president's veto power.[42] In response, they proposed a line-item veto so that the president would no longer depend on Congress' good-faith framing but could instead target particular abuses by striking just offensive provisions.[43] The critics warned that when legislators beholden to military suppliers micromanaged national defense through hyperdetailed authorization and spending statutes, the predictable result was "waste, inefficiency, and absurdity."[44] When Congress micromanaged domestic policy, again to serve favored constituencies such as farm aid recipients, it stealthily inserted instructions to agencies in continuing resolutions that received no legislative scrutiny.[45]

Against this combined aggression from the legislative branch, conservatives rallied around a wide-ranging intellectual defense of a presidency empowered to exercise discretion in serving the public good. Like Woodrow Wilson in his later years, Reaganites believed the president's singularity gave him a unique form of legitimacy in the American constitutional system. He was the only official with the wherewithal to vindicate the people's interests against their corrupted, parochial representatives. Separation-of-powers concerns were thus directly connected to substantive policymaking goals, and especially the promise that conservatives could deliver lean, business-like government where liberals had nurtured bloat. In a 1991 speech, Vice President Dan Quayle contrasted the presidency's democratic legitimacy against "the iron triangle—special-interest groups, bureaucrats, and Congressional staff—[who] are elected by nobody."[46] This point was ready-made for populist politicking against an elite, out-of-touch "government" that preyed on Americans, siphoning off ever more of their tax dollars without solving their problems.[47]

Conservatives were essentially accusing the Democrat-controlled Congress of enforcing a corrupt bargain with favored interest groups, forfeiting its claim to representativeness. Republican legislators, on the other hand, were mostly locked out, and their worsening marginalization slowly but surely convinced most of them to embrace the outsider critique of Congress as an institution.[48]

What should we make of this anti-Congress, pro-executive synthesis that conservatives came to embrace over the course of the 1980s? One might dismiss their complaints as a repackaging of perennial anti-Congress tropes to suit their own needs. Recall Speaker Longworth's 1925 caution that an active Congress would be denounced as meddlesome, and a reflective one as "do-nothing." The material needed to attack Congress is, in some sense, ubiquitous, and perhaps the conservatives of the late 1980s were simply adept at selling it. But conservatives' subsequent success in contesting Democrats' control of Congress is more readily explained by simply acknowledging that their critique packed a mighty punch. The openness the 1970s liberals had achieved allowed particularistic interests to more reliably get attention for their pet issues. The shift to oversight steered legislators toward interfering in administrative affairs rather than working through the leading problems of the day. And, to the extent that House Democrats had begun to operate more cohesively, haranguing the Reagan and George H. W. Bush administrations was indeed a top priority.

The executive tilt of conservatives' response is understandable given Republicans' successes in winning the White House (five out of six times from 1968 to 1988) and continued failures in recapturing the House. An earlier generation of conservatives, who formed their views in opposition to Franklin Roosevelt, had celebrated Congress as the preserver of "lowly," mundane virtues against the nascent Caesarism of the executive. Willmoore Kendall and James Burnham, especially, condemned presidency worship as an un-American form of "democratism" tracing its lineage to the French Revolution. If Congress were to recede, they warned, America would be at the mercy of the "masses" and unable to respect the people's differences.[49] But by the time of the Reagan administration, conservatives viewing the American constitutional dispensation from the vantage point of the Oval Office regarded the anti-Caesarist view as a relic of a more innocent time in which Americans' natural (little-c) conservatism expressed itself through Congress. Now, though, media and well-organized interests alike pushed legislators to embrace the very utopian impulses Kendall had said legislators were naturally immune to, and only the president possessed sufficient stature to bring an effective counternarrative to the American people.[50] If George H. W. Bush found himself wildly popular after the brief Persian Gulf War, why should he waste his political capital trying to barter with an intransigent Democratic Congress rather than figuring out ways to work around them?[51]

Like their Wilsonian forerunners, conservatives believed in an executive branch capable of operating above the din of congressional politics. But their favored brand of executive dominance was quite distinct from that of the progressives, who had valued "independent" executive branch instrumentalities meant to sit outside of electoral politics entirely and govern based on expertise. The 1980s proponents of the unitary executive had "scoop[ed] up the progressive legacy of national power" but largely rejected "the extra-constitutional mechanisms that the progressives had relied upon to surround and regulate their presidency-centered system," in the words of political scientist Stephen Skowronek.[52] Wilson's vision of a president as a prime minister–like figure supposed he would work through a pliant legislature, rather than needing to go around it. Nevertheless, in their suspicion of congressional manyness, the contemporary conservatives shared Wilsonians' belief that representation might work best through the simplest possible electoral contests available to the public—namely, presidential elections.

If the conservatives' intellectual moves were understandable, they also created unappreciated vulnerabilities. Most importantly, even as Gingrich plotted a way for conservatives to regain the majority that had so long been out of reach, conservatives' anti-Congress vision made it difficult for them to imagine how Congress, in all of its pluralistic splendor, might be made an instrument of productive conservative reform. Instead, they were committed to truncating congressional power and lining up behind a single leader capable of reversing decades of Democratic depredations.

## Crusading against the Speaker and Corruption

During this period, conservatives also took Congress to task for its inappropriate meddling in foreign policy. In the complicated Iran-Contra scandal and its investigation, they argued that congressional Democrats were undermining a Republican president's foreign policy for partisan gain while using slippery statutory language to avoid taking responsibility for hard calls. A Select Committee minority report supervised by Rep. Dick Cheney (R-WY) criticized the "boundless view of Congressional power [that] began to take hold in the 1970s."[53] Members of the administration had made errors of judgment, the report conceded, but most blame for the scandal belonged to Democratic legislators and their "aggrandizing theory of Congress' foreign policy powers" that had unnecessarily escalated the incident.[54] Cheney's work raised his profile, and after the 1988 elections he was elected minority whip, making him heir apparent to Minority Leader Michel. But, in a fateful turn, after Bush's first nominee for defense secretary was rebuffed by the Democratic Senate, Cheney was tapped to head the Pentagon instead. None other than Newt Gingrich took his place in the House GOP leadership after a hard-fought, narrow victory over one of Michel's moderate allies.[55] By that time, Gingrich (pictured in Figure 5.1 with GOP leadership) had already launched a broad attack on Wright that would indelibly transform the House.

When Gingrich came looking for ammunition against the Speaker, Wright's record gave him an embarrassment of riches. There were rumors

**Figure 5.1**  Rep. Newt Gingrich (R-GA) after his elevation to minority whip with House Minority Leader Bob Michel (R-IL), President George H. W. Bush, and Senate Minority Leader Bob Dole (R-KS) in September 1989.
*Source:* Robert H. Michel Collection, Dirksen Congressional Center.

that local businesses had been strong-armed into donating to retire a large campaign debt.[56] Both of Wright's wives' professional lives were awkwardly entwined in his commercial ventures. A business partner gave Wright several large loans. He rather tactlessly interceded with the Federal Savings and Loan Insurance Corporation on behalf of a number of Texas firms it regulated. Most infamous was a scandal surrounding a book of Wright's speeches published in 1984, for which the majority leader received an unheard of 55 percent royalty. Those who wished to ingratiate themselves bought in bulk, "just trying to make a contribution to Jim's income" as one purchaser of 1,000 copies artlessly put it.[57] Although legal—House limits on outside income had an exception for book royalties—it stank of corruption.

Gingrich picked up that scent and identified it as Democrats' biggest weakness. "Just as Spiro Agnew had discovered that the style of corruption taken perfectly for granted in 1960 Maryland would destroy him as Vice President a decade later," Gingrich wrote in his memoir, "the habits and practices that were perfectly survivable in Texas a generation earlier would not pass the national standards of the late 1980s."[58] After prolonged courting,

Gingrich convinced John Gardner, president of the good-government organization Common Cause, that Wright needed scrutiny. Gardner's support gave Gingrich's accusations the imprimatur of a neutral observer. Before long, the House Ethics Committee ordered a special counsel to investigate the Speaker's activities.[59] The counsel's report, running to almost 500 pages, painted an unequivocal picture of corruption. In April, the Ethics Committee found 69 different charges worth pursuing further, and in May it was reported that the IRS would conduct a criminal investigation. Realizing he was effectively crippled, Wright resigned on June 6, 1989.

Having toppled a Speaker—a tyrant, in their thinking—conservatives redoubled their campaign against institutional corruption in the House. Ambitious young members, such as the "Gang of Seven" in the 102nd Congress, schooled themselves in Gingrich's techniques. As one of them, John Boehner (R-OH), later reflected, "Seven freshmen have about as much power around here as the lint on the carpet. Our only chance of succeeding was to get America as mad as we were."[60] They were not much calmed by the less brash style of Wright's successor, Tom Foley (D-WA). In 1990, they generated a firestorm around legislators' ability to make overdrafts on their accounts at the House Bank, a practice whose cost to voters was hard to make out but which seemed abusive. More straightforwardly salacious was the revelation that workers at the House post office had been selling drugs on the job and facilitating staffers' conversion of their offices' postal stamps into hard cash they could spend freely.[61] Amidst this petty corruption, members of Congress sought a pay raise—and conservatives predictably turned that into another bludgeon against the chamber's majority. (Voters' pique at the pay raise led four states to ratify what became the 27th Amendment to the Constitution, a founding-era rule prohibiting legislators' pay raises from taking effect during the Congress in which they are passed.[62])

Alongside the focus on corruption, a few Republicans leveled a Madisonian critique against the Democratic majority. The ranking member of the House Rules Committee, Gerald B. H. Solomon (R-NY), lamented that Congress had lost its character as a truly deliberative body. In 1994 he and his counsel, Don Wolfensberger, wrote that leadership's restrictive procedures kept most members, even those in the majority, from meaningful participation in crafting laws. They were especially concerned by proxy voting and "drop-in" voting in committees and subcommittees, Democratic innovations that allowed business to be done without most members of the majority even being present. Though they conceded that Democrats were coping with centrifugal forces making legislating more difficult, they averred that the forms of deliberation produced "are not broadly representative of the House or the electorate, they are not conducted in the open, there is little or no accountability for members, and they neither serve to enlighten the public nor contribute to the development of a national consensus for the policy decisions made."[63] A "restoration of deliberative democracy" could only come with the "restoration of a strong, effective, representative, responsive, and open committee system."[64]

But it was Gingrich's anti-corruption message, rather than Solomon's Madisonian critique, that garnered headlines as Republicans finally achieved victory in the 1994 midterm. Their 54-seat pickup in the House was the largest swing since 1948 and gave them 230 seats, the GOP's first majority in the chamber since 1954. Their 8-seat pickup in the Senate also gave them a slim majority of 52 seats. But these numbers understate the momentum that Republicans and conservatives felt. They regarded Bill Clinton's 1992 election as a fluke attributable to H. Ross Perot's huge impact, and they imagined Perot's supporters had rallied to Republicans' cause and would help deliver an easy win over the then-unpopular Clinton in 1996.

Just as important to House Republicans' understanding of their victory was the Contract With America, an unusually detailed campaign document that nearly all Republican candidates for the House signed on to in October 1994. The Contract, masterminded by Gingrich and his associates, promised to reform Congress itself and pledged votes on various policy and constitutional changes within 100 days of taking office. Some members felt the Contract was superfluous, preferring to focus on Bill Clinton's failed health care plan and tax increases, but others insisted it was instrumental in convincing voters that Republicans would be reformers.[65] As he rose to the Speakership (with Michel having retired), Gingrich was totally committed to fulfilling the terms of the Contract.

## Congress Rebuked, but Not Reimagined

Because of the Contract With America, because Republicans were so energized by their unexpected return to the majority, and because Gingrich self-consciously viewed himself as a world-historical figure, the ambition to overhaul government reached an apex in the 104th Congress.[66] At the same time, conservative suspicion of Congress as an institution persisted, steering

Republicans away from embracing the full reforming potential of Congress and toward strengthening the presidency in spite of their low regard for Clinton.

First among the Contract's promises was a commitment to purge Congress of corruption and run the House more like a business.[67] First came the Congressional Accountability Act, which subjected members of Congress and their staff to federal labor and workplace safety laws just like private employers. Also at the outset of the new Congress, Republicans created a new officer of the House, the chief administrative officer (CAO), to handle a range of back-office functions that the (usually highly partisan) Committee on House Administration had previously handled. The memory of Wayne Hays' capricious favoritism was to be buried deeply, rather than revived in Republican garb. The first CAO met resistance and was gone by 1996, charging Republicans with failing to stay true to their vision of professionalism.[68] But the CAO has, for the most part, been an enduring institutional success story, exercising a stabilizing influence on House affairs through several partisan reversals. The House today is undoubtedly a more business-like environment than before the Republican Revolution.[69]

Determined to destroy cozy relationships between committee staff and the bureaucrats they oversaw, Republicans immediately cut House committee staff by one-third. They defunded legislative service organizations, mainly to kill off the decades-old Democratic Study Group.[70] They also zeroed out appropriations for the Office of Technology Assessment, a congressional support agency they believed had become duplicative and too beholden to liberals.[71]

Other rules changes sought greater congressional accountability, in some cases reflecting the Madisonian concerns voiced by Solomon, now chairman of the Rules Committee. Committees would have to publish their votes and end proxy voting. Legislators were prohibited from revising their remarks in the *Congressional Record*. A ban on commemorative legislation sought to keep Congress focused on important policymaking.[72]

But the more sweeping theme was a continued redistribution of power away from committees and toward the Speaker. Indeed, according to Rep. Dennis Hastert (R-IL), whom Republicans chose as chief deputy whip, Gingrich gathered his leadership team and told them: "Well, from now on, the six of us are going to make all the decisions."[73] Ambitious plans to restructure committee jurisdictions mostly fizzled, though three full committees and 31 of 115 subcommittees were abolished.[74] More importantly, Republicans gave Gingrich control over committee chairmanships. Rep. Christopher Cox (R-CA) observed: "You don't have to change the head of every committee when you change just a few. Gingrich has given them a renewed sense that chairs serve at the Speaker's pleasure."[75] Term limits for chairmanships further created an expectation that the Speaker and other leaders would dictate how committee power was used.

Even House Republicans skeptical of Gingrich had to admit that he had led the way out of the wilderness, and so their party committed itself to pursuing his vision. The concerns about Wright's tyranny had apparently evaporated, and for a short time Gingrich basked in the perception that he had become the center of American government. A *New York Times* story with the breathless headline "With Political Discipline, It Works Like Parliament" explicitly invoked the memory of Woodrow Wilson's Westminster yearnings and credited Gingrich with bringing them to life— neglecting, along with Gingrich, the foundations of legislator independence in the American system that would hinder univocal action.[76] Among the obstacles for Gingrich would be the Senate, where Majority Leader Bob Dole did not share the new Speaker's seething contempt for Congress' folkways. Gingrich had once called Dole "the tax collector for the welfare state," but he would need his cooperation to make changes that reached beyond the House.[77]

One shared priority was deregulation, where Republicans seemed poised to fundamentally alter the architecture of the New Deal state. Rhetoric on the subject flew freely within the conference, with Boehner describing the Occupational Safety and Health Administration (OSHA) as the "Gestapo of the federal government."[78] Leading the deregulatory push was the new majority whip, Tom DeLay (R-TX), whose years as an exterminator left him constantly frustrated by federal environmental regulations. He loudly courted business interests looking to devise a new regulatory order. In February, DeLay shepherded a bill to freeze all ongoing regulatory efforts through the House. The Senate passed its own bill with a moratorium, but the two chambers failed to coordinate, perhaps because GOP lawmakers had undertaken actions on so many other deregulatory fronts, apparently trying to do everything at once. They worked on a Clean Water Act reform, a strengthening of the Regulatory Flexibility Act, a Democrat-sponsored bill to sunset agency rules on a regular basis, a major reform of the Administrative Procedure Act, an OSHA reform, and a restriction of the Environmental Protection Agency.

The last of these caused a rift. Led by Sherwood Boehlert (R-NY), 51 House Republicans joined with Democrats to vote down the bill. Gingrich and other leaders engineered a revote and won because of Democratic absences, but moderates' defection had signaled that Republicans' vaunted unity was not all it was cracked up to be. Ambitious bills stalled in Senate committees and Gingrich was eventually forced to acknowledge reality, telling his conference: "Those bills aren't going anywhere this year. Let's regroup and get started in a more appropriate way next year."[79] Ironically, even as their bid for long-lasting deregulatory change ended up yielding very little, Republicans' control of committees' oversight powers did induce federal agencies to slacken their regulatory pace during the 104th Congress.[80]

Republicans failed to refashion America's regulatory state because they acted as if a single election victory would, all on its own, ring in a new age. House Republican leaders had believed Congress would behave like Parliament, with its legislative leader effectively commanding the government, and in the process had utterly failed to contend with the complexity of public opinion on these complicated issues—including among members of their own party. As the great observer of Congress Richard Fenno pointed out, four decades in the minority had apparently left House Republicans unable to think clearly about what an election victory would support in terms of practical governing. They perceived a resounding mandate, when in fact the 1994 midterms could just as easily be read as a simple repudiation of Clinton administration overreach. Their failure to contend with continuing manyness led them to squander their energies on unrealistic, and probably unpopular, plans.[81] To put it bluntly, Republicans had lost the constitutional plot; their indictment of the status quo was powerful, but they had the wrong answer to "why Congress?"

Republicans were in a stronger position in regards to several popular structural reforms promised by the Contract With America. They got off to a promising start by passing the Unfunded Mandates Reform Act of 1995 with little opposition. By making it harder for Congress to foist new responsibilities on state governments without providing them any new funding, Republicans made good on their commitment to federalism. They continued to pursue that goal, especially through the block granting of federal spending programs, and had some notable successes, especially the landmark welfare reform in 1996. Federalism was the one area where Republicans could claim to have made significant progress in restructuring American government in the 1990s, although, with hindsight, their achievements in this vein seem both incremental and temporary.

Republicans came very close to success on another reform that would have had a deep impact on the federal government's operation: a constitutional balanced budget amendment. House leaders devised a special rule that would let the chamber decide between two versions: one that would require a three-fifths supermajority for actions raising revenues, favored by conservatives, and one without that provision, which had greater bipartisan support and moved on to the Senate with a vote of 300–132.[82] After some maneuvering, the Senate set up a dramatic vote on passage on March 2, 1995. Sen. Mark Hatfield (R-OR), chairman of the Appropriations Committee, cast the lone Republican dissent, which left the amendment one vote short of passage.[83] It was a vote of conscience; he said that while he agreed with the goal, he did not believe a simple constitutional requirement provided sufficient guidance.[84] Conservative freshmen were furious at Hatfield and sought to have him censured or stripped of his chairmanship, but Dole repelled their efforts.[85] Republicans had come ever so close to a major constitutional overhaul—one that would have tied Congress' hands—but fell just short. (State ratification would still have been required as well.) Another of their major attempts at structural reform of Congress, though popular with the general public, was much more obviously destined to fail: the push for term limits. With senior Republicans implacably opposed—Rep. Henry Hyde (R-IL) said he would not "be an accessory to the dumbing down of democracy"—that bill predictably failed to clear the House.[86]

Finally, Republicans undertook two major changes designed to strengthen the presidency. The line-item veto was conservatives' favored antidote to Congress jamming the president with must-pass omnibus bills. As the next section details, when Republicans pushed their own omnibuses on Clinton, their ardor for the line-item veto cooled, but they nevertheless eventually passed it into law. House Republicans also pushed for repeal of the War Powers Resolution, which Gingrich believed unwisely hindered strong presidential responses to crises abroad. He took to the House floor to ask his fellow legislators to "allow the Commander in Chief to be the Commander in Chief." The bill failed, 201–217, as the older strain of conservative anti-Caesarism reared its head and 44 Republican members, mostly older ones, disappointed their Speaker. Said Rep. Toby Roth (R-WI), "Every President finds Congress inconvenient. But we're a democracy, not a monarchy."[87]

## Republicans' Anti-Congress Philosophy Bites Back

For all the energy Republicans directed toward deregulation and structural reform, they concentrated their firepower most heavily on fiscal policy. They believed, sensibly enough, that using the power of the purse was the best way to take a stand for limited government, with budget reconciliation giving them the tool they needed to avoid a Senate filibuster and push for a balanced budget by 2002. Happily leaving behind their complaints about the Democratic omnibus bills of the late 1980s, Republicans explicitly planned to advance this agenda via omnibus appropriations bills that (they thought) would be impossible for Clinton to veto.[88] Here, apparently, turnabout was fair play.

While President Clinton was willing to accept some modest cuts in entitlement programs, including Medicare, Republicans wanted much deeper cuts paired with tax reduction. Characteristically, Gingrich believed the public could be won over if Republicans pursued the right sort of confrontation and chose the right communication strategy. (In 1990, a memo entitled "Language: A Key Mechanism of Control" had instructed GOP House members to use 133 words and phrases that would let them "Speak Like Newt," including characterizing Democrats as "corrupt," "traitors," and "sick."[89]) He and his allies sought to brand their plan for Medicare as a way to "preserve and protect it" from bankruptcy and strenuously avoided the word "cuts." Meanwhile, Democrats (and especially organized labor) connected the Republicans' proposed $270 billion reductions to the $245 billion they proposed for tax relief.[90] The two parties stood at an impasse, each waiting for the other side to blink.

Faced with an impending government shutdown if no spending deal was reached, Republicans believed the president would have little choice but to accept their terms. Clinton, though, was willing to exercise his veto, even at the cost of a government shutdown. Determined to make a point, he told top Republicans at the White House:

> I am not going to agree to your Medicaid package no matter what. I am not going to agree to education cuts. If you want to pass your budget, you're going to have to put somebody else in this chair. I don't care what happens. I don't care if it all comes down around me. I don't care if I go to five percent in the polls. I am not going to sign your budget. It is wrong. It is wrong for the country.[91]

A partial shutdown began on November 14. Gingrich then made what became an infamous blunder. After Clinton and his team chose not to speak with him on the long Air Force One flight returning from Israeli Prime Minister Yitzhak Rabin's funeral, the Speaker complained to the press about the administration's lack of courtesy. Political cartoonists and commentators alike had a field day, depicting him as a crybaby. Shortly after, Republicans passed a new continuing resolution to open the government through mid-December in exchange for the White House's commitment to negotiate terms for balancing the budget within seven years. That ended the shutdown on November 19, and many Republicans felt they were making progress, but press accounts overwhelmingly depicted the president's team controlling events.

Legislators were learning that pitting a univocal House majority against a president was no sure recipe for success—and Gingrich, for his part, started to advocate for some sort of compromise.[92] But enraged Republican freshmen wanted nothing short of capitulation from the White House. To avoid being eaten by his own revolution, Gingrich adopted their intransigent stance. Clinton maintained his unwillingness to accept sharp entitlement cuts, and so a new government shutdown began on December 16, this time lasting for weeks.[93] Finally, on January 5, 1996, Gingrich dragged his conference into passing a pay bill and an interim spending bill, contingent on the White House offering a concrete plan to balance the budget by 2002. In a terrific anti-climax, the White House promptly produced such a plan—though, of course, not one that was to Republicans' liking.[94]

Republicans were, by then, totally discombobulated. They had assumed their power of the purse would let them dictate fiscal terms to Clinton. Gingrich had basically tried to make himself legislator-in-chief, claiming a mandate to set the national policy agenda even on the most high-salience spending policies. He had brought along the House, no mean feat, but he lacked the resources to overawe the White House. He also paid surprisingly little attention to the Senate, where Republican members were much less committed to rapid change. With Gingrich's frontal assault parried, the term "revolution" went from branding coup to political liability. Leadership initiative passed to the compromise-minded Senate, which was expected to pick up the pieces in a way that more accurately reflected what Americans wanted.[95]

Although their revolution was exhausted, Republicans demanded a few symbolic concessions from the president in exchange for passing longer-term spending and debt limit increase bills. In March 1996, Clinton signed the grandiose-sounding Contract With America Advancement Act, which conceded two small Republican priorities: an increase in the allowable earnings limit on Social Security (effectively a tax cut for seniors) and a modest regulatory reform measure for small business. The deal also advanced two more ambitious reforms.[96]

The first was the Congressional Review Act, a sort of poor man's replacement for the Supreme Court–eliminated legislative veto. The three principal Senate sponsors of the congressional review language, including Sen. Harry Reid (D-NV), offered a statement that explained, "This legislation will help to redress the balance, reclaiming for Congress some of its policymaking authority, without at the same time requiring Congress to become a super regulatory agency."[97] But whereas the legislative veto really had given Congress a tool to stop the executive branch in its tracks, the joint resolution mechanism embedded in the Congressional Review Act can be overridden by a presidential veto. Only in the case of a presidential transition from one party to the other is the president likely to assent.[98] Congress had other options available to it, including a "Congressional Responsibility Act" introduced in December 1995 that attracted 58 House cosponsors, which would have created a system of prospective approval for major new regulations.[99] That might have created genuine legislative accountability for rules, but the Congressional Review Act falls well short of doing so.[100]

The second was the line-item veto, a president-empowering change conservatives had long sought and which had been included in the Contract. Naturally, Clinton regarded this change as his own victory. His signing speech pulled straight from 1980s conservative discussions on the "constitutional balance of powers" and the evils of overlarded omnibuses.[101] Republicans may have supposed that the line-item veto power could only bias spending downward, though that is doubtful. Because the line-item veto provides a kind of security blanket for congressional irresponsibility, members would probably have felt liberated to include more pet projects, as Andrew Rudalevige has pointed out.[102] Actual experience with the federal line-item veto was limited, as the Supreme Court soon enough ruled it unconstitutional.[103]

The 104th Congress' dynamic shifted after the March–April denouement. Clinton was reinvigorated and trumpeted his taming of Republicans to whomever would listen.[104] After Dole resigned to concentrate on his presidential campaign in May 1996, new Senate Majority

Leader Trent Lott (pictured with Gingrich in Figure 5.2) became the "de facto leader of the demoralized congressional GOP," which was ready to accept some bipartisan compromises.[105] Far from reaffirming their revolutionary commitments as they campaigned against Clinton in 1996, Republicans turned toward the center and focused on the particular needs of their districts in order to save their majorities even as Clinton handily dispatched Dole in November.[106]

What lessons about congressional reform generally can be drawn from the Republican Revolution's repulsion? Was Republicans' inability to achieve most of their ambitious agenda inevitable, or should the episode be viewed as a missed opportunity? Were they doomed from the start or merely outmaneuvered?

Most observers seem to agree that, as Clinton's aide George Stephanopoulos put it in the midst of the budget showdown, "Newt's very good. . . . But he has a very bad hand."[107] The Republican House freshmen were committed to policies more conservative than the American people actually wanted, and Clinton demonstrated the presidency's overall superiority for shaping media

**Figure 5.2** Speaker of the House Newt Gingrich (R-GA) and Senate Majority Leader Trent Lott (R-MS) pictured during a joint GOP leadership meeting in August 1997.

*Source*: CQ Roll Call Photograph Collection, Library of Congress Prints and Photographs Division.

narratives of politics and policy alike. Gingrich had much less momentum upon becoming Speaker than he realized.

But it is worth considering how much Republicans were handicapped by their own cramped understanding of the institution they controlled. Gingrich, in particular, was never a congressional institutionalist; given his dramatic leadership of a nationalized campaign in 1994, the superior legitimacy of a Madisonian legislature never interested him much at all. Rather, he was a quintessential anti-institutionalist working within Congress. His time as Speaker pushed him slightly toward a compromise-oriented way of thinking, but he chafed at the role of negotiator. After one difficult and fruitless session with the White House, he admitted: "This is draining stuff. I like to give speeches. It's more fun."[108] He had ample opportunity to "educate" the American people. He lacked realistic endgame strategies for dealing with those who remained unpersuaded.[109]

Gingrich rose to power by promising to throw the bastards out, and he remade the House as an emanation of his own will as much as possible. His uncompromising stance faithfully delivered on the Wilsonian ideal of giving the electorate a clear choice. But he never considered how a less partisan, less top-down, more deliberative approach might have strengthened Congress' hand in negotiating with the president or in making the case for reform to the American people. If Republicans were constantly surprised by the public's reactions to their proposals, that reflected poorly on their deliberative method or lack thereof. Having prejudged congressional Democrats as corrupted protectors of the bureaucracy they wanted to upend, Republicans made themselves less able to build the broad coalitions capable of delivering lasting structural reforms. Having determined the Great Society a failure, they did too little to explore which parts of it enjoyed deep support in the electorate. Decentralized congressional action might have given them the means to discover a viable strategy, but that was a road not taken.

Despite the clear shortcomings of the 104th Congress, during the ensuing quarter century leaders of both parties, in both chambers, have emulated Gingrich's example more than they have rejected it. Maximal partisan differentiation and confrontation would be the watchwords of 21st-century American politics.

# 6

# The Triumph of Partisan Posturing
# over Politics

The core problem here is that my good friend the majority leader as a practical matter is running the whole Senate because everything is centralized in his office, which diminishes the opportunity for Senators of both parties to represent their constituents. Look, we all were sent here by different Americans who expected us to have a voice, to have an opportunity to effect legislation. I would say to my good friend the majority leader, we don't have a rules problem, we have an attitude problem. When is the Senate going to get back to normal?
  —Senate Minority Leader Mitch McConnell (R-KY), July 18, 2012[1]

The majority . . . risks turning this body into a colosseum of zero-sum infighting—a place where the brute power of the majority rules, with little or no regard for the concerns of the minority party, and where longstanding rules have little or no meaning.
  —Senate Minority Leader Chuck Schumer (D-NY), April 3, 2019[2]

On October 8, 1998, the House of Representatives voted to launch a formal impeachment inquiry against President Bill Clinton for perjury, obstruction of justice, and abuse of power. After Clinton's re-election in 1996, Republicans in Congress lost some of their reforming zeal, but Speaker Newt Gingrich remained committed to maximizing the contrast between the two parties in hopes that the American people would give Republicans a clear mandate. Clinton's affair with White House intern Monica Lewinsky and his subsequent cover-ups gave Gingrich what he believed was a golden opportunity to attack Democrats' character problem.[3] But the move backfired. Democrats gained five House seats and fought to a draw in the Senate in the

November midterms, an unexpectedly good performance for a party whose president had been in the White House for six years. Within days, facing widespread Republican dissatisfaction, Gingrich announced he would resign the Speakership and leave Congress.

Gingrich was, unquestionably, a singular presence—a prophetic bringer of doom to the old congressional order, who held truly unusual ideas about governing, leadership, and the appropriate role of Congress. It was possible, then, that his political exit could have created an opportunity for a course correction in American politics. But nothing of the sort happened. Instead, impeachment careened onward, with the House voting to impeach Clinton on three counts in December. Just as they were doing so, Gingrich's presumed successor, Rep. Bob Livingston (R-LA), imploded. *Hustler* magazine had offered up $1 million for dirt on congressmen, which turned up several women prepared to expose the would-be Speaker's extramarital affairs.[4] Livingston had wanted to move beyond Gingrich's "revolutionizing" to the work of "day to day governing," but now he withdrew, saying that he could no longer effectively lead Republicans in their quest to hold Clinton accountable.

Eager to replace Gingrich and end this drama, Republicans turned to Rep. Dennis Hastert (R-IL), a former wrestling coach whose avuncular persona made it easy to imagine a friendlier, less poisonous version of American politics. Hastert explicitly promised such a turn as he assumed the Speakership, praising the leadership of his fellow Illinoisan Bob Michel and telling members of both parties that "solutions to problems cannot be found in a pool of bitterness" but in a recognition "that each Member is equally important for our overall mission of improving the life of the American people." He hearkened back to his days as a wrestling coach for some pertinent homespun wisdom: "Above all, a coach worth his salt will instill in his team a sense of fair play, camaraderie, respect for the game and respect for the opposition. Without those, victory is hollow, and defeat represents opportunities lost. I've found this to be true around here, too."[5]

Hastert presented a reassuring image. (Nearly two decades later, Hastert's irregular financial activities led to the exposure of blackmail payments made to cover up molestation of his one-time students, exposing his reputation as a caring mentor to be counterfeit.) But his Speakership was not a time of healing for the House. Instead, the lower chamber became even more acrimonious, subordinated itself to the executive branch, and incubated Republican ethics scandals rivaling the Democratic capers of the 1970s. Remarkably, the once famously individualistic Senate followed this example, developing practices that enabled tight leadership control of the agenda through restrictions on open debate and amending. This model has the virtue of facilitating certain kinds of action, even in a time of bitter partisanship, but it comes at a grave cost. On the most consequential issues, our legislature has become positively hostile to the strange bedfellow coalitions that allow fluid interactions between factions and prevent the entrenchment of enmities.

The first part of this chapter chronicles the triumph of centralized processes, which have progressed steadily even as partisan control of both chambers of Congress has seesawed. As of the early 2020s, the pendulum has swung so decisively toward tight central control that the organizational problems of the anarchic late 1970s seem almost incomprehensible. While many legislators criticize the current regime, the prospects of swinging the pendulum back toward openness do not currently seem bright.

The second half of the chapter explores the consequences of this regime for American policymaking. In recent years, "partisan gridlock" has become almost synonymous with Congress. It is true that legislators have found themselves unable—or unwilling—to pass legislation addressing some of the most important challenges of our era, so that policymaking on these matters has migrated into the executive branch and judiciary. But on many other issues, partisan majorities have found ways to work their will even in the face of determined and united opposition. Elsewhere, bipartisan coalitions continue to carry on vital functions, though often in ways that leave much to be desired. Finally, when faced with crises, Congress is usually capable of rapid and ambitious action, as strong bipartisan majorities rally around deals brokered by legislative leaders.

We should not imagine Congress as a body suffering from complete paralysis. Yet contemporary modes of policymaking reveal a Congress that has almost given up on meaningful debate—with disastrous consequences. When bureaucrats and judges are asked to supplant Congress' representative function, they excite bitter resentments, a sense of arbitrary rule, and feelings of political exclusion. When partisan majorities enact major statutes without conciliating their opponents, the resulting laws are often undermined when Congress changes hands, or suffer later Congresses' inability to revise troublesome sections. However ambitious a single statutory enactment may be, it is relatively much less potent than the establishment of a broad coalition capable of enduring through electoral changes. When leaders dictate responses to crises without deliberation, important questions are often left unresolved.

Although Congress has readily provided cash and discretionary power to the executive branch, it has failed to secure broadly acceptable arrangements for sharing the burdens of national misfortunes, leaving a deep sense of unfairness hanging over even some of their more successful interventions.

Members of Congress have gone along with changes to their institution for understandable reasons. Diminished opportunities for amendments mean legislators are spared hard votes. Messaging bills help core partisans understand the stakes in the next election, the better to energize them and open their wallets. As more policymaking authority migrates into the executive and judiciary, winning the next election to gain (or retain) the president's power of nomination and the Senate's power of confirmation does become more important. And, in a tensely divided nation where many voters resent the party in power, it is true that the losing side could wrest back power as soon as the next election.

The current organization is nevertheless failing us. Dug into their respective trenches, both parties suffer from stagnant orthodoxy, rewarding members who distinguish themselves through rhetorical bomb throwing instead of dutiful coalition building. Our expectations of Congress have plummeted, and we have almost forgotten the institution's potential to support the kind of unpredictable politics that allow the nation to benefit from its stunning diversity.

## Centralized Control in the 21st-Century House

By the turn of the millennium, leadership dominance had already gained momentum in the House, especially during the Speakerships of Jim Wright and Newt Gingrich. Hastert projected a friendly, aw-shucks image, and his partisanship was far less flamboyant and combative than Gingrich's. Nevertheless, he and his leadership team continued Gingrich's consolidation of power in the House. Through the Steering Committee, they aggressively utilized their ability to choose committee chairmen, withholding gavels from those members who had broken with leaders on campaign finance reform and extending their control to subcommittee chairmen on the Appropriations Committee.[6] Later, they began to interview candidates for chairmanships—as the ascendant Democratic freshmen had once done in 1975. Now, though, it was leadership asserting itself rather than the broader caucus, and the deciding factor in their choices of who should become chair

was often who contributed to the party's central coffers most lavishly and reliably. Even once committee chairs were installed, leaders made it clear they
would not be beholden to them. If chairs threatened to hold up the party's
priority legislation, the leadership would simply bypass them with ad hoc
task forces of loyalist members.[7]

Hastert and his leadership team were unusually punctilious when it came
to using their power to conform the agenda to their party's priorities. In
2003, Hastert declared that a central principle of his leadership was to "please
the majority of the majority" and never to "expedite legislation that runs
counter" to its wishes. This "Hastert rule" grants extra leverage to the majority party's less moderate members, who can effectively block bipartisan
measures that would otherwise command majority support in a chamber.[8]

Political scientist James Curry illustrates Republican leaders' use of their
agenda-setting powers to keep their caucus together on a favored bill. In
2005, Rep. James Sensenbrenner (R-WI), chairman of the House Judiciary
Committee, cooperated closely with leadership to move a bill tightening federal standards for personal identification and strengthening border control.
To gain GOP support, he needed to sell the bill as a continuation of anti-
terrorism efforts responding to 9/11, not as a foray into the complicated
immigration debates then dividing Republicans. Leaders therefore sought
to frame the debate and speed the bill's passage by bypassing normal committee procedures, giving "various perquisites" to the sponsor of a potentially rival bill in exchange for his support, and compelling the president's
assent by threatening to abandon his larger immigration agenda. Finally,
they used two special rules to control proceedings on the House floor, first
limiting debate to 60 minutes and then implementing some strategically
chosen amendments through a self-executing rule released late in the eve-
ning. House members then had to vote on the amended bill, without any further chance for reflection or debate and with just a few specified amendments
allowed—the most important of which had been set up to fail. The hurried
last-minute changes and vote meant that "rank-and-file Republicans had to
rely on their leaders for information, while simultaneously making it more
difficult for Democrats to effectively oppose or amend the bill."[9] This kind of
leadership dominance has become typical in the 21st-century House.

As Hastert tightened the majority leadership's power, House Democrats
countered with their own leadership consolidation. They transformed the
large, inclusive whip system pioneered by Tip O'Neill into an even larger and
more hierarchical organization, pulling in a significant share of Democratic

members while simultaneously increasing centralized leaders' control.[10] Minority Leader Nancy Pelosi (D-CA) worked fervently to unify her party in opposition, sharply rebuking members of her party who joined Republicans in adding prescription drug coverage to Medicare in 2003.[11]

Democrats were well positioned to gain seats in the 2006 midterms, given the unpopularity of incumbent president George W. Bush. But, like the Republican Revolutionaries of the previous decade, they also painted the congressional majority as corrupted by special interests and out of touch with the concerns of ordinary Americans. Following the example of the Contract With America, their reform agenda included inward-looking changes to the House, such as ethics reforms and a promise to return to regular order. Democrats picked up 31 seats and gained a narrow majority.

With the House secured, Pelosi became America's first "Madam Speaker," and promises of regular order faded away. Her new leadership team was just as enthusiastic about centralized control of the agenda as their Republican predecessors.[12] Democrats completely bypassed committees to move a significant package of legislation at the beginning of the new Congress. Pelosi used her power over committee assignments to reward party loyalty and fundraising. And the Rules Committee, which included four Democratic freshmen, worked closely with (read: "under") the new Speaker. During Pelosi's (first) Speakership, the portion of "unreported" bills (those receiving floor action without ever having been reported out by the committee of jurisdiction) rose to more than a quarter. Such bills were often shielded from floor debate through tightly restrictive rules—meaning that, from drafting to passage, they were shaped almost entirely by leadership.[13]

Democrats achieved a remarkably high level of party unity under Pelosi's command—92 percent in the 110th Congress and 91 percent in the 111th.[14] Moreover, leadership was able to hold their members together even as they pushed the party in a more progressive direction.

The trend toward leadership consolidation in the House, established in the 1990s and the aughts, would continue through two more changes in party control in the 2010s. After the GOP took back the majority in the 2010 midterms, the Republican Steering Committee actively used its committee assignment power to ensure obedience by promoting nonsenior members to chairs, putting select freshmen on powerful committees, and punishing defectors by rebuffing their requests.[15] Democrats after 2019 again maintained tight party discipline, enabling them to impeach President Donald Trump on terms that maximized their own partisan solidarity.

Throughout this period, changes in the allocation of resources also contributed to the dominance of leadership. Financial resources and staff available to members and House committees have stagnated, while resources and staff of leadership have grown considerably. Consistent with the emphasis on political differentiation, staff roles in all three types of offices have shifted away from legislative functions toward communications.[16] Committee oversight activities have transformed into tools for scoring partisan points within the framework of leaders' messaging campaigns, with shorter but more frequent investigations used to uncover fodder for short-term attacks rather than informing the long-term reorientation of agency activities.[17]

The move toward tightly controlled debate becomes even more evident if we consider House floor activity holistically. Figure 6.1 charts this transformation. Through the late 1990s, open rules and modified open rules were about as common as closed and structured rules. In the 21st century,

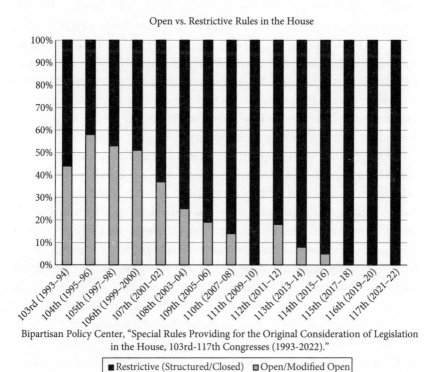

Open vs. Restrictive Rules in the House

Bipartisan Policy Center, "Special Rules Providing for the Original Consideration of Legislation in the House, 103rd-117th Congresses (1993-2022)."

■ Restrictive (Structured/Closed)   □ Open/Modified Open

**Figure 6.1** The decline of open rules in the House.

*Source:* Bipartisan Policy Center.

however, they gradually became all but extinct. They were entirely absent in the 115th and 116th Congresses. Rules Committee structuring of debate, along lines approved by the Speaker, is now ubiquitous.

Under this regime, voting patterns of Democratic and Republican members have diverged to an extent not seen in a century. While this trend of partisan polarization is often understood as a function of an increasingly polarized electorate, it is important to remember that the chances for re-corded votes are now much more tightly controlled by leaders than in the past. Those leaders have an active interest in creating the impression of dif-ferentiation.[18] Partisan polarization, as measured by roll-call voting patterns, is indicative of the exercise of leader power in a political environment geared toward keeping legislators tightly bound to their own party.[19]

Unsurprisingly, leadership's tight grip of the agenda has generated in-ternal dissension, which has occasionally boiled over. Most dramatically, a group of 40 frustrated conservatives formed the House Freedom Caucus in January 2015, hoping to force Speaker of the House John Boehner (R-OH) to adopt a more confrontational stance toward the Obama administration. The desire to disrupt the establishment generally, rather than any particular policy demand, animated the group. In service of that goal, Freedom Caucus members sometimes raised Madisonian complaints about the operation of the contemporary House, and especially the absence of opportunities for amendments. As cofounder Raúl Labrador (R-ID) put it, "We have a lot of people here who feel they are not being heard."[20]

But rather than finding opportunities to build coalitions that could out-flank leadership, Freedom Caucus members focused almost exclusively on lodging grievances with and creating difficulties for their party's existing leaders. Indeed, in registering their dissatisfaction, they were frequently willing to push Boehner into cutting deals with moderate Democrats. Over the course of 2015, standoffish distrust curdled into outright enmity, to the point where Freedom Caucus member Mark Meadows (R-NC) introduced a resolution to declare the Speakership vacant, threatening a revote on the Speakership. Boehner expected to survive the challenge but thought it would create electoral vulnerabilities for many Republican members. Rather than fight, he announced his retirement in late September. The Freedom Caucus declared victory, but the changing of the guard gave them little leverage to change the way the House operated. They came to resent the new Speaker, Paul Ryan (R-WI), even more than Boehner despite his more frequent com-munication with caucus members. Ironically, for all their interest in changing the operation of the House, the caucus' members achieved their greatest influence by turning toward the opposite end of Pennsylvania Avenue. Having courted Donald Trump as he marched toward their party's nomination, and casting themselves as fellow scourges of the swamp, numerous members became important confidants to the president. Mick Mulvaney (R-SC) and Meadows would each end up serving Trump as chief of staff; Jim Bridenstine (R-OK) would become administrator of NASA. A reversal of the pendulum in the House, meanwhile, remained light years away.

## Centralized Control Comes to the Senate—The Demise of Amendments

In the 1980s and early 1990s, norms of bipartisan comity in the Senate had frayed, though the chamber could still broker major deals in a fairly decentralized way. By the late 1990s, partisan warfare in the Senate intensified, and the majority party came to see the minority as a serious threat to the chamber's ability to do any business at all. In response to this perceived threat, the majority party supported its leader's exercise of control over the flow of debate in the chamber. The minority doubled down on its complaints of systematic exclusion, justifying further escalation of tactical warfare—and the majority responded with even greater power for its leader. The Senate's pendulum swung toward central control, and each change of majority only accelerated that trend.

Majority Leader Trent Lott (R-MS) pioneered various techniques to bypass minority obstruction. In July 1996, Lott complained, "We are now in a rolling filibuster on every issue, which is totally gridlocking the U.S. Senate.... [W]e have an obligation to allow the Senate to do its work. That is not happening."[21] Lott candidly spelled out his perspective on open debate when defending his decision to limit amendments on a bill being considered in 1999. "I have learned a lesson. If we are going to pass legislation," he told his colleagues, "I am going to have to take actions to block irrelevant, nongermane amendments that are just part of a political agenda."[22]

Amendments on spending bills were a special concern for the majority. Since these bills were understood as must-pass legislation, the opportunity to amend them gave the minority a chance not only to further its substantive priorities but also to force members of the majority to take difficult votes they would rather avoid on primarily symbolic measures. In May 2000, Lott and

Republicans moved to shut down the ability to offer one such type of amendment, those that declared the "Sense of the Senate," as nongermane and therefore out of order. Expressing Democrats' dismay, Sen. Chuck Schumer (D-NY) declared: "I fear if we are throttled any further, the whole order and comity of this body will break down."[23] Republicans judged this risk worth taking, swinging the pendulum toward centralized control in hopes of securing their party's hold on the power of the purse.

Lott also ramped up use of another technique to shut out minority amendments, known as "filling the tree." Because the Senate majority leader has the right of first recognition, he can offer amendments before any other senator. Normal parliamentary procedures create a particular structure—a "tree"—of consideration for amendments to the underlying bill (first degree) and amendments to those amendments (second degree perfecting or substitute). If he chooses to do so, the majority leader can offer his own amendments and "fill" every one of the available amendment slots, effectively shutting other senators out. Eventually, the Senate could work through all of the leader's amendments, giving other senators a chance to offer their own, but the strategy can impose significant delays and give the leader the chance to close off debate entirely through a cloture motion. This technique had been used once in 1993, but Lott relied on it eight times in the 106th Congress of 1999–2000. His Republican successor, Bill Frist (R-TN), used it at a similar rate.

When Democrats regained the majority, Sen. Harry Reid (D-NV) took filling the tree from an occasional tactic to a nearly routine way of conducting business on important bills, using it 95 times over his eight years as leader (2007–14). Republicans were sometimes almost entirely shut out of floor activity; during half of 2013, their members received votes on just four amendments.[24] To the minority's bitter complaints, Reid answered that their pattern of "obstruction, obstruction, obstruction" left him no real choice.[25] Mitch McConnell, who became majority leader in 2015, pledged that a Republican majority would leave more room for open consideration of amendments. In practice, he resorted to filling the tree nearly as often as Reid had.

To the extent amendments are allowed in the contemporary Senate, they are often tightly controlled through complex unanimous consent agreements (UCAs) negotiated by the two party's leaders. In a manner closely analogous to rules for debate passed by the House Rules Committee, such UCAs often prescribe exactly which amendments will be considered and for how long before sending the chamber to votes "with no intervening action or debate" allowed.[26] Since these agreements do require unanimous consent, any single senator who feels like a crucial matter is being neglected has the power to block them—a stark contrast to the decisions made by the House Rules Committee. In practice, then, the majority leader has to make some concessions, allowing some amendment opportunities that will satisfy all members. But, in the current regime, senators in both parties feel pressured to go along with the UCAs that their leaders negotiate. The more demand for amending activity has pent up, the more plausible it becomes that opening a bill to amendments will derail it. As demonstrated by their willingness to rally behind a leader monopolizing the agenda, most members appear to believe that the alternative to tightly controlled debate is a completely broken Senate.

As in the House, quantitative data vividly corroborates the story of diminishing openness in the Senate. Senate amendments considered on the floor, tracked in Figure 6.2, have fallen dramatically in our hyperpolarized era. In the 104th Congress, the newly Republican-controlled chamber considered more than 1,700 amendments on the Senate floor. Under Reid's control in the

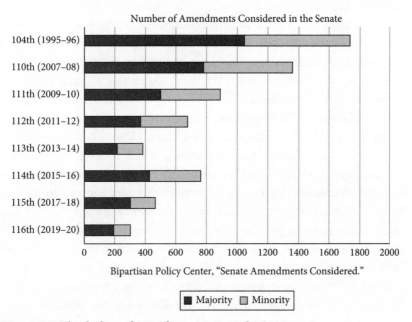

Bipartisan Policy Center, "Senate Amendments Considered."

**Majority** ☐ **Minority**

**Figure 6.2** The decline of amending activity in the Senate.
*Source:* Bipartisan Policy Center.

110th Congress, that figure fell by roughly a quarter. By the 113th Congress, it dropped all the way to 384 amendments. When Republicans regained control, McConnell trumpeted the return of a more open Senate, and the 114th Congress did consider 763 amendments on the floor. But by the end of McConnell's six-year run as majority leader, amending activity had fallen to an all-time low, with just 303 amendments considered in the 116th Congress.

As Adam Jentleson, one of Reid's former aides, puts it in his blistering indictment of the contemporary Senate, "What used to be a place where deals were struck is now a place where orders are handed down, the Senate's power more like that of a soul-crushing bureaucracy than of a great deliberative body."[27]

## Limiting Debate in Response to the Degraded Filibuster

The threat of procedural chaos led Senate leaders to suppress amendment activity, notwithstanding the long Senate tradition of open debate. But even more important to the evolution of 21st-century Senate dynamics has been the routinization of other forms of obstructionism by the minority, especially the filibuster.

Today's filibuster bears very little resemblance to the grand, attention-focusing spectacle depicted in Chapter 3. As Chapter 4 explained, in 1975 the Senate had shifted the number of votes needed to cut off debate with cloture from 67 to 60 and created a "tracking" system that allowed the Senate to consider other business during filibusters. This was intended to make filibustering less capable of paralyzing the chamber, and it succeeded in that regard. But obstructive entrepreneurs like Jesse Helms (R-NC) and James Allen (D-AL) soon learned that filibustering, which no longer jeopardized their colleagues' priorities, had become nearly costless. Not surprisingly, the tactic proliferated, as did the cloture motions that now became decisive on many of the most important issues. While the Senate of the 1960s saw just a few cloture motions per Congress, in the 1970s they were up to around 30, in the 1980s around 40, and in the 1990s and early 2000s around 70 (see Table 6.1).[28] Throughout this period, senators struggled to deal with the filibuster's effects on their chamber's ability to operate, periodically changing the chamber's rules and precedents to make debate more manageable.

As filibusters became commonplace, individual members found their ability to block legislation magnified. By custom, senators had long been able

Table 6.1  Cloture motions filed in the Senate, 1961–2022

| Years | Cloture Motions Filed per Congress (rounded) |
|---|---|
| 1961–70 | 6 |
| 1971–80 | 32 |
| 1981–90 | 41 |
| 1991–2000 | 72 |
| 2001–6 | 67 |
| 2007–12 | 130 |
| 2013–22 | 243 |

*Source:* US Senate, Cloture Motions, https://www.senate.gov/legislative/cloture/clotureCounts.htm

to place a "hold" on a bill, but that had only guaranteed them a day's notice if the bill was going to come to the floor. But with a tighter schedule and increasingly assertive behavior, a hold in the 1980s became a kind of de facto one-man veto.[29] An obligation to accommodate other senators may sound salutary, but individuals' power reached absurd heights; one senator went so far as to say, "When you prepare an amendment or a bill, subconsciously you're thinking about Howard Metzenbaum. Will it pass the Metzenbaum test?"[30] Senators' willingness to place holds became nearly indiscriminate by the 2000s, with senators often expressing their intent to block all actions relating to a particular issue.[31]

In the first decades of the 21st century, the minority's ability to obstruct bills and presidential nominees has combined with the larger trend of partisan combat to produce a series of dramatic confrontations over the limits of the filibuster, with both parties escalating the stakes by expanding what they were willing to block over time. When Democrats relied on holds and filibusters to block the confirmation of many of George W. Bush's highest-priority nominees to appellate courts, denouncing them as "radicals in robes," Republicans began a years-long consideration of what Frist called "the constitutional option." That would entail modifying the Senate's cloture threshold on judicial nominees to a simple majority by means of overruling the Senate's presiding officer enforcing its precedents—a change easier to make than formally amending the chamber's rules, because it requires only a simple majority and cannot itself be filibustered. The tactic is also known as the "nuclear option" because of fears that triggering it would lead to a kind of parliamentary mutually assured destruction, with the disadvantaged minority resorting to every possible means of preventing the Senate from functioning. Republicans nearly took that risk in 2005, but a bipartisan group of senators struck a deal to preserve the filibuster by allowing votes on three of Bush's controversial nominees.[32] A continued trend toward obstructionism and reflexive invocation of cloture continued, however. Cloture motions skyrocketed to an average of around 130 per Congress from 2007 to 2010.

Dealing with the 60-vote cloture threshold had become all but automatic, keeping the temptation to go nuclear strong. Under the leadership of Reid, who warned that a "broken" Senate was in danger of becoming "obsolete," Democrats finally pulled the trigger in 2013 and instituted a 51-vote cloture threshold for executive branch and non–Supreme Court judicial nominees.[33] McConnell, then minority leader, said Democrats were using procedural wizardry to achieve policy results that the American people had decisively rejected at the polls. They would try to achieve their agenda "through the bureaucracy and through the DC Circuit" rather than reckoning with the reality of a Republican House.[34] But if McConnell was willing to suggest that the Democrats were becoming dangerously undemocratic, he and his colleagues were unwilling to bring on the nuclear winter that some had feared. Although they increased their use of dilatory tactics, they also continued to cooperate on many of the unanimous consent agreements that allowed the Senate to operate smoothly, and Democrats worked through a backlog of nominees. GOP leaders felt that "it would be a mistake to make ourselves the issue" ahead of the 2014 midterm elections.[35] That may have been a sensible calculation; Republicans gained nine seats that November and McConnell finally achieved his decades-old ambition of becoming majority leader, at which point he abandoned his earlier paeans to an open process and the value of unlimited debate.

As majority leader, McConnell continued to base his procedural arguments on the assumption that elections, rather than debate, should decide the most important questions. When Antonin Scalia's death in early 2016 created a Supreme Court vacancy, McConnell declared that it would remain empty until after the next presidential election, invoking a striking plebiscitary understanding of American democracy: "The American people are perfectly capable of having their say on this issue, so let's give them a voice," McConnell declared. "Let's let the American people decide."[36] After that election went Republicans' way, McConnell and his colleagues were happy to operate under the assumption that the election had made prolonged debate unnecessary. They routinely availed themselves of the 51-vote threshold for cloture on Trump's nominees—bringing overall invocations of cloture to around 200 per Congress from 2017 to 2020.[37] And they executed two nuclear maneuvers of their own, adopting a 51-vote threshold for Supreme Court nominations in 2017 and reducing postcloture debate for federal district court judges from 30 hours to just 2 in 2019. Minority Leader Chuck Schumer (D-NY) denounced the change in terms that echoed McConnell's 2013 arguments: "Underneath all of the statistics, what Leader McConnell, President Trump, and Republicans in the Senate are trying to do is use the courts to adopt the far-right agenda that Republicans know they cannot enact through the legislative process."[38] The Senate, meant to be the world's greatest deliberative body, was reduced to a forum in which each side accused the other of stacking the courts to achieve what a straightforward debate among legislators could not.

Inasmuch as gaining control of the federal courts was taken as the metric, McConnell and Republicans had some striking successes. Having frozen out Obama's Supreme Court nominee in 2016, they pulled off the *opposite* feat in 2020, when Ruth Bader Ginsburg's death gave Trump the opportunity to nominate a third Supreme Court justice. The Republican-controlled Senate then managed a lightning-quick confirmation of Amy Coney Barrett—*before* the election. McConnell did not profess a thoroughgoing democratism then—it was whatever it takes to get the job done, with the job defined as facilitating conservative control over the real commanding heights of policymaking, now to be found in the judiciary rather than the legislature.

The opportunism so starkly on display in handling these Supreme Court nominations has poisoned any high-minded attempt to stake out a procedural principle on which the Senate should stand. So where does that leave the filibuster in the 2020s?

While the filibuster has been done away with for presidential nominations, the legislative filibuster survives and indeed thrives, for now, which means that most legislation effectively requires 60 votes to pass. That has its benefits: the prod to building broader coalitions sometimes helps produce more legitimate policies, as the grinding process that eventually led to the Infrastructure Investment and Jobs Act of 2021 receiving 69 votes in the Senate revealed.

But the Senate is hardly uniform in its respect for supermajorities. The body has increasingly relied on what political scientist Molly Reynolds has called "majoritarian exceptions," various statutory provisions that allow the Senate to avoid the threat of filibustering and pass statutes with bare majorities.[39] Most important among these is budget reconciliation, a procedure put in place by the Congressional Budget Act of 1974, which both parties now see as the best vehicle for implementing any part of their agenda related to taxes or spending. Reconciliation has facilitated the passage of numerous important pieces of legislation, but it also limits and distorts debate, as senators tie themselves into pretzels attempting to figure out what policy changes can comply with the Byrd rule—a germaneness requirement discussed in the "Partisan Legislating" section below.

That rule is named for Robert C. Byrd (D-WV), who was perhaps the last principled defender of the filibuster in the Senate. As recounted in Chapter 3, Byrd filibustered the Civil Rights Act in 1964, capping off that months-long affair with a 14-hour speech. He went on to serve as Senate majority leader in the late 1970s and again in the late 1980s. During both stints, he was distressed by what he saw as harmful overreliance on filibustering and sought to put limits on the practice. At one point in 1988, frustrated by a filibuster of a campaign finance measure he favored, he kept debate going through a 53-hour legislative day and seven unsuccessful cloture votes, and even went so far as to have the Senate's sergeant-at-arms drag members to the chamber when they sought to evade debate. As he wrote in a 1988 reflection on the filibuster's history, Byrd fervently believed that "the right of extended, even unlimited, debate is the main cornerstone of the Senate's uniqueness." Without it, the Senate would "lose its special strength and become a mere appendage of the House of Representatives."[40]

Far from embodying the right of unlimited debate, the modern-day version of the filibuster, unfortunately, does not promote debate at all. A form detached from principle, it now embodies obstruction detached from persuasion. Debate on the Senate floor is all but moribund, and the very idea of persuasion is in disrepute.[41] The filibuster as we now know it is, therefore, difficult to defend.

Byrd's defense nevertheless still resonates, if we can recover the principles that animated it. Many of those most eager to see the filibuster eliminated—that is, to see the Senate move to a majority threshold for cloture on all matters—do, in fact, wish to see the Senate reduced to an appendage of the House because they view the representation of states embodied in the Senate's structure as basically undemocratic. Others focus on segregationists' decades-long reliance on the filibuster, hoping to doom the practice through guilt by association. But as Chapter 3 showed, the old, rare version of the filibuster, which completely stopped up the Senate, served as a mechanism for focusing the nation's attention and forcing difficult decisions, often in compromise but sometimes in decisive victory for the supermajority. Segregationists relied on the filibuster—but the politics it enabled led to their complete rout. Without any substitute, today we lack the ability to feel we have decisively confronted a pressing question. Instead, we have only the sense of which side is able to impose its will today and the losing side's determination to change the conditions for tomorrow—by winning elections or changing the rules.

Of course, policymaking goes on. Our system has evolved several distinct methods for dealing with novel challenges that take for granted the Senate's transformation to a body in which a 60-vote majority is required to legislate. In the shadow of gridlock, Congress is often simply cut out of the loop. Other times, when the partisan stars align, legislators take their opportunities to push through major laws, even with single-party support. Finally, there are still many situations in which bipartisan deals prevail, although increasingly these are worked out away from the legislature and simply ratified there without much substantial committee input or floor debate. The following sections explore each of these patterns.

## Policymaking under Gridlock

As we have seen, each party has accused the other of making policy in courts because they could not command majorities in Congress. These complaints capture a real dynamic, one subtler than denunciations of "judicial activism" suggest. Typically, Congress is aware of some important problem—often *caused by* previous congressional actions—and legislators then introduce and debate legislation to address the problem, but they lack the wherewithal to shepherd their bills through to passage. When Congress fails to act, the executive branch steps into the vacuum, and the judiciary is forced to either acquiesce to or reject policies, even if no legislative replacements are in the offing.

Now, legislating is supposed to be hard in our constitutional system. And those who hold our contemporary legislature in low regard may say that the less legislating Congress does, the better for the rest of us. But in the contemporary era, in which dozens of statutes have created a reservoir of vaguely defined powers at the executive's disposal, stalled legislation does not freeze the policymaking process. Instead, the president and executive branch agencies take initiative to fill the void, creatively interpreting existing statutory authorities to justify their actions. President Obama famously declared, "I've got a pen, and I've got a phone," giving him the power to set ambitious policymaking efforts in motion without any cooperation from Congress.[42] The president's opponents invariably denounce such actions but rarely can pass legislation to decisively clarify or limit executive branch powers. Instead, the most important form of opposition comes from litigation challenging the legality of the executive branch's action. Statutory interpretation and administrative law, two subjects that sound deadly dull to most people, form the front lines of contemporary policymaking battles. If courts stymie the executive branch, that is not necessarily the end of the story; subnational policymakers (including state attorneys general[43]) may step forward to fill the gap, or trial lawyers acting through the tort system may come to shape their own policy regime.

American climate change policy presents a clear illustration of the shortcomings of trying to fashion policy without congressional action.[44] Congress took some modest first steps on climate issues, asking the Environmental Protection Agency (EPA) to formulate a plan in 1987 and unanimously ratifying a nonbinding United Nations agreement in 1992. But it declined to create a regulatory scheme for carbon emissions in its Clean Air Act amendments of 1990 and overwhelmingly rejected efforts to join a binding treaty in 1997. During the George W. Bush administration, the EPA rejected environmental groups' petitions for rulemaking under the Clean Air Act, explaining that the statute was a poor fit for addressing climate change—but the Supreme Court rejected the agency's reasoning in *Massachusetts v. EPA* (2007).

It thus fell to Barack Obama's administration to devise an administrative response to climate change. Since a new statute would be better suited to deal with carbon emissions, many hoped that initiating executive action would force disparate factions to compromise on new legislation. House Democrats passed an ambitious cap-and-trade bill in 2009, but an effort to assemble a coalition of 60 votes around a Senate version floundered, as it proved impossible to reconcile the demands of so many different kinds of interests, especially while congressional leaders prioritized other issues.[45]

Congress' inaction meant the EPA's regulations took center stage. While rules for automobiles were relatively easy to fashion, regulating power plants proved a much more awkward fit for the Clean Air Act. Finally, in 2015, the EPA promulgated a byzantine scheme requiring fossil-fuel plants to subsidize renewable energy generation.[46] This "Clean Power Plan" was immediately challenged in court. In February 2016, the Supreme Court took the unusual step of enjoining the policy—ordering it be held in limbo while a fuller consideration of its legal merits played out. Before that could ever happen, Donald Trump would rescind and replace the rule—only to see *those* efforts eventually ruled impermissible. Finally, in 2022, the Supreme Court ruled that the EPA's 2015 scheme could not be supported by a fair reading of the Clean Air Act. The six conservative justices in the majority emphasized that Congress needed to be the institution deciding such "major questions"[47]—an appealing precept, but one hard to swallow for the many observers convinced that Congress had more or less permanently abdicated its responsibility on this issue. Subnational policymaking has partially sought to provide substitute regimes, but those efforts have their own serious difficulties.

Similar dynamics play out in other policy issues Congress faces. Congressional stalemate on immigration, one of the most difficult and pressing issues of the 21st century, has led to a fragmented and sometimes contradictory set of subnational policies with significant legal uncertainty for millions of long-time residents without legal status; Chapter 7 takes up that story in detail. Congress has mostly punted the question of whether internet service providers must treat all types of content identically, so-called net neutrality, leaving the Federal Communications Commission to set policy and courts to adjudicate disputes. As in the case of climate change, changes in control of the White House led to sharp reversals of policy (one of which, in December 2017, was delayed because of a bomb threat called in to a meeting of the commission). That was also the case with regulation of American universities' sexual misconduct policies, undertaken through "Dear Colleague" letters sent out by Obama's Department of Education. The Trump administration reversed those policies; the Biden administration may well bring them back. Bureaucracies designed to navigate this shifting legal terrain, meanwhile, tend to accumulate power.[48]

At least some policies initiated in the executive branch are less subject to partisan whiplash and may be effective on their own terms. Still, when engineered apart from the legislative process, they tend to lack broad legitimacy. To help push economic recovery in the early 2010s, for example, the Federal Reserve undertook a massive bond-buying program that transformed its balance sheet and operations. It easily justified this "quantitative easing" by reference to its mandate to support full employment, but the sense that it was operating without Congress' support dented its above-the-fray reputation. Or consider the evolution of the so-called government-sponsored entities, the secondary mortgage market giants Fannie Mae and Freddie Mac, which were placed in a public conservatorship under the terms of a 2008 statute that seemed to envision a short period of public control followed by reprivatization. Nearly 15 years on, the two institutions remain in public hands. Legislators have debated but never significantly advanced bills to resolve the considerable ambiguity that hangs over this important market. This limbo may suit politicians, but it leaves taxpayers exposed to considerable risk. By failing to decide, we still make a decision of sorts. Legislators avoid responsibility—but they may well take the blame if the current arrangement contributes to later difficulties.

## Policymaking through Partisan Legislating

Policymaking through executive fiat is unsatisfactory. But policies resulting from congressional action are not necessarily more stable or legitimate if the majority party short-circuits the deliberative process to avoid accommodating the minority's concerns.

As noted above, that dynamic has often played out with the help of the budget reconciliation process, put in place by the Congressional Budget Act of 1974. That law's architects envisioned the congressional budget process giving fiscal conservatives a chance to plot out a sustainable, deficit-reducing path with reconciliation giving them a sure way to follow that path without procedural obstacles. Votes on reconciliation bills would be guaranteed by law—with no need to invoke cloture in the Senate. In an early use in 1980, the process worked roughly as planned, but from the presidency of Ronald Reagan onward, legislators used it just as often to enact deficit-increasing policies backed by the president and a narrow congressional majority.

Once Republicans retook control of Congress in 1995, they made aggressive use of budget reconciliation. In 1996, they used the process to pass welfare reform. Democrats objected that this ran afoul of the so-called Byrd rule—a germaneness requirement stating that reconciliation can only be used for genuinely budget-related legislative changes. That requires some judgment, and generally legislators rely on the rulings of an appointed parliamentarian who is supposed to act as a neutral arbiter of established rules. To overcome any procedural hurdles, Republicans installed a new Senate parliamentarian, who ruled that the proposed law was sufficiently budgetary to fit into reconciliation.[49] Five years later, after George W. Bush was sworn in, Republicans controlled a 50–50 Senate—with Vice President Dick Cheney casting the tie-breaking vote. Republicans once again turned to reconciliation to pass major tax cuts in 2001 and 2003. The Byrd rule also requires that a reconciliation law not increase the deficit outside of a 10-year budget window, so these tax cuts were designed to abruptly sunset after a decade. That seems like an eternity to legislators, but, sure enough, time passed, and the scheduled end of the Bush tax cuts created a mini-crisis for Congress ("the fiscal cliff") in 2013. Working through reconciliation has serious disadvantages for making sound policy.

Not all partisan lawmaking relies on reconciliation—but it tends to require procedural cunning of some sort. That was the case with the health care reform law Democrats pushed through against unified Republican opposition in 2010.[50] After significant gains in the 2008 election and a party switch by Sen. Arlen Specter (R → D-PA), Democrats briefly found themselves with 60 votes in the 111th Congress, enough to end a Republican filibuster if they stuck together. Thanks to some heavy-handed steering by Reid, Democrats made the most of their opportunity, passing the Patient Protection and Affordable Care Act in December 2009. However, after the death of Ted Kennedy (D-MA), Scott Brown (R-MA) won Kennedy's seat in a January 2010 special election, leaving Democrats with 59 votes—not enough to invoke cloture to merge the Senate and House versions of the bill.

House Democratic leaders, including committee chairmen, had labored mightily to pass their own bill in November, using a complicated, partially self-executing rule to control debate. To avoid a second Senate vote, House Democrats decided that they had no choice but to simply pass the Senate's version, discarding much of the work done in their own chamber and leaving plenty of unresolved questions. At that point, Democrats would switch gears, utilizing budget reconciliation procedures to amend some of the new law's provisions in order to bypass a filibuster. To ease passage, the House Rules Committee unusually created a rule that "deemed" the House to have passed both the Senate version and the reconciliation amendments simultaneously—without debate. Then-minority leader John Boehner denounced the process for ignoring and excluding the many voices opposed to the bill: "No matter how they engage in this debate, this body moves forward against their will. Shame on us. Shame on this body. Shame on each and every one of you who substitutes your will and your desires above those of your fellow countrymen."[51] Obama signed the Affordable Care Act (ACA) into law, and a few days later Senate Democrats passed the reconciliation bill—with a few minor items dropped because of Byrd rule violations. The House passed the slightly amended reconciliation bill, and by the end of March 2010, Obamacare was on the books.

That partisan success hardly ended the story, however. From the moment of its passage, Republicans campaigned against the legitimacy of the law, attacking the manner of its passage alongside many of its substantive provisions. Repealing Obamacare became the central campaign message of Republican politics in the years to come, with considerable success in 2010 and 2014. The law also immediately became the target of an unprecedented amount of litigation, including constitutional challenges to its individual mandate to purchase health insurance and its employer mandate to provide emergency contraception.[52] But a different legal challenge would later emerge based on a flaw in the text of the act itself, the language of which seemed to throw into doubt the ability to direct subsidies to any states relying on federal health care exchanges. With some interpretive heroics (or villainy, depending on one's perspective), the Supreme Court upheld the administration's saving interpretation, but the general problem would recur. When the Republican-controlled Congress refused to provide appropriations for another of the law's subsidies in its 2014 appropriations, the administration repurposed funds to make up the shortfall. Members of Congress then sued the president for improperly circumventing the legislature's power of the purse and won their case in the district court in 2016.

Clearly, then, passing a major statute on the basis of a purely partisan majority generates serious policymaking difficulties once the coalition that passed the law leaves the scene. The hazards are even greater once an administration of the opposite party comes in and can work from the inside to reorient the law, as the Trump administration did.[53]

In an attempt to repeal the ACA, Republicans mounted their own attempt at purely partisan lawmaking. In control of both the House and Senate in 2015, they used budget reconciliation to pass a repeal law and ran into Obama's expected veto. But once Trump was elected, they could play with live ammunition, using reconciliation. House Republicans dramatically failed in an attempt to pass a bill in March 2017 but then regrouped, with House leaders getting different factions within the party to openly negotiate with each other.[54] To great fanfare, they passed a repeal bill in May. The Senate then sought to push its own version through, with McConnell relying on an extraordinary degree of secrecy in fashioning a compromise almost completely out of public view, without committee involvement.[55] As a number of Republican senators began to air concerns about that bill, McConnell came up with another tactic: he would get the Senate to vote on two different bills, one the comprehensive repeal he had assembled, and one a "skinny repeal" that would do away with the ACA's controversial individual mandate (which the Supreme Court had upheld as constitutional) and delay a mandate for employers to provide coverage. In this case, process wizardry was the effort's undoing. Sen. John McCain (R-AZ), dying of brain cancer, dramatically cast the decisive vote against skinny repeal with a thumbs down on the Senate floor. He expressed grave misgivings about the attempt to meet Democrats' partisan power in kind, saying:

> We must now return to the correct way of legislating and send the bill back to committee, hold hearings, receive input from both sides of the aisle, heed the recommendations of the nation's governors, and produce a bill that finally delivers affordable health care for the American people. We must do the hard work our citizens expect of us and deserve.[56]

That didn't happen. Instead, Republicans' second use of reconciliation in 2017, on the Tax Cuts and Jobs Act, included a repeal of the individual mandate. Most of the ACA would survive, albeit sometimes repurposed by the Trump administration.

Go-it-alone partisan legislating also limits congressional ambition. Not everything worth legislating on can be included in a reconciliation bill, given the limitations of the Byrd rule. Legislators then look for other statutes that ensure their ability to secure final votes without being blocked by a filibuster. In recent years they have favored the Congressional Review Act (CRA), discussed in Chapter 5 as a kind of bargain-basement resuscitation of the legislative veto. When the political stars align—when a congressional majority wants to overturn an agency regulation, when the sitting president does not want to protect that rule, and when the relatively short statutory window is still open—the CRA gives a congressional majority a way to force action to overturn an agency regulation. While the CRA knocked out only one rule in the first 20 years of its existence, during Trump's administration Congress passed 16 resolutions negating regulations, and Democrats passed 3 such resolutions in 2021.[57] But CRA resolutions tend to be products of happenstance, making them a sorry substitute for considering changes to underlying regulatory statutes. By limiting itself to the partisan lawmaking mode on regulatory matters, Congress makes itself into a weak second-guesser of the executive, rather than a Madisonian body whose ability to balance tradeoffs gives it a superior claim to determine the overall contours of the regulatory system.

In short, partisan lawmaking may gain short-term victories through legislative hardball, and these may include important policy achievements; Democrats in the 111th Congress amassed an impressive record working against nearly unified Republican opposition. But the costs in terms of bad feelings and lingering legitimacy problems for the legislation are great. Instead of building a coalition that could flexibly and repeatedly respond to the challenges of the Great Recession in the 2010s, Democrats spent their political capital all at once and made it much more difficult to produce legislative action of any kind in the following years. Figure 6.3 shows one of

**Figure 6.3** President Barack Obama hosts a May 2012 lunch to pitch his legislative agenda to congressional leaders: House Minority Leader Nancy Pelosi (D-CA), Speaker John Boehner (R-OH), Senate Majority Leader Harry Reid (D-NV), and Senate Minority Leader Mitch McConnell (R-KY).
*Source:* Obama White House.

many fruitless attempts to find bipartisan common ground in this era of bad feelings.

## What Remains of Bipartisan Legislation

As the previous two sections have shown, an unusual amount of 21st-century policymaking has been characterized by circumvention of Congress or highly partisan enactments. That does not mean bipartisan enactments have disappeared from the scene, however. Even in today's Congress, there are still a number of areas in which bipartisanship is alive and well—though deliberation and carefully wrought compromise are ailing.

First, commonplace descriptions of our Congress as "completely dysfunctional" are hyperbolic. In what political commentator Matt Yglesias has dubbed "secret Congress," because of how little press coverage it receives, committees still deliberate, incremental amendments to statutes are still worked up into free-standing bills or riders on omnibuses, and problems still often get solved with relatively little drama. Indeed, most of the hundreds of laws Congress passes each year continue to be bipartisan; political scientists James Curry and Frances Lee have shown that "robust minority party support characterizes lawmaking in the contemporary Congress at roughly the same level as in the 1970s and 1980s."[58] All of the procedural rules that make advancing legislation complicated can and frequently are suspended in both chambers when consensus prevails, so that noncontroversial matters can be addressed with little fuss. We may fairly suppose that such issues must not be politically momentous—but that doesn't mean we should take these actions for granted. As Chapter 9 plays out, it is certainly possible to imagine a *more* dysfunctional Congress making such mundane work much more difficult, or even impossible.

Bipartisanship has also persisted to a significant degree in three highly consequential areas: defense authorizations, annual appropriations, and crisis responses.

America's military retains more confidence than just about any other institution in the country, so both parties eagerly position themselves as supportive of our troops.[59] As a result, the Armed Services committees in both chambers have uniquely managed to maintain a strong bipartisan culture, including passing an annual authorization bill with strong bipartisan support nearly every year.[60] For the country with the world's most expensive military, highly functional committee deliberations are essential to creating a sense of political accountability for top uniformed leaders. Again, although we may take this functionality for granted, there is no guarantee it will endure.

Congressional appropriations are another area where the cost of breakdown is high. If spending bills do not pass, the government shuts down. If the debt ceiling is not raised in a timely manner, we could default on the nation's debt, which would likely cause a global financial catastrophe. Getting to bipartisan agreements to avoid these eventualities is the expectation, and it is generally fulfilled—but not always. Shutdowns have recurred in 2013, 2018, and 2019, with near misses routine; debt ceiling standoffs led to frayed nerves in 2011, 2013, and 2021. If all this drama were simply the cost of sensibly rendering difficult decisions, perhaps it would generate less angst. But the overall fiscal situation of the United States has rapidly deteriorated in the 21st century. Total public debt stood at around 50 percent of the nation's annual economic output in 2000, while today it is around 100 percent and on track to rise to 180 percent by 2050.[61] Congress has kept regular appropriated spending in check but has utterly failed to discipline mandatory health care spending. Just as in 1974, when Congress felt it necessary to reset its fiscal deliberations, there is widespread consensus that our overall budgetary process is broken. As discussed above, budget resolutions these days are passed in large part because of the reconciliation process they enable. In years where the majority does not hope to use reconciliation, they often decide not to bother with the trouble of passing a budget at all; in the 2010s, Congress passed budgets in only three years.[62]

Working through the conflicting interests involved in federal spending decisions is bound to be difficult, and we should not expect smooth sailing. But shutdowns, near shutdowns, and debt ceiling confrontations consume huge amounts of legislative energy and create serious administrative difficulties—not to mention being deeply embarrassing. Many reformers seek to eliminate them entirely, perhaps by automating spending in the event of a congressional impasse (a subject taken up in Chapter 10). There is a serious danger that the conspicuous failures of Congress' current fiscal policymaking will lead people to decide that these decisions are too important to be left to unreliable legislators. Regularly operating bipartisan negotiations are not, clearly, themselves a panacea.

Responses to crises reveal another area of broad but deeply flawed bipartisanship in the contemporary Congress. While gridlock may have stalled progress on some of the nation's most pressing long-standing problems, bipartisan coalitions of legislators have regularly emerged to pass legislation in response to newsier needs, from hurricanes to an infant formula shortage.[63] Supplemental spending, negotiated outside of the annual appropriations process, encompasses a growing share of total outlays, and "emergency" spending exempt from self-imposed spending caps has shot up especially fast.

We have also seen remarkable banner headlines of emergency government in the 21st century. When a bipartisan Congress quickly approved $40 billion in aid in response to the September 11 attacks, lawmakers pushed the frontier of what the federal government could do in a crisis. But 2008 was the watershed year in which Congress voted through emergency spending in amounts previously unimaginable: more than $150 billion for stimulus in February 2008, $300 billion in July 2008 for Fannie Mae and Freddie Mac, $700 billion in October 2008 for the Troubled Asset Relief Program (TARP), and $787 billion in February 2009 for stimulus (only the latter being a strictly partisan enactment). Much of the money spent in response to the financial crisis was used to further priorities that had little to do with overcoming the emergency. And the responses to the coronavirus in 2020 and 2021, discussed in Chapter 8, have made these figures look modest.

To a remarkable extent, the responses to the financial crisis and the coronavirus crisis were worked out by congressional leaders negotiating with executive branch officials, with the president playing a secondary role. Leaders have repeatedly shown their ability to put aside their mutual partisan animosity to massively empower appointed officials in the executive branch. Many emergency laws commanded overwhelming bipartisan support, including the Authorization for Use of Military Force and USA PATRIOT Act passed after September 11 and the coronavirus responses of 2020. Even where legislators were split, as with the responses to the financial crisis in 2008, the cleavage tracked a leadership vs. populist dimension rather than partisan allegiance.

This style of bipartisan crisis legislating is vastly superior to paralysis, but it does not serve us well overall. Robust partisan competition could produce public deliberations with real gravity, helping the nation work through difficult choices forced by crisis. When instead we end up with massive deals rapidly whipped up by the two parties' leaders, we get little meaningful debate. Indeed, the leadership makes sure that members understand how very unwelcome deliberation is, threatening to treat any member who insists on debate as a dangerous obstructionist. As Chapter 8 discusses, Congress often almost completely ignores difficult questions, generating a particularly toxic politicization unmoored from legislative bargaining.

Even relatively successful laws suffer from legitimacy problems when the process that produced them excludes important interests. The TARP, for example, ultimately saw most of its loans paid back in full, with interest, much to the surprise of those who condemned it as a hasty giveaway. But its anemic and tardy efforts to directly support struggling homeowners convinced many people that it only benefited Wall Street at the expense of the rest of the country. (Recall Madison's opposition to the National Bank in the 1790s.) The narrowness of the congressional debate, as well as the limited political perspective of the Treasury secretaries who ran the program, made it one of the most unpopular programs in American history.[64]

## Consequences of Centralized Control: Worse Policy, Less Durable Policy, and Endless Litigation

As Chapters 4, 5, and 6 have shown, Congress is not what it used to be because legislators themselves have supported a reorganization of power in America's legislature. They have swung the organizational pendulum from the radical decentralization of the late 1970s to the tight centralized control of the 2010s. Though their reasons for doing so are understandable, the institution they have created is failing in its constitutional responsibilities.

Today, Congress flattens the country's diversity rather than representing it. A functional representative assembly's legislative work ought to reflect the diversity of the concerns of its members, both in the process of generating laws and in the enactments themselves. Congress as currently structured, however, tends to reduce the nation's complexity into two polarized, warring camps. Party leaders who view politics as a zero-sum struggle for control arrange the legislative agenda accordingly, suppressing free-flowing and provisional coalition building that would force factions to see each other as potential collaborators and allies. Instead, leaders marshal the interests on their "team" to gain every advantage possible in service of tactical victories today and electoral victories tomorrow. This serves the Wilsonian end of giving voters a clear choice, but at the cost of wrecking the policymaking process.

The nature of the electoral connection, between legislator and constituents, changes profoundly in this environment. Whereas we generally think of legislators as beholden to their constituents' particular, parochial concerns, legislators in the current environment come to see their political fortunes as functions of their party's ability to control the national narrative. That means they need to act as team players most of all—and if they manage to do so with sufficient verve and vitriol, demonstrating a talent for social media virality, they may find themselves rewarded with donations from true believers across the nation. Some personality types thrill to this challenge, but many lawmakers understandably resent these pressures as detracting from their ability to practice Madisonian politics on behalf of their districts.

The unending partisan battle has hampered another one of the representative legislature's most distinctive purposes: generating trust. Incremental, detail-oriented policymaking builds trust over time, as legislators who may passionately disagree with each other are forced to cooperate—often in real face-to-face encounters—to achieve some shared goal. Team-based combat, on the other hand, stokes mistrust, since, if the two sides are engaged in a zero-sum struggle, what basis for trust can be found?

As the parties have differentiated themselves from each other, we have not gotten anything like the "responsible government" that Woodrow Wilson and his followers promised. Indeed, we have something much more like "irresponsible government." We have achieved the clear choice between near-monolithic parties, but thanks to constitutional features differentiating our system from a Westminster model, we have much less accountability than we did when we had far messier parties. We can (and very frequently do) find ourselves with different parties in control of Congress and the presidency. That clouds responsibility, making it unclear who should be held accountable for policy failures. Each side blames the other, and elections become a contest to see which side can make the other sound worse. In the next part's two examples, this dynamic is distressingly clear.

# PART III

# THE COSTS OF A FAILING CONGRESS

Having surveyed the reality of our policymaking process in the era of a highly centralized and polarized Congress, we now turn to look more closely at how this institution has fared in instances of serious stress.

Each of these chapters can be read as a funhouse-mirror inversion of the case studies in Part I. In those earlier cases, lively debates in Congress helped pull the country together in the face of adversity. In these contemporary cases, congressional dysfunction and passivity instead leave festering political sores.

In Chapter 3, we saw legislators work within their institution's onerous processes to pass the Civil Rights Act of 1964. Building a coalition that could break through the resistance of Southern segregationists was a real burden, but success in navigating that process brought rich rewards in the form of widespread acceptance of the law's legitimacy, even among its opponents. In contrast, Chapter 7 relates how proponents of immigration reform, including congressional leaders, tried and failed to secure a victory through manipulation of the legislative process, only to then abandon Congress in favor of executive action. That delivered short-term results, but it opened the door to a decades-long fight over the propriety of the executive actions that still rages today. It also impeded reformers' ability to mobilize a massive coalition in favor of change, as civil rights activists had done.

In Chapter 2, we saw legislators find a way to distribute the enormous burdens of World War II. While the executive branch and military handled America's engagement with the enemy, Congress reigned on the home front, and legislators' ability to ensure fairness in the wartime economy helped to keep the country united. They also checked the president's most ambitious demands for societal transformation and charted a return to normalcy as the war wound down. In Chapter 8, we see contemporary lawmakers following their World War II predecessors' example in quickly uniting against a common enemy. In spring of 2020, Congress put massive resources at the executive's disposal for fighting the virus and minimizing its economic harms. But, unlike in the 1940s, the Congress of the early 2020s did very little to create a sense of fairness on the home front. Instead, lawmakers simply ignored many of the most difficult questions posed by the virus and repeatedly deferred to public health bureaucracies, notwithstanding clear signs of those institutions' practical failures and limited ability to handle political questions.

Having a healthy Congress would not have made it easy to work through either immigration or COVID-19. But it would have helped us confront these issues without tearing America's social fabric.

# 7

# Failing to Compromise on Immigration

As you said last week, "What we can't do is just keep on waiting. There's a cost for waiting." ' .... We agree with you, Mr. President. We can no longer afford to wait.

As you have said, it is ultimately the job of Congress to reform our broken immigration system by enacting legislation. But by failing to do their job—and repeatedly interfering with your efforts to do your job—congressional Republicans threaten to take our immigration system hostage and preserve a status quo that everyone agrees is unacceptable. Their failure to act must not inhibit your commitment to governing.

—Letter of 116 House Democrats to President Barack Obama,
November 13, 2014[1]

When he ran for president, Sen. Barack Obama (D-IL) promised to prioritize immigration reform. The American people, he said, were counting on political leadership with the ability to "rise above the fear and demagoguery, the pettiness and partisanship, and finally enact comprehensive immigration reform."[2] Once elected, however, Obama had to grapple with the worst economic downturn in decades. He and Democratic congressional leaders addressed health care reform, climate change, and an overhaul of the nation's financial regulations before immigration. That left many Democrats bitterly disappointed and many immigrants in legal limbo.

Ahead of the 2010 midterms, Democrats focused their energy on the most sympathetic set of victims of America's faltering immigration system: those brought into America illegally as children, who lacked legal status through no fault of their own. Bipartisan legislation to provide options for schooling and create a path to citizenship, the Development, Relief, and Education for Alien Minors (DREAM) Act, had been circulating on Capitol Hill since 2001.[3] But Republicans, who felt frozen out by Democrats throughout the

111th Congress and sensed an electoral breakthrough coming, were in no mood to cooperate with the majority.

In September of 2010, Majority Leader Harry Reid (D-NV) sought to force the Senate to vote on the DREAM Act through parliamentary maneuvering. He attached the provision (as well as a repeal of the military's Don't Ask, Don't Tell policy) to the must-pass National Defense Authorization Act (NDAA) then being considered. But nearly all Republicans, and a few red-state Democrats, blocked the bill from moving forward.[4] Reid promised to deliver another vote after the election, helping him retain his own seat with the strong support of Hispanic Nevadans, even as Republicans made significant gains. In December, he twice sought to fulfill his promise, first with another push on the NDAA, still containing the DREAM Act, and then by moving a House-passed immigration bill. But cloture failed both times (57–40 and 55–41).[5]

In 2011, Obama renewed his pledge to pass the DREAM Act. In March of that year, at a town hall organized by the Spanish-language television station Univision, the president was asked whether he could unilaterally solve the problem. He demurred, insisting, "For me to simply through Executive order ignore those congressional mandates would not conform with my appropriate role as President."[6] The message at that point was unambiguous: given the legal situation and the importance of the policy, only a congressional enactment would do, and so a coalition capable of pushing one through would have to be formed.

Within months, though, the Obama administration took actions that belied the president's professed dedication to the legislative process. A June 2011 memo instructed Immigration and Customs Enforcement (ICE) employees on factors they should consider when exercising "prosecutorial discretion" in immigration enforcement, including whether an immigrant had been present in the country since childhood. In June 2012, that policy of "deferring action" was elaborated in greater detail by the secretary of the Department of Homeland Security, Janet Napolitano, who gave subordinates criteria that looked very much like those contained in the DREAM Act. In this articulation, the policy included not just nonenforcement but affirmative eligibility for employment authorization. The president himself characterized the new policy as "a temporary stopgap measure that lets us focus our resources wisely while giving a degree of relief and hope to talented, driven, patriotic young people."[7] The stopgap, however, would survive for many years, and hundreds of thousands of people would end up building their lives around the Deferred Action for Childhood Arrivals (DACA) program, as the supposedly temporary measure came to be called.

The Obama administration had decided that a DREAM deferred was too painful to endure. It hoped that deferring immigration actions could heal what many people saw as a festering sore. The executive branch had at its disposal the means of effecting change, and plenty of members of Congress, including Reid, urged them to use it.[8] The policy could not wait for the legislative politics to be neatly worked out—after all, Congress had tried and failed to deal with the issue as far back as the George W. Bush administration too.

Does it matter that the political process was short-circuited in this manner?

It is hard to argue against offering some relief to young people who found themselves essentially stateless. But we must situate this relief within the larger context of Congress' failure to achieve immigration reform in the first two decades of the 21st century. By correcting what may have been the most glaring injustice, the Obama administration removed the strongest impetus for reform. The contrast with the civil rights movement discussed in Chapter 3 is striking: whereas the galling delay of justice led to the formation of an overwhelming coalition for durable reform in the early 1960s, the provision of partial and uncertain progress through nonlegislative means in the 2010s impaired the country's ability to work through one of its most difficult problems.

Throughout this book, I have argued that Congress' most important function is to bring the nation's disparate factions together, put them into dialogue with each other on the nation's most pressing challenges, and then push them to accommodate each other in a way that all parties can live with. As we saw in Chapter 6, if Congress fails to perform this function, policy choices still get made, either in the executive branch, in the courts, or at some subnational level of government. But, especially for challenges of a truly national character, policy created this way is likely to be fragmented, unreliable, and illegitimate.

Immigration presents an especially stark case of the consequences of congressional failure. Congress has repeatedly taken up the issue, and all sides seem to agree that the legal status quo is undesirable. Bipartisan coalitions of lawmakers have repeatedly come together to advance legislation that would improve our nation's border policies, strengthen work-site enforcement, and clarify the status of millions of people currently living without the full protection of the law. But the leader-dominated processes in Congress have not managed to facilitate the success of any of these coalitions—even in the cases where leaders fully backed them.

When subnational governments respond by taking immigration policy upon themselves, they produce a disordered kaleidoscope of conflicting policies. Some states, most famously Arizona in 2010, dedicated their own resources to enforcing federal immigration laws, directing their police to identify and arrest unlawful immigrants. On the other hand, hundreds of American cities and states declared themselves "sanctuary" jurisdictions, instructing their law enforcement officers not to concern themselves with immigration status or cooperate with federal immigration authorities to facilitate deportations. Since both types of decisions raised difficult questions of constitutional federalism, this policy dispute has unfolded in federal courts, which have searched for some viable regime of "immigration federalism."[9] Meanwhile, messy border policies have contributed to periodic surges of refugees attempting to enter the country, troubling presidents of both parties and placing millions more people in a legal gray zone, waiting for processing by a system obviously overwhelmed by its task.

Immigration is inevitably a difficult issue because of the intense passions surrounding questions of who is, or ought to be, an American. We shouldn't expect compromise to come easily. But with decades worth of legislative failures, the American people and their representatives in Congress have become distressingly accustomed to believing that legislative action on this pressing matter is never going to come. Advocates turn to the executive branch, the courts, and subnational governments, even when it comes to this quintessentially national policy issue. Immigration policy reveals a Congress that is failing to live up to its constitutional responsibility, and we must investigate why.

## Background—Immigration Lawmaking in the Late 20th Century

The prominence of immigration in our time is, in part, a direct consequence of a policy choice made by Congress in 1965. At that time, the share of foreign-born Americans had fallen to an historic low, under 5 percent of the total population. Having successfully received many refugees from Europe after World War II, Americans were ready to welcome more immigrants from more countries. Strong bipartisan majorities in both chambers passed the Immigration and Nationality Act—though many Southern representatives voted in opposition, an ominous foreshadowing of later developments. The law relaxed country-specific quotas and also created a preference system that prioritized relatives of US citizens, people with specialized professional skills, and refugees. It would significantly change the demographics of the United States over the next half century. Today, around 14 percent of Americans are foreign born, nearly matching the highest levels in the nation's history.

Immigration authorized by the 1965 act was only partially responsible for that shift, however. Alongside elevated levels of legal immigration, America received a major influx of unauthorized immigrants, who either crossed one of the country's borders illegally or (more typically) overstayed their temporary visas. A significant portion of immigrants—roughly a quarter as of 2017—entered without legal status, creating the potential for an underclass cut off from normal avenues of social mobility and crowding out legal workers.[10]

Because immigrants are present in nearly every facet of American life and because there are so many potential ways to productively confront the problems of illegal immigration, legislators historically addressed the issue by assembling a broad coalition of disparate factions willing to support a compromise package.[11] In the term most often used today, "comprehensive immigration reform," we can read an implicit invitation to practice Madisonian politics, in which many factions' concerns are addressed simultaneously.

The Congress of the 1980s managed, with some difficulty, to assemble such a coalition in 1986. After an unsuccessful Carter administration push in 1977, a congressionally created Select Commission on Immigration and Refugee Policy published a set of recommendations in 1981. One of the commission's members, Sen. Alan Simpson (R-WY), then teamed up with Rep. Romano Mazzoli (D-KY) to frame a comprehensive package that would enhance enforcement against employers who knowingly hired illegal immigrants, strengthen border control, and provide amnesty and a path to citizenship for all who had resided in the United States since before 1980. The two legislators, who chaired their respective chambers' Judiciary Committee subcommittees on immigration and refugees, first sought to advance a bill in 1982. Despite Reagan administration concerns about burdening business with administrative requirements, they secured easy passage in the Senate. But House leadership was not committed to moving the bill. The Rules Committee sent it into a virtually unrestricted debate in the lame duck session, in which members would need to work through roughly 300 amendments. Facing increasingly well-organized opposition from employers who resented the law's administrative burdens and civil rights groups worried about the effect of the law on vulnerable populations, the bill died without a House vote.[12] During the next Congress, a similar story played out as a new Senate-passed bill met with reluctance from House leaders and organized opposition. This time, the House narrowly passed its own bill in June 1984, but the conference committee convened that fall could not fashion a mutually acceptable vehicle, and the effort stalled again.[13]

Finally, on their third try, the reformers found a way through. After the Senate again passed a bipartisan bill in 1985, another failure seemed likely in September 1986 when the House voted down a rule to take up a committee-reported bill (a highly unusual occurrence). Some members worried about a farm worker program and resented that they were being frozen out of shaping the law. But the bill's champions, including Rep. Chuck Schumer (D-NY), managed to restart negotiations. In October, the House passed a rule that automatically amended the farm programs to take into account various concerns and tightly restricted amendments and debate on the compromise package. The House passed the bill by a healthy margin, 230–166, and an October conference worked quickly to frame a report that both chambers accepted. The Immigration Reform and Control Act of 1986, better known as Simpson-Mazzoli, became law.[14]

Since Simpson-Mazzoli, no equivalent display of legislative maneuvering has managed to secure another package of comprehensive immigration reform. The way it came to fruition demands appreciation: a diligent process of incubating ideas in the DC ecosystem, working bills through committees for some years, and finally selling congressional leadership on the worthiness (and political advantage) of the bill so they would help a law across the finish line. This was a fine Madisonian process of interests prodding each other as they sought to deal with difficult problems before finding an accommodation.

But process is not the sole important factor in determining a law's ongoing legitimacy. And, unfortunately, the immigration regime put in place by Simpson-Mazzoli was unable to fundamentally alter the troubling dynamics that brought the various parties to the bargaining table in the first place. The crucial flaw was in the employer sanctions—the main attraction of the compromise for those worried about illegal immigrants displacing native-born Americans in the workforce. In practice, the system established was all but toothless. Employers were required to collect papers from new employees, but there was hardly any system to ensure the information they provided was accurate. Immigration skeptics who had supported the bill ended up feeling duped. With Republicans more attuned to the concerns of big business and Democrats worried first and foremost about pleasing minority advocacy groups, neither party would adequately represent the skeptics' concerns in a negotiation for a future comprehensive reform package. Those who had opposed the bill but not resorted to serious obstructionist tactics resolved to take a more aggressive approach in the future.

Consequently, all that turned out to be politically possible in the 1990s was a 1996 law meant to strengthen enforcement, in part by implementing an "E-Verify" system to check documents, but adoption of that system proved slow.[15] An attempt by California voters to deny social services to undocumented immigrants passed in 1994 but was blocked by courts. Meanwhile, individuals who had received amnesty from Simpson-Mazzoli helped their family members immigrate legally. Skeptics pointed out that the overall regime sent a clear message to potential migrants: finding a way into America without following the rules would be rewarded. Illegal immigration increased, with the estimated unauthorized population more than doubling in the 1990s to more than 8 million in 2000. It would rise to more than 12 million by 2007.[16]

## How Failures of Representation Doomed Bush-Era Reforms

That increase in unauthorized immigration led to renewed demands for comprehensive immigration reform in the 21st century. After winning re-election in 2004 with an unusually strong showing among Hispanic voters for a Republican, President George W. Bush made immigration reform a top priority. He sought to assemble a broad coalition behind a bill that would once again include an amnesty provision, but immigration opponents in his own party rejected that approach. They pushed a narrow enforcement bill, which would have made illegal entry a felony, through the House in 2005. Their hope was that if living without documentation became difficult enough, most undocumented immigrants would find it necessary to "self-deport."[17] Immigrants' rights groups, outraged by this bill, organized protests and pushed the Senate to adopt a much broader and less punitive approach.

The resulting bill, negotiated primarily by Sens. John McCain (R-AZ) and Ted Kennedy (D-MA) and supported by leaders of both parties, passed 62–36 in May 2006. It would have created a complicated path to citizenship, requiring back payment of taxes, for those living and working in America without documentation.

Republican House leaders, however, did not wish to see the Senate's bill taken up in a conference, fearing that it would divide their party. Many members insisted that creating any path to citizenship would replay the same dynamic as Simpson-Mazzoli. Refusing to advance the bill, Speaker Dennis Hastert insisted that among his most important roles as leader was ensuring that the House voted only on bills supported by a majority of Republicans—a commitment that became known as "the Hastert Rule."[18] Instead of pursuing a deal on the comprehensive bill, the House leadership arranged to pass a series of narrower bills. The Senate ignored most of those, though a bipartisan majority did agree to the Secure Fence Act of 2006, authorizing the construction of 700 miles of fencing along the southern border.[19] The cause of broader reform was left for the next Congress.

At that point, after Democrats won both chambers in the midterms, a number of prominent legislators made a renewed push for a compromise bill in 2007. McCain and Kennedy led a bipartisan "Gang of 12" in structuring negotiations. As in the 1980s, this group assembled a seemingly broad coalition of supporters including business lobbies, Hispanic and civil rights organizations, and labor unions. They understood that the deal they were striking was fragile, and therefore sought to shield it from most amendments as it worked its way through the legislative process.

As one news story observed at the time, relying on such a small group was "a risky strategy on an issue as contentious as immigration. Lawmakers in both parties are eager to express themselves and bristle at accepting a measure developed by a small group of senators in private with the White House." An outspoken critic of the bill's legalization provisions, Sen. Jim DeMint (R-SC), declared of the group, "A lot of us don't feel like they're speaking for us, that this idea that we can't offer an amendment or it's going to blow up the deal is a bunch of nonsense." He continued, "This is something that every member of the Senate should be participating in—not a small group."[20] DeMint and other opponents believed they spoke for Americans who suspected that the bargain being struck primarily benefited special interests—agribusiness that wanted cheap labor and immigrant groups more interested in entrenching a particular community than in serving the common good. They bitterly remembered Simpson-Mazzoli's unkept promises of enforcement and organized a grassroots campaign to pressure lawmakers to stand against a repeat performance. Conservative Republicans in Congress took their calls to reject a new amnesty to heart.

At one point, Senate Republicans had assembled almost 300 amendments to the proposed deal. Majority Leader Harry Reid, fearing that the issue had become unmanageable, moved for cloture on June 7. Three different times the vote failed, never garnering more than 45 votes, far short of the 60 required.[21] Reid and his Republican counterpart, Mitch McConnell (R-KY), sought to revive negotiations with a new bill later that month, which would bypass the committee process and receive quick consideration with just a dozen amendments allowed for each party. None of the permitted amendment votes would incorporate the concerns of the hardline conservative opponents, who castigated the deal as the product of an unrepresentative elite.[22] Reid's staff director told reporters that "Republican obstructionists" would have to decide: "Are they going to stand for efforts to provide increased funding for border security along with comprehensive immigration reform? Or are they going to continue to block one of the top priorities of the president?"[23] But this attempt to reduce the debate to a binary choice only hardened resistance. A cloture vote seeking to end debate on the revised deal failed again, 46–53, with 37 of 49 Republicans voting to block the bill.[24]

For Madisonian politics to succeed, legislators must do more than broker deals between full-time activists and advocacy groups, who only perform a specialized variety of representation. A representative coalition capable of supporting an enduring social bargain must pull in a much broader swath of the American people, including those whose concerns may seem outrageous to some potential bargaining partners. If they are excluded, those silenced may indeed come to think "obstructionism" is an appealing strategy. Those hoping to secure new legislation must either find a way to incorporate them or, as in the civil rights movement in the 1960s, build a coalition so broad and united that it is able to change electoral calculations and isolate and defeat opponents.

## Circumventing Legislation in the Obama Administration

Many would-be immigration reformers hoped that President Barack Obama would be exactly the kind of leader who could galvanize such a broad coalition. Rising to prominence largely because of his vision of a more united America, Obama promised to broker a deal on immigration reform that had eluded Bush. But, as laid out in this chapter's introduction, Obama found it difficult to make space in his agenda for comprehensive immigration reform. He also confronted increasingly strident denunciations of illegal immigrants. Condemning "anti-immigration" Republicans "who are out there engaging in rhetoric that is divisive and damaging," Obama claimed the opposition only strengthened his resolve to find a way.[25]

As we saw in this chapter's introduction, when Republicans gained 63 seats and control of the House in the 2010 midterms, Obama responded by working around them rather than figuring out a way to conciliate them. Opponents of the 2010 DREAM Act had condemned the bill as overinclusive, susceptible to fraud, and likely to lead to a cascade of new legalizations without deterring future illegal immigration.[26] Not surprisingly, they leveled the same kinds of complaints at Obama's DACA program, while also expressing alarm that the president was willing to distort the policymaking process. The 112th Congress therefore made no attempt at broad reform.

After Obama's re-election in 2012, though, congressional leaders made another serious push for comprehensive reform. As in 2006 and 2007, a small group of senators—this time, a "Gang of Eight"—sought to broker a deal between the many contending factions. Their bill contained the DREAM Act and a pathway to citizenship for many of those who had come illegally. In an attempt to win the support of immigration hawks, the bill committed to doubling the number of Border Patrol agents on the Mexican border and to making the E-Verify system harder for employers to dodge. This time around, the bill's architects methodically worked their legislation through the Senate's committees. After a number of significant amendments, the Judiciary Committee reported it favorably in June 2013. It easily won cloture, 84–15, after which the Senate conducted an unusually full floor debate. The final bill passed 68–32, with the support of all Democrats and 14 Republicans.

While this bill had undergone a much broader and more involved process than in 2007, many dissenters were unmoved. Sen. Jeff Sessions (R-AL) said the bill "came about as a direct result of the fact that the forces that shaped it had goals that were important to them, but these goals are not coterminous with, they're not in harmony with, the nation as a whole. The realpolitik gang that put it together seemed fine with that."[27]

A sizable number of House members concurred with Sessions, so the bill's chances in the lower chamber were poor. Following the same "Hastert rule" that had frustrated comprehensive reform in 2006, Speaker John Boehner (R-OH) committed to only take up an immigration bill that had the support of the majority of his conference.[28] Before long, it became quite clear that no such support was forthcoming. House leaders issued a statement indicating their party's unwillingness to work off of the Senate's bill:

> The American people want our border secured, our laws enforced, and the problems in our immigration system fixed to strengthen our economy. But they don't trust a Democratic-controlled Washington, and they're alarmed by the president's ongoing insistence on enacting a single, massive, Obamacare-like bill rather than pursuing a step-by-step, common-sense approach to actually fix the problem. The president has also demonstrated he is willing to unilaterally delay or ignore significant portions of laws he himself has signed, raising concerns among Americans that this administration cannot be trusted to deliver on its promises to secure the border and enforce laws as part of a single, massive bill like the one passed by the Senate.[29]

Their argument, reminiscent of the GOP's Congress-skeptical critiques of the 1980s and the 1994 revolution, was that Democratic officials were so untrustworthy as to make any grand bargain with them fundamentally impossible. We might well take that as a basic rejection of Madisonian politics, but these Republicans believed they were merely reflecting broader public opinion on the topic. In opinion polls, supporters and opponents of the Senate bill just about equaled each other, but 30 percent strongly opposed it compared to just 19 percent who strongly supported it.[30] The reform coalition for immigration had not achieved anything like the civil rights movement's success in convincing their fellow citizens of the urgency of their cause.

Conservatives' declaration of distrust led to another round of executive-led policy change by the Obama administration. "If Congress will not do their job, at least we can do ours," Obama declared, announcing in June 2014 that his administration would greatly extend its use of prosecutorial discretion to shield many undocumented immigrants from deportation, especially those who were parents of American citizens. He sharply criticized those who said his executive actions made it harder for Congress to pass a law, saying that he would prefer to work through the legislative process but that "America cannot wait forever for" lawmakers to act.[31] Obama's action, known as Deferred Action for Parents of Americans (DAPA), was made official in November of that year (after another midterm loss for Democrats) and potentially affected some four million people.

Both DACA and DAPA faced numerous legal challenges. DAPA was blocked in 2015, and a divided 4–4 Supreme Court left it in legal limbo at the end of the Obama administration.[32] It was rescinded by the Trump administration without ever taking effect. Courts were divided, however, on the permissibility of DACA. When Donald Trump became president, he sought to terminate Obama's policies—only to find that courts were also divided on whether that reversal was permissible. Ultimately, the Supreme Court ruled that Trump's withdrawal of DACA protections was undertaken arbitrarily, meaning that the policy remarkably survived into the Biden administration—only to be enjoined by another federal judge in July 2021.[33]

## Leadership in Control—With Nothing to Show for It

These tangled proceedings hung over legislative negotiations during the Trump administration. At one point, as the original DACA program's expiration approached, the famously immigration-skeptical president seemed willing to make a push for a path to citizenship in exchange for a hefty sum dedicated to border wall construction. In practice, however, he and the majority of Republicans were unwilling to support even a bill that fit that basic outline.

In January 2018, McConnell had promised Democratic senators that he would allow some floor votes on immigration bills in exchange for their support on a spending bill that ended a brief government shutdown. Given the chance, Democrats wanted consideration of a "clean" bill to extend DACA—one that was narrowly confined to that purpose without taking up other difficult immigration issues.

But although he had promised "open and freewheeling" deliberations, the majority leader imposed sharply restrictive procedures, including a 60-vote threshold for all amendments. He sought to have the Senate consider four alternatives in a strategically chosen sequence: one to clamp down on sanctuary cities, which was understood as a partisan measure included to embarrass Democrats; one combining a DACA extension with some money for President Trump's top priority, extension of the southern border wall; a comprehensive reform package that provided no wall funding; and one bill teeing up the Trump administration's own preferred combination of wall funding, DACA extension, and also new restrictions on *legal* immigration. Democrats viewed this sequence as unacceptable. They did not want to vote on the sanctuary city bill at all, and they preferred to see the second and fourth alternatives directly pitted against each other. McConnell and Minority Leader Schumer failed to come to any agreement, ending the chances for any robust debate—precisely the result that many felt McConnell was angling for all along.[34] To fulfill his pledge that the Senate get to votes, McConnell sought to invoke cloture on all four proposals. After minimal debate, none of his motions received 60 votes (though all but the one on the Trump-favored proposal received more than 50). The issue was effectively dead in the Senate, even though a majority of senators wanted to see some kind of solution enacted.[35]

Legislators in the House later mounted their own push to reauthorize DACA. More than a dozen moderate Republicans and most Democrats committed to sign a discharge petition to force a floor vote on a bill against leadership's will.[36] A discharge petition allows a majority of the House to override the Speaker's control of the agenda. In practice, successful petitions are quite rare, since leaders are likely to take a very dim view of members of their party working with members across the aisle to force their hand. The effort in 2018 was no exception: Republican House leaders vehemently denounced it. In a closed-door meeting in May 2018, Majority Leader Kevin McCarthy (R-CA) reportedly told members that if they hoped to retain their majorities in the upcoming midterm election, "we cannot disrupt ourselves" through a display of disunity over DACA. He warned: "Discharge petitions release the power of the floor that the American people gave us the responsibility to hold. . . . When you release that power, the majority goes to Nancy."[37]

This is a remarkably clear illustration of how tight leadership control of a majority party tends to function. Leaders see their primary job as ensuring that political questions are framed in terms that will favor their party at the next election. To the extent that bipartisan coalition building will complicate their efforts to paint the other party as opposed to constructive change, leaders have incentives to directly discourage it and instead to shift the agenda to questions that emphasize division.[38] They tell their copartisans that any effort to bypass leadership's control amounts to a complete renunciation of their party's worthiness to exercise "the power of the floor," and therefore an invitation to the American people to install their rival party in power. The prospect of returning to the minority—which, of course, the other party's leadership can be expected to freeze out of policymaking, just as their own party's leadership has done—is so grim that most members willingly put their trust in their own party leaders' control.

In the case of the DACA discharge petition, leaders managed to dissuade just enough members to prevent it from gaining majority support. They did so by promising to bring a leadership-assembled bill to a vote, assuring moderate members that this package would contain a DACA renewal. They offered such a bill in June, but while it contained a three-year extension of DACA's legal protections, it also included a number of elements meant to appeal to immigration hardliners, including a sharp reduction of legal immigration and a crackdown on sanctuary cities. That bill failed, 193–231, opposed by all Democrats and a few dozen Republicans, including moderates who opposed its reductions in legal immigration and a few skeptics committed to opposing any extension of DACA.[39] Leaders then put together a second attempt at compromise, which took a somewhat softer line and bore Trump's endorsement, and brought it to the floor a week later. But this time, most Republican conservatives defected, joining Democrats in opposition, and the bill suffered a lopsided 121–301 defeat.[40]

Leadership had promised that by keeping Republicans together, they would avoid an embarrassing rift. But in the end, their aggressive use of agenda control failed to deliver a show of unity on one of the most pressing issues of the day. Their warning about ceding control to Pelosi proved more accurate, as Democrats gained 41 seats and retook the majority in the 2018 elections.

Before the 115th Congress drew to a close, however, another immigration-related drama began—this one over the funding of the southern border wall.

## Congress at a Loss: Trump's Big, Beautiful Wall

From the beginning of his candidacy for president in 2015, Donald Trump had promised to build a wall along the length of America's southern border. Hundreds of miles of fencing already existed, much of it authorized by the Secure Fence Act of 2006 and paid for in the Consolidated Appropriations Act of 2008. Those bipartisan statutes were enacted before wall building became a symbol, at a time when a construction project was easier to compromise on than other questions of immigration policy. Between 2006 and 2009, Customs and Border Patrol (CBP) put up significant stretches of fencing. In the early 2010s, the agency received smaller appropriations to help maintain existing infrastructure.

Trump hailed the wall as a great solution to America's immigration problems, but sometimes his commitment seemed more symbolic than focused on actually jumpstarting construction—his promise to make Mexico pay for it played well to his base but was not a realistic plan. He pushed for $1 billion for wall funding in a fiscal year (FY) 2017 supplemental appropriations bill and got $341 million to replace 40 miles of existing barriers. He then pushed somewhat harder for $1.6 billion in FY 2018 spending, threatening to veto spending bills and bring on a government shutdown if they withheld funding. After extended negotiations, prolonged by continuing resolutions and spanning a weekend-long government shutdown in January 2018, Congress eventually approved $1.375 billion.[41]

As negotiations over FY 2019 appropriations got underway, Trump's official budget once again sought $1.6 billion. But with a Democratic House incoming after the November election, members of the administration apparently decided they needed to push harder. They privately urged Republican congressional leaders to up the amount to $5 billion in the continuing resolution that needed to be passed in the lame duck session to avoid another government shutdown. Passing that resolution was the only thing standing between senators and their Christmas breaks, however, so the chamber's Republicans were not particularly eager to open the potentially explosive question of wall funding just then. On December 19, 2018, they passed a continuing resolution with no reference to wall funding and suggested Trump take his stand over the main appropriations bills coming early in the new year.

The House, still under GOP control until the swearing in of the 116th Congress at the beginning of January 2019, appeared to be on its way to passing an identical bill. But conservative House members, normally staunch Trump allies, began suggesting that the president's base would be furious if Trump failed to secure wall funding in this bill, the last in which a Republican House majority could cooperate with him. They urged Trump to veto any bill lacking wall funding, and the president threatened to do so. The House then passed a funding bill that included the administration's requested $5 billion for wall funding—but since it diverged from the Senate's bill, it could not avert a partial government shutdown from beginning on December 22. That further raised the pressure for an agreement—but Senate Democrats now sensed an opportunity to dig in their heels and reset negotiations with a

Democratic House incoming in January. Both chambers adjourned for their Christmas breaks without any solution, and indeed the Congress came to an end without any resolution in sight.

With Nancy Pelosi reinstated as Speaker of the House, and Democrats having loudly denounced the wall as a symbol of Trump's xenophobia, the new House majority did not want to gratify the president by offering him wall funding. For his part, Trump thought his position was a winner and said he was "proud" to force the government shutdown and let it linger until wall funding could be secured. For most of January, this impasse continued; at the president's urging, the (still-Republican-controlled) Senate refused to take up new House-passed spending bills that lacked wall funding.

Not until January 25, after the shutdown had gone on for a record 35 days, did Trump change his strategy.[42] He encouraged a three-week continuing resolution without any wall funding, which was passed without delay, fully reopening the government. In the negotiations that followed, the president indicated that if Congress failed to provide him with his desired wall funding, he would declare a national emergency to accomplish the same goal with other money. In other words, he would demonstrate that he possessed his own power of the purse.

In February, the House and Senate negotiated a spending deal that included $1.375 billion for border fencing—a level identical to the previous fiscal year. Putting aside his earlier veto threat, Trump signed this bill into law on February 15. But at the same time, he declared a national emergency on the southern border. "We're going to do it one way or the other—we have to do it," he said. Of the device of declaring a national emergency under the National Emergencies Act of 1976, he continued: "There's rarely been a problem. [Previous presidents] sign it; nobody cares."[43] Trump promised that by repurposing various emergency funds available to the Department of Homeland Security and the Department of Defense, he could find some $8 billion for construction of the wall. Congress' attempt to limit him to $1.375 billion was to be treated as a mere speed bump.

Legislators did not take Trump's move lying down. Bipartisan majorities in both the House and Senate passed a joint resolution pursuant to the National Emergencies Act to declare Trump's emergency declaration invalid.[44] But on March 15, 2019, Trump issued the first veto of his administration, which his allies in the House easily sustained, and the resolution did not take effect.[45] Congress had tried to prevent the president's action but found that majorities in favor of doing so were insufficient.[46] Trump's Republican supporters competed in showing their zeal for the president's Congress-circumventing strategy. Sen. Ted Cruz (R-TX) made headlines by suggesting that the president might use money seized from recently convicted drug kingpin El Chapo, thereby fulfilling his pledge that Mexico would pay for the wall.[47]

The House (at the behest of the Democratic majority), various advocacy organizations, and numerous states filed suit in April 2019, seeking to have Trump's actions declared unconstitutional. But their legal challenges did not stop the administration from reprogramming funds and commencing construction. Although a federal judge ruled against the administration and would have enjoined all spending while litigation proceeded, the Supreme Court issued a stay on that injunction, meaning that money could be spent pending final legal resolution.[48] Before the Supreme Court ever reached the merits of the case, Trump's re-election bid was defeated and President Joe Biden froze all federal spending on wall construction.[49]

Congress, meanwhile, might have taken matters into its own hands, given House Democrats' expressions of outrage over the unconstitutional abuse of power. House spending bills passed in June 2019 contained riders that would have prevented all funds from being used for a border wall unless specifically appropriated for that purpose—but the riders were dropped before final passage. More targeted measures were introduced in the Senate but unsurprisingly failed to advance in the GOP-controlled chamber.[50] Legal challenges notwithstanding, the Trump administration spent billions of dollars beyond what Congress specifically appropriated for border wall construction and apparently finished some 458 miles of fencing (some of it replacing existing structures) before leaving.[51] Both parties played the circumvention game with some success.

## Why Congress Has Failed on Immigration

It took considerable persistence to build the coalition that finally passed the Simpson-Mazzoli Act in 1986 after years of false starts. Why has the 21st-century Congress failed to pass a comparable comprehensive reform package, even as the salience of immigration has risen?

As the events described in this chapter make clear, it is not for lack of trying. Legislators from both parties made significant pushes for a major deal in 2006, 2007, 2013, and 2018, each time with support from the president. Nor can we blame that familiar culprit, the filibuster, given that compromise packages assembled in 2006 and 2013 received 62 and 68 votes in the Senate, respectively.

What has prevented a breakthrough is a mutual lack of trust between proponents of reform and skeptics of immigration—the dynamic here is devilishly self-reinforcing.

Conservatives, who correctly understood themselves to be reflecting the views of a broad swathe of the American public, felt almost completely excluded from Bush-era negotiations, and they came to believe that their kind of people would be the losers of all "comprehensive immigration reform" deals. By demanding bills that were almost exclusively devoted to border control, they managed to win some modest victories, but nothing even vaguely proportionate to the problem they claimed to want to solve. When potential bargaining partners on the other side represented themselves as willing to take more ambitious steps to control the flow of immigrants, the skeptics simply were not able to treat their offers as being in good faith. With Republicans internally divided on the matter, John Boehner in 2013 and Paul Ryan in 2018 prioritized moving on from the issue rather than pushing to get to a deal. Conservatives hailing from the most immigration-hostile districts believed—not without reason—that their constituents would appreciate their refusal to get fooled again, probably more than any compromise.

There is a genuine conundrum. Leaders who want a deal look at this group of legislators and think: *It is impossible to work with them at this point. The only thing to do is design even more restrictive rules for debate that deprive them of the ability to mess things up. If those fail, and we end up with legislative stalemate, we will see what we can get done through executive-initiated measures, and the blame will rightly fall on the intransigent minority.*

Meanwhile, members of the holdout group look at leaders and think: *These people just think of us as a problem they wish would go away. They may occasionally pay lip service to our concerns, but they will ultimately do everything they can to marginalize and work around us. So, the only thing left for us is to blow up their deals.*

There is truth in both sides' perspectives, but together they create a destructive cycle that inhibits Congress from functioning.

Legislative leaders justify their restrictive procedures by claiming the alternative is procedural chaos. That isn't a frivolous or cynical concern—indeed, when we consider the House during the late 1970s, as described in Chapter 4, it seems like a fair description. But their willingness to limit debate in service of a particular compromise is no guarantee of results.

Why, then, did champions of immigration reform fail to build an overwhelming coalition for change?

One might object that maybe there was simply no potential for such a coalition at all—that the process was irrelevant, because the problem was intractable. Such doubts cannot be completely dispelled. Prediction is hard, especially about the future, the old saying goes, but penetrating the haze of counterfactual histories can be even harder. There is no way to be sure that a healthier debate in Congress would have produced a bill that was mutually acceptable to the differing, sometimes diametrically opposed, interested factions.

But saying that a deal was impossible is a peculiar sort of claim, given the nature of the questions involved. Immigration policy offers so many dimensions on which to forge compromise. To name a few: border security and wall spending, capacity for interdiction, capacity for processing asylum claims, numbers of available visas for skilled workers, welfare restrictions for new immigrants, penalties for those who broke earlier laws, penalties for employers who flout the law, the question of where immigrants will go once they have been admitted to the country. If our legislators had exhausted themselves combining these alternatives, only to find that none could command the support needed to get a law passed, then we might well conclude that no path forward existed. Instead, only the Senate's 2013 process allowed a really extensive process of mutual exploration to take place—and it managed to produce a package that won 68 votes in support. In the House that year, and in both chambers on other occasions, leaders sharply limited members' ability to maneuver.

In the case of the civil rights movement, allowing the legislative process to play out in the fullest manner possible focused the attention and generated the urgency needed to pass the 1964 act. Limiting debate on immigration did not produce a similar success—nor did it facilitate building broader support behind the policy changes. Instead, the tendency to reject legislative politics once they proved too frustrating, in favor of executive or judicial action, only made viable compromise in Congress more difficult. With executive action seemingly addressing the worst of the policy failures, the moral urgency and burning injustice that could motivate legislative action faded from view. Madison scholar Greg Weiner puts this point eloquently: "The farther we recede from majoritarian institutions, the likelier they are to disappoint us."[52]

To put the complaint plainly: we have not gotten the conflict we deserve when it comes to immigration policy. Rhetoric on both sides has intensified (even as immigration, both legal and illegal, fell through most of the 2010s), but we have had no clarifying moment of truth. Congress ought to have given us that—even if doing so would have been challenging to internal partisan cohesion. Instead, legislators repeatedly steered away from the issue, content to say that they had tried and would pursue other avenues.

Meanwhile, our immigration policy today is a worse mess than ever. Border apprehensions are at an all-time high, and there is now a backlog of more than 9 million asylum claims waiting to be processed, translating into years-long delays for those seeking refugee status; immigration courts have queues of more than 1.5 million cases.[53] Texas has taken to busing asylum seekers to Washington, DC, and New York City.[54]

Perhaps a moment of reckoning is not so far off, then. But at this point, our frustration with Congress' failures is so longstanding that it seems an act of lunacy to hope for a reassertion of legislative politics on immigration. As I write, no major effort to form a broad coalition for immigration reform is in the works. Biden administration allies have offered legislation clearing the path to citizenship for many undocumented migrants, but these bills have absolutely no Republican support. No one has attempted to win by making concessions on other fronts. Instead, Republicans have focused their messaging on restarting construction of the southern border wall; one 2022 Senate campaign document promises to finish it and "name it after President Donald Trump."[55]

With this dispiriting divide in mind, one might be excused for thinking that Congress in the 2020s would be incapable of dealing with just about anything serious. Happily, as the next chapter shows, that would be unfair. In a pinch, Congress could act with real decisiveness—though it is unclear whether they could do so in a way that would prevent the country from falling to pieces.

# 8

# Congress and COVID

Struggling people have waited and waited and gotten nothing. That has been the Democrats' decision. Reporters can call it "hardball," like this was some ordinary standstill, but families are suffering. Americans are dying. This is not a Washington game; it is a national crisis. It would serve the Nation better if the Democratic leaders would act like it is a crisis.

—Senate Majority Leader Mitch McConnell (R-KY),
August 11, 2020

Facing the greatest domestic crisis in the 21st century, where Americans are hurting healthwise and economically, the Senate Republican majority ran down the clock, tossed up an air ball, and then subbed themselves out of the game.

—Senate Minority Leader Chuck Schumer (D-NY),
August 11, 2020[1]

Rep. Cori Bush (D-MO) was first elected to Congress in 2020. Her primary victory over sitting Rep. William Lacy Clay Jr., a 20-year incumbent who had succeeded his father, came in the midst of a global pandemic and nationwide unrest and protests sparked by the police killing of George Floyd. Bush had herself been a leader in similar protests going back to 2014, and her victory was hailed as a sign of "the return of the protester-politician."[2]

A year later, Bush made headlines protesting—this time, as a member of the House, conducting a "nearly round-the-clock sit-in" on the steps of the US Capitol lasting five days. She was drawing attention to the impending lapse of a federal moratorium on evictions of renters, put in place because of the COVID-19 virus that was still sickening millions of Americans more than a year after it first arrived in the country. Bush, who had herself been evicted three times, was determined to make a difference. "I'm an organizer.

I'm an activist. That is what I do. I fell back on what I know to do, which was be visible, put your body on the line, use whatever you have," she declared.[3] And her efforts succeeded, at least temporarily: within days, President Joe Biden's administration announced it would extend the moratorium, in spite of worries about its shaky legal basis. In less than a month, the Supreme Court struck the policy down, insisting, "It is up to Congress, not the CDC, to decide whether the public interest merits further action here."[4]

It is telling that Bush looked not to her own constitutional branch—even though her party controlled both chambers of Congress—but to executive action. This was not because she had not sought congressional action, but because her own leader determined it was not worth pursuing. Speaker Pelosi told her that because Senate action was unlikely and a House majority was uncertain, it would be folly to seek a floor vote on the issue. "We're not calling the members back" from their August recess, Pelosi reflected at a weekly press conference.

> We wanted our energies focused on the president, the administration extending the moratorium. But the value of what she did, and I, again, I say, as a grassroots organizer myself, the public awareness is very important. You've heard me say a million times—President Lincoln said, "Public sentiment is everything. With it, you can accomplish almost anything. Without it practically nothing."

The Speaker seemed confident that the House was not the place to cultivate debate, change minds, or build a winning coalition. Instead, its members had the opportunity to put pressure on the government's more active decision makers. That sense of the legislature's secondary role is entirely consistent with Congress' performance during most of the coronavirus pandemic.

In the first, most frightening phase of the country's response to the virus in March and April of 2020, Congress itself showed admirable resolve. Huge bipartisan majorities of legislators put aside their differences and passed four statutes in quick succession with little partisan debate. Those laws provided tens of billions of dollars for combating the virus' spread, developing medicines to treat it, and speeding the development and manufacture of the vaccines that would ultimately render the virus less deadly. And they offered trillions of dollars in economic relief, providing support for individuals and firms whose incomes were threatened by nationwide economic shutdowns.

As impressive as Congress' early consensus efforts were, our legislature's ability to bypass debate came at a serious cost as the pandemic persisted and spread. On the hardest and most divisive questions, Congress essentially excused itself, failing to give serious consideration to any legislation that would have addressed the thorny conflicts over testing, vaccines, business closures, and mask wearing. Members of Congress had plenty of criticism for the Centers for Disease Control and Prevention (CDC), Food and Drug Administration (FDA), and other public health authorities, but they rarely acted like it was their job to seriously intervene. Their failure to act meant that the country as a whole had no way to seek compromises allowing different groups to get some of what they wanted. Instead, discourse centered on who was "following the science," and policy responses in the states were characterized by symbolic stand-taking—dishearteningly, our political system turned COVID into just another front in our tense, bipolar culture war.

If representatives had more actively sought compromise on these issues, we might have seen a greater willingness to pursue experiments such as massive rapid testing, public provision of quarantine housing, and outdoor schooling. Acting together, through Congress, to find ways to meet the challenges of the pandemic would have helped create a sense of national unity as we grappled with the enormous challenges imposed by the pandemic. We might have sought to learn from our collective failures, going beyond criticizing public health authorities to actually figuring out how to reform them—an effort that has been absent as of this writing. Instead, legislators limited themselves to determining how much more money ought to be spent, and COVID-19 nearly fell off the congressional agenda in 2021, despite killing nearly half a million Americans and continuing to profoundly disrupt normal life in that year. Unlike in World War II, Americans found themselves with no good ways to argue over the fair allocation of burdens as we confronted difficult tradeoffs, and our country nearly fell to pieces.

In short, we needed leadership, and they gave us cash.

Finding common ground on these issues would have been difficult, but real possibilities for accommodation existed. Many would have entailed changing the way the government's public health regulators operate, but legislators were remarkably timid in broaching these issues. Unless they find the courage to do so, there is little reason to hope that our next pandemic experience will be any less politically divisive.

This chapter proceeds to offer an abbreviated chronicle of Congress' COVID-19 legislation, with special attention to questions of deliberation. It then turns to an examination of why Congress did so little to attempt to resolve thorny conflicts.[5]

## Pandemic Preparedness and COVID Early Warnings

Congress had, over the years, done a good deal to create a statutory framework for dealing with pandemics. As early as 1944 it gave the federal government some quarantine authority and organized disparate public health agencies to combat epidemic disease. More recently, Congress responded to concerns about bioterrorism and Asian epidemics with further bipartisan enactments. The Project Bioshield Act of 2003, passed at the urging of the George W. Bush administration, made it easier for the Department of Health and Human Services (HHS) to procure supplies, hire experts, and award grants in response to an emergency; created a framework for government purchase guarantees meant to facilitate private investment in various countermeasures that might otherwise not be commercially viable; and, most importantly, put in place the procedure for emergency use authorizations, by which the FDA can give accelerated temporary approval to countermeasures in response to a public health emergency. The Public Readiness and Emergency Preparedness Act, included in a 2005 supplemental emergency spending bill, created a liability shield for businesses administering countermeasures during a public health emergency. Another key series of 21st-century statutes authorized spending for various preparedness activities, including the Pandemic and All-Hazards Preparedness and Advancing Innovation Act of 2019. A 2006 act created an agency charged with developing and readying medical countermeasures for public health emergencies and created the Office of the Assistant Secretary for Preparedness and Response in HHS, ensuring that a high-level federal executive would devote his or her full attention to these issues. Together, these laws created a detailed National Health Security Strategy meant to prepare the country to respond quickly to any public health threat.

With these tools at their disposal, various federal agencies responded energetically to the outbreak of Ebola in West Africa in 2014–15, successfully limiting it and preventing its spread in the United States. That relatively easy success unfortunately led to a false sense of security. Funds went unspent, and, in the words of one participant in this effort, "we were left with a complacency that capacity would be sufficient to deal with an outbreak or epidemic."[6]

Most experts agree that, despite the recent laws Congress passed, pandemic preparedness was severely underfunded in the 2010s.[7] A Public Health Emergency Fund was meant to provide support for meeting a fast-moving challenge, but it had a zero balance since 2012.[8] Bills to restore its funding had gone nowhere. The CDC's prevention budget had been cut three consecutive years before 2020. The 2019 act had created a separate fund, the Infectious Disease Rapid Response Reserve Fund, but its $105 million available was used up by early February 2020.[9] A steady parade of Cassandras had been warning that the United States was not adequately preparing itself for a pandemic, but their warnings had gone unheeded. By failing to provide sufficient resources for the programs it had launched, Congress hamstrung its own preparations.

Such a failing may be unsurprising for democratic governments preoccupied with more pressing issues, but some other developed countries readied themselves significantly better for the threat of a novel virus. South Korea, in particular, distinguished itself with efficient suppression of the virus and relentless contact tracing.[10] Its parliament also proved quite nimble in updating the powers available to public health officials once the pandemic arrived.[11] Wise preparation and efficient response should not be considered unattainable, then.

In the event, Congress overestimated our level of preparedness in January and February 2020, when members showed a clear awareness of the threat of coronavirus but did little to actively combat it. Lawmakers were busy with other matters—"coronavirus" was first mentioned on the Senate floor on January 23, 2020, when Senate Majority Leader Mitch McConnell (R-KY) briefly interrupted the (first) impeachment trial of President Trump to tell his colleagues that they would have an off-the-record briefing on the matter.[12] But legislators (like most of the country) remained largely complacent through February, when some hearings began to focus attention on the issue. Even then, despite strong warnings, most members responded with professions of confidence in the country's public health officials.

Appropriators began working with the administration on a supplemental spending package, but normal partisan jousting also found its place. Democrats criticized the administration's budget proposal, which had included cuts to HHS accounts needed to combat the pandemic; later, members would trade accusations as to which side was delaying the first funding bill.

Perhaps it is too much to hope that Congress could have significantly shaped the early federal response to COVID. After all, legislators had built infrastructure for dealing with epidemic disease and did not yet see signs it was overwhelmed. They worked to make more funding available in a timely manner. Still, Congress shed remarkably little light on the failing processes that led to February becoming a "lost month" in America's fight against coronavirus.[13] When the CDC's development of a working test seemed to be failing, members of Congress were repeatedly satisfied with assurances that a fix was just a week away. One might have thought that Democrats in Congress, who were so openly hostile to the Trump administration by this point, would have taken a less accommodating stance, but in fact both parties exhibited remarkable, and unwise, patience with the bureaucracy.

## Massive Response—Congress Rescues the Economy: March–April 2020

Congress' next stage of COVID response was extraordinarily energetic. Congressional leaders made deals and moved them through their respective chambers with exceptional speed, foregoing almost all formal debate. Given the nature of the emergency and the acuteness of economic distress, prioritizing speed over deliberation made a great deal of sense.

As it became clear, in the first week of March, that the virus had begun to spread widely in the United States, Congress advanced the supplemental appropriations bill it had been negotiating in February, going from a $1.5 billion Trump administration request to $8.3 billion in the final version. The House passed the bill under suspension of the rules on March 4, 415–2. The Senate was close behind. While Sen. Rand Paul (R-KY) refused to support a unanimous consent request to vote immediately on the bill, he was mollified with a chance to introduce an amendment that would offset spending by cutting international aid. Once that was tabled, 80–16, the Senate adopted the unamended bill, 96–1. Congress, not generally thought of as speedy, had acted sooner than most major American institutions.

Even as the first supplemental bill was being hurried into law, Congress turned its attention to a much more ambitious sequel: the Families First

Coronavirus Response Act (FFCRA). Staffers in several House committees quickly drafted a bill that guaranteed no-cost testing for all Americans (with payment coming either through their health insurer or the federal government), mandated and funded paid sick leave and paid family leave (both broadly defined) through the end of 2020, supported unemployment benefits, boosted food stamps, ensured school lunch programs would continue despite school closures, and increased Medicaid matching rates to provide fiscal relief to states, among other provisions.

All told, the bill was estimated to cost $192 billion over 10 years, just $2.5 billion of which was through additional discretionary spending. Much of the cost would come through increases in mandatory spending—in other words, by expanding existing entitlements and creating new ones, including additional obligations for all American businesses. Those obligations created immediate partisan controversy, with Republicans arguing that new requirements for small business would prove ruinous in the short term, even if the federal government would eventually reimburse employers for their COVID-19-related leave costs. Those concerns were met by quickly negotiating a second version of the bill, which included additional opportunities for businesses to claim tax credits on their employment tax returns, filed quarterly, and immediately reduce their payroll tax deposits to offset payments made for leave. That new version of the bill was brought to the House floor late Friday night, March 13. Again voting to suspend the rules, the House passed the bill entirely without debate, 363–40. Rep. Justin Amash (I-MI) voted "present," complaining that members were given almost no time to comprehend the revised bill before being asked to vote it through, but most members were willing to put their trust in the deal negotiated by their leaders.

Senators conducted a somewhat more substantial debate, considering three amendments, all of which fell well short of the 60-vote threshold required. That meant the Senate could vote to adopt the House version in its entirety, sending the bill to the president. The FFCRA, primarily the House's creation, impressively showcased Congress' ability to negotiate a complex emergency statute quickly, and the bill's main programs seem to have worked well in ensuring that Americans could take paid leave.

The Senate took the lead on the next and most ambitious "phase three" response bill. Indeed, the House recessed after passing the FFCRA, with a plan to reconvene only once the next bill was ready to pass, presumably without any alteration by the lower chamber.

To start negotiations, Senate Majority Leader McConnell introduced a bill on March 19 with a headline value of $1 trillion. It featured a direct payment of $1,200 to all American adults (with an income-sensitive phaseout); a $500 payment for each child; $300 billion in federally guaranteed loans for small business; and more than $200 billion in support for struggling industries such as airlines. Although they agreed on many of the fundamentals, Democrats quickly protested that they had had almost no input in shaping this huge bill and began working on their own alternative. McConnell created five bipartisan task forces to develop his plan, which yielded a revised bipartisan bill on March 22.[14] Many Democrats still felt it lacked sufficient support for schools and hospitals and characterized the money it made available to support industries as a "slush fund."[15] Some additionally demanded a $15 minimum wage and corporate board diversity requirements for recipients of federal aid, as well as student loan forgiveness. Senate Republicans responded with derision, objecting that Democrats were trying to hijack the crisis as an opportunity to pass their own agenda.

Despite the two parties' differences, McConnell sought to move directly into debating his bill. He was rebuffed on two consecutive days, though, when his cloture motions fell well short of the 60 votes needed.[16] For a moment, it looked like the divide between the parties might be unbridgeable, and financial markets responded by falling to their lowest levels in years.

On the Senate floor, Sen. Joe Manchin (D-WV) made a revealing observation about the bill's progress during this impasse. He said that while taking up the bill and working to improve it sounds appealing, the Senate in his 10 years of service had never operated like that. Instead, the minority expects to be effectively deprived of all opportunities to change a bill once it has been taken up—on the floor, it would be "out of our jurisdiction, if you will." As a result, he continued, all negotiation has to happen before a bill is formally considered, and any attempt to move a bill before an agreement is worked out among leaders is simply "political posturing." Manchin expressed confidence that a deal would soon be reached and that no Democrat would stand in the way of its speedy adoption at that point.[17]

He turned out to be correct. With Pelosi and Treasury Secretary Steven Mnuchin playing central roles, behind-the-scenes negotiations soon yielded a deal. Rather than substituting some of Democrats' priorities instead of Republican ones, the bill became a massive agglomeration of both, with a staggering headline price tag of $2.2 trillion. Leaders of both parties were eager to speed the compromise to passage.

Four Republican senators slowed their progress, slightly, by seeking to delay the bill because of a concern that its generous unemployment benefits would discourage low-wage workers. To satisfy them, McConnell arranged for consideration of an amendment prohibiting payments higher than the recipient's prepandemic wages. After some debate, it failed on a party-line vote, 48–48.[18] Other than that, there was almost no debate of substantive issues. The Senate passed the Coronavirus Aid, Relief, and Economic Security (CARES) Act, as embodied in an amendment submitted by McConnell, 96–0, and promptly adjourned until April 20, leaving the House to also agree to the bill without amendment.

The bill's House passage included a bit of high drama. Pelosi hoped to pass it by unanimous consent, sparing members who had returned to their districts a trip back to Washington. But Rep. Thomas Massie (R-KY) frustrated this desire by signaling his intent to object, forcing the House to rely on other procedures. On the morning of Friday, March 27, the House passed a rule taking up the bill with three hours of debate. A few Republicans objected to miscellaneous spending, and a few progressives, including Rep. Alexandria Ocasio-Cortez (D-NY), lamented that the Senate had crafted "one of the largest corporate bailouts with as few strings as possible in American history."[19] But these dissenting voices were overwhelmed by members expressing their gratitude and institutional pride that Congress had moved so quickly and done so much.

When the House proceeded to a voice vote, Massie came forward to object: "I came here to make sure our republic doesn't die by unanimous consent in an empty chamber, and I request a recorded vote." His motion, however, lacked sufficient support (one-fifth of members present would have been necessary) and therefore failed. By unrecorded voice vote, with members socially distanced throughout the chamber (including the galleries normally reserved for press and spectators), the "ayes" had it. Massie again objected, suggesting the absence of a quorum, but the chair announced that a quorum was present and the vote stood. Massie's colleagues were furious at his actions, as was President Trump, who called on Kentucky voters to vote Massie out in the fall election.[20]

Together, the Treasury secretary and Fed chair wielded an incredible amount of discretion in allocating the CARES Act's funding. For all the anger inspired by the bailouts of 2008 and the concerns about President Trump and his anti-democratic ambitions, overwhelming bipartisan majorities in Congress once again chose to empower the executive branch.

One part of the CARES Act proved so popular that the considerable re-sources originally allotted rapidly came to seem insufficient. The Paycheck Protection Program (PPP), which originated in the Senate Small Business Committee, funneled federal dollars to ordinary workers through forgiv-able loans to their employers. With huge uptake across the country, the program ran through the $349 billion allotted by the CARES Act by mid-April. Without much fanfare, Mnuchin and congressional Democrats once again negotiated, producing a $484 billion bill whose main purpose was to re-fund the PPP but which also made substantial allocations to hospitals, emergency disaster grants and loans, and COVID-19 testing. With just a small fraction of the body in attendance, the Senate passed the bill by voice vote on April 21—just hours after the deal was struck and less than two hours after legislative text became available.[21] House members, on the other hand, returned to Washington to debate the bill and cast a re-corded vote two days later. After some back-and-forth accusations as to which side had been holding the bill's passage up, the House voted the bill through, 388–5.

Congressional leaders justifiably look back on this record of ambitious legislation with pride. Far from being paralyzed by partisanship, Congress erected a massive crisis response apparatus in weeks, on a bipartisan basis, even as many legislators quarantined. The central provisions of these laws, designed to provide economic support for a country suffering soaring shutdown-induced unemployment, allowed Americans to maintain their standard of living during the pandemic. This record of accomplishment deserves appreciation.

Some features of Congress' massive response in March and April ought to nevertheless give us pause. Especially given the massive size of the bills under consideration, they received strikingly little public deliberation. The leadership negotiations that produced these deals iced out most members. If this were simply an affront to the dignity of rank-and-file members of Congress, it would be of little concern. But in fact it left many of the most important questions roiling the country totally unresolved. That was forgiv-able in the fog of war that characterized this period. But it was a defect that Congress never squarely confronted. The overwhelming bipartisanship of the March and April actions thus laid the stage for the bitter, fruitless par-tisanship that dominated the country's thinking about COVID-19 by the summer.

## Disappearing Act: Summer and Fall 2020

From May until December 2020, Congress passed just a few small and un-controversial bills related to the COVID-19 emergency. After its unani-mous passage of the CARES Act, Sen. Dan Sullivan (R-AK) cheered his chamber's work but lamented that senators were going to take a 30-day re-cess. "Because if there's one thing about this crisis that we've already seen is that new challenges pop up every day, every minute, every hour," he said.[22] Notwithstanding that concern, lawmakers' presence on Capitol Hill was rarer than usual.

Democrats sought to make it easier for the House to function in spite of their absence by allowing members to designate a proxy who could cast their vote in their absence. The Rules Committee held nine hours of meetings to work out the details of these proxy voting rules and a brief debate on the House floor. Republicans proclaimed that bringing people together for in-person interaction sits at the heart of representative democracy—as Rep. Tom McClintock (R-CA) said, "The word 'congress' literally means the act of coming together and meeting"[23]—and that the proxy voting regime would jeopardize the chamber's social dynamics. They also questioned the move's constitutionality. Democrats insisted that protecting the health and safety of members and staff made the move nec-essary, and they carried the day. Initially set to last 45 days, proxy voting was repeatedly extended all the way through to the end of 2022. Indeed, al-though Republicans initially united against the practice and even brought an (unsuccessful) lawsuit against it,[24] members of both parties came to rely on the system.[25] Meanwhile, an acrimonious debate over properly health-conscious rules of conduct on Capitol Hill itself became a microcosm of the national debate.

On the legislative front, both chambers were active in framing what was billed as the next big relief bill, with expiration of federal support for un-employment insurance expected to bring both sides to the table. But the two chambers, controlled by opposite parties, went in opposite directions. House Democrats pushed through their opening bid on a party-line vote in May, with a whopping $3 trillion in spending billed as extending COVID-19 relief. Republicans, however, claimed the package merely dressed up Democratic agenda items as pandemic response and adamantly opposed it. In the Senate, after it became clear that negotiations between Democrats and the White House were not leading to a compromise, Republicans assembled a much more modest package of bills in July, including $1.1 trillion in spending commitments and liability protection for businesses, a Republican priority. They had difficulty coming to terms even with the White House, however, and by August they had basically abandoned their effort. With an eye on the November election, Democrats passed a revised version of their own package in September, but at that point efforts at compromise were nonexistent.

Congress could not move any small- or medium-size legislation targeted directly to specific defects in the federal government's COVID-19 response. A few bills meant to improve the rather half-hearted contact-tracing efforts around the country circulated in the House and seemed to gain traction, but none ultimately advanced. The House passed a bill that would have bulked up the Strategic National Stockpile meant to ensure availability of personal protective equipment in September, but the Senate did not take it up. Some House-passed Democratic messaging efforts were branded as responses to COVID, including a bill to expand childcare funding, a bill to require continuity in Postal Service operations during the pandemic, and a resolution condemning anti-Asian discrimination related to COVID-19; the latter two were widely interpreted as swipes at the president.

The Trump administration responded to the lack of substantive policymaking from Congress with a series of four executive actions in August 2020: (1) an extension of a CDC eviction moratorium originally sanctioned by the CARES Act for 120 days; (2) a deferral of student loan payments; (3) a commitment to continue federal support for increased unemployment payments, previously $600 per week under the CARES Act, at a level of $400 per week, using money allocated to the Federal Emergency Management Agency; and (4) a rule change allowing individual tax filers to defer their payroll tax payments until 2021, with the announced hope that Congress might forgive these payments later.[26] The public mostly ignored this payroll tax change.[27] The eviction moratorium, discussed in this chapter's introduction, would be continued by the Biden administration until the Supreme Court finally declared it unlawful. Far from questioning why the administration was circumventing Congress, many legislators (including Republicans on the House Ways and Means Committee) cheered on executive action.[28]

## More Economic Relief and Then Silence:
## December 2020–2022

Congress returned to playing fiscal provider in December. With the election behind them, a bipartisan group of senators negotiated the outlines of a roughly $900 billion spending package, including another round of economic relief checks, additional federal support for unemployment payments, a liability shield for corporations acting in good faith to prevent the spread of COVID-19, and money for schools and local government. Most of those provisions (though not the liability shield) were attached to the omnibus spending package passed that month, after four continuing resolutions in a row gave negotiations time to conclude. At 5,593 pages, the resulting law was the longest statutory enactment in American history. It passed both chambers on December 21, with votes of 359–53 and 92–6.

The question of the size of the checks to be sent out nearly derailed the bill. Democrats sought to build on the CARES Act's payments of $1,200 with a new $2,000, and they soon recruited President Trump, by then a lame duck, to their cause. Congressional Republicans, including in leadership, drew the line at $600 this time around, however, and prevented any increase. Much to their surprise, President Trump then said he was considering vetoing the bill, citing the insufficient size of the relief checks and a failure to include two other unrelated provisions he now wanted to insist on; the timing of its passage meant that he could utilize a pocket veto simply by not acting, which would have led to a government shutdown.

As the nation awaited Trump's decision, his demand for larger checks came to dominate the runoff election campaigns for Georgia's two Senate seats, which would take place on January 5, 2021; all candidates professed their commitment to $2,000 checks. A strange coalition emerged for immediate action, before the 116th Congress came to an end on January 3. Trump confusingly signed the spending bill into law on December 27 but simultaneously threw his support behind a Democratic bill to increase the checks, which passed 275–134, with 44 Republicans joining all but two Democrats the next day. The bill had an apt title, reflecting the COVID-19-fighting role that Congress had come to prefer: the Caring for Americans with Supplemental Help Act, or CASH.

CASH did not rule everything around it, however, as McConnell did not feel obliged to play along. The Senate, he insisted, would reject providing "another fire hose of borrowed money," including for the best off, and would accept only more targeted relief. With the two Georgia Republican candidates getting bashed over the issue, he conceded that the Senate would be willing to consider a bill that addressed all three of Trump's objections to the December act in a single bill—but he well knew that Democrats would flatly refuse Trump's other two demands. The Senate did not take up any bill before the end of the session, and so there was no extra cash. Both of Georgia's GOP senators were defeated on January 5, leading to Democratic control of the Senate after Vice President Kamala Harris' swearing in. It was a new administration's and a new Congress' turn to grapple with COVID-19.

In January 2009, Biden had become vice president in the midst of a serious economic crisis and was part of a team that pushed an $800 billion economic stimulus bill through a Democratic Congress within a month with only three Republican votes. Twelve years later, having been sworn in as president, he nearly repeated that accomplishment. Just seven weeks after Biden's inauguration, Democrats used budget reconciliation to push through a $1.9 trillion rescue plan without a single Republican vote—including $1,400 checks. Cash ruled, if belatedly. Critics of the law complained that, far from being a targeted rescue plan, it represented a giveaway to favored interest groups, especially state and local governments that demanded aid despite their relatively healthy finances after receiving some $360 billion in previous relief bills. Warnings that this unrestrained spending could contribute to inflation would come to seem prescient.

The political dynamics of these bills differed substantially from those of the earlier crop. Whereas leadership had been able to more or less dictate terms back in March and April, moderate senators from both sides of the aisle brokered the December bill. Democrats' American Rescue Plan Act, on the other hand, hearkened back to the 111th Congress of 2009–10, which pushed through Democratic priorities despite Republican intransigence. But whereas Democrats had 60 votes in 2009–10, allowing them to carry cloture motions on their favored legislation, in Biden's first term their bare majority of 50 senators plus the vice president forced them to rely on budget reconciliation.

After March, the 117th Congress was remarkably inactive regarding COVID-19. Democrats focused their energy on moving President Biden's nominees through the Senate and assembling two mega bills to advance their agenda: the Infrastructure Investment and Jobs Act (IIJA), negotiated on a bipartisan basis in the Senate, which passed in November 2021, and a huge spending package that became known as "Build Back Better," meant to pass using reconciliation without any Republican votes, which eventually struggled across the finish line as the Inflation Reduction Act of 2022.

Just a few COVID-19-related provisions found their way into these bills. The IIJA contains a provision requiring that long-term production contracts for personal protective equipment go to American firms. It also rescinds or repurposes tens of billions of dollars in previously obligated COVID-19 money.[29] The Democrats' budget plan promised to renew and deepen some of the cash commitments of the CARES Act but suggested nothing like a major overhaul of the federal government's COVID-19 policy. The law finally passed contained nothing COVID related. Various other bills have circulated, and a few modest measures have even passed, but neither party focused on the issue in spite of its huge prominence in Americans' lives.

## Why Did Congress Defer?
## Nonpharmaceutical Interventions

So, what should legislators have been doing? I contend that they should have sought compromises on difficult questions surrounding nonpharmaceutical interventions, testing, and vaccines and been much less willing to defer to the judgments of existing government agencies, especially the CDC and the FDA, on these questions.

This strikes many people as counterintuitive. Hadn't previous Congresses created expert bureaucracies precisely to take the lead in dealing with complicated public health issues? If the generalists on Capitol Hill have no advantage over trained professionals in making sense of the pandemic, why would we wish for them to intrude into matters beyond their competency? Whatever trust issues bureaucrats ended up having, wouldn't they have been even worse if legislators tried to settle such thorny issues?

This way of thinking misjudges how much can reasonably be crammed into the category of "public health" and fails to appreciate politicians' comparative advantage. Because they are representative and forced to take in all manner of considerations, including *but not limited to* public health concerns, compromises they broker with broad coalitions can possess a degree of political legitimacy that decisions made by bureaucrats lack. Some policy elements of their arrangements may well be suboptimal, but their ability to attend to social cohesion is as important as any particular outcome. At the same time, lawmakers' willingness to disregard a narrowly professional point of view is likely an asset when dealing with a novel phenomenon; bureaucrats are creatures of routines and believe in the integrity of those routines, even when an emerging threat makes it sensible to establish a new way of acting. On some issues, the kinds of "outsider" concerns that Congress brought to the table could have been a goad to better policy, including by taking risks bureaucrats found unacceptable.

Let us make this more concrete by turning to specific examples, beginning with so-called nonpharmaceutical interventions. Our first line of defense against COVID-19 was a set of behavioral modifications meant to reduce the opportunities for the virus to spread, including mandatory closures of businesses, public facilities, and schools; "stay at home" orders; social distancing requirements; and, eventually, mask mandates.

Given our constitutional structure, state governments retain the primary responsibility for protecting public health, which they frequently delegate to local governmental units. To some extent, our federal structure required that most of these interventions would not originate in Congress.[30] But imagining that such policies were none of the federal government's business requires ignoring the decisive role federal policymakers played in shaping them around the country. Perhaps unsurprisingly, given the fast-moving and national dimensions of the pandemic, most local officials were eager to defer to centralized expertise, such that "follow the CDC guidance" be-came a mantra around the country, one that many in Congress were happy to endorse. Unfortunately, CDC guidance was often substantively flawed and presented in a garbled form that was anything but clarifying.

Masks provide an infamous example. In the pandemic's early days, the CDC advised against masking before later changing its tune and recommending mask mandates.[31] Congress was in no position to provide clarity on the sci-ence while the CDC's interpretation of the available evidence wobbled, but lawmakers could have pursued various plausible compromises. For instance, legislators could have made a deal purchasing American-manufactured masks and sending them to all households, as some in the Trump admin-istration briefly sought to do. It might have emphasized that mask quality was something worth focusing on and sought to make N95 masks cheaply available to the public, something that state and local government only got around to doing very belatedly in 2022.[32]

Forging a coalition to support such actions might have required simul-taneously discouraging mandatory masking, at least in some types of business environments, perhaps through conditions on funding. Instead, with legislators rejecting compromise, masking became a yes-no partisan loyalty test, including in the Capitol itself. This is a natural consequence of "keeping politics out of" such decisions, a formulation that most Americans find attractive. Putting politics in, as legislative bargaining would have done, would have left more room for maneuvering.

School closures provide a less-remarked-on example in which compromise was possible but not energetically sought. After replacing in-person classes with hastily improvised virtual ones in the spring of 2020, many US schools reopened in person in late summer, even as most of the country's largest school districts kept their doors shut for most of that school year. Both public and private schools that reopened showed considerable ingenuity in altering their operations to maximize safety, including holding outdoor classes. As it poured out money to support school districts' adaptations to COVID-19, Congress could have actively incentivized such experimentation by attaching conditions to its funding. Congressional Republicans made some moves in this direction, seeking to tie money for schools to commitments to in-person reopenings, both in their summer 2020 bill and in the Biden administration. But they never found a way to bring teachers' unions or their allies to the bargaining table, and these ideas were simply frozen out. School reopening decisions ended up reflecting political affiliations rather than on-the-ground COVID-19 conditions.[33] Even worse, federal dollars to support schools ended up providing ammunition for intrastate fights over masking and other issues; in Arizona, the governor threatened to withhold relief money from any schools implementing mask mandates.[34]

Social distancing guidelines offer another example in which Congress made its unhappiness known but took few actions to effect change. The CDC's strict, inflexible, and arbitrary recommendation of six feet of distancing was at least defensible as long as people assumed COVID-19 was a droplet-spread disease.[35] But that assumption was wrong. The scientific record came to overwhelmingly support an understanding of COVID-19 as an airborne disease, but the CDC was painfully slow to even acknowledge that possibility.[36] Members of Congress pressured the agency to explain itself when it confusingly admitted the possibility and then retracted the change.[37] By October 2020, it was advising Americans that aerosolized spread was a mechanism of the disease's spread.[38] If airborne spread was the primary mechanism, then extra-thorough cleaning of surfaces was a waste, greater attention to ventilation was probably the key, and the fixation on six feet of social distancing did not make much sense. Many of the CDC's recommendations needed updating, but they mostly remained the same; not until May 2021 would the CDC fully catch up with the scientific evidence.[39]

Even as the agency's reputation sank, many organizations around the country continued to treat its guidance as authoritative. That meant that many schools went on insisting that full reopenings were impossible, given the inability to ensure that students would remain six feet apart throughout their school days. Meanwhile, the CDC continued to advise schools to take actions such as extra cleaning that were unsupported by evidence.

Members of Congress finally swung into action in response to this. In March 2021, Rep. Virginia Foxx (R-NC), the ranking member of the House Education and Labor Committee, led a push to get the CDC to change its guidance such that it would actually be helping schools realize the goal of reopening, as President Biden said was his administration's goal.[40] That campaign paid off, quickly, with the CDC revising its guidance to recommend three feet of distancing for students on March 19. Nevertheless, the CDC continued to make dubious representations about precautions needed outdoors and for children's summer camps. Sen. Susan Collins (R-ME) sharply questioned the CDC's director on these issues at a hearing in May 2021.

Congress translated its concerns into legislative proposals for reform remarkably rarely. In the 117th Congress, various bills proposed to alter the CDC's authority by *adding* new responsibilities. To this observer, that seems like the quintessence of failing upward. A few bills sought to penalize the CDC, including Sen. Marco Rubio's (R-FL) Restore Public Health Institution Trust Act of 2021, which would have required a Government Accountability Office review of CDC guidance. But, although the CDC's disastrous COVID performance seems to offer the perfect opportunity to overhaul a fundamentally dysfunctional agency and thereby better prepare the country for public health emergencies, Congress has not seen fit to pursue such ambitions.

## Why Did Congress Defer? Testing and Vaccines

Throughout the first two years of the COVID crisis, the United States consistently lagged behind its peer nations in testing capacity. That claim was sometimes disputed, but the crucial metric of tests per case unambiguously showed lower levels of American testing.[41]

This failure is mostly attributable to the public health bureaucracy. The CDC infamously botched its effort to develop the country's first test in February 2020. Then the FDA blocked decentralized innovation in developing an alternative test,[42] refused to approve American-developed and -manufactured rapid at-home tests because they did not meet the existing medical device standards, and failed to create a more appropriate standard for public health tests.[43] Bureaucrats also never managed to detach testing from our byzantine system of health care provision and billing.

Obviously, members of Congress were in no position to develop a COVID-19 diagnostic test or figure out precise criteria for determining which tests were acceptably accurate. But it would nevertheless have been easy for them to improve America's testing efforts by demanding an answer to a simple question: Why were Americans so much worse off, in their access to tests, than citizens of peer countries?

Congress provided a great deal of funding to support state efforts to make COVID-19 testing widely available. But legislators did not relieve the states of the incredible burdens that our public health laws and regulations put on health-related enterprises, and so states were painfully slow in utilizing financial support. Providing money is sometimes no substitute for directly addressing bottlenecks.

These issues did not escape legislators' attention. Indeed, Rep. Kim Schrier (D-WA), a pediatrician, pushed the bureaucracy to make at-home tests more readily and cheaply available to consumers for many months.[44] But her method of advocacy is once again revealing: members of Congress act as petitioners hoping to influence the government, rather than members of a body meant to collectively decide what actions government should take.

America's vaccine story is in many ways a happier one, so perhaps there is less to be desired from Congress' efforts. Thanks to massive public investment—supplied, quickly and without much difficulty, by Congress—and a thriving private-sector capacity for drug development, the United States led the world in developing high-quality vaccines. Within about 14 months of the virus' arrival in force in America, Americans had access to free vaccines, usually at a pharmacy near their home. This miraculous success seemed all but impossible back in March 2020.

Yet there is still plenty to criticize. First, the FDA often seemed oblivious to the costs of normal bureaucratic foot-dragging in a country losing thousands of lives each day to a deadly virus. In the fall of 2020, President Trump assured the nation that vaccines would become available imminently. But the

FDA stretched out the data collection process with Pfizer, and the company waited until a week after the November election to release news of its success. After that release, more than four weeks passed before the FDA granted an Emergency Use Authorization, during which time the most severe wave of the virus to date was spreading. For outsiders, the delay was utterly incomprehensible. Then, throughout 2021, when it was clear that both the Pfizer and Moderna shots had its full confidence, the agency withheld its full approval of these vaccines for no clear reason.

At a more fundamental level, it should give us pause that the vaccines were developed within days of the drug companies receiving the gene sequencing of the SARS-coV-2 virus, all the way back in January 2020, before a single American ever died.[45] Given the importance of safety and efficacy testing, and given the difficulties in transitioning from synthesizing small quantities in a lab to manufacturing at scale, some lag was inevitable. Weighing the risks of moving too quickly against the risks of moving too slowly was not an easy calculation. Still, it seems almost bizarrely complacent to believe that the best way of balancing these risks was simply to accept the processes in place before we knew anything about the novel coronavirus. Why did our legislators shy away from debating whether we could create a COVID-specific approval process for these drugs rather than hewing so faithfully to our normal procedures? Why did they not consider sanctioning more risks to establish safety faster, such as human challenge trials, in which healthy adults volunteer to be infected with the virus after receiving the vaccine, which the United Kingdom eventually used as part of its vaccine testing?[46] Their near-total silence undoubtedly contributed to a national sense of helplessness, as if the only thing we could do was wait.

Members of Congress have shown some awareness of the potential for improvement here, circulating several bills in the 117th Congress meant to provide Americans quicker access to vaccines in the case of a future pandemic. The chair and ranking member of the Senate's Health, Education, Labor, and Pensions Committee cosponsored a bill making some reasonable improvements, and the "Secret Congress" managed to include some of its provisions in an omnibus spending bill.[47] But it is disheartening how little members of Congress, from leaders to backbenchers, have been willing to make FDA reform a prominent issue, such that we could expect better performance when confronted with a new pandemic.

Given that the federal government provided the resources to support the vaccine rollout, it might well have been better for Congress to work through the difficult questions relating to who became eligible for shots first. The CDC recommended that scarce shots be allocated first to health care personnel and nursing home residents, then to Americans age 75 and older and "essential workers"—an elaborately defined and politically contestable category.[48] States, however, exercised a free hand in determining who would be eligible for the vaccine. They sometimes made shots available for people with different health conditions or potential comorbidities.[49] In some places, to combat racial inequities in vaccination rates, they even created explicit race-based priorities.[50] Setting these parameters often created bitter resentments and contributed to the sense that the public health establishment was being given political powers that far exceeded what their expertise could justify. A nationally legislated compromise might well have created a smoother path in the months of vaccine scarcity.

Another important vaccine issue was determining optimal dosage and timing of vaccines. Each vaccine was approved to be administered subject to a certain schedule that was chosen for the FDA's safety and efficacy testing. But those schedules—which varied considerably for the different vaccines—had not been proven medically or socially optimal in comparison to other possible ones, and the FDA proved remarkably incurious about potential alternatives. The United Kingdom pursued a "first doses first" strategy to speed up availability of at least one shot for all who sought to be vaccinated, and many argued for the merits of that strategy in the United States, including seven Republican members of Congress, all of whom were medical doctors, who in March 2021 urged the HHS to consider it.[51] They made no headway at the time, although in the fall of 2021, the Biden administration did begin to allow more flexibility on the timing of booster shots.

Once vaccines became superabundant in America, the political fight shifted to whether governments, schools, and businesses could or should mandate that their employees, customers, or students receive the vaccine. In the fall of 2021, as President Biden announced that the Occupational Safety and Health Administration would move to require large employers to administer vaccine mandates, arguing about the justice and propriety of vaccine "passports" and mandates became a mainstay of national politics, including for members of Congress. But there was no indication whatsoever that either side was interested in working out some kind of compromise that could de-escalate these issues.

What would such a compromise have looked like? Given that Democrats saw mandates as attractive ways of fighting the virus but undoubtedly recognized their political costliness, Republican skeptics of mandates might have figured out some other way to address their concerns. Since Democrats focused on "barriers to access" for working-class Americans, there should have been an opening. "Maximize real choice for everyone" was a compromise frame that would have offered something for both sides, with a focus on sweeping away bureaucratic obstacles to fighting COVID-19, for both the individual (as with paperwork requirements or complicated medical billing or with access to drugs) and the community (as with projects to improve school ventilation, build up supplies of crucial equipment around the country, and ensure clinical capacity in all areas).

In part, such an agenda would have involved yet another round of dispersing cash. But it would have also involved listening more to the concerns of the American people and taking seriously the idea that their representatives might have been in a position to accommodate many of their disparate concerns in ways that reduced conflict rather than exacerbating it.

## Money Is Not the Problem or the Answer

Our political system managed to produce huge bipartisan majorities to mobilize a response to the COVID-19 emergency, with unprecedented sums used to blunt the economic harms of the pandemic and its response as well as supporting the successful development and rollout of a vaccine. Yet, our legislature avoided taking on the divisive questions about COVID-19 that roiled the nation. Legislators had plenty of criticism for public health agencies that ended up as on-the-spot decision makers, but they did not actively assert legislative responsibility for answering these questions. Indeed, through their various enactments, they tended to shovel more money into these same agencies and add to their remits.

We should be grateful that Congress was not, in fact, so dysfunctional as to choke off all federal action during the crisis. Massive federal deficit spending helped fend off a prolonged economic downturn and undoubtedly alleviated massive amounts of human suffering. Historic support for our public health efforts was entirely appropriate. But a good deal of Congress' spending under the heading of its COVID-19 response did not focus on combating the virus. According to a professor of education finance, the American Rescue Plan's $122 billion for schools was "*for sure* the largest one-time federal investment in public education in this country."[52] Some of that money would be spent on air filtration and testing to help keep schools open; some on educational programming to make up for students' lost time. But—largely because of arcane federal disbursement laws—much of that money will sit idle for years, acting as a boon for the educational sector, which might mean providing more money for teachers, swelling the ranks of paraprofessionals, or piling up computing equipment that is supposedly crucial to American students' educations. Other COVID-19 spending that did flow out in the short term is best understood in the context of a longer-term fight over the shape of American social welfare spending. The temporary child tax credit enacted as part of the American Rescue Plan, for example, was clearly intended to be made permanent at a later date, and with the innovation of having it paid out monthly, it was also intended to alter the on-the-ground politics of federal spending.[53]

In other words, especially as the pandemic wore on, Congress used its relief bills as vessels for other priorities. Even as it did this, it failed to seek any kind of resolution on some of the most difficult political questions, ones that public health officials were poorly suited to handle. Former FDA commissioner Scott Gottlieb, my American Enterprise Institute colleague, puts it this way: "I learned at the FDA that people are often willing to confront risks that they can adequately measure for themselves, but balk when forced to embrace risks that seem open-ended, ambiguous, or hard to measure."[54]

Generalist representatives are best qualified to grapple with exactly these kinds of risks, because they can pull in the full variety of human concerns as they make their way through ambiguous situations. When such uncertainty is compounded by deep concerns about fairness and justice, the need for political leadership only deepens. Congress should have been the body to provide it—and still should be today.

If this suggestion somehow seems offbeat, that is a stinging indictment of our low expectations for Congress today.

# PART IV
# THREE FUTURES FOR CONGRESS

The great economist and political commentator Herb Stein famously quipped: "If something can't go on forever, it will stop." Does that mean that the current evolution of Congress away from substantive compromise and toward symbolic confrontation must come to an end soon? Should we expect that, any day now, members will swing the pendulum away from tight leader control and toward more open deliberation? Will "ambition counteracting ambition" revive a lively interplay of diverse factions, regardless of leaders' attempts to impose rigid partisan lines?

With each passing year, it takes a bit more wishful thinking to suppose such a reversal is imminent. Maybe the trend toward members of Congress acting as partisan foot soldiers is here to stay. Maybe congressional marginalization in the policymaking process *can* go on forever—maybe Congress' best days are long gone.

The purpose of Part IV is not to develop detailed or quantified predictions about Congress' future. Rather, by imagining three different ways that Congress could develop in the 2020s and beyond, I seek to once again force readers to consider what is at stake. What will we lose if we choose to accept congressional dysfunction as an indelible aspect of our constitutional fabric? If we face up to our legislature's shortcomings head on, might formal reforms that reduce its responsibilities improve our system of governance? Or, alternatively, what must change for Congress to experience a renaissance?

In each of the three short chapters that follow, I begin by taking some creative license, sizing up Congress from the perspective of hypothetical observers in 2039, the year of its 250th anniversary. Returning to an analytical viewpoint from our present, I go on to explain how the developments I have imagined align with existing trends and discuss their implications for American politics. This is, in some ways, easier for the first two scenarios, "Decrepitude" and "Rubber Stamp." In both cases, Congress comes to be viewed as an also-ran institution, perhaps even an irrelevancy. But plenty of observers render that judgment already. In contrast to their cynicism, my own fond hopes for a Madisonian Congress reborn are embodied in the vision of "Revival" offered in Chapter 11. In the book's postscript, I directly address our legislators, enjoining them to understand that any realization of those hopes must start with them.

# 9

# Decrepitude

This place sucks.

—Sen. Joe Manchin (D-WV), to his Senate colleagues, before
announcing his intention to pursue re-election in 2018[1]

### Reflections on Congress at 250: An Institution Hollowed Out but Capable of Mischief

by A Disappointed Observer

*Congress is turning 250. That seems like something to celebrate, but most Americans in 2039 find themselves wishing that the institution could have died of old age by now. Instead, it lingers on like someone suffering serious dementia: sometimes enjoying stretches of calm and good feeling but just as often violently disrupting more vital goings-on.*

*Congress may have once been a place for disparate factions to work together, but today it is a holding pen for "legislators" who make a high art of abuse. Bottom-up, bipartisan collaborations are a thing of the past. While top-level leaders may sometimes call a truce to move deals, they have all but completely obliterated more pedestrian forms of cross-partisan coalition building. Members used to tease each other about "fraternizing with the enemy," but now they level that grave charge without any hint of irony.*

*It may once have been true that "Congress in its committee rooms is Congress at work," as Woodrow Wilson observed so long ago, but today committees are well understood as mechanisms for photo-ops, allowing senior members to coordinate a bit of pageantry for social media. Today, dozens of newer members deliberately provoke their own banishment from all committee assignments, judging there are better places to stir up confrontations and grab attention. On both sides of the aisle, these anti-establishment agitators bask in the enmity of congressional leaders of both parties. They* know their core supporters value their performances of alienation more than any modest substantive policy gain they might deliver by playing nice. Leaders, meanwhile, have become ever-more adept at talking out of both sides of their mouths, casting themselves as consummate outsiders even as they hold the levers of power.

Unfortunately, our inflexible Constitution ensures this body of ingrates still matters, however much we might yearn for its silence. When even the narrowest House majority impeaches the president, the commander-in-chief must respond (though the routinization of this once-rare procedure has made it less of a news event than earlier in the 21st century). When congressional resources flow to increasingly elaborate investigations meant to humiliate the minority party's members, subpoenas must be answered. Sitting in the congressional dock has come to be regarded as one of cabinet officials' central duties, although a growing number of judges are willing to validate expansive claims of executive privilege if they allow our executive branch offices to focus on their more meaningful work. When Congress fails to pass a defense authorization bill—once as reliable as clockwork—our military isn't entirely crippled, but resulting bureaucratic headaches distract our leaders from external threats.

When Congress fails to approve government spending, we still get government shutdowns. Of course, these aren't what they used to be: the category of "essential" personnel authorized to soldier on in the absence of funding has swollen to include most federal workers. But the missed paychecks shutdowns cause inconvenience workers enough to dissuade many people from taking government jobs. Much more damaging than any quotidian government shutdown was Congress' willingness to mess around with the debt ceiling, which led directly to the financial panic of '32. Congressional leaders whose intransigence caused that mishap insisted it was only a "technical default," and bondholders received the interest due to them within the month. Nevertheless, global investors treated the incident as a sign of American unreliability and now demand higher interest rates to induce them to lend to the United States.

With total public debt now above 150 percent of GDP and such shenanigans likely to recur, the dollar, once almighty, now finds itself in a struggle for global supremacy with the yen, the yuan, and the euro. Debt payments swallow an ever-larger portion of our economic output, and our politics have only gotten nastier as appropriators fight over an ever-shrinking slice of the pie. There is, of course, no chance of Congress providing a systemic solution. The congressional budgeting process is a farce, having long ago abandoned *any pretense of imposing overall coherence. Congress passes budgets only to enable reconciliation, a procedure now expanded to facilitate important legislative priorities on any topic.*

*With Congress so incompetent to address the normal work of government, it is no wonder that American policymaking has evolved to leave Congress out of the loop. Back in the 2010s, there were signs that judges might defer less to agencies' interpretations of their enabling statutes. But they soon realized that when they wrote that "if there is a problem, it is up to Congress to fix it," they were committing to a permanently broken statute. Agencies now very nearly have a free hand to do what they like, so long as they go through the motions of providing a vaguely plausible legal justification. In emergencies, the executive's position has become near unassailable. What judge wants to say that America's survival ought to depend on a clear statement by Congress, when the body is such a mess?*

*Administrators and presidents do still worry what voters will think of their policies at the next election time, and they rely more than ever on polling and propagandizing the public to ensure a warm reception. But the executive now faces only a very hypothetical possibility that Congress might hold them accountable. In practice, the legislators of their own party will likely shield them from serious consequences.*

*If deference to the executive has become the norm, it is not without exceptions. In particular, the Supreme Court has emerged as a kind of super-legislature in recent years. Everything is litigated, and in fact members of Congress have become increasingly common litigants, having bulked up their capacity for legal combat even as their policymaking capacities atrophy. And so the court has a chance to decide most every front-page conflict if the justices want it. More than two decades ago, Supreme Court action figures began to be marketed, but today they are hot sellers with many demographics. With so much riding on justices' idiosyncratic outlooks, each of the nine justices is treated as an avatar of certain causes and groups. Needless to say, the court's abilities as a representative body remain limited; while the justices frequently resort to plurality opinions employing complicated balancing tests, in most cases they still send one side or the other home as decisive losers. That in turn only heightens people's sense that getting their justices on the bench justifies just about any political tactic.*

*Members of Congress still keep themselves busy, dashing after donors and making sure they don't miss the daily two minutes hate, whatever its object may be. They sometimes push policy tweaks to help their constituents, mostly by attaching them to one of the few giant omnibuses negotiated by leaders each year. But because everything depends on the leaders' goodwill, the skills needed to thrive in this environment are those of the courtier. It is hard to understand why anyone would wish for a job demanding the practice of such ingratiation. But there is no shortage of office seekers. After all, putting in time on Capitol Hill is a tried-and-true resume booster for those aspiring to be star political personalities on social media. The congressional platform is especially valuable for those willing to actively provoke their colleagues, with fisticuffs returning to the chamber after a hiatus of more than a century. Videos of middle school brawls have serious competition these days, especially given the influx of members who cut their teeth in mixed martial arts or professional wrestling. Embarrassing dance wars attract even more eyeballs.*

*There is no denying that Congress is a stupid place these days, even if a few earnest plodders do what they can for the seriousness of the institution. Intelligent people everywhere understand this and wish it could be otherwise. But attempts at major institutional overhauls inevitably get branded as partisan maneuvers. If it was once possible to conceive of the legislature as having its own distinctive institutional interests, now only the most naïve are taken in by such claims.*

*We can only hope that this institution does not end up being the downfall of our nation, and take whatever steps we can to ensure it never gets the chance.*

## Like Our Current Congress, Only More So

To some readers, that fanciful future retrospective may sound eerily similar to the Congress we already have. That is no accident. For Congress to descend into full-on decrepitude, all that is necessary is for current trends to continue without correction.

Chapter 6 noted that the description of our contemporary Congress as "completely dysfunctional" is hyperbolic. Things could still become more dysfunctional, and there is a good chance they will—things can always get worse. The scenario described gives a sense of what that would mean:

- leader dominance squeezing out all cross-partisan activity;
- even fewer attempts at incremental problem-solving through legislation;

- a further weaponization of oversight, alongside a routinization of impeachments;
- an even more broken-down budget process, made subordinate to the reconciliation tool that has become the central tool for passing legislation;
- more government shutdowns and worse debt ceiling difficulties, with a good chance an episode would finally lead to delayed payments;
- increasing incidents of political violence; and
- saturation levels of isn't-the-other-side-atrocious posturing.

Realistically, if Congress' fecklessness is obvious enough, our policymaking processes will adapt to work around the legislature rather than through it. Such circumvention may be constitutionally and legally awkward—but that is already true in the early 2020s, and its awkwardness does not make it impossible. Carl Sandburg famously advised lawyers: "If the facts are against you, argue the law. If the law is against you, argue the facts. If the law and the facts are against you, pound the table and yell like hell." Government lawyers facing obvious absurdities or governance disasters if they follow the law will find ways of justifying other action. Judges will find reasons to accept their justifications. None of this is good, but it makes considerably more sense than society hitching its fate to a plummeting institution until impact.

Even without knowing what substantive issues would dominate the politics of 2039, we can say with some certainty that the decrepit Congress described here would be unlikely to show any creativity, charity, or even common sense in figuring out how to deal with them. Because its leaders focus single-mindedly on embarrassing their political rivals, the Congress described lacks spontaneous encounters between diverse communities' trusted representatives; all action is carefully stage-managed. (As in professional wrestling, another carefully choreographed simulation of real conflict, the only really compelling surprises come when something goes horribly wrong.) Strange bedfellows coalitions have become a thing of the past. In this Congress there is no cure for the mischiefs of faction; there is no pursuit of a mutually acceptable understanding of the public good. This is an institution that persists not because of any virtues, but simply because our constitutional architecture makes formally abandoning it practically impossible—a "relic," as two of its critics have called it.[2]

What would happen to representation, broadly speaking, in the America burdened by this body?

Perhaps the public's ideas about representation have shifted, so that what matters is that all kinds of interests and ideas have their say in our virtual public square. Since "the discourse" is now online, representation can and should happen there—with public decisions somehow emerging from the fray. The next section takes up the (many) problems with this idea.

But, less speculatively, the other branches would attempt to take over the representative function that Congress had neglected by extending processes already in motion.

Executive branch agencies already invest significant resources in notice and comment rulemaking. As they formulate rules that interpret their mandates and translate them into concrete actions, they give all comers a chance to weigh in. That process opens them to input from whichever "stakeholders" involve themselves and frequently leads to significant learning on the part of the agency before a rule is finalized. With the internet making it possible for citizens around the country to engage this process at a fairly low cost, some enthusiasts have argued that rulemaking would become a more vital representative process than exists in America's legislature, or at least a very attractive complement.[3] If the legislative process itself has bogged down completely, there would surely be an attempt to turn notice-and-comment rulemaking into a more thoroughgoing substitute.

Courts, too, can try to dress up some of their proceedings in representative garb by including more voices. They can cultivate the filing of amicus briefs, gathering the input of a variety of interests far beyond those directly involved in litigation, a practice that has become far more coordinated and sophisticated in recent years.[4] Judges can even go so far as to appoint intervenors who will participate in proceedings, representing the interests of certain groups affected by litigation if they are systematically neglected. By liberalizing standing rules, they can ensure that all types of prospective litigants have functional access to courts. State legislation can also open courts to new kinds of actions meant to promote policy goals that might instead have been pursued directly through statutory law. Texas' legislature recently made creative and controversial use of this technique to create a civil cause of action against abortion providers and anyone else who enables abortions, and California's legislature followed by creating a civil cause of action against gun dealers who sell to underage purchasers.[5] Such relocations of political struggles into courts will multiply if federal lawmaking channels are hopelessly clogged.

And of course, to the extent descriptive representation is prioritized, both the executive branch and judiciary can be made to resemble the population, in terms of whatever demographic or personal characteristics people believe are most salient.

Should we expect such attempts at representativeness to be good substitutes for what Congress used to provide?

We should be very skeptical. However much agencies may emphasize their formal openness, in practice well-organized, directly interested parties dominate comment processes.[6] Normal people do not perceive these proceedings as "democratic." Just as problematic, receiving the chance to offer inputs does not necessarily translate into any opportunity for genuine influence. An agency is required to listen to, but not to conform their proceedings in accord with, the comments they receive. Indeed, the logic of bureaucrats' work disposes them to be dismissive, especially of outright dissent. Courts may pile up amicus curiae briefs, attempting to create a sense that they hear from every perspective, but they are acutely limited in their capacity to even notice, much less digest and accommodate, all of the considerations in complex areas.

Of course, legislators are not even required to listen, and access to them is very much skewed toward well-organized interests.[7] But there is a crucial difference: the electorate still has the chance, crude as it may be, to pass judgment on the elected official and convince other members of their community of the importance of doing so. Against the courts or the bureaucracy, citizens have no such recourse. As sterile and stage-managed as the degraded Congress may be, the kind of politics possible within the confines of bureaucratic procedure is even worse. If a group feels like the process has been "rigged" against them, they may be driven to cynical apathy—or dangerous despair. Judge-made law is little better, as legal decisions (especially if made by the Supreme Court) have a finality unknown to the products of legislative bargaining. As we saw in Chapter 3, that does not necessarily make them effective at securing on-the-ground change. But it does make it difficult to pursue half-a-loaf compromises of the sort that Madisonian politics enables.

## The Pathologies of Twitter Representation

If old institutions cannot make up for the decline of legislative representation, what about new technologies? Can the free-flowing talk facilitated by social media make up for the sclerosis of debate in the halls of the Capitol?

Techno-optimists hail the possibilities, excited by the ways in which social media increases elected officials' accessibility and responsiveness. A 2015 report by the Congressional Management Foundation, a group that works closely with congressional offices, found that most staffers felt that social media activity helped their members have "more meaningful interactions with constituents," and that this activity also made them "more accountable to constituents." About a third of staffers indicated that their offices "pay attention to" interactions even if they involve fewer than 10 comments, and another half said 10 to 30 comments would be sufficient—perhaps evidence that social media was becoming a low-barrier-to-entry way for citizens to meaningfully influence their representatives.[8] A small community on Capitol Hill envisions social media, "virtual town halls," and other innovative communications techniques bringing members closer to their swelling constituencies, helping to renew and update what representativeness means in the 21st century. This approach has real potential, and countless constructive interactions between constituents and their representatives already take place online.

Nevertheless, several characteristics of the broader social media environment ought to make us very worried about our representatives shifting their attention to the virtual public square and away from their colleagues in Congress—and potentially from their actual district-based constituents. The first is the very open-endedness of most social media engagement. Rather than engaging with a particular audience, social media makes the whole world the audience. The potential to reach so many may feel exhilarating, but communication with an unclear audience is inherently difficult. A message intended for one group of interpreters becomes actually subject to interpretation by everyone, including many people with very different assumptions. Communication breakdown, misunderstanding, and increased levels of distrust can easily result. A lawmaker's ability to tailor their message to the sensibilities of their own state or district is rendered useless if outsiders make an aspect of the message fodder for controversy. Even the intended in-district audience may end up learning of the legislator's message not in its original context, but rather as an outsider's example of a stupid/insensitive/blinkered/oblivious thing to say.

The second concerning aspect of social media is who gets influence. Being an elected representative does not grant any special status on social media; plenty of House members have only a few thousand followers on Twitter. For members to gain a large audience, they must attract attention just like anyone else, with their elected status giving them just a small advantage. And anyone who has spent any time on social media has a sense of what qualities make political tweets go viral: sarcasm, intense emotion or moral judgment, a clear target for derision, evocation of people's deep fears, flattering certain people's sensibilities. Also highly rewarded is joining in to an existing discourse with a large existing audience—which often means the highly nationalized culture war. For all the promise of openness, the incentives push toward sticking to well-established scripts. Offbeat relationship building is possible and sometimes realized, but the amorphous "liking" crowd values "dunking" more highly than conciliation. Recent empirical research confirms that members' tweets have trended toward negativity, with a striking jump in that direction in 2018.[9] The representatives whose social media performances have won them top-tier celebrity are those most skilled at denouncing (and trolling) their political enemies.

Of course, as we saw in Chapter 5, figuring out how to use new media to embarrass your political enemies is nothing new. But if we recall how control of C-SPAN cameras became so controversial in the 1980s, we can begin to appreciate why control of online discourse is likely to be an explosive political issue in the 2020s and beyond. A third serious difficulty with relying on these platforms as foundations for our democratic representation is that each must define and enforce its own norms, which necessarily entails "policing" the discourse and excluding persistent violators. "Somebody" having to make rules is not necessarily a problem, but the power of just a few powerful companies to determine who gets attention is concerning, especially since these platforms tend to flock together in their decisions.

In January 2022, Twitter permanently banned Rep. Marjorie Taylor Greene (R-GA) for repeated infractions of its COVID-19 misinformation ban. During 2021, several other members of Congress received temporary suspensions from YouTube for similar violations. The official justification of these decisions was undoubtedly public-spirited: the companies said that questioning the efficacy of vaccines or promoting the use of unproven medications would lead to more infections and deaths from the global pandemic, and they wanted to do whatever they could to prevent those deaths. But even if one agrees that the best way to reduce the influence of these messages is to exclude them from the most widely used platforms (a highly debatable proposition), this is an intimidating display of these platforms' power to control what kinds of ideas are even open to political contestation. Can we simply hope that they will use that power wisely and justly, and leave it at that? Certainly they are trying, making massive investments in sensitizing their algorithms to subtleties of meaning and usage, and hiring small armies of content moderators who apply a human touch to sorting wheat from chaff. But, as Jon Askonas and Ari Schulman have persuasively argued, neutral adjudication is an impossible task. As platforms adjust their rules, "The people who most need to be convinced will see a game of Three Card Monte, in which blame and responsibility are displaced to different parts of the same irredeemably flawed system, designed not for real fairness and neutrality but only for their appearance." The platforms may insist that they play straight, but for those on the wrong end of their exclusions, it will be glaringly obvious that there is no such thing as an apolitical platform.[10]

Forcing our political deliberation to conform to whatever terms massive social media platforms choose to impose has not brought on an immediate crisis. Some voices have always been excluded, and the angry complaints of their supporters may not matter so much. But there is a danger that cutting out certain kinds of people or viewpoints will become a default maneuver to settle contentious policy debates. Persuasion then gives way to a raw exercise of power in determining what views are to be deemed permissible. Given the underlying context of a deeply divided nation, that ought to strike us as genuinely frightening—even for those who believe the filtration will be consistent with their commitments. This is the very opposite of a system designed to negotiate civil peace through a process of accommodation.

## Rejecting Cohesion and Cultivating Unrest

When we think about this chapter's scenario of a washed-up Congress—that is, when we imagine continuing down the path we are currently on, with our representative legislature no longer working through our conflicts but instead heightening our contradictions—it is hard to avoid the specter of total social breakdown, or even civil war.

Admittedly, it isn't obvious what that would look like in today's world. A unified bloc of states seceding, as happened in 1861, is difficult to imagine. So is an attempt by one political party to declare opponents enemies of the state. To be anything other than self-destructive, the party in power would need overwhelming dominance of major cultural, political, and military institutions, and that does not seem likely to happen any time soon.

But other, less dramatic forms of socio-political dysfunction do now seem alarmingly possible, especially after the politically motivated shooting at a Republican congressional baseball practice in June 2017 and the storming of the US Capitol on January 6, 2021. When any large group of Americans develops a deep sense that their government does not represent people like them, some tiny fraction will conclude that the appropriate recourse is violence. That is terrible and must be condemned without ambiguity. But it should not shock us. It seems all too likely that we might look back from the 2040s at these early turns toward violence and see in them a prelude to much worse troubles.[11]

That is a frightening enough possibility to make drastic reforms look attractive, even if they openly abandon the Founders' vision of Congress as the central organ of political decision-making. Perhaps what we need is a drastic overhaul of our system, one that will deliver us from dissolution by focusing on delivering good governance. That leads us to the next potential future.

# 10

# Rubber Stamp

Democracy is one element in politics; if it seeks to be everything, it destroys politics, turning "harmony into mere unison," reducing "a theme to a single beat."

—Bernard Crick[1]

## Congress at 250: Finally, Democratic and Grown-Up Government for the 21st Century

by A Lover of Good Government

*Not so long ago, Congress was a place where good ideas went to die, consumed as it was by the worst kind of partisan squabbling. Its sorry state threatened the very viability of American government, and plenty of doom-and-gloom types pronounced the institution unsalvageable.*

*Now, as we mark Congress' 250th birthday, we celebrate an institution reborn: modernized for the 21st century, expanded to represent America's diversity, and streamlined to actually get things done. After years of letting rabble-rousers in the House turn our whole government upside down, we have finally adopted sensible reforms that ensure the American people's will reigns supreme in Congress. Instead of accepting the inevitability of obstruction and dysfunction, we have entered a new era in which American government is marked by action. Let us review how this happy transition has unfolded.*

*The first major shift began during the coronavirus pandemic of 2020, when the House of Representatives began to allow proxy voting and virtual hearings to limit members' exposure to the disease. Originally intended as temporary, these measures opened people's eyes to the advantages of relying on 21st-century communications technology, and before long the House adopted fully remote deliberation and voting. Once they could make speeches by video (and later hologram) and vote using their phones, representatives were able to spend more time among their constituents and less time being socialized into the dubious ways of Washington. "Floor" votes were no longer a confusing ordeal once it became possible for representatives to precommit to voting with their party's leadership. Legislator "independence" has now become a thing of the past, but our experience of more responsible parties has shown that it was always overrated.*

*A protracted government shutdown in 2024 led to another salutary change: the adoption of Sen. Mark Warner's (D-VA) Stop STUPIDITY Act, first proposed in 2019.[2] Whereas lapses in federal funding previously disrupted government operations, this law ensures that appropriations remain level if the legislature fails to act. No more would there be shameful attempts to force policy changes with threats of paralyzing the whole government. Quite rightly, students of contemporary American government now regard the shutdowns of the 1980s through the early 2020s as a bizarre historical curiosity and marvel that we were willing to tolerate such a haphazard approach to funding the federal government.*

*Next came a more dramatic change for Congress. With voting and deliberation enhanced by new technologies, leaders of the House saw that expanding the number of representatives would present no insuperable logistical difficulties. In 2029, riding high on their second consecutive wave election, the Democratic majority updated the Permanent Apportionment Act of 1929, which had locked in the number of representatives at 435 for a century, to set the number of representatives at 1,776. That gave each House member a district of about 200,000 people, making it much more common for members to represent coherent communities. (It also has the happy side effect of making the Electoral College much less distortionary. California now has around 225 electoral votes to Wyoming's 5—still skewed in favor of the smaller state, but only slightly. From now on, only in the case of a historically close race could there be a divergence between the popular vote and electoral count winner.) The demographic diversity of this enormous body has finally come to reflect the nation it represents.*

*The tradition-bound Senate was slow to follow the House's example on remote voting, but it finally came around in the early 2030s. Senators are rarely seen mingled with stuffed shirts in Washington any longer, and gone are the tedious quorum calls that once took up much of the institution's time. It turns out that the fiction that senators are speaking and listening to each other is just as easily sustained through the virtual rendering of the Senate chamber as through the selective placement of C-SPAN cameras.*

*Most important of all for the health of our democracy, the Senate has left behind its obstructionist past. Senators did away with the filibuster—it was only fair for a majority of 58, representing 70 percent of the American public, to work its will. The American people themselves imposed the next, more dramatic change. Responding to the unexpected shock of China's Great Disengagement, the president put together a wildly popular plan for reorienting America's economy back toward manufacturing, assigning all underemployed Americans to jobs. But the Senate majority leader stubbornly refused to bring the Made in America Recovery Act to the floor, claiming it would jeopardize Americans' economic liberties—quite an abstract concern to prioritize amid stagflation twice as severe as that of the 1970s. Americans rebelled, and the Unleash Democratic Productivity (UDP) grassroots movement took off around the country, energizing the public and scrambling the country's political parties. To overcome the Senate's obstruction, the group pushed a constitutional amendment reforming America's political processes, and the necessary two-thirds vote in Congress was secured thanks to an unprecedented pressure campaign. (The roughly 80 House members and 20 senators who decided to defy UDP soon learned the extent of the group's bottom-up democratic power—not one was re-elected.) More than 40 state ratifying conventions approved the transformative 29th Amendment within a year.*

*The 29th Amendment only modestly changes the Constitution, but in doing so it rebalances American government so that it finally works for the American people by empowering the president to govern. It operates through two simple mechanisms. The first: all presidential nominees must still be submitted for the advice and consent of the Senate, but now they are automatically confirmed if the Senate does not act on their nomination within 30 days (60 at the beginning of a new Congress). The second: the president can now introduce one bill to the House of Representatives on the first business day of each month (excepting election months and lame duck sessions), and the House must give that bill an up or down vote on the second Tuesday of the month, with the Senate following on the third Tuesday.*[3]

*These monthly bills have sensibly become the main mechanism of American policymaking. Naturally, the president's first bill was the Made in America Recovery Act, which set the nation on a path to full employment and strategic self-reliance. But the regular work of government generally happens through presidential bills too. Decisions on spending and debt get made decisively, without interminable delays or the ridiculous hostage-taking maneuvers of earlier times. Our various regulatory regimes get updated regularly and leg-islation now encompasses much of what the cumbersome system of the past forced into substatutory executive actions. In leading the economic reorgan-ization mandated by the Made in America Recovery Act, the president has also speedily built up the more professional and independent civil service needed to make this effort successful. The newly created Improvement through Machine Learning Agency has been a particular success in making job alloca-tion orders more efficient and satisfactory.*

*When crises arise, presidential legislation quickly empowers our executive branch officials, and they bring their world-class credentials to bear on diffi-cult issues that baffled legislators. Laws standing in the way of successful ad-aptation get changed in a hurry.*

*There are those who whine that, with most nominees coming to their posts without votes and Congress having rejected a presidential law only once (only to pass a nearly identical law the next month), our legislature has become a "mere rubber stamp." Nonsense. Our newly expanded cadre of representatives provides better service for their constituents than their predecessors ever did. With the help of artificial intelligence–enhanced screening, people who have trouble navigating any government program get the help they need from their district office in a matter of hours. Through their innovative public discussion forums, representatives' lively debates are more accessible to the public than ever before. Besides, in truth, legislators haven't been the ones writing legis-lation since the 19th century. The people's will is still embodied in Congress' votes—indeed, far more faithfully than it was in earlier decades. The enlarged House has already become a wonderful incubator of talent for those who go on to fill important executive branch positions.*

*With so much going right, it seems almost unnecessary to mention the per-sistent misbehavior of a malcontented minority, whose irrational devotion to outdated ideas make them hate our country's progress. They have plenty of chances to persuade their fellow citizens of the merits of their positions, and of course Congress has its loyal opposition that plays this role honorably. But far too often critics of our reformed system instead resort to misinformation and dirty tricks meant to embarrass honest public servants. Thankfully, our re-sponsible media platforms have developed advanced techniques for containing such misbehavior. (Although human content moderators proved insufficient to quell the tide of disinformation, fortunately instant-fact-checking tech-nology has helped clamp down on such ridiculous and verifiably false claims as "everything is more expensive today than it used to be" or "life was better before we gave so much power to computers.") And our domestic terrorism investigators are better than ever at infiltrating potentially violent groups before they ever have a chance to carry out traitorous plots. Dissent is, and will always be, an undying part of America's political culture—and intraparty debate today is thriving, informing the president's choices of what to include. But honoring that tradition doesn't mean that people trying to drag us back to the hateful ways of the 20th century should be allowed to distort our whole democratic system. They have no right to do so, and we are better off having adopted a system that lets us move forward in spite of their revanchism.*

*Congress ain't what it used to be? Well, so what? Nostalgia for simpler times doesn't create jobs for everyone. Our current system does, and Congress plays an important part in making its programs work for everyone. That is something to celebrate as the institution turns 250.*

## Choosing Democracy over Representation

The foregoing scenario obviously involves several leaps of imagination, but it plausibly depicts one way America's politics might evolve. A large portion of the American public already denounces aspects of our system of government that fall short of a full commitment to democracy, including our "anti-majoritarian Senate" and the overrepresentation of rural citizens in the House. Many Americans today think our current realization of representative government improperly frustrates the will of democratic majorities, and they associate that offense with a deep and troubling strand of injustice in American history. Sen. Elizabeth Warren (D-MA), for example, has said, "The filibuster has deep roots in racism, and it should not be permitted to serve that function, or to create a veto for the minority. In a democracy, it's majority rules."[4]

Right now, these concerns are mostly voiced by Democrats, who have lacked the political power to resolve them through major structural changes. But any number of factors could easily break us out of our age of partisan parity, which is atypical of American history. Either one of our parties could opportunistically reorient itself to become a clear majority party, perhaps by championing a popular policy that has been kept off of the agenda as a solution to an emergency. If conditions align, a grassroots movement could upend familiar political battle lines and open the door to structural changes.

The focal policy in this reform scenario recalls Franklin Roosevelt's push to implement a far-reaching "manpower" program as World War II came to an end. As Chapter 2 described, Roosevelt's program was broadly popular; even among legislators, the general idea seemed to command clear majority support. And yet, in the process of asking representatives to put together a program that they would actually vote into law, the inherent tensions and difficulties of a system in which the government assigned civilian work came to the fore. Our representative assembly sensed trouble and steered us clear of it by insisting that hard questions be answered. When they were not, the effort stalled, preserving Americans' freedom to choose which economic opportunities to pursue.

Today, it is easy to imagine that things might go differently. A jobs guarantee has flitted around the edges of political discourse, not quite securing a place on the agenda. But it has sometimes received the support of as many as three-quarters of Americans (depending, of course, on how the question is put).[5] If a deeply troubled economy faces an additional adverse shock, it is easy to imagine a demand for government-provided jobs spreading quickly. And perhaps, if the leaders of that movement became sufficiently influential and found that stubborn legislators were all that stood between them and success, they would undertake and achieve major structural reform of America's policymaking process.

If they did so, they might well come up with something like the 29th Amendment I have described here, inspired by the reform program advanced by William Howell and Terry Moe, two self-described Wilsonians who argue that our parochial Congress stands between America and good governance.[6] Howell and Moe quite reasonably assume that Americans will be reluctant to massively overhaul our Constitution, but they make the case for radically altering the balance of power between the branches by ensuring the president has the power to force votes on pieces of legislation that he controls.

The constitutional transformation considered here seems to leave the United States with something like the Westminster-style parliamentary system Woodrow Wilson once idealized—but Americans under this regime would find themselves far less empowered than modern Britons. As in that system, the majority party would exercise near-complete control of the legislative agenda while also directly controlling the government. But, because he retains his own electoral base (and the ability to claim he is still "the only official elected by the whole people"), the American president in this system would actually be much more powerful than the prime minister of the United Kingdom. The occupant of 10 Downing Street formally serves at the pleasure of the constitutional monarch and practically serves at the pleasure of the majority party in Parliament, which can decide to replace him for any reason and at any time. The American president is generally secure in office for a whole four-year term.

The president's power to control the agenda would also outstrip the prime minister's. A failed legislative push could not end with a vote of no confidence from his own party or with the dissolution of the government and the calling of a new election. Instead, as the scenario hints at, the president could push the same proposal repeatedly, employing carrots and sticks to improve his position between successive votes, until passage was finally secured.

What should we make of the resultant political system? Let us first try to understand its appeal, then consider why it would entail a decisive break from the American tradition of political liberty.

## "Politicians Ruin Everything"—A Refrain with a Broad Appeal

Why might the American people willingly embrace a clearly subordinate role for our legislature?

Perhaps, as a practical matter, recent episodes of legislative dysfunction are enough to convince them. Self-inflicted crises like government shutdowns really are hard to stomach, and they have driven a number of serious legislators to the possibility of changing the default rule for spending. Senator Warner's (very real) Stop STUPIDITY Act is only the most colorfully named of a long line of bills going back to the 1990s that have proposed "automatic continuing resolutions." The bills mandate that in the absence of congressional action, government funding continues at (or near) previous levels rather than going to zero.[7] Some would also impose punitive measures on members of Congress, such as preventing use of official funds on travel, to force them to come to a spending agreement—but the dominant impulse here is to minimize Congress' ability to make a nuisance of itself through a failure to compromise. Of course, as former House Appropriations chair Nita Lowey (D-NY) noted, by creating the possibility of "indefinite autopilot," these bills would also risk rendering Congress' power of the purse notional.[8] But the more trouble Congress makes, the easier it is to put aside such abstract concerns about the nature of our institutions, and the more attractive this sort of marginalizing reform becomes.

Alongside such good government concerns, there are deeper reasons why minimizing Congress' role appeals to many Americans. They derive from the persistent and difficult questions about the nature of representation, discussed in Chapter 1, which have hung over Congress' work since the beginning of the republic.

The Anti-Federalists and their intellectual heirs thought a legislative body should precisely mirror the community at large and that a federal legislature of Congress' scale could never live up to that ideal. They believed that in a true democracy, the people must get their way "immediately"—without delay, and also without any intermediating body distorting or corrupting their wishes. Representation in an extended republic seemed to them, as it seems to many people today, to be a kind of flim-flam designed to appease the people and distract them from self-interested actions of the powerful.

A seemingly contrary line of thinking reaches a similar endpoint. If we imagine that the general interest is an objective, well-defined reality and that we simply must determine the best way to put it into practice, the debates of generalist, vote-seeking legislators do not have much to recommend them. Instead, it seems that specialists "outside of" or "above" the concerns of "petty politics" should be given the chance to serve the public by drawing on their professional training and superior aptitude. Because of their disinterested commitment to knowledge, such experts are elevated above base politicians as the only truly loyal servants of the people.

These populist and technocratic impulses are complements rather than opposites. In their shared anxiety about "politicians ruining everything" and their shared sense that disintermediation can purify democracy, they have a common reform cause around which to rally. This combination defined the Progressive movement and is also evident in many reform circles today. It has undeniable appeal: the people express their will through the national election of the president, and then the experts of the administrative state labor to carry out their will in a maximally efficient manner, supplementing the people's judgments about justice with their own governing prowess.[9]

This appeal will only grow alongside our increasing reliance on algorithmic computations beyond human comprehension. As Chapter 8 relates in the context of COVID-19 responses, communities of human experts can lose their reputation for being above politics. And while computer algorithms created by humans, for human purposes, should be seen as imbued with their creators' biases, in practice the work of artificial intelligence(s) is often treated as the embodiment of technical neutrality. Machine learning, in particular, seems to promise a kind of purely empirical knowledge we can use to order society. If what people want out of government is a black box that outputs good things, artificial intelligence offers the ultimate black box. The transcendence of human understanding is its selling point—one likely to be paired with a righteous refusal to give legible reasons for decisional outputs.[10]

"Democracy is the theory that the common people know what they want, and deserve to get it good and hard," H. L. Mencken contemptuously suggested.[11] But many Americans today seem ready to sign onto that bargain. Before long, they may be ready to cut out any middlemen who insist on complicating the deal.

## What Legislators Do in a Dressed-Down Legislature

To be sure, the "cutting out" of the intermediaries is not likely to be literal. Almost every nation has a legislature that meets and does business, regardless of whether it is an autocracy or a free country, and regardless of whether anyone believes that its proceedings have any substantive importance for shaping the country's laws.

To put the point even more sharply, even the Roman Empire had a functioning Senate, whose members continued to enjoy an exalted status for *centuries* after the emperor had taken over nearly all of the body's important functions. As a matter of formal procedure, they were still the ones who passed the laws. Tacitus, imperial Rome's great historian, observed that in a free state as the republic had been, "the national eloquence will be prompt, bold, and animated," whereas

in a state of polished society, where a single ruler sways the sceptre, the powers of the mind take a softer tone, and language grows more refined. But affectation follows, and precision gives way to delicacy. The just and natural expression is no longer the fashion. Living in ease and luxury, men look for elegance, and hope by novelty to give a grace to adulation.[12]

We should expect Congress' history to go on, then, even if its members' speeches concern themselves primarily with flattering the right people, even if policymaking authority migrates almost entirely to the executive branch and judiciary, even if citizens regard the legislature as a rubber stamp. But what would the job of a legislator look like in a Congress that has been rendered nearly subordinate or irrelevant?

As the scenario above suggests, a shift toward constituent service would build on existing trends. For decades, congressional offices have built up their capacity to help their in-district constituents navigate the many challenges of dealing with the bureaucracies of the federal welfare state. This can be as simple as helping someone figure out why their social security checks went missing or as complicated as seeking trade adjustment compensation from the US Department of Labor. Congressional intervention tends to produce real results for constituents.[13] Receiving a helping hand can turn someone into a loyal supporter of the incumbent, whether or not she supported the member at the last election. Treating a constituent coldly, on the other hand, might create an enemy for life. Unsurprisingly, then, congressional offices have invested heavily in their capacity to help constituents. According to one study, median House office spending on office staff dedicated to providing constituent services rose 67 percent between 1994 and 2009—and even still, staffers whose focus is supposed to be on legislative work are often asked to pitch in on constituent service.[14]

Note that there is nothing especially political in the idea that every citizen ought to find some help in dealing with the sometimes forbidding bureaucracy. Indeed, many believe that staffers can acquire a neutral competency at constituent service, with the same training applicable to everyone. Congress has taken on this function not so much because it is vital to fulfilling its core constitutional responsibilities, but because it offers incumbents the ability to take credit for providing customer service. Political scientist Morris Fiorina famously argued that getting the chance to correct the bureaucracy's errors was one of the chief benefits legislators saw in pushing responsibility out to executive agencies in the first place.[15] The executive branch can handle the political headaches, while congressional offices offer constituents much-needed direct relief. Unfortunately, the ad hoc, apolitical nature of this engagement between the legislative branch and the bureaucracy makes it unlikely to create concerted pressure for needed policy change; if Fiorina imagined efficacious control by congressional committees, in fact legislators may end up seeking solidarity with their voters through bitter complaints, without even managing to steer policy.[16]

Even if legislators have very little political power, the legislature as a whole may perform various useful functions for a ruling regime. It may be able to deal with minor, basically nonpolitical problems about which the regime is indifferent. By conducting low-stakes debates and airing constituents' concerns, the legislature's members may help keep the government apprised of various social trends and what different factions think of them. Legislators can also act as cheerleaders for administration initiatives. Handing out legislative positions can function as a useful form of patronage or (as alluded to in the scenario) as a training ground and testing stage for rising party functionaries. Finally, genuine political questions that divide the ruling party may sometimes be fought out in the legislature, within appropriately controlled bounds.[17]

Legislative leaders in such chambers may seem powerful, at least in their ability to keep their members in line, but they are themselves merely top-level functionaries, easily replaceable if they seem too interested in establishing their independence.

Finally, it is worth noting the synergy between these functions and legislators' increasing use of social media. Just as in the previous chapter's scenario, the opportunity to partake in mass political discourse will be more attractive to a legislator the less his or her specifically legislative role matters. Whether the representative assembly is utterly broken or subordinated to some other channel of democratic control, we end up with a system oriented toward mass politics and away from fluid coalition building. Legislators in these worlds may as well seek to influence the influencers, rather than fancying that they have anything to gain from fraternizing with their colleagues.

## Congressional Vitality and Political Freedom

We come now to the crucial question: If Congress becomes the handmaiden of an empowered executive branch, will we really lose anything so important? After all, the government described in this scenario still seems to have free and fair elections. The people still get to decide which party will rule. This system is still unquestionably a democracy.

And yet, such a system has nearly done away with politics. The right to disagree, and to make that disagreement the basis of effective political resistance, has withered and become irrelevant to the work of government. Rather than working through differences, this system is set up to suppress them. As James Madison warned, the two methods of "removing the causes of faction" employed here are worse than the problem: "destroying the liberty that is essential to its existence" and "giving to every citizen the same opinions, the same passions, and the same interests."[18] The people have become the online masses.

Perhaps some readers find that description melodramatic, and perhaps they think that jettisoning old-fashioned political values would be worth it if we got Singapore-caliber efficient governance in return. Even if we could obtain that (and there is no serious reason to believe we can), American history ought to make us doubtful that the American people would accept this bounty if it were produced without meaningful consideration of their concerns, however little or base they might be. Good laws that lack legitimacy may not last, nor do much good.

What might work for the small city-state of Singapore is hopelessly maladapted to the circumstances of the United States, with its huge variety of interests and communities. It would be convenient if Americans could distill their national will into clear directions simply through the process of their national elections, but there is no sign that they can actually do so. Indeed, as we saw in Chapter 5, politicians who try to interpret the results of a single election as conferring a strong mandate for abrupt change are likely to find themselves utterly disoriented by the complexity and diversity of concerns found even in their own coalition. Political scientist James Morone warns, "Reforms introduced amid celebrations of the people are rarely designed to accommodate conflict among them."[19]

Congress is the organ of American government designed to make pluralism work. If we collectively decide to subordinate it to a purely majoritarian conception of popular will embodied by the president, we are essentially abandoning pluralism. That would not *necessarily* entail tyranny; the forbearance of ruling parties might lead them to real conscientiousness, especially if rotation in office seemed certain.

But forcing all political conflict to express itself through plebiscitary elections is entirely consistent with the end of freedom. Conversely, maintaining the health of Congress as something more than a rubber stamp is, as James Burnham insisted, the only way to ensure the preservation of political liberty in the modern United States. He reflected that in earlier times, a representative assembly may not have been needed to maintain political balance, because "the traditional 'orders'—nobles, clergy, elders, communes"—or immovable beliefs provided a counterpoise against a grasping executive. Those old orders and beliefs are gone now, though, making the representative assembly "inseparable from constitutional government, juridical defense, and liberty."[20]

What, then, might the restoration of Congress look like?

# 11

## Revival

The people cannot be represented by or embodied in a single leader precisely because of the people's diversity. Their representation, if it is to be more than a masquerade, must have some sort of correspondence to their diversity.

—James Burnham[1]

### Congress at 250: Gloriously Full of Fight

by A Constitutional Believer

*As recently as the early 2020s, Congress had become little more than a venue for a partisan death match while the president, executive agencies, and courts shouldered policymaking responsibility. Strong party leaders in both the House and Senate successfully managed their coalitions in tight ranks, keeping them marching together—which in retrospect looks like a stunning, if corrosive, display of organizational dominance. A remarkable number of intelligent people believed Americans really were split into two distinct tribes, each fervently devoted to the platforms of the respective parties, whose enmity seemed destined to last forever. American politics seemed dully, depressingly predictable.*

*Oh, how quickly things can change!*

*After several dominant congressional leaders finally aged out in the mid-2020s, their Generation X successors had difficulty maintaining a similar level of partisan unity, especially in the face of the great migrations of 2026. After a devastating volcanic eruption in Guatemala laid waste to the Central American country's economy, millions migrated northward through Mexico, hoping to reach the United States. At the same time, the Chinese government intensified its persecution of Christians. Millions made harrowing escapes, by land, air, and sea, to South Korea and Japan, both of which asked the United States to accept many of these religious refugees.*

*America was faced with a stark decision: accept a huge number of refugees or risk an acute crisis on its southern border, as well as the condemnation of many of its Christian faith leaders. To some members of both parties, this moment seemed like an opportunity to reassert America's moral authority in the world and gain millions of potentially productive citizens (an attractive proposition given rising wages). To other members, also found among the ranks of both Democrats and Republicans, the prospect of prioritizing these foreigners (however sympathetic) ahead of working-class Americans' needs seemed like a betrayal of epic proportions. Chaotic midterm elections of 2026 featured an unexpected number of cross-party endorsements as "Welcomers" and "Real Nationers" forged connections that defied the old party lines. Indeed, although our historians have yet to fully penetrate the whirlwind of activity at this moment, anti-refugee forces in each party organized themselves and developed extensive hierarchical leadership structures, though they were largely kept secret.*

*This new factional struggle had an immediate, dramatic impact. Districts previously regarded as locks for one party or the other suddenly saw tight contests between Democrats and Republicans, many of whom appended extra adjectives to their party labels—"People's Democrat," "American Republican," and the like. That fall, the Senate saw an unusual level of turnover, with 8 incumbents defeated and 5 open seats flipping parties. But a veritable tsunami swept over the House, where a shocking 78 House incumbents were defeated. Coupled with 64 retirements, roughly a third of the House members were freshmen in the next session. Strikingly, unlike a typical wave election where one party gains, there were dozens of unexpected switches in both directions.*

*On January 3, 2027, the members of the new 120th Congress convened, and they began their congressional careers with a bang. Rather than re-electing Speaker of the House Jeffries (D-NY),[2] as their December caucus vote bound them to do,[3] 53 Democrats broke away. No member received a majority on that first ballot, and pandemonium broke out. Only on the ninth vote did a bipartisan majority coalesce around the "True Democrat" freshman, Rep. W___ (D-AZ). Stunning the pro-immigrant Democratic establishment, a "Real Nationer" now had control of the House.*

*Joining Henry Clay and William Pennington as a freshman-elected Speaker, W___ presided over a dramatic shift in the chamber's operation, enacted partly through a dramatically altered Rules package. To gain support from members of both parties, W___ pledged to fight for committee chairs who reflected her coalition's priorities on immigration and mostly prevailed in tense Democratic Steering Committee struggles. She then committed to granting significant independence to committee chairs, polled the membership of the whole House before making appointments to the Rules Committee, and pledged that all reported legislation on immigration would receive extensive floor debates with open rules. Democrats would keep control of the chamber, but anti-immigration forces were clearly emboldened.*

*The Great Immigration Debate of '27 that followed will be forever marked as the beginning of a new era for Congress. Discussing its many ins and outs is beyond the scope of this reflection, but what distinguished it most of all is that nobody really had any idea where it would end up. Congress engaged the leading issue of the day, and members' votes actually stood in the balance as debate proceeded. As members turned their attention toward their colleagues, instances of successful persuasion proliferated. Representatives were listening to each other ahead of taking many "hard votes"—hard because the issues were hard, and the certainty of incumbency advantage seemed to have evaporated. After four months of sometimes agonizing proceedings, the fractured House managed to frame a compromise with surprisingly broad appeal; funding to complete the southern border wall helped bring many Republicans along.*

*The Senate had been deeply affected by the results of the '26 elections but, naturally, it was much less transformed than the House. Senators conducted their own debate, with new members vocally denouncing the majority leader's attempts to confine votes to a few narrow alternatives. Their bipartisan filibuster, combined with a coordinated effort to grind all of the chamber's confirmation activity to a halt, attracted the whole nation's attention like no debate since the Civil Rights Act of 1964. Finally, after months of negotiations and surprisingly memorable floor speeches, a compromise found its way to 60 votes. An old-fashioned conference committee went to work in search of a deal that could command both House and Senate majorities—followed by a narrow Senate defeat of cloture, then the dramatic revival and passage of a slightly amended version, followed finally by House acceptance. The final law was an incongruous, but nevertheless somehow inspiring, product of broad coalition building. It featured an ambitious and creative, if strictly capped, refugee resettlement program that forced "Welcomer" regions of the country to directly bear the costs of supporting so many new Americans; a denial of access to many federal welfare programs, not just for the new refugees but for previously settled immigrants; official "amnesty" for some long-time* residents, provided they paid steep fines; and, of course, funding to complete the southern border wall.

Once this immigration debate had so thoroughly disrupted Congress' previous arrangements, wide-ranging and unpredictable debates broke out on a whole host of other issues previously kept off the agenda. Speaker W_ __ delighted in personally presiding over raucous, fiery displays of oratory from both sides. As the two parties' grips on their members loosened, well-organized blocs proliferated, which facilitated negotiations in the new, sometimes confusing fray. After much cross-partisan coalition building, we have seen landmark laws addressing antitrust, the power of Big Tech firms, trade, and protections for religious communities. The coalitions supporting passage of these bills varied considerably, and a sense of fluidity has returned to American politics.

On both extremes of the political spectrum, loud voices denounce these compromises as corrupt, and anti-system conspiracy theories continue to attract millions of followers online. But, thankfully, the overwhelming majority of Americans have dismissed those who devote themselves to these groups as fantasists, disconnected from the reality of our newly vital politics.

Re-energized by their successes in working through some of the country's most difficult issues, Congress has come to take itself more seriously and invest accordingly. As both chambers have cultivated their once again powerful committee systems, they have invested deeply in those committees' staff, bringing a surprising number of world-class experts in with new residency programs and generally making it more realistic for young people to build full careers on Capitol Hill. Congress also created two new support agencies in the 2030s: the Congressional Regulation Office, designed to help legislators frame reforms of existing regulatory programs in light of evidence about their real-world policy impacts,[4] and the Congressional Artificial Intelligence Lab, which seeks to develop innovative artificial intelligence–based tools to make legislative policymaking more sensitive to knowledge widely dispersed throughout electronic sources.

With the Congressional Budget Act of 2033, Congress took another crack at getting its arms around the country's daunting fiscal challenges. By turning the budget committees into convenings of other committee chairs, carefully delineating what kinds of changes can be made through the budget process, and guaranteeing votes on their budgets, the new law has given us reason to be hopeful that the spirit of coalition building now at work can help avoid a crack-up over inevitably painful questions about health care entitlements.

*Of course, Congress' revitalization has not made it wildly popular—its ap-*
*proval rating has never broken 45 percent in recent years, and it boasts plenty*
*of easily mocked characters. But if they do not universally love their legisla-*
*ture, all kinds of Americans generally do have the sense that their people are*
*mixing it up in Congress, where the action is. We can only hope that Congress*
*continually earns that reputation as it works through the country's next*
*250 years.*

## Making Factional Struggle Fertile

Is this scenario a form of escapism? If a volcanic eruption or some other *deus ex machina* is required, can we really believe that a dramatic reordering of political alliances is in the offing?

There are plenty of reasons for skepticism. In this case, though, history should be a source of hope. Insurgent coalitions have toppled towering leaders and broken the hold of stifling orthodoxies in the past. For years, "Boss" Cannon and his Republican majority seemed every bit as invincible as our own set of tenacious leaders and the evenly matched duopoly over which they preside. But the unity of his own party decayed, leading to his dramatic overthrow in 1910. The pendulum of congressional organization has reversed course before, and there is no reason to believe it cannot do so again.

That is easy enough to say, but perhaps a Madisonian competition of interests has somehow become outmoded in our nationalized, polarized age? If Americans really have become sortable into two big partisan camps, bitterly hating each other, then prospects are grim. But, given that a plurality of American voters registers as political independents—and given a commonsense look at the continuing complicated diversity of our population—we ought to reject that possibility without too much consternation.[5]

Getting from our present malaise to a Congress of free-flowing factional negotiations will nevertheless take a great deal of work, and perhaps also the intervention of fortune. In the scenario I have sketched out, a desperate sense of crisis calls forth organizations that operate perpendicular to the existing parties, opening the door to a successful comprehensive immigration reform package and then to action in many other areas. A shock snaps legislators out of their sense that partisan loyalties trump all others, which makes them appreciate the benefits of embracing openness.

Of course, I may have the issue all wrong—perhaps by this point immigration issues are not so cross-cutting as they were even a decade ago. Change could also come about through a years-long development of a new coalition, rather than a rapid reconfiguration. Sens. Elizabeth Warren (D-MA) and Josh Hawley (R-MO) sound remarkably similar when they talk about the menace of the nation's big tech companies, and they both admire Teddy Roosevelt, to boot. Perhaps they could put aside their (many!) differences to build up a Bull Moose Against FAANG Coalition, and perhaps the cross-partisan connections they develop would force the issue onto the agenda even over the objections of congressional leaders.[6]

In recent years, both parties' extremes have had real successes organizing as blocs, including the Progressive Caucus and Freedom Caucus. Another live possibility is that more moderate factions in each party will tire of being outmaneuvered by intraparty rivals and cultivate their own factional organizations. As Steve Teles and Robert Saldin have argued, "Moderates will have new opportunities to carve footholds within the party system and shape the country's future," if they embrace the need for disciplined cooperation.[7] If moderates can build their own distinctive "brands," they will also be in a good position to bring meaningful partisan competition to the "dark red" and "dark blue" districts that seem beyond one or the other party's control right now. Massachusetts and Maryland have had Republican governors for long stretches now, but there is not yet a good model for running competitive Republican congressional candidates in those states. Advertising oneself as belonging to a well-established moderate subgroup, like the now-dwindling Blue Dog Coalition, could alleviate this problem and thereby expand political competition to more regions.[8]

Of course, if such bloc building can unlock our politics, we must ask why it has not already occurred (or why the organizing we have now has not shaken things loose). Teles and Saldin suggest that the absence of well-organized moderates is the key factor; moderates often fail to organize because they believe they have the "broader public . . . already on their side," such that they should naturally win out.[9] At the same time, many potential backers of such organizing are distracted by efforts to promote generic bipartisanship, or even by quixotic efforts to build a viable third party, a cause that has consistently proven fruitless in the context of modern campaign rules. It may take something disorienting—an eruption of some sort, if not like the one in the scenario—to force a new dynamic.

## Do We Need Structural Reform?

It is also possible, of course, that the pressures toward conformity in each party are simply too strong in the modern era for any kind of intraparty differentiation to swing the pendulum. Do our legislative bodies then need stronger medicine if they are to return to vitality? Must we fundamentally reshape our political processes or institutions to succeed in reviving representation in Congress?

Political scientist Lee Drutman argues a revival of meaningful factional struggle is impossible under the crushing weight of today's duopolistic arrangements, so that America's only hope for a healthier politics is a shift to proportional representation, which would give smaller parties a real chance to win seats in Congress.[10] That vision could be at least partially realized through statutory electoral reform. By amending the Uniform Congressional District Act of 1967, which requires all House members to win office through single-winner elections, Congress could open the door to multimember districts. If a district has five seats to allocate, a party winning 20 percent of the vote would win one of them. Such opportunities to win seats even without commanding local majorities might facilitate the emergence of brand-new third parties (especially if ranked-choice voting rules were also adopted), but it would also allow the two dominant parties to break apart into factions. They might provisionally reunite to elect a Speaker, but nobody would mistake them for a monolithic force. Their plurality would enable a much more free-flowing politics to evolve, which would consequently enliven Senate politics even absent a change in the manner of electing senators.

To realize this vision, a broad-based reform movement would need to take hold, putting intense pressure on politicians of both parties to re-engineer America's electoral institutions. As a citizen frustrated with the choices offered by our current politics, I am enthusiastic about making such an experiment and recommend that my fellow citizens get on board. As an observer of American politics, I will not be holding my breath. Even if they are frustrated by our current political system, Americans seem more comfortable complaining about the status quo than overhauling it.

Reformers also sometimes suggest a radical expansion of the House of Representatives. As the "rubber stamp" scenario in Chapter 10 suggests (following Madison's Federalist No. 58), a truly enormous body would, almost necessarily, be dominated by strong central leaders and struggle with complicated negotiations between factions. As Madison pointed out, as it grows larger, at some point an assembly starts looking like a mob.

Nevertheless, expanding the House more modestly might be salutary. A recent report published by the American Academy of Arts and Sciences recommends increasing the House to 585 seats, with further expansion to track population growth after each census.[11] A change of that magnitude would not make representatives utter strangers to each other, and the influx of new members might conceivably give the institution just the sort of shot in the arm it needs.

Plenty of other attractive reform ideas exist that might help representation flourish. I am a skeptic that "money in politics" is as poisonous as many reformers seem to believe, but it is true that in both the House and the Senate—and even in races for state and local offices—fundraising has become an increasingly nationalized function.[12] That encourages legislators to cultivate donors across the country rather than focusing on their local constituencies. To counteract that distorting dynamic, as Michael Malbin argues, we ought to consider proposals that would effectively magnify the influence of small local donors.[13] Others point to small primary electorates, dominated by the ideologically extreme, as a major distortionary force in our politics and recommend shifting to nonpartisan primaries combined with ranked-choice voting to shake things up, as Alaska has recently done.[14] That too seems well worth trying.

Unfortunately, focusing attention on structural reforms may cause our representatives in Congress to feel that change is beyond their power. They may excuse their complacent acceptance of the status quo by pointing to the persistence of our institutions, as if that is all to be said about the matter. We should not let them so easily duck responsibility.

## Rediscovering Regular Order and Committees

As this book makes clear, our current electoral institutions are consistent with a huge variety of arrangements in congressional organization. Congress may seem stuck with dominant leadership and restricted debate, but in fact members must continually reaffirm these choices in order for them to hold. Simply put: members can demand that their chambers function differently.

That case is especially easy to make for the Senate, in which nothing prevents an individual senator from effectively grinding the chamber's business to a halt by preventing the adoption of unanimous consent agreements that structure proceedings. Forcing the Senate to operate by its formal rules is a rarity, but it is a choice available to senators just about any time. Especially if a handful of senators banded together to ensure continuous floor presence, they could effectively decide to make the Senate operate very differently from what its leaders might try to negotiate, including affording many more opportunities for amendment activity.[15] Tight control and limited debate is a choice, not a property of the institution or its formal rules, which indeed often facilitate unlimited debate.

Of course, a small group could not do away with the most reviled aspect of Senate procedure, the legislative filibuster. To take that most momentous nuclear option, a solid majority willing to overrule the chamber's precedents would be needed. Democrats mustered 48 votes in favor for using the maneuver to pass their voting rights bill in 2021, but not 50.

Should we be rooting for the filibuster's ultimate demise? As Chapter 3 and this chapter's scenario both make clear, a "real" filibuster has the power to focus the nation's attention on a political problem like almost nothing else. By forcing the Senate to put every other priority on hold, filibustering legislators can reveal the intensity of their constituents' preferences on an issue, and there is something wonderful about making their physical ability to sustain debate on the Senate floor the test of their mettle.

But ever since Democrats moved filibusters onto a "dual tracking" system in the 1970s, we have not seen filibusters that look anything like this. Today, "the filibuster" is simply a floating expectation that 60 votes are required to invoke cloture and move legislation. This supermajority requirement has some benefits. As Chapter 6 explained, forcing through important legislation on narrow, party-line votes invites continuing policy dysfunction. A need to assemble a broad coalition sometimes leads to bipartisan cooperation where none might otherwise have taken place, as with the ambitious Infrastructure and Jobs Act of 2021. But all of this is routine rather than focusing, and there are plenty of matters for which a 60-vote threshold seems too high—where the ability to decide expeditiously is more important than the assembling of a broad coalition. When we think about filibuster reform, then, we should appreciate the force of the majoritarian position, but that should not be the end of the discussion; instead, we should wish to rehabilitate the practice as one that can force us to come to terms with some of our most divisive issues.

Much more important than the filibuster is the question of "regular order" in both chambers. The exact meaning of this phrase is contested, but its essence is clear: bills should be worked through committees and extensively debated on the floor, such that many members have a chance to contribute to a bill's final form and many combinations of ideas can be considered before moving to a final vote. If most back-bench members feel they are basically irrelevant in today's Congress, it is because regular order has disappeared; there is no guarantee that committee work will feed into final bills that actually get considered, and there are few chances to amend bills on their way to passage.

There are a great many ways to rehabilitate regular order and the committees that make it work; the particulars are less important than members' determination. But, as the scenario suggests, one of the most promising ways is to broaden the process for selecting chairs, lessening their dependence on party leadership.[16] This could be especially important in the case of the House Rules Committee, which, under the Speaker's thumb, exercises so much power to shape the agenda. If Rules became a rival power center, coalitions would have an avenue to bypass recalcitrant Speakers.[17] Another promising rules change is to allow committees to force floor consideration of a bill they passed, perhaps triggered by supermajority support of the committee's members. Or, to take the opposite tack, the rules could make it in order to table bills that had not been reported by a committee with the support of some minority of the chamber. That would make it harder for leaders to work up their own legislation bypassing the committee system.

For my purposes, it is not necessary to settle on any one of these reform alternatives. Members themselves are in a better position to judge which rules changes might win support. The main thing is that they decide to decentralize power. They can't win if they don't play.

## Focusing on the Biggest Things, Not Everything

In envisioning a revived Congress, it is worth saying something about what legislators should aspire to do, as well as the processes of deliberation on which they will rely. One of James Burnham's final words of counsel for Congress was that it must find a way to concentrate on essentials. If it is to continue to be a partner and peer within the central government, then its principal energies must go to deciding major issues of policy, not to the critique of details.[18]

This recommendation is at odds with the prescriptions of many conservative critics of the administrative state. They suggest that American government can only be made legitimate if Congress decides nearly every question of policy for the federal government—in other words, if we entirely curtail delegation to the executive to underline that all responsibility remains with the legislature.[19] Burnham sensed that, given the size and scope of the modern federal government *as he wrote in 1959*, asking generalist legislators to shoulder the burden of making every decision was simply a fantasy. The situation is much starker today. The truth is, lawmakers have neither the will nor the ability to take on that role—they cannot be quite that "responsible." Indeed, to the extent that Congress can load-shed truly minor issues, it should do so, even if it means legislators miss out on a few small opportunities for endearing themselves to constituents. Post office namings really should not involve legislators at all.

What legislators can and should do is demand that the nation's most pressing issues run through them. As we saw in Chapters 6, 7, and 8, presidents and executive branch agencies have become adept at finding ways to launch ambitious policy initiatives without congressional action, including on plenty of matters that make front-page news. At this point, even legislators themselves take this pattern for granted, and they end up acting as advocates for executive actions rather than seeking compromises that could survive the legislative process. But, as we have seen, this is a pathological form of policymaking, one that almost ensures the resulting decisions will be tied up for years in litigation. At best, if they survive in the courts, they are often reversed at the first opportunity when the White House changes control.

Legislators need to recognize how harmful this pattern is and reverse it. Republicans made an attempt in the early 2010s, when they passed the Regulations in the Executive In Need of Scrutiny (REINS) Act out of the House on several occasions. That law would have turned all economically significant rulemakings into legislative proposals requiring an up-or-down vote in Congress. Nearly all Democrats dismissed REINS as an anti-regulatory assault, and it is fair to ask whether there is presently any support in their party for subjecting executive branch agencies to greater legislative control. But REINS would have imposed a serious burden on Congress, since many dozens of qualifying regulations are promulgated each year. A similar proposal could be much more attractive if it required Congress to weigh in on the 10 most important rules each year. More broadly, Congress should reflect back on its experiences with legislative vetoes and think about constitutional ways of reconstructing them, possibly requiring that some presidential (or agency) actions receive congressional approval if they are to become permanent.[20] Again, legislators should be seeking responsibility on major decisions, rather than indiscriminately multiplying their opportunities to intervene in less important administrative matters.

## Congress and Self-Government

What will we gain if our legislators collectively heal their institution?

First is a negative power. "The revival of congressional power, if it ever does come about, will be outwardly and unmistakably marked for the nation by a shattering congressional No," Burnham prophesied.[21] Members of Congress can, if they so choose, insist that Congress act as an institution that squarely addresses differences, rather than papering them over. If they are unsatisfied, they can sink the program of any president who believes he is above such distractions as the politics of a diverse nation. That strikes many people as a nuisance, but it is one of the greatest treasures of our political inheritance.

Second, and even more important, is a positive power. It is through Congress' deliberations that we come to feel that the country's future is *ours*. Our fundamental human sense of fairness makes us fearful that those who know what we do not and who have the power to make the rules will do so in their own interests rather than in ours, precisely because we do not know enough to hold them accountable. The danger is that we, the people, come to believe that they, the government, do not act as we would because they see the world in some entirely different way from how we do. When the government fails, as its humanity makes inevitable, it needs the trust and loyalty of the people to weather the difficulties.

If *they* are not *us*, if we come to think of government as an alien oppressor, we cannot help but begin to hope for their incompetence. Tocqueville put this point eloquently:

> It is doubtless important to the good of nations that those who govern have virtues or talents; but what is perhaps still more important to them

is that those who govern do not have interests contrary to the mass of the governed; for in that case the virtues could become almost useless and the talents fatal.[22]

Self-government in the modern sense means that when we look at the men and women who make the big decisions about our country's future, we think: *these people are us*. It is much easier to think that about elected officials, whose primary qualification is that we have chosen them—but the power of the sentiment does not come from believing that each member of our legislature is faithfully communicating their constituents' preferences, delegate style. Instead, we judge representativeness more broadly; we want assurance that our own concerns are shared by some of the people in power, but most of us also genuinely wish to see an assembly that includes all of the most important of the diverse elements in our society, taking each of their concerns seriously. This is something very different than wishing for majorities to work their will. Blunt majority rule is about domesticating brute political force into a somewhat gentler form; but effective representative government reveals to us which of our interests can be joined together to support shared public endeavors and which cannot.

The self-government that representative government can deliver is likely to disappoint many people. It is not a path to a sense of personal political efficacy for all; there are too many of us for that. It is not even a bold commitment to having the people's representatives make most of the decisions; there are too many decisions to be made, so delegation to the much larger executive branch is inevitable.

But a vital Congress is a realization of political freedom worth having. It is a bulwark against tyranny. It is the only way we know to make our extended republic thrive. That is why Congress.

# Postscript

## An Open Letter to America's Legislators

I write as a scholar of your proud institution and its place in our nation's constitutional system, who wishes to remind you of something you already know: Right now, to our nation's great detriment, Congress is on its way to obsolescence.

This is a humble plea directed at you—yes, you. You need to do something different if you want your chamber to punch at its constitutional weight. You need to think differently about the body you are part of and about the responsibility that comes with the privilege of holding your office.

If you imagine yourself as a loyal soldier for your party, that isn't enough. If you think breaking with your party leaders on some votes makes you a maverick, that isn't enough. You owe your constituents more than your hard work, more than your determination to show up and vote the right way. You have an obligation to engage in *politics*.

Even though you have chosen this vocation, the word itself may still repel you. Members of Congress are wont to denounce actions they do not like as "just part of a political agenda."[1] Is that really such a forceful accusation to level against US representatives or senators? Aren't you supposed to have a political agenda? Still, we all know what the phrase means. "Political" means flattering your supporters' assumptions, belaboring your side's talking points to make the other side look bad, rather than working to get things done.

Politics can be that, of course. But it can also be a form of realism. As the great public commentator Walter Lippmann put it almost a century ago, the best politicians "penetrate from the naïve self-interest of each group to its permanent and real interest," that which can be harmonized with the needs of society's other groups. "What you think you want is this. What is possible for you to get is that. What you really want, therefore, is the following."[2] He called that "statesmanship," but we shouldn't need such a fancy word. Politics is the art of the possible.

You sit in Congress because you represent your district's voters, well enough at least that they elected you. But for Congress to maintain its credibility as a representative institution, it needs to do more than contain multitudes. It needs to put America's many factions into motion, let them poke and prod and appease and accommodate each other, to collectively find our way forward on the biggest issues of our time. The interests you represent must be made to confront each other, face to face, sharing their deepest concerns and most intensely desired aspirations. If you practice politics correctly, these encounters will generate new ways of understanding our country's challenges, new ways for citizens and government to relate to each other, new ways to turn our country's collective might toward pursuit of a more perfect union. Your ultimate accountability to the voters is bedrock, but it is by arguing and deciding together with your peers that you provide the focal point of our political freedom.

That is the aspiration. The reality, of course, is more often sterile. You and your fellow legislators are stuck in a terrible equilibrium, where you have surrendered most of the really important decisions to the executive branch or judiciary. That means the most important thing Congress does today is confirm the president's nominees to federal agencies, commissions, and the judiciary. That, in turn, means that the most important thing you can do is play your small part in helping your party win the next election, so that it will be your team deciding who occupies those positions of real power. So you make the phone calls and shake the hands to raise the money for the campaigns, not just your own but across the country. You exercise the message discipline needed to excite your party's base voters without putting off those rare persuadable swing voters. When your leaders tell you not to muddy the waters by collaborating with those on the other side, you mostly listen. When they tell you that now is not the time to take up big and confusing questions, not with the election hanging in the balance, you don't object.

Your leaders aren't crazy or obviously wrong for thinking this way. You aren't crazy or obviously wrong if you listen to them. For that matter, you probably can appreciate that members across the aisle aren't crazy to think much the same.

Reasonable as it might be, this way of thinking is destroying the vitality of your institution. And, hard as it might be to step out of today's news cycle and look history in the face, if you can do it, you will realize that the next election is just not that important compared to having a representative government that is something more than an ornament to bureaucratic decisions and presidential decrees.

So we need you to get out of your partisan trenches and make things happen. Now. Not "after this election, which *really is* so important." The next election will always seem so important. Meanwhile, Congress has dithered as massive challenges have gathered. Immigration. Stagnant productivity and real wages. The disintegration of so many of our communities, and the decay of our schools.

Your leaders will tell you that if you want to see Congress make progress on these issues, you must trust in their ability to control the agenda. They say that your respective chambers will devolve into chaos if given over to open debate—that you and your copartisans are ready to be constructive representatives, but they, on the other side, just want to jam you up with "political" amendments.

They're surely right that your political adversaries want to force you to take hard votes, ones that will anger some of your constituents no matter what you do. Honestly, though, that shouldn't sound so frightening. You'll probably win your next election anyway. And we need you to take some hard votes because there are hard issues that have to get decided. When Congress shirks those decisions, they get made elsewhere, by people who aren't charged with being the people's representatives. That may feel like a relief, but it is poisonous to our nation's ability to collectively work through our problems.

Breaking out of the institutional straitjackets that have constrained and belittled both chambers on Capitol Hill will require you to take some real risks. It will require uniting some rank-and-file members committed to breaking the hold of leaders in the face of their vindictive retaliation.

But you aren't the first representatives to find yourselves in this spot. Speaker Joseph Cannon seemed all but invincible in the first decade of the 20th century, personally chairing the Rules Committee and using it to enforce a strict party line. He was the undisputed "Boss"—until he wasn't. Led by Rep. George Norris, 42 members of his party conspired to overthrow him, joining with their partisan rivals to break open the House agenda and pursue policies they believed were ultimately more important than the next election. The particulars of their parliamentary maneuvering are not so important—if you and your colleagues have a willingness to organize in pursuit of common interests, and to push forward to action, you will find a way.

The choice, and the responsibility for deciding what kind of institution Congress will be, really is *yours*. Small hordes of well-meaning outsiders hope to push congressional reform along, but giving them (us!) polite hearings doesn't change anything. Some of the ambitious and talented staffers employed in your offices harbor visions of a livelier politics, but it isn't up to them either. And much as we like to think that a commitment to self-government means that the American people have the ultimate say over all this, we shouldn't kid ourselves. The public has a great many unfulfilled substantive demands, but there is not going to be a groundswell of grassroots energy around the health of our legislature. The American people can get used to a Congress that doesn't work. To an alarming extent, they already have.

You might agree with all of this in the abstract—but then think it just isn't your problem. You've got the phone calls to make, the floor votes to take, the dollars to raise, the meetings to attend. You've got plans to ascend to a position of real power—maybe in the executive branch, maybe as the president of some NGO, maybe as an appropriations subcommittee chair someday. And maybe that will all work out.

But if Congress is going to become the sort of institution that a free American people needs it to be, someone will have to reject that kind of reasonableness. Someone will have to stick their neck out. Easy for me to say, I know! Nevertheless, there it is. We put our hope in you.

# Acknowledgments

This book has been years in the making and I have acquired many debts. My former institutional homes, the Brookings Institution and the R Street Institute, provided me excellent opportunities to develop ideas in this book. The C. Boyden Gray Center for the Administrative State at Scalia Law School invited me to write for a roundtable on the subject of Congress and the administrative state, which led to a paper that became the basis of Chapter 5.

The American Enterprise Institute (AEI), which I rejoined in September 2020, has offered an ideal environment to debate and refine my ideas and has been incredibly supportive of my book writing. I feel extremely fortunate to be included in the excellent group of scholars Yuval Levin has brought together under the auspices of the Social, Cultural, and Constitutional Studies program, and even more fortunate to be working for someone as sympathetic and clear-eyed as Yuval.

James Wallner first introduced me to the basic argument contained Chapter 3 and taught me a great deal else about the purpose and potential of a Madisonian Congress. Kevin Kosar steered me toward a deeper engagement with Congress and taught me a great deal about Capitol Hill—to say nothing of Potomac shad.

Many friends and colleagues read and commented on versions of the manuscript: Doug Arnold, Tyler Cowen, Matt Green, Vera Krimnus, Yuval Levin, Michael Malbin, Shep Melnick, Joe Postell, Jeremy Rabkin, Connor Raso, Molly Reynolds, Gary Schmitt, Daniel Stid, Adam White, Thomas Chatterton Williams, and Will Wilson. I am especially indebted to Sarah Binder, Lee Drutman, Matt Glassman, and Kevin Kosar for steering me early on in my writing. I also thank two anonymous reviewers for their constructive criticism and encouragement. An AEI roundtable discussing the future scenarios also yielded excellent advice from Joel Alicea, Karlyn Bowman, Tim Carney, Kevin Kosar, Yuval Levin, Nicole Penn, Jeff Rosen, Gary Schmitt, and Chris Stirewalt. My friends Ben Kay and Justus Myers have been invaluable sounding boards.

I am grateful to Steve Teles for helping plan and launch this book. At Oxford University Press, Dave McBride and his team have smoothly guided me through the publication process.

AEI has also given me the privilege of putting many excellent young people to work on this book. Interns Matt Malec, Lily Kincannon, Sanseong Yang, Sophie Callcott, and Matt Cochis provided research and editing help beyond their years. Mikael Good offered invaluable research assistance, especially on the meaning and history of representation. J. R. Roach has provided most of the project's organizational glue. More importantly, he has been a true intellectual partner throughout, and this would be a much lesser book without his contributions.

Finally, I thank my family, and especially my wife, Vera Krimnus, for everything. I could not begin to say enough.

# Notes

## Introduction

1. This is a fairly common slur against members of the House. For an exposition of its meaning by Rep. David Jolly (R-FL), see Norah O'Donnell, "Are Members of Congress Becoming Telemarketers?," *CBS News*, April 24, 2016, https://www.cbsnews.com/news/60-minutes-are-members-of-congress-becoming-telemarketers/.
2. Irving Kristol, "American Historians and the Democratic Idea," *American Scholar* 39, no. 1 (1969): 89–104, 91.
3. Reproduced in William Henry Smith, *Speakers of the House of Representatives of the United States* (Baltimore, MD: S. J. Gaeng, 1928), 261.

## Chapter 1

1. Woodrow Wilson, *Congressional Government: A Study in American Politics* (Boston: Houghton, Mifflin, 1885), 93.
2. Speech delivered in the Senate, May 7, 1834, reproduced in *The Works of Daniel Webster*, vol. 4 (Boston: Charles C. Little and James Brown, 1851), 122.
3. Jorge Luis Borges, "On Exactitude in Science," in Jorge Luis Borges, *Collected Fictions* (trans. Andrew Hurley) (New York: Penguin Books, 1998), 325.
4. From Aristotle, *The Politics of Aristotle*, ed. Sir Ernest Barker (Oxford: Clarendon Press, 1946), 51; quoted in Bernard R. Crick, *In Defence of Politics* (London: Weidenfeld & Nicolson, 1992), 17.
5. Kenneth A. Shepsle, "Congress Is a 'They,' Not an 'It': Legislative Intent as Oxymoron," *International Review of Law and Economics* 12, no. 2 (June 1, 1992): 239–56.
6. Hanna Pitkin, *The Concept of Representation* (Berkeley: University of California Press, 1967), 8–9.
7. Ibid., 83.
8. Robert A. Dahl, *On Democracy* (New Haven, CT: Yale University Press, 1998), 23–25, 103–5.
9. Marc Morris, *A Great and Terrible King: Edward I and the Forging of Britain* (New York: Pegasus Books, 2016).
10. Joseph R. Strayer, *On the Medieval Origins of the Modern State* (Princeton, NJ: Princeton University Press, 1970), 44.
11. Alfred Frederick Pollard, *The Evolution of Parliament*, 2nd ed. (London: Longmans, Green & Co., 1926), 120.

12. Winston S. Churchill, *A History of the English-Speaking Peoples*, vol. 1 (London: Bantam Books, 1958), 288.

13. Pollard, *The Evolution of Parliament*, 133.

14. Ibid., 160–61.

15. Ibid., 135.

16. For a helpful discussion, see "A Medieval Parliament (Part 1): Dropping the Writs," Order of the Coif, November 6, 2018, https://orderofthecoif.wordpress.com/2018/11/06/a-medieval-parliament-part-1-dropping-the-writs/.

17. James Conniff, "Burke, Bristol, and the Concept of Representation," *Western Political Quarterly* 30, no. 3 (1977): 329–41, 338–39; Also see Edmund Burke, *Edmund Burke's Speech on Conciliation with America*, ed. Albert S. Cook (New York: Longmans, Green, and Co., 1906), 51, https://books.google.com/books?id=tuk9lTzkTiMC&newbks=0&vq=electric+force&source=gbs_navlinks_s.

18. Crick, *In Defense of Politics*, 31.

19. Michael Zuckert, "Natural Rights and Imperial Constitutionalism: The American Revolution and the Development of the American Amalgam," *Social Philosophy and Policy* 22, no. 1 (January 1, 2005): 27–55, 42–44.

20. James Wilson, "Considerations on the Nature and Extent of the Legislative Authority of the British Parliament," in *Collected Works of James Wilson,* vol. 1, ed. Kermit L. Hall and Mark David Hall (Indianapolis: Liberty Fund, 2007), 5.

21. Forrest McDonald, *E pluribus unum* (Boston: Houghton Mifflin, 1965).

22. Ibid., 218.

23. James Madison, "Federalist No. 63," in *The Federalist Papers*, ed. George W. Carey and James McClellan (Indianapolis: Liberty Fund, 2001), 325–31.

24. Noah Webster, "An Examination into the Leading Principles of the Federal Constitution," in *Pamphlets on the Constitution of the United States*, ed. Paul Leicester Ford (Brooklyn, 1888), 25, 31.

25. James Madison, "Federalist No. 14," in *The Federalist Papers*, 62–67.

26. James Madison, "Federalist No. 10," in *The Federalist Papers*, 42–48.

27. James Madison, "Federalist No. 58," in *The Federalist Papers*, 300–304.

28. Richard Henry Lee, "Letters of a Federal Farmer," in *Pamphlets on the Constitution of the United States*, 290.

29. George Mason, "The Objections of the Hon. George Mason to the proposed Federal Constitution. Addressed to the Citizens of Virginia," in *Pamphlets on the Constitution of the United States*, 329, 332.

30. David P. Currie, *The Constitution in Congress: The Federalist Period 1789–1801* (Chicago: University of Chicago Press, 1999), 116.

31. Ibid., 16.

32. Quoted in Fergus M. Bordewich, *The First Congress: How James Madison, George Washington, and a Group of Extraordinary Men Invented the Government* (New York: Simon and Schuster, 2017), 93.

33. Currie, *The Constitution in Congress*, 107–10.

34. Quoted in Jay Cost, *James Madison: America's First Politician* (New York: Basic Books, 2021), 211.

35. Ibid.

36. Quotations from ibid., 214.

37. Norman K. Risjord, "Partisanship and Power: House Committees and the Powers of the Speaker, 1789–1801," *William and Mary Quarterly* 49, no. 4 (1992): 628–51, 640.

38. Joanne B. Freeman, *Affairs of Honor: National Politics in the New Republic* (New Haven, CT: Yale University Press, 2002), 101.

39. James Parton, "The Quarrel of Jefferson and Hamilton," *The Atlantic*, March 1, 1873, https://www.theatlantic.com/magazine/archive/1873/03/the-quarrel-of-jefferson-and-hamilton/537411/.

40. George Washington, "Farewell Address," *Founders Online*, September 19, 1796, https://founders.archives.gov/documents/Washington/05-20-02-0440-0002.

41. Pietro S. Nivola, "How, Once Upon a Time, a Dogmatic Political Party Changed Its Tune," *Brookings*, November 14, 2012, http://www.brookings.edu/research/opinions/2012/11/14-war-1812-nivola; "What the War of 1812 Can Teach Us about the Fiscal Cliff Debate," *The Atlantic*, November 26, 2012, http://www.theatlantic.com/politics/archive/2012/11/what-thewar-of-1812-can-teach-us-about-the-fiscal-cliff-debate/265488.

42. Henry Adams, *Democracy: An American Novel* (New York: Penguin Classics, 2008), 90.

43. Ibid., 84.

44. Woodrow Wilson, *Congressional Government: A Study in American Politics* (Boston: Houghton, Mifflin, 1885), 324.

45. Ibid., 79.

46. Ibid., 82.

47. Ibid., 58.

48. Ibid., 326.

49. 10 Cong. Rec. 2661 (1880).

50. Robert V. Remini, *The House: The History of the House of Representatives* (New York: Smithsonian Books/Collins, 2007), 248–49.

51. Wilson, *Congressional Government*, x.

52. On the evolution of Wilson's position, see Daniel Stid, *The President as Statesmen: Woodrow Wilson and the Constitution* (Lawrence: University Press of Kansas, 1998), 6–26.

53. Woodrow Wilson, *Constitutional Government in the United States* (New York: Columbia University Press, 1908), 70; see also 68.

54. Ibid., 56.

55. Jeremy D. Bailey, *The Idea of Presidential Representation: An Intellectual and Political History* (Lawrence: University Press of Kansas, 2019).

56. Both quotes from Remini, *The House*, 269.

57. For related thoughts on the tradeoff between representativeness and efficiency, see Kenneth R. Mayer and David T. Canon, *The Dysfunctional Congress?* (Boulder, CO: Westview Press, 1999), 9, 27–30, 101.

58. William G. Howell and Terry M. Moe, *Relic: How Our Constitution Undermines Effective Government, and Why We Need a More Powerful Presidency* (New York: Basic Books, 2016), xv.

59. William G. Howell and Terry M. Moe, *Presidents, Populism, and the Crisis of Democracy* (Chicago: University of Chicago Press, 2020).

60. Douglas L. Kriner and Andrew Reeves, *The Particularistic President: Executive Branch Politics and Political Inequality* (Cambridge: Cambridge University Press, 2015).

61. Nadia Urbinati, *Representative Government: Principles and Genealogy* (Chicago: University of Chicago Press, 2006), 5.

62. David R. Mayhew, *The Imprint of Congress* (New Haven, CT: Yale University Press, 2017), 100.

63. John Dunn, *Interpreting Political Responsibility: Essays 1981–1989* (Princeton, NJ: Princeton University Press, 1990), 5.

64. Thucydides, *History of the Peloponnesian War*, Book II, 60. This translation is presented by Ronald Beiner, *Political Judgment* (London: Methuen, 1983), 83.

65. Bryan Garsten, *Saving Persuasion: A Defense of Rhetoric and Judgment* (Cambridge, MA: Harvard University Press, 2009), 3.

# Chapter 2

1. Quoted in Nancy Beck Young, *Why We Fight: Congress and the Politics of World War II* (Lawrence: University Press of Kansas, 2013), 17.

2. 72 Cong. Rec. 9644 (1932); quoted in Ira Katznelson, *Fear Itself: The New Deal and the Origins of Our Time* (New York: Liveright Publishing, 2013), 12.

3. Ibid., 8.

4. Ibid., 20.

5. Geoffrey Kabaservice, *The Guardians: Kingman Brewster, His Circle, and the Rise of the Liberal Establishment* (New York: Henry Holt and Co., 2004), 69–83, 79.

6. Quoted in Mariano-Florentino Cuellar, "Administrative War," *George Washington Law Review* 82 (2014): 1343–445, 1360.

7. See J. Garry Clifford and Samuel R. Spencer Jr., *The First Peacetime Draft* (Lawrence: University Press of Kansas, 1986).

8. Mark R. Wilson, *Destructive Creation: American Business and the Winning of World War II* (Philadelphia: University of Pennsylvania Press, 2016), 131.

9. Richard Overy, *Why the Allies Won* (New York: W. W. Norton & Company, 1995), 290.

10. John Morton Blum, *V Was for Victory* (New York: Harcourt Brace Jovanovich, 1976), 16.

11. Richard R. Lingeman, *Don't You Know There's a War On? The American Home Front, 1941–1945* (New York: Capricorn Books, 1970), 94, 97, 162, 260–61.

12. Mark H. Leff, "The Politics of Sacrifice on the American Home Front in World War II," *Journal of American History* 77, no. 4 (1991): 1296–318, 1297.

13. Beck Young, *Why We Fight*, 23.

14. Overy, *Why the Allies Won*, 191.

15. Ibid., 254.

16. Carolyn C. Jones, "Class Tax to Mass Tax: The Role of Propaganda in the Expansion of the Income Tax during World War II," *Buffalo Law Review* 37 (1988): 685–737, 693.

17. My discussion of tax policy changes relies heavily on John F. Witte, *The Politics and Development of the Federal Income Tax* (Madison: University of Wisconsin Press, 1985).

18. Leff, "The Politics of Sacrifice," 1299–301.

19. Richard Polenberg, *War and Society: The United States, 1941–1945* (Westport, CT: Greenwood Press, 1980), 28. Notably, a young economist named Milton Friedman, then working at the Treasury Department, was instrumental in developing the technical details of withholding.

20. Polenberg, *War and Society*, 28.

21. Young, *Congressional Politics in the Second World War*, 136.

22. Witte, *The Politics and Development of the Federal Income Tax*, 121.

23. Quoted in Beck Young, *Why We Fight*, 96.

24. Statement of Rep. Eugene Cox (D-GA), 90 Cong. Rec. 1995 (1944).

25. Statement of Rep. Charles Dewey (R-IL), 90 Cong. Rec. 2005 (1944).

26. Quoted in Beck Young, *Why We Fight*, 96.

27. Ibid., 50, 96.

28. Statement of Sen. Alben Barkley (D-KY), 90 Cong. Rec. 1965 (1944).

29. Of those who paid income taxes in 1943, just 11 percent supported higher taxes in May 1943; National Opinion Research Center (NORC), NORC Survey 1943-0124: Inflation, Question 31, USNORC.430124.Q24A, NORC (Cornell University, Ithaca, NY: Roper Center for Public Opinion Research, 1943). Just 17 percent of poll respondents in June 1943 thought it would be reasonable to raise all of the president's revenue demands through increased taxes. Gallup Poll # 1943-0297: World War II/Cost of War, Question 11, USGALLUP.43-297.QKT06A (Roper Center, 1943).

30. Quoted in Beck Young, *Why We Fight*, 73.

31. Quoted in Katznelson, *Fear Itself*, 319.

32. Although this remark is sometimes cited as coming in 1947 on the floor of Congress, in fact Vandenberg delivered it as part of a speech in Mackinac, Michigan, on September 22, 1943; it was entered into the Congressional Record by Rep. Roy Woodruff (R-MI) on September 23, 1943, see 89 Cong. Rec. A3984 (1943).

33. Quoted in Blum, *V Was for Victory*, 27.

34. Quoted in ibid., 40.

35. Cornelius P. Cotter and J. Malcolm Smith, "Administrative Accountability to Congress: The Concurrent Resolution," *Western Political Quarterly* 9, no. 4 (1956): 955–66. The authors note that Congress never actually utilized one of these resolutions, and from this they conclude that they were not particularly effective as constraints. But such a conclusion is, at least, not obvious on the evidence provided; the possibility of congressional termination of a program must have cast a shadow over executive-congressional interactions.

36. Elias Huzar, "American Government and Politics: Congress and the Army: Appropriations," *American Political Science Review* 37, no. 4 (1943): 661–76, quotation at 668, transfer authorities discussed at 675.

37. David M. Levitan, "The Responsibility of Administrative Officials in a Democratic Society," *Political Science Quarterly* 61, no. 4 (1946): 562–98, 582.

38. For an explanation of how Congress sought to extend and refine this principle in the Legislative Reorganization Act of 1946 after the war, see David H. Rosenbloom, *Building a Legislative-Centered Public Administration* (Tuscaloosa: University of Alabama Press, 2000), chapter 3.

39. Blum, *V Was for Victory*, 244.

40. The continuity between the Select Committee's work and that of the Joint Committee on the Organization is not well documented in secondary literature. For its most important report in this regard, see "Seventh Intermediate Report of the Select Committee to Investigate Executive Agencies: Recommendations and Proposed Legislation to Improve the Organization of Congress," House Report, United States Congress Serial Set 10848 (Washington, DC: House of Representatives, November 20, 1944). In reflecting on the early experience under the Legislative Reorganization Act, its principal architect, George Galloway, chose to conclude his remarks with a reference to this report; George Galloway, "Hearings on the Evaluation of the Legislative Reorganization Act of 1946," Committee on Expenditures in the Executive Departments (February 18, 1948), 155. Also relevant is the testimony of Howard Smith, "Hearings before the Joint Committee on the Organization of Congress," March 28, 1945, 186–99. For early appreciation of the Select Committee's work, see Leonard D. White, "Congressional Control of the Public Service," *American Political Science Review* 39, no. 1 (1945): 1–11; Aaron L. Ford, "The Legislative Reorganization Act of 1946," *American Bar Association Journal* 32, no. 11 (1946): 741–809, at 741.

41. This discussion is informed by the definitive study of the committee, Donald H. Riddle, *The Truman Committee* (New Brunswick, NJ: Rutgers University Press, 1964).

42. Quoted in Leff, "The Politics of Sacrifice on the American Home Front in World War II," 1297.

43. Riddle, *The Truman Committee*, 38.

44. Roland Young, *Congressional Politics in the Second World War* (New York: Columbia University Press, 1956), 44–46.

45. Henry Wallace, "Where I Was Wrong," *Week Magazine*, September 7, 1952.

46. Blum, *V Was for Victory*, 282; Edward L. Schapsmeier and Frederick H. Schapsmeier, *Prophet in Politics: Henry A. Wallace and the War Years, 1940–1965* (Ames: Iowa State University Press, 1971), 27–29, 44–45.

47. Schapsmeier and Schapsmeier, *Prophet in Politics*, 65–71.

48. Ibid., 122–24.

49. Wilson, *Destructive Creation*, 197.

50. Blum, *V Was for Victory*, 232.

51. Wilson, *Destructive Creation*, 197.

52. 89 Cong. Rec. 2197 (1943).

53. Sen. John Rankin (D-MS) quoted in Beck Young, *Why We Fight*, 68.

54. Quoted in Ibid., 64.

55. Meg Jacobs, "'How about Some Meat?': The Office of Price Administration, Consumption Politics, and State Building from the Bottom Up, 1941–1946," *Journal of American History* 84, no. 3 (1997): 910–41, 918.

56. Franklin Roosevelt, "Message to Congress on Stabilizing the Economy," September 7, 1942, The American Presidency Project, https://www.presidency.ucsb.edu/docume nts/message-congress-stabilizing-the-economy.

57. Quotations from Beck Young, *Why We Fight*, 68.

58. Jacobs, "'How about Some Meat?,'" 937–40.

59. Franklin Roosevelt, State of the Union Address, (January 11, 1944, http://www.fdrlibr ary.marist.edu/archives/address_text.html.

60. Franklin Roosevelt, State of the Union Address, January 6, 1945, http://www.let.rug. nl/usa/presidents/franklin-delano-roosevelt/state-of-the-union-1945.php.

61. Young, *Congressional Politics in the Second World War*, 76–82; quotation from Senator O'Mahoney at 79.

62. 91 Cong. Rec. 2765 (1945).

63. Blum, *V Was for Victory*, 140.

64. Public opinion polling clearly demonstrates Americans' unease with organized labor during the war. For example, in 1942, half of respondents thought labor unions were not doing their utmost to help secure victory. Gallup Poll # 1942-0265: War Effort/ Taxes/1944 Presidential Election, Question 3, USGALLUP.041742.RK01B (Cornell University, Ithaca, NY: Roper Center for Public Opinion Research, 1942). A plurality thought that Roosevelt listened to labor leaders too much. Gallup Poll # 272, Question 36, USGALLUP.42-272.QT08B (Roper Center, 1942). A remarkable 85 percent thought strikes should be banned, and a similar number said they had lowered their opinion of unions. Gallup Poll # 1942-0276: Military Draft/Elections/Effects of the War/Movies, Question 6, USGALLUP.42-276.QKT05 (Roper Center, 1942), and Gallup Poll # 1943-0294: Peace Terms with Germany/War Effort/Labor Unions/ Presidential Election, Question 2, USGALLUP.051443.RK10B (Roper Center, 1943).

65. Young, *Congressional Politics in the Second World War*, 63–65; quotation from Bruce J. Dierenfield, *Keeper of the Rules: Congressman Howard W. Smith of Virginia* (Charlottesville: University of Virginia Press, 1987), 100. Congress had the support of 47 percent of poll respondents for its override, while the president was supported by just 31 percent. Office of Public Opinion Research, OPOR Poll # 1943-013: Roosevelt Survey # 13, Question 1, USOPOR.43-013.Q01 (Cornell University, Ithaca, NY: Roper Center for Public Opinion Research, 1943).

66. George Sirgiovanni, *An Undercurrent of Suspicion: Anti-Communism in America during World War II* (New Brunswick, NJ: Transaction Publishers, 1990), 62.

67. "Special Report on Subversive Activities Aimed at Destroying Our Representative Form of Government. 2 Pts. Doc. No. 2277," *U.S. Congressional Serial Set* 10664 (1942): 1–22, quotations at 2.

68. Sirgiovanni, *An Undercurrent of Suspicion*, 51–55, quotation at 55.

69. John Earl Haynes and Harvey Klehr, *In Denial: Historians, Communism & Espionage* (San Francisco: Encounter Books, 2005).

70. David Witwer, "The Racketeer Menace and Antiunionism in the Mid-Twentieth Century US," *International Labor and Working-Class History* 74 (Fall 2008), 124–47.

71. David R. Mayhew, "Wars and American Politics," *Perspectives on Politics* 3, no. 3 (2005): 473–93. Mayhew notes that scholars generally seem disappointed that Congress tends "to make use of industries rather than to confront them," 481.

72. Overy, *Why the Allies Won*, 68.

73. Ibid., 99.

74. Ibid., 185.

75. Calvin M. Longue and Dwight L. Fresley, eds., *Voice of Georgia: Speeches of Richard B. Russell: 1928–1969* (Macon, GA: Mercer University Press, 1997), 58.

76. Aaron Friedberg, *In the Shadow of the Garrison State: America's Anti-Statism and Its Cold War Grand Strategy* (Princeton, NJ: Princeton University Press, 2000). His succinct statement of his thesis is: "By preventing some of the worst, most stifling excesses of statism, these countervailing tendencies made it easier for the United States to preserve its economic vitality and technological dynamism, to maintain domestic political support for a protracted strategic competition and to stay the course in that competition better than its supremely statist rival," at 4.

# Chapter 3

1. 110 Cong. Rec. 2883 (1964).

2. Quoted in Clay Risen, *The Bill of the Century: The Epic Battle for the Civil Rights Act* (New York: Bloomsbury Press, 2015), 102.

3. E.g., Lawrence Glickman, "How White Backlash Controls American Progress," *The Atlantic*, May 21, 2020, https://www.theatlantic.com/ideas/archive/2020/05/white-backlash-nothing-new/611914/.

4. Jon Meacham, *The Soul of America: The Battle for Our Better Angels* (New York: Random House, 2019), 266.

5. Ibid., 287. A more egregious offender is the HBO movie *All the Way*, in which Bryan Cranston's Lyndon Johnson is portrayed as the source of every strategic and tactical move used to get the Civil Rights Act through Congress, as if legislators were simply marking time waiting for the president to figure things out.

6. Denton L. Watson, *Lion in the Lobby: Clarence Mitchell, Jr.'s Struggle for the Passage of Civil Rights Laws* (New York: Morrow, 1990), 648.

7. Hubert Humphrey, speech delivered to the Democratic National Convention, Philadelphia, PA, July 14, 1948, https://www.americanrhetoric.com/speeches/PDFFiles/Hubert%20Humphrey%20-%201948%20DNC.pdf. When he delivered the speech, Humphrey was still mayor of Minneapolis, and would be elected to the Senate in November 1948.

8. Risen, *Bill of the Century*, 12.

9. In some cases, Southerners simply hoped to evade *Brown v. Board* by ignoring it. A member of the Selma, Alabama, school board said: "A ruling had been

made but there were no guidelines as to how it was going to be interpreted, and it seemed like a bad dream. . . . Our initial thought was: 'Well, that's what they decided in Washington, but it may not affect us that much.'" Quoted in Jason Sokol, *There Goes My Everything: White Southerners in the Age of Civil Rights, 1945–1975* (New York: Vintage Books, 2007), 48.

10. Sally Russell, *Richard Brevard Russell, Jr.: A Life of Consequence* (Macon, GA: Mercer University Press, 2011), 208.

11. Robert Mann, *The Walls of Jericho: Lyndon Johnson, Hubert Humphrey, Richard Russell, and the Struggle for Civil Rights* (New York: Harcourt Brace, 1997), 255–60.

12. Julian E. Zelizer, *The Fierce Urgency of Now: Lyndon Johnson, Congress, and the Battle for the Great Society* (New York: Penguin Press, 2015), 34–35.

13. Some of the portraits in Kennedy's 1956 book, *Profiles in Courage*, make for strange reading today; he celebrated Sen. Edmund Ross of Kansas for his vote to acquit impeached President Andrew Johnson, and Sen. Lucius Q. C. Lamar of Mississippi for his attempts to maintain comity with his Northern colleagues even as he denounced attempts to dismantle white supremacy in the South. John F. Kennedy, *Profiles in Courage* (New York: Harper & Brothers, 1956). Also see Risen, *Bill of the Century*, 21.

14. Mann, *Walls of Jericho*, 301.

15. Ibid., 320–25.

16. Ibid., 341. See also Zelizer, *Fierce Urgency of Now*, 38–39.

17. Risen, *Bill of the Century*, 89–92.

18. Ibid., 85.

19. McCulloch and other Republicans insisted that the law contain no racial balance requirements that would require busing or reconfiguring school districts, for example. Hugh Davis Graham, *The Civil Rights Era: Origins and Development of National Policy, 1960–1972* (New York: Oxford University Press, 1990), 135.

20. Zelizer, *Fierce Urgency of Now*, 51.

21. Shamira Gelbman, "'The Unity among These Groups Is Truly Tremendous': The Leadership Conference on Civil Rights and the Civil Rights Act of 1964," in *Congress and Race* (18th Annual Congress and History Conference, Radcliffe Institute of Advanced Studies, Harvard University, 2019), https://www.dropbox.com/s/7hog 4iwsuqzuujz/Gelbman%20-%20The%20Unity%20among%20These%20Groups%20 Is%20Truly%20Tremendous.pdf?dl=0.

22. Risen, *Bill of the Century*, 106–7.

23. Ibid., 63, 92.

24. John F. Kennedy, "Televised Address to the Nation on Civil Rights," June 11, 1963, http://www.jfklibrary.org/learn/about-jfk/historic-speeches/televised-address-to-the-nation-on-civil-rights.

25. Mann, *Walls of Jericho*, 373; Graham, *Civil Rights Era*, 127–28.

26. Risen, *Bill of the Century*, 135.

27. The quotation was the headline of a *Washington Post* editorial on December 6, 1963, cited in Zelizer, *Fierce Urgency of Now*, 90–91.

28. See Katherine Krimmel, "Rights by Fortune or Fight? Reexamining the Addition of Sex to Title VII of the Civil Rights Act," *Legislative Studies Quarterly* 44,

no. 2 (2019): 271–306; Louis Menand, "How Women Got In on the Civil Rights Act," *New Yorker*, July 14, 2014, https://www.newyorker.com/magazine/2014/07/21/sex-amendment; Risen, *Bill of the Century*, 161; Graham, *Civil Rights Era*, 136–38.

29. Watson, *Lion in the Lobby*, xvi, 605–9, 603.

30. For an excellent discussion of the Leadership Conference on Civil Rights' conscious turn toward this strategy, see Gelbman, "'The Unity among These Groups Is Truly Tremendous.'"

31. Risen, *Bill of the Century*, 149, 162.

32. James F. Findlay, "Religion and Politics in the Sixties: The Churches and the Civil Rights Act of 1964," *Journal of American History* 77, no. 1 (1990): 66–92, https://doi.org/10.2307/2078639.

33. Risen, *Bill of the Century*, 204.

34. Ibid., 204.

35. Ibid., 211.

36. Don Oberdorfer, *Senator Mansfield: The Extraordinary Life of a Great Statesman and Diplomat* (Washington, DC: Smithsonian Books, 2003), 230.

37. Dirksen's involvement did lead to some minor improvements in the bill. For example, he worried that the use of the phrase "massive resistance" in Title II was too legally ambiguous and had it replaced with the phrase "pattern or practice," which became the text of the final law. Liberal worries notwithstanding, Dirksen never pushed business opposition to Title VII especially hard. Risen, *Bill of the Century*, 217, 221. It is also worth noting that while the Equal Employment Opportunity Commission was made less powerful than many civil rights advocates would have liked, at Dirksen's behest private citizens were empowered to bring lawsuits to enforce the Civil Rights Act's employment provisions, and they were given the chance to collect attorneys' fees. That provision proved to be among the most momentous in the history of Title VII. See Sean Farhang, *The Litigation State: Public Regulation and Private Lawsuits in the U.S.* (Princeton, NJ: Princeton University Press, 2010), especially 113–21.

38. Zelizer, *Fierce Urgency of Now*, 120. Journalist Murray Kempton, writing in the *New Republic*, captured the dynamic in another way. "When Lyndon Johnson was majority leader of the Senate, there used to be complaints that he passed weak laws by bemusing the liberals into thinking them strong. Now Everett Dirksen seems to be moving toward the passage of a strong civil rights law by telling the conservative that it is weak," he wrote. Quoted in Risen, *Bill of the Century*, 213.

39. Francis R. Valeo, *Mike Mansfield, Majority Leader: A Different Kind of Senate, 1961–1976* (Armonk, NY: M. E. Sharpe, 1999), 124–25.

40. Oberdorfer, *Senator Mansfield*, 228.

41. Ibid., 59, 20–51, 56.

42. Ibid., 109–10, 147–48.

43. Valeo, *Mike Mansfield*, 34–37.

44. Keith M. Finley, *Delaying the Dream: Southern Senators and the Fight against Civil Rights, 1938–1965* (Baton Rouge: Louisiana State University Press, 2008), 251.

45. Risen, *Bill of the Century*, 169; Russell, *Richard Russell*, 211, 232. Russell himself preferred an effort to divide the bill's supporters with strategic amendments rather than

all-out resistance, but hardliners like Eastland and Thurmond pushed him into an all-or-nothing strategy of pure obstruction. Finley, *Delaying the Dream*, 253–56.

46. Zelizer, *Fierce Urgency of Now*, 104. There was actually a preliminary filibuster, lasting from March 9 to March 26, on the question of whether to take up the bill at all.

47. Valeo, *Mike Mansfield*, 67–71.

48. "Outstanding Senate Filibusters from 1841 to 1962," Appendix to *Proposed Amendments to Rule XXII of the Standing Rules of the Senate (Relating to Cloture): Hearings before the Subcommittee on Standing Rules of the Senate of the Committee on Rules and Administration*, 89th Congress, 1st Session, 1965, 149, https://books.google.com/books?id=ZAbTNZ8OUkwC&newbks=0&printsec=fro ntcover&pg=PA148#v=onepage&q&f=false.

49. Risen, *Bill of the Century*, 224; Valeo, *Mike Mansfield*, 156–58.

50. 110 Cong. Rec., 13308 (1964).

51. Ibid., 13310.

52. Ibid., 13319.

53. Risen, *Bill of the Century*, 215, 229.

54. Russell, *Richard Russell*, 235.

55. Watson, *Lion in the Lobby*, 641–42.

56. Hubert H. Humphrey, *The Education of a Public Man: My Life and Politics* (Minneapolis: University of Minnesota Press, 1991), 211. See also Mann, *Walls of Jericho*, 430; Risen, *Bill of the Century*, 231.

57. Sen. George Smathers (D-FL), quoted in Oberdorfer, *Senator Mansfield*, 235; Mann, *Walls of Jericho*, 429.

58. The nine were Weltner, Richard Fulton of Tennessee, Claude Pepper of Florida, Carl Perkins of Kentucky, Ross Bass of Tennessee, Jack Brooks of Texas, Albert Thomas of Texas, Jake Pickle of Texas, and Henry Gonzalez of Texas; for the full roll call vote, see https://www.govtrack.us/congress/votes/88-1964/h182.

59. 110 Cong. Rec., 15894 (1964).

60. Calvin M. Longue and Dwight L. Fresley, eds., *Voice of Georgia: Speeches of Richard B. Russell: 1928–1969* (Macon, GA: Mercer University Press, 1997), 357.

61. Ibid., 354.

62. Russell, *Richard Russell*, 240.

63. Risen, *Bill of the Century*, 246; Finley, *Delaying the Dream*, 279.

64. Sokol, *There Goes My Everything*, 204–11.

65. *Heart of Atlanta Motel, Inc. v. United States*, 379 U.S. 241 (1964); *Katzenbach v. McClung*, 379 U.S. 294 (1964).

66. The remarkably smooth roll-out of the act was, of course, not merely the product of the defeated opponents' urging of compliance. To head off any efforts at "massive resistance," the Department of Justice had coordinated with a network of Southern business and civic leaders as well as clergy. They hoped to broadcast a clear message of inevitability and the seriousness of their intention to enforce the law. See Risen, *Bill of the Century*, 192.

67. Zelizer, *Fierce Urgency of Now*, 217–18.

68. When the Voting Rights Act was passed, its objective was clearly understood as ensuring that black Americans would be allowed to register to vote. On that front, it has been an unambiguous and overwhelming success. What became more controversial over time was the preclearance provision, which requires covered jurisdictions to get the assent of federal authorities before changing their voting procedures. See Abigail M. Thernstrom, *Whose Votes Count? Affirmative Action and Minority Voting Rights* (Cambridge, MA: Harvard University Press, 1987), 18–22. For a definitive statement of the law's effectiveness in extending registration in its early years, see James E. Alt, "The Impact of the Voting Rights Act on Black and White Voter Registration in the South," in *Quiet Revolution in the South: The Impact of the Voting Rights Act, 1965–1990*, ed. Chandler Davidson and Bernard Grofman (Princeton, NJ: Princeton University Press, 1994), 351–77.

69. Gerald N. Rosenberg, *The Hollow Hope: Can Courts Bring about Social Change?* (Chicago: University of Chicago Press, 1991), Table 2.1, 50. For exploration on how Brown mobilized Southern opposition to desegregation, see Michael J. Klarman, *From Jim Crow to Civil Rights: The Supreme Court and the Struggle for Racial Equality* (Oxford: Oxford University Press, 2006).

70. At their peak in 1972, these schools enrolled just 4.3 percent of Southern students. "Note: Segregation Academies and State Action," *Yale Law Journal* 82, no. 7 (1973): 1436–61.

71. Quoted in John David Skrentny, *The Ironies of Affirmative Action: Politics, Culture, and Justice in America* (Chicago: University of Chicago Press, 1996), 3.

72. Ibid., 91.

73. Nixon's approach to civil rights was characterized by a "deeds not words" strategy, in which the president offered rhetorical comfort to aggrieved Southerners while his administration worked effectively to advance desegregation through enforcement of existing laws, often insisting that courts were primarily responsible. See Dean J. Kotlowski, *Nixon's Civil Rights: Politics, Principle, and Policy* (Cambridge, MA: Harvard University Press, 2001), 184; Kevin J. McMahon, *Nixon's Court: His Challenge to Judicial Liberalism and Its Political Consequences* (Chicago: University of Chicago Press, 2011), 73–75.

74. Skrentny, *Ironies of Affirmative Action*, 196–212.

75. Over the long history of affirmative action, Congress has sometimes been drawn into active debate over aspects of the policy. Legislators fought heated battles in the 1980s over the federal government's preferences for minority-owned contractors, and the debate over the Civil Rights Act of 1991, addressing the conditions needed to prove employment discrimination, saw a spirited but not altogether decisive exchange over hiring quotas. Voters, for their part, have almost always registered their dislike of affirmative action policies when given the chance in state referenda. See Melvin I. Urofsky, *The Affirmative Action Puzzle: A Living History from Reconstruction to Today* (New York: Pantheon Books, 2020).

76. That the triumph of civil rights was so long in coming may have also made it easier for Southerners to adjust themselves to the idea of desegregation's inevitability. By 1963,

83 percent of Southerners told pollsters that they expected public accommodations to be desegregated. Finley, *Delaying the Dream*, 277–79.

77. "Dedication and Unveiling of the Statue of Richard Brevard Russell, Jr.," Proceedings in the Rotunda of the Russell Senate Office Building (US Government Printing Office), January 24, 1996, 8, https://www.govinfo.gov/content/pkg/CDOC-105sd oc8/pdf/CDOC-105sdoc8.pdf.

# Chapter 4

1. 119 Cong. Rec. 13170 (1973).
2. Quoted in James L. Sundquist, *The Decline and Resurgence of Congress* (Washington, DC: Brookings Institution Press, 1981), 458.
3. Nelson W. Polsby, *How Congress Evolves: Social Bases of Institutional Change* (New York: Oxford University Press, 2004), 15.
4. American Political Science Association, "Toward a More Responsible Two-Party System," *American Political Science Review* 44, Supplement (September 1950): i–99, v, 13. For helpful discussions, see Daniel Stid, "Two Pathways for Congressional Reform," in *Is Congress Broken?: The Virtues and Defects of Partisanship and Gridlock*, ed. William F. Connelly, John J. Pitney, and Gary J. Schmitt (Washington, DC: Brookings Institution Press, 2017), 11–36, and Lee Drutman, *Breaking the Two-Party Doom Loop: The Case for Multiparty Democracy in America.* (New York: Oxford University Press, 2020), 35–47.
5. Austin Ranney, "Toward a More Responsible Two-Party System: A Commentary," *American Political Science Review* 45, no. 2 (June 1951): 488–99, 498.
6. Roger H. Davidson and Walter J. Oleszek, *Congress against Itself* (Bloomington: Indiana University Press, 1977), x.
7. Such was the advice given by Sen. Hubert Humphrey (D-MN) to fellow liberal Sen. Joseph Clark (D-PA) in 1957. Quoted in Michael Foley, *The New Senate: Liberal Influence on a Conservative Institution, 1959–1972* (New Haven, CT: Yale University Press, 1980), 121.
8. Ibid., 129.
9. Emily Baer, "Organizing for Reform: The Democratic Study Group and the Role of Party Factions in Driving Institutional Change in the House of Representatives" (doctoral dissertation, University of Minnesota, 2017), http://conservancy.umn.edu/han dle/11299/191403, 69–78; Julian E. Zelizer, *On Capitol Hill: The Struggle to Reform Congress and Its Consequences, 1948–2000* (Cambridge; New York: Cambridge University Press, 2006), 54.
10. Polsby, *How Congress Evolves*, 63.
11. Richard Bolling, *House Out of Order* (New York: E. P. Dutton & Co., 1964), 12–14, 21.
12. Ibid., 238. For an account of the APSA report's influence on the vision of Bolling and the DSG reformers, see Sam Rosenfeld, "A Choice, Not an Echo: Polarization and

the Transformation of the American Party System" (doctoral dissertation, Harvard, 2014), 227, https://dash.harvard.edu/handle/1/12274614.

13. Quotation in John Jacobs, *A Rage for Justice: The Passion and Politics of Phillip Burton* (Los Angeles: University of California Press, 1995), 177.

14. Burton D. Sheppard, *Rethinking Congressional Reform: The Reform Roots of the Special Interest Congress* (Cambridge, MA: Schenkman Books, 1985), 41.

15. Zelizer, *On Capitol Hill*, 136.

16. John A. Lawrence, *The Class of '74: Congress after Watergate and the Roots of Partisanship* (Baltimore: Johns Hopkins University Press, 2018), 95, 107.

17. Jacobs, *A Rage for Justice*, 244.

18. Zelizer, *On Capitol Hill*, 147.

19. Davidson and Oleszek, *Congress against Itself*, 47–49.

20. Norman J. Ornstein, "Causes and Consequences of Congressional Change: Subcommittee Reforms in the House of Representatives, 1970–1973," in *Congress in Change: Evolution and Reform*, ed. Norman J. Ornstein (New York: Praeger Publishers, 1975), 88–114, 102.

21. Tip O'Neill with William Novak, *Man of the House* (New York: Random House, 1987), 283–84.

22. Sheppard, *Rethinking Congressional Reform*, 305–6.

23. Select Committee on Committees, Committee Reform Amendments of 1974, H.R. Rep. No. 93–916, pt. 1, 26.

24. Davidson and Oleszek, *Congress against Itself*, 194; Sheppard, *Rethinking Congressional Reform*, 187.

25. Davidson and Oleszek, *Congress against Itself*, 202–3, 248–50; Jacobs, *A Rage for Justice*, 245–46.

26. Sheppard, *Rethinking Congressional Reform*, 117, 121, 159–87.

27. These were the Obey Commission (1976–77) and the Patterson Select Committee on Committees (1979–80). See ibid., 257–71.

28. Polsby, *How Congress Evolves*, 69–70; Zelizer, *On Capitol Hill*, 158–59.

29. Polsby, *How Congress Evolves*, 70; Davidson and Oleszek, *Congress against Itself*, 266.

30. Eric Schickler, *Disjointed Pluralism: Institutional Innovation and the Development of the U.S. Congress* (Princeton, NJ: Princeton University Press, 2001), 227.

31. The parliamentary maneuvering around this change was arcane and dramatic, with Vice President Nelson Rockefeller playing a pivotal role. See Zelizer, *On Capitol Hill*, 173–75.

32. Steven S. Smith, *Call to Order: Floor Politics in the House and Senate* (Washington, DC: Brookings Institution, 1989), 97–99.

33. Steven S. Smith, *The Senate Syndrome: The Evolution of Procedural Warfare in the Modern U.S. Senate* (Norman: University of Oklahoma Press, 2014), 148–49.

34. Michael J. Malbin, "Compromise by the Senate Eases Anti-Filibuster Rule," *National Journal*, March 15, 1975.

35. 124 Cong. Rec. 20813-20847 (July 13, 1978).

36. Quoted in Schickler, *Disjointed Pluralism*, 218.

37. Ibid., 204–9; Zelizer, *On Capitol Hill*, 187–89.

38. Smith, *Senate Syndrome*, 145.

39. Quoted in Jacobs, *A Rage for Justice*, 273–74.

40. Lawrence, *The Class of '74*, 238.

41. Jacobs, *A Rage for Justice*, 318–22. See also J. Brooks Flippen, *Speaker Jim Wright* (Austin: University of Texas Press, 2018), 258–60; Matthew N. Green and Douglas B. Harris, *Choosing the Leader* (New Haven, CT: Yale University Press, 2019), 122–38.

42. Zelizer, *On Capitol Hill*, 100–103.

43. Schickler, *Disjointed Pluralism*, 214–17.

44. Quoted in ibid., 209; see also Smith, *Call to Order*, 26–27.

45. Smith, *Call to Order*, 27, 32.

46. Quoted in Schickler, *Disjointed Pluralism*, 210.

47. Sheppard, *Rethinking Congressional Reform*, 277–80; Zelizer, *On Capitol Hill*, 112–24.

48. Zelizer, *On Capitol Hill*, 136.

49. 122 Cong. Rec. 15344–15346 (1976).

50. Zelizer, *On Capitol Hill*, 183.

51. Ibid., 186.

52. Sheppard, *Rethinking Congressional Reform*, 305–6.

53. "Notes and Comment," *New Yorker*, April 28, 1973.

54. Don Oberdorfer, *Senator Mansfield: The Extraordinary Life of a Great Statesman and Diplomat* (Washington, DC: Smithsonian Books, 2003), 436.

55. Davidson and Oleszek, *Congress against Itself*, 122–23; Schickler, *Disjointed Pluralism*, 195–98.

56. Sundquist, *The Decline and Resurgence of Congress*, 201–36.

57. Philip G. Joyce, *The Congressional Budget Office: Honest Numbers, Power, and Policymaking* (Washington, DC: Georgetown University Press, 2011).

58. Thomas E. Mann and Norman J. Ornstein, eds., *The New Congress* (Washington, DC: American Enterprise Institute for Public Policy Research, 1981), 141–42; Morris P. Fiorina, *Congress, Keystone of the Washington Establishment* (New Haven, CT: Yale University Press, 1977), 56–60.

59. Davidson and Oleszek, *Congress against Itself*, 240, 267; Schickler, *Disjointed Pluralism*, 217–20.

60. Brookings Institution, Vital Statistics on Congress, Table 5-5, www.brookings.edu/VitalStats.

61. Kevin R. Kosar, "Legislative Branch Support Agencies: What They Are, What They Do, and Their Uneasy Position in Our System of Government," in *Congress Overwhelmed*, ed. Timothy M. LaPira, Lee Drutman, and Kevin R. Kosar (Chicago: University of Chicago Press, 2020), 127–41.

62. Adam Keiper, "Science and Congress," *New Atlantis*, Fall 2004–Winter 2005, https://www.thenewatlantis.com/publications/science-and-congress.

63. James R. Naughton, "The Origin and Implementation of the Inspector General Act," *Government Accountants Journal* 47, no. 3 (Fall 1998): 12–19.

64. Joel D. Aberbach, *Keeping a Watchful Eye: The Politics of Congressional Oversight* (Washington, DC: Brookings Institution, 1990), 27, 35.

65. Quoted in Lawrence, *Class of '74*, 222.

66. Michael J. Berry, *The Modern Legislative Veto: Macropolitical Conflict and the Legacy of Chadha* (Ann Arbor: University of Michigan Press, 2016), 22–42.

67. James H. Cox, *Reviewing Delegation: An Analysis of the Congressional Reauthorization Process* (Westport, CT: Praeger, 2004), 56–57.

68. Michael W. Kirst, *Government without Passing Laws: Congress' Nonstatutory Techniques for Appropriations Control* (Chapel Hill: University of North Carolina Press, 1969).

69. Cox, *Reviewing Delegation*, 57–58. Also see Richard E. Cohen, "Hitching a Legislative Ride," *National Journal*, May 13, 1978, 769.

70. John A. Farrell, *Tip O'Neill and the Democratic Century* (Boston: Little, Brown, and Co, 2001), 463–71.

71. First passed in each chamber's rules, these would be codified in statute in the Ethics in Government Act of 1978. Zelizer, *On Capitol Hill*, 189–90, 199–200; also Farrell, *Tip O'Neill*, 474–75.

72. Farrell, *Tip O'Neill*, 450; Paul Clancy and Shirley Elder, *Tip: A Biography of Tip O'Neill, Speaker of the House* (New York: MacMillan Publishing Co., 1980), 215–16.

73. Quoted in David W. Rohde, *Parties and Leaders in the Postreform House* (Chicago: University of Chicago Press, 1991), 142.

74. Burdett A Loomis, *The New American Politician: Ambition, Entrepreneurship, and the Changing Face of Political Life* (New York: Basic Books, 1988), x.

75. Jimmy Carter, "Address to the Nation on Energy," April 18, 1977, https://www.preside ncy.ucsb.edu/documents/address-the-nation-energy.

76. Quoted in "Carter Energy Bill Fails to Clear," CQ Almanac 1977, https://library.cqpr ess.com/cqalmanac/document.php?id=cqal77-1204123.

77. Charles O. Jones and Randall Strahan, "The Effect of Energy Politics on Congressional and Executive Organization in the 1970s," *Legislative Studies Quarterly* 10, no. 2 (1985): 151–79, 166–68.

78. Farrell, *Tip O'Neill*, 506–9.

79. Bryan D. Jones, Sean M. Theriault, and Michelle Whyman, *The Great Broadening: How the Vast Expansion of the Policy-Making Agenda Transformed American Politics* (Chicago: University of Chicago Press, 2019), 55–64.

80. Ibid., 151–54.

81. Lawrence, *Class of '74*, 265.

82. Richard E. Cohen, "Filling the Leadership Vacuum," *National Journal*, January 12, 1980.

83. Dennis Farney, "Student of Power: Bolling Ponders a Role for Democrats, Broods about Country," *Wall Street Journal*, April 2, 1981.

84. Michael J. Malbin, *Unelected Representatives: Congressional Staff and the Future of Representative Government* (New York: Basic Books, 1980), 251, 240–41.

85. Farrell, *Tip O'Neill*, 481–91; Zelizer, *On Capitol Hill*, 194–97.

86. Zelizer, *On Capitol Hill*, 200–204.

87. "Congress and the Public," Gallup, https://news.gallup.com/poll/1600/congress-pub lic.aspx.

88. Clancy and Elder, *Tip*, 206–7.

89. Farrell, *Tip O'Neill*, 534.
90. Sundquist, *The Decline and Resurgence of Congress*, 441–57.
91. Richard Fenno, *Home Style: House Members in Their Districts* (Glenview, IL: Scott, Foresman and Company, 1978), 164–68.

# Chapter 5

1. Gordon S. Jones and John A. Marini, eds., *The Imperial Congress: Crisis in the Separation of Powers* (New York: Pharos Books, 1988), ix, x.
2. Quoted in Andrew Rudalevige, *The New Imperial Presidency: Renewing Presidential Power after Watergate* (Ann Arbor: University of Michigan Press, 2005), 7.
3. Julian E. Zelizer, *Burning Down the House: Newt Gingrich, the Fall of a Speaker, and the Rise of the New Republican Party* (New York: Penguin Press, 2020), 25.
4. Michael Barone, "The Senate the Staff Built," *Washington Post*, April 14, 1981, A21.
5. Roger H. Davidson and Walter J. Oleszek, "Changing the Guard in the U.S. Senate," *Legislative Studies Quarterly* 9, no. 4 (1984): 635–63, 655–57, 656.
6. Matthew S. Mendez, "Leading Gently on Taxes," in *Robert H. Michel: Leading the Republican House Minority*, ed. Frank H. Mackaman and Sean Q. Kelly (Lawrence: University Press of Kansas, 2019), 140–58, 144.
7. Daniel J. Palazzolo, "From 'Exhilarating Days' to Pragmatic Politics," in *Robert H. Michel*, 159–85, 164.
8. Quoted in Douglas B. Harris and Matthew N. Green, "Michel as Minority Leader," in *Robert H. Michel*, 94–114, 97.
9. James S. Fleming, *Window on Congress: A Congressional Biography of Barber B. Conable, Jr.* (Rochester, NY: University of Rochester Press, 2004), 296–300.
10. Michael Peter Bobic, *With the People's Consent: Howard Baker Leads the Senate 1977–1984* (Lanham, MD: University Press of America, 2015), Chapter 6.
11. Philip Wallach, "How Social Security Was Saved—and Might Be Again," *The American Interest*, November 26, 2019, https://www.the-american-interest.com/2019/11/26/how-social-security-was-saved-and-might-be-again/.
12. Jackie Calmes, "Idea Rebounds: Automatic Cuts to Curb Deficits," *New York Times*, May 15, 2011, http://www.nytimes.com/2011/05/16/us/politics/16fiscal.html?pagewanted=all.
13. *Congressional Quarterly Almanac* 41 (1985): 457–59.
14. Jeffrey H. Birnbaum and Alan S. Murray, *Showdown at Gucci Gulch: Lawmakers, Lobbyists, and the Unlikely Triumph of Tax Reform* (New York: Vintage Books, 1988); see also R. Douglas Arnold, *The Logic of Congressional Action* (New Haven, CT: Yale University Press, 1992), 212–23.
15. David W. Rohde, *Parties and Leaders in the Postreform House* (Chicago: University of Chicago Press, 1991), 86, 88; Scott R. Meinke, *Leadership Organizations in the House of Representatives: Party Participation and Partisan Politics* (Ann Arbor: University of Michigan Press, 2016), 143–48.

16. Ibid., 136–37.

17. Steven S. Smith and Stanley Bach, *Managing Uncertainty in the House of Representatives: Adaption and Innovation in Special Rules* (Washington, DC: Brookings Institution Press, 1988), Table 3–3.

18. Smith, *Call to Order*, 76–77.

19. Eric Schickler, *Disjointed Pluralism: Institutional Innovation and the Development of the U.S. Congress* (Princeton, NJ: Princeton University Press, 2001), 234–38; Rohde, *Parties and Leaders*, 98–103.

20. Nelson W. Polsby, *How Congress Evolves: Social Bases of Institutional Change* (New York: Oxford University Press, 2004), 114–24; Rohde, *Parties and Leaders*, 128.

21. Polsby, *How Congress Evolves*, 126–30; Rohde, *Parties and Leaders*, 122–23; Smith, *Call to Order*, 65–69; Zelizer, *Burning Down the House*, 58–64.

22. Smith, *Call to Order*, 62–69; Julian E. Zelizer, *On Capitol Hill: The Struggle to Reform Congress and Its Consequences, 1948–2000* (New York: Cambridge University Press, 2006), 190–94.

23. Zelizer, *Burning Down the House*, 71.

24. Ibid., 74. See also "Interview of Vin Weber," PBS Frontline, https://www.pbs.org/wgbh/pages/frontline/newt/newtintwshtml/weber.html; William F. Connelly Jr., "Newt Gingrich—Professor and Politician: The Anti-Federalist Roots of Newt Gingrich's Thought," *Southeastern Political Review* 27, no. 1 (1999): 103–27, 112; Polsby, *How Congress Evolves*, 127–28.

25. Jim Wright, *Balance of Power: Presidents and Congress from the Era of McCarthy to the Age of Gingrich* (Atlanta, GA: Turner Publishing, 1996), 39. See also Philip Wallach, "The Fall of Jim Wright—and the House of Representatives," *The American Interest*, January 3, 2019, https://www.the-american-interest.com/2019/01/03/the-fall-of-jim-wright-and-the-house-of-representatives/, which reviews J. Brooks Flippen, *Speaker Jim Wright: Power, Scandal, and the Birth of Modern Politics* (Austin: University of Texas Press, 2018).

26. Flippen, *Speaker Jim Wright*, 356.

27. Ibid., 359; Polsby, *How Congress Evolves*, 134; Zelizer, *Burning Down the House*, 115–18.

28. Rohde, *Parties and Leaders*, 114–15.

29. Polsby, *How Congress Evolves*, 133–34; Rohde, *Parties and Leaders*, 105–13; Schickler, *Disjointed Pluralism*, 238–42; Zelizer, *Burning Down the House*, 86, 106.

30. Wright, *Balance of Power*, 446.

31. Ibid., 474.

32. Quoted in Eric Pianin, "House GOP's Frustrations Intensify," *Washington Post*, December 21, 1987, A10.

33. Jones and Marini, eds., *The Imperial Congress*, ix, x.

34. Gordon Crovitz and Jeremy Rabkin, eds., *The Fettered Presidency* (Washington, DC: American Enterprise Institute, 1989).

35. The party's 1992 platform contained a condemnation of the "Imperial Congress." Craig Green, "Deconstructing the Administrative State: *Chevron* Debates and

the Transformation of Constitutional Politics," *Boston University Law Review* 101 (2021): 619–704, 646.

36. Stanley M. Brand and Sean Connelly, "Constitutional Confrontations: Preserving a Prompt and Orderly Means by Which Congress May Enforce Investigative Demands against Executive Branch Officials," *Catholic University Law Review* 36 (1986): 71–91, 78–80; Ronald L. Claveloux, "The Conflict between Executive Privilege and Congressional Oversight: The Gorsuch Controversy," *Duke Law Journal* 1983, no. 6 (1983): 1333–58.

37. David C. W. Parker and Matthew Dull, "The Weaponization of Congressional Oversight," in *Politics to the Extreme*, ed. Scott A. Frisch and Sean Q. Kelly (New York: Palgrave Macmillan, 2013), 47–69.

38. Joel D. Aberbach, *Keeping a Watchful Eye: The Politics of Congressional Oversight* (Washington, DC: Brookings Institution, 1990), 200–201.

39. For discussion of the politics around inspectors general, see Paul Charles Light, *Monitoring Government: Inspectors General and the Search for Accountability* (Washington, DC: Brookings Institution Press, 1993).

40. J. Gregory Sidak, "The President's Power of the Purse," *Duke Law Journal* 1989, no. 5 (1989): 1162–253.

41. For example, see William P. Barr, "Common Legislative Encroachments on Executive Branch Authority," Memorandum Opinion for the General Counsels' Consultative Group, July 27, 1989, 255.

42. Smith, *Call to Order*, 53–59; Smith, *Senate Syndrome*, 155–56, 183–87.

43. Charles Tiefer, *The Semi-Sovereign Presidency: The Bush Administration's Strategy for Governing without Congress* (Boulder, CO: Westview Press, 1994), 15–16.

44. Herman A. Mellor, "Congressional Micromanagement: National Defense," in *The Imperial Congress*, 107–29; Mackubin Owens, "Micromanaging the Defense Budget," *Public Interest*, no. 100 (1990): 131–46; L. Gordon Crovitz, "Micromanaging Foreign Policy," *Public Interest*, no. 100 (1990): 102–15.

45. John Hiram Caldwell, "Congressional Micromanagement: Domestic Policy," in *The Imperial Congress*, 130–50; Jeremy Rabkin, "Micromanaging the Administrative Agencies," *Public Interest*, no. 100 (1990): 116–30.

46. Quoted in Tiefer, *Semi-Sovereign Presidency*, 4. Also called "subgovernments," iron triangles were a major focus of political scientists in the 1980s. See Thomas L. Gais, Mark A. Peterson, and Jack L. Walker, "Interest Groups, Iron Triangles and Representative Institutions in American National Government," *British Journal of Political Science* 14, no. 2 (1984): 161–85; Jeffrey Berry, "Subgovernments, Issue Networks, and Political Conflict," in *Remaking American Politics*, ed. Richard A. Harris and Sidney M. Milkis (Boulder, CO: Westview, 1989), 239–60; Amitai Etzioni, *Capital Corruption: The New Attack on American Democracy*, 1st ed. (San Diego: Harcourt Brace Jovanovich, 1984).

47. Richard A. Viguerie, *The Establishment vs. the People: Is a New Populist Revolt on the Way?* (Chicago: Regnery Gateway, 1983); James L. Payne, "The Congressional Brainwashing Machine," *Public Interest*, no. 100 (1990): 3–14.

48. Matthew N. Green and Jeffrey Crouch, *Newt Gingrich: The Rise and Fall of a Party Entrepreneur* (Lawrence: University Press of Kansas, 2022), 68–70.

49. Willmoore Kendall, "The Two Majorities," *Midwest Journal of Political Science* 4, no. 4 (1960): 317–454; James Burnham, *Congress and the American Tradition* (New York: Henry Regnery Company, 1959).

50. Jeffrey Hart, "The Presidency: Shifting Conservative Perspectives?," *National Review*, November 22, 1974, 1351–55.

51. See Tiefer, *Semi-Sovereign Presidency*, 1, 13.

52. Stephen Skowronek, "The Conservative Insurgency and Presidential Power: A Developmental Perspective on the Unitary Executive," *Harvard Law Review* 122 (2009): 2070–103, 2095. See also Stephen Skowronek, John A. Dearborn, and Desmond King, *Phantoms of a Beleaguered Republic: The Deep State and the Unitary Executive* (New York: Oxford University Press, 2021), 44.

53. *Report of the Congressional Committees Investigating the Iran-Contra Affair: With Supplemental, Minority, and Additional Views* (U.S. House of Representatives Select Committee to Investigate Covert Arms Transactions with Iran, U.S. Senate Select Committee on Secret Military Assistance to Iran and the Nicaraguan Opposition, 1987), https://archive.org/details/reportofcongress87unit/page/10/mode/2up?view=theater, 457.

54. Ibid., 437. On leaks, see 576–79.

55. Polsby, *How Congress Evolves*, 137; Green and Crouch, *Newt Gingrich*, 72.

56. Flippen, *Speaker Jim Wright*, 147.

57. Ibid., 334.

58. Newt Gingrich, *Lessons Learned the Hard Way: A Personal Report* (New York: HarperCollins, 1998), 92.

59. Green and Crouch, *Newt Gingrich*, 66.

60. Quoted in C. Lawrence Evans and Walter J. Oleszek, *Congress Under Fire: Reform Politics and the Republican Majority* (New York: Houghton Mifflin, 1997), 35.

61. Ibid., 35–37.

62. Richard L. Berke, "1789 Amendment Is Ratified but Now the Debate Begins," *New York Times*, May 8, 1992, A1.

63. Gerald B. H. Solomon and Donald R. Wolfensberger, "The Decline of Deliberative Democracy in the House and Proposals for Reform," *Harvard Journal on Legislation* 31, no. 2 (1994): 321–70, 349.

64. Ibid., 369.

65. See James G. Gimpel, *Legislating the Revolution: The Contract with America in Its First 100 Days* (Boston, MA: Allyn & Bacon, 1996), 5–15; Nicol C. Rae, *Conservative Reformers: The Republican Freshmen and the Lessons of the 104th Congress* (Armonk, NY: Taylor & Francis, 1998), 42–43.

66. On Gingrich's ambitions, see Lois Romano, "Newt Gingrich, Maverick on the Hill," *Washington Post*, January 3, 1985, https://www.washingtonpost.com/archive/lifest yle/1985/01/03/newt-gingrich-maverick-on-the-hill/46aab64f-7752-493d-b28b-9b675c0775b5/.

67. Lloyd Grove, "PAYBACK," *Washington Post*, November 28, 1994, https://www.was hingtonpost.com/archive/lifestyle/1994/11/28/payback/4a4d7fba-a3f1-44c0-a8e7-279c6d9200a7/.

68. Scot M. Faulkner, *Naked Emperors: The Failure of the Republican Revolution* (Lanham, MD: Rowman & Littlefield, 2007).

69. One might wonder whether the less professional system may have been more favorable to producing political compromises; see Philip Wallach, "Congress Rebuked but Not Reimagined," *Law & Liberty*, January 15, 2020, https://www.lawliberty.org/2020/01/15/congress-rebuked-but-not-reimagined/.

70. Gimpel, *Legislating the Revolution*, 38.

71. Warren E. Leary, "Congress's Science Agency Prepares to Close Its Doors," *New York Times*, September 24, 1995, A26.

72. Rae, *Conservative Reformers*, 76.

73. Dennis Hastert, *Speaker: Lessons from Forty Years in Coaching and Politics* (Washington, DC: Regnery, 2004), 115.

74. Rae, *Conservative Reformers*, 68.

75. Gimpel, *Legislating the Revolution*, 36.

76. Adam Clymer, "With Political Discipline, It Works Like Parliament," *New York Times*, August 6, 1995, https://www.nytimes.com/1995/08/06/weekinreview/the-nation-with-political-discipline-it-works-like-parliament.html.

77. Steve Kornacki, *The Red and the Blue: The 1990s and the Birth of Political Tribalism* (New York: Ecco, 2019), 273.

78. Maraniss and Weisskopf, *Tell Newt*, 56.

79. Ibid., 144, 92.

80. See David Hedge and Renee J. Johnson, "The Plot That Failed: The Republican Revolution and Congressional Control of the Bureaucracy," *Journal of Public Administration Research and Theory* 12, no. 3 (2002): 333–51.

81. See Richard F. Fenno Jr., *Learning to Govern: An Institutional View of the 104th Congress* (Washington, DC: Brookings Institution Press, 1997), 6–8 (arguing that House Republicans' interpretation of their electoral victory in 1994 suffered badly from their party's institutional unfamiliarity with winning House elections).

82. Gimpel, *Legislating the Revolution*, 46–47.

83. 104th Congress, 1st Senate Session, roll call vote 98, on H.J. Res. 1. The vote was actually 65–35, two short of the needed 67, but Senate Majority Leader Dole voted "nay" for procedural reasons and would have voted "yea" had Hatfield voted in the affirmative.

84. John H. Cushman Jr., "Dole Says Hatfield Offered to Quit Over Balanced-Budget Vote," *New York Times*, March 6, 1995, A11.

85. Rae, *Conservative Reformers*, 154.

86. Congressional Record, 104th Congress, 1st Session, March 29, 1995, H3905; Gimpel, *Legislating the Revolution*, 99–104.

87. Katharine Q. Seelye, "House Defeats Bid to Repeal 'War Powers,'" *New York Times*, June 8, 1995, https://www.nytimes.com/1995/06/08/world/house-defeats-bid-to-repeal-war-powers.html.

88. Maraniss and Weisskopf, *Tell Newt*, 88. Dubbed the "Armey protocols" after House Majority Dick Armey (R-TX), the Republican plan to push substantive policy changes into the appropriations process was the leadership's way of coping with the calendar jam that the Contract With America's strict timeline had created. Of course, it also helped leaders further empower themselves at the expense of committees.

89. Green and Crouch, *Newt Gingrich*, 85.

90. Maraniss and Weisskopf, *Tell Newt*, 129–40.

91. Ibid., 148.

92. Rae, *Conservative Reformers*, 119.

93. Maraniss and Weisskopf, *Tell Newt*, 165, 176.

94. Ibid., 198–200.

95. Rae, *Conservative Reformers*, 161.

96. Elizabeth Drew, *Showdown: The Struggle between the Gingrich Congress and the Clinton White House* (New York: Simon & Schuster, 1996), 169.

97. Congressional Record, April 18, 1996, S3683.

98. For helpful commentary on the limitations and uses of the Congressional Review Act, see Note, "The Mysteries of the Congressional Review Act," *Harvard Law Review* 122 (2009): 2162–83.

99. H.R. 2727, 104th Cong.

100. For an elaboration, see the discussion of the Regulations from the Executive in Need of Scrutiny (REINS) Act in Philip Wallach, "LegBranch Conversations: An interview with David Schoenbrod," *LegBranch.org*, June 12, 2018, https://www.legbranch.org/2018-6-12-legbranch-conversations-an-interview-with-david-schoenbrod/.

101. William J. Clinton, "Statement on Signing the Line Item Veto Act," online by Gerhard Peters and John T. Woolley, American Presidency Project, April 9, 1996, https://www.presidency.ucsb.edu/node/223132.

102. Andrew C. Rudalevige, "Deficit Politics and the Item Veto: Serving the Public, or the Congress?," Paper prepared for the Annual Meeting of the American Political Science Association, Washington, DC, August 28–31, 1997.

103. *Clinton v. City of New York*, 524 U.S. 417 (1998). Some observers believe that the form of the line-item veto that Congress finally passed was intended to be struck down by the court.

104. Fenno, *Learning to Govern*, 47.

105. Rae, *Conservative Reformers*, 187.

106. Ibid., 196.

107. Quoted in Maraniss and Weisskopf, *Tell Newt*, 142.

108. Ibid., 182. Gingrich's limitations can be conceptualized in other ways too. Reflecting on the Speaker's orientation to committee jurisdiction reforms, one Republican staffer said: "Newt isn't a nuts and bolts guy. He wants to know how [realigning committees] will affect his goals. Will it help elect a dozen new Republicans? Will it help win the White House?" Quoted in Evans and Oleszek, *Congress Under Fire*, 94.

109. Fenno, *Learning to Govern*, 20–21, 41–43.

# Chapter 6

1. 158 Cong. Rec. S5095 (daily ed. July 18, 2012).

2. 165 Cong. Rec. S2217 (daily ed. April 3, 2019).

3. Ceci Connolly and Howard Kurtz, "Gingrich Orchestrated GOP Ads Recalling Clinton-Lewinsky Affair," *Washington Post*, October 30, 1998, https://www.washing tonpost.com/wp-srv/politics/special/clinton/stories/ads103098.htm.

4. Adam Cohen, "The Speaker Who Never Was," *CNN*, December 21, 1998, https://www.cnn.com/ALLPOLITICS/time/1998/12/21/livingston.html.

5. Quoted in Dennis Hastert, *Speaker: Lessons from Forty Years in Coaching and Politics* (Washington, DC: Regnery, 2004), 176–77.

6. Scott R. Meinke, *Leadership Organizations in the House of Representatives: Party Participation and Partisan Politics*, Legislative Politics and Policy Making (Ann Arbor: University of Michigan Press, 2016), 163.

7. Kathryn Pearson, *Party Discipline in the U.S. House of Representatives* (Ann Arbor: University of Michigan Press, 2015), 114–15.

8. Charles Tiefer, *The Polarized Congress: The Post-Traditional Procedure of Its Current Struggles* (Lanham, MD: University Press of America, 2016), 58–63, quotation on 59.

9. James M. Curry, *Legislating in the Dark: Information and Power in the House of Representatives* (Chicago: University of Chicago Press, 2015), 167–68.

10. Meinke, *Leadership Organizations in the House*, 148.

11. Pearson, *Party Discipline*, 174.

12. Donald R. Wolfensberger, *Changing Cultures in Congress: From Fair Play to Power Plays* (New York: Columbia University Press, 2018), 119–21.

13. Tiefer, *Polarized Congress*, 65–67.

14. Ibid., 175. Meinke, *Leadership Organizations in the House*, 159.

15. Meinke, *Leadership Organizations in the House*, 164–65.

16. Molly E. Reynolds, "The Decline in Congressional Capacity," in *Congress Overwhelmed: The Decline in Congressional Capacity and Prospects for Reform*, ed. Timothy M. Lapira, Lee Drutman, and Kevin R. Kosar (Chicago: University of Chicago Press, 2020), 34–50; "Chapter 5: Congressional Staff and Operating Expenses," in *Vital Statistics on Congress: Data on the U.S. Congress*, Brookings Institution, updated February 2021, https://www.brookings.edu/multi-chapter-rep ort/vital-statistics-on-congress/.

17. Jonathan Lewallen, *Committees and the Decline of Lawmaking* (Ann Arbor: University of Michigan Press, 2020). For a useful counterpoint, demonstrating that partisan point scoring is hardly a recent oversight innovation, see Josh Chafetz, "Congressional Overspeech," *Fordham Law Review* 89 (2020): 529–96.

18. Laurel Harbridge, *Is Bipartisanship Dead?: Policy Agreement and Agenda-Setting in the House of Representatives* (Cambridge: Cambridge University Press, 2015).

19. Frances E. Lee, *Beyond Ideology: Politics, Principles, and Partisanship in the U.S. Senate* (Chicago: University of Chicago Press, 2009).

20. Quoted in Matthew Green, *Legislative Hardball: The House Freedom Caucus and the Power of Threat-Making in Congress* (New York: Cambridge University Press, 2019).

21. Quoted in Steven S. Smith, *The Senate Syndrome: The Evolution of Procedural Warfare in the Modern U.S. Senate* (Norman: University of Oklahoma Press, 2014), 178.

22. Ibid., 182.

23. Ibid., 185.

24. Adam Jentleson, *Kill Switch: The Rise of the Modern Senate and the Crippling of American Democracy* (New York: Liveright Publishing Corporation, 2021), 175–77.

25. 113 Cong. Rec. S116 (daily ed. January 8, 2014).

26. Tiefer, *Polarized Congress*, 90.

27. Jentleson, *Kill Switch*, 2.

28. C. Lawrence Evans and Wendy J. Schiller, "The U.S. Senate and the Meaning of Dysfunction," in *Congress Reconsidered,* 12th ed., ed. Lawrence C. Dodd, Bruce I. Oppenheimer, and C. Lawrence Evans (Thousand Oaks, CA: CQ Press, 2021), 10.

29. Sarah A. Binder and Steven S. Smith, *Politics or Principle? Filibustering in the United States Senate* (Washington, DC: Brookings Institution, 1997), 12.

30. Steven S. Smith, *Call to Order: Floor Politics in the House and Senate* (Washington, DC: Brookings Institution, 1989), 113.

31. Walter J. Oleszek et al., *Congressional Procedures and the Policy Process* (Thousand Oaks, CA: CQ Press, 2016).

32. James I. Wallner, *On Parliamentary War* (Ann Arbor: University of Michigan Press, 2017), 114–20.

33. 159 Cong. Rec. S8414 (daily ed. November 21, 2013).

34. 159 Cong Rec. S8415 (daily ed. November 21, 2013).

35. Quotation from Sen. John Cornyn (R-TX), in Wallner, *On Parliamentary War*, 165.

36. 162 Cong. Rec. S1524 (daily ed. March 16, 2016).

37. Evans and Schiller, "Meaning of Dysfunction," 10.

38. 165 Cong. Rec. S2217 (daily ed. April 3, 2019).

39. Molly E. Reynolds, *Exceptions to the Rule: The Politics of Filibuster Limitations in the U.S. Senate* (Washington, DC: Brookings Institution Press, 2017).

40. Robert C. Byrd, *The Senate, 1789–1989,* vol. 2 (Washington, DC: US Government Printing Office, 1988), 162–63. Quoted in Gregory Wawro and Eric Schickler, *Filibuster: Obstruction and Lawmaking in the U.S. Senate* (Princeton, NJ: Princeton University Press, 2006), 7.

41. Jentleson, *Kill Switch*, 7–8.

42. Jennifer Epstein, "Obama's Pen-and-Phone Strategy," *Politico*, January 14, 2014, https://www.politico.com/story/2014/01/obama-state-of-the-union-2014-strategy-102151.

43. Paul Nolette, *Federalism on Trial: State Attorneys General and National Policymaking in Contemporary America* (Lawrence: University Press of Kansas, 2015).

44. For a more detailed account, see Philip A. Wallach, "When Can You Teach an Old Law New Tricks," *New York University Journal of Legislation and Public Policy* 16 (2013): 689–755, 732–49.

45. Ryan Lizza, "As the World Burns," *New Yorker*, October 3, 2010, http://www.newyorker.com/magazine/2010/10/11/as-the-world-burns.

46. Philip A. Wallach, "Where Does US Climate Policy Stand in 2019?," Brookings Institution, March 22, 2019, https://www.brookings.edu/2019/03/22/where-does-u-s-climate-policy-stand-in-2019/.

47. West Virginia v. Environmental Protection Agency, 597 US ___ (2022).

48. R. Shep Melnick, *The Transformation of Title IX: Regulating Gender Equality in Education* (Washington, DC: Brookings Institution Press, 2018).

49. Smith, *Senate Syndrome*, 190–93.

50. Wolfensberger, *Changing Cultures in Congress*, 38–58.

51. Quoted in Ibid., 56.

52. Josh Blackman, *Unraveled: Obamacare, Religious Liberty, and Executive Power* (New York: Cambridge University Press, 2016).

53. Frank J. Thompson, "Six Ways Trump Has Sabotaged the Affordable Care Act," Brookings Institution, October 9, 2020, https://www.brookings.edu/blog/fixgov/2020/10/09/six-ways-trump-has-sabotaged-the-affordable-care-act/.

54. For one account of that process, see Michael A. Needham and Jacob Reses, "How Republicans Stopped Pretending and Started Getting Real," *Politico Magazine*, May 16, 2017, https://www.politico.com/magazine/story/2017/05/16/how-republicans-stopped-pretending-and-started-getting-real-215141/.

55. Andrew Prokop, "'Stealth and Speed': Senate Republicans' Health Care Strategy Is a Massive Political Gamble," *Vox*, June 21, 2017, https://www.vox.com/policy-and-politics/2017/6/21/15804768/republican-health-bill-secret.

56. Michael Mathes, "McCain's Moment: A 'No' on Health Care," *Yahoo News*, July 28, 2017, https://www.yahoo.com/news/mccains-moment-no-health-care-164533822.html.

57. "Congressional Review Act," George Washington Regulatory Studies Center, https://regulatorystudies.columbian.gwu.edu/congressional-review-act.

58. James M. Curry and Frances E. Lee, *The Limits of Party: Congress and Lawmaking in a Polarized Era* (Chicago: University of Chicago Press, 2020), 24.

59. "Americans' Trust in Military, Scientists Relatively High; Fewer Trust Media, Business Leaders, Elected Officials," Pew Research Center, March 22, 2019, https://www.pewresearch.org/ft_19-03-21_scienceconfidence_americans-trust-in-military/.

60. Amanda Chuzi, "Defense Lawmaking," *Columbia Law Review* 120 (2020): 995–1034.

61. "The 2022 Long-Term Budget Outlook," Congressional Budget Office, July 2022, https://www.cbo.gov/publication/58340.

62. Kate P. McClanahan et al., "Continuing Resolutions: Overview of Components and Practices," Congressional Research Service, updated April 19, 2019, https://sgp.fas.org/crs/misc/R42647.pdf.

63. This discussion is adapted from Philip A. Wallach, "Crisis Government," *National Affairs* 44 (Summer 2020): 31–47, https://nationalaffairs.com/publications/detail/crisis-government.

64. See Philip A Wallach, *To the Edge: Legality, Legitimacy, and the Responses to the 2008 Financial Crisis* (Washington, DC: Brookings Institution Press, 2015).

# Chapter 7

1. For reporting, see Sean Sullivan, "House Democrats Urge Obama to Take 'Bold' Action on Immigration," *Washington Post*, November 13, 2014, https://www.washing tonpost.com/news/post-politics/wp/2014/11/13/house-democrats-urge-obama-to-take-bold-action-on-immigration/; for full text of the letter, https://titus.house.gov/news/documentsingle.aspx?DocumentID=2216.

2. "Remarks at the 2008 National Council of La Raza Annual Meeting in San Diego, California," American Presidency Project, UC Santa Barbara, July 13, 2008, https://www.presidency.ucsb.edu/documents/remarks-the-2008-national-council-la-raza-annual-meeting-san-diego-california-0.

3. Elisha Barron, "The Development, Relief, and Education for Alien Minors (DREAM) Act," *Harvard Journal on Legislation* 48 (2011): 623–55.

4. 156 Cong. Rec. 16055 (2010), https://www.senate.gov/legislative/LIS/roll_call_votes/vote1112/vote_111_2_00238.htm.

5. 156 Cong. Rec. 19431 (2010), https://www.senate.gov/legislative/LIS/roll_call_vo tes/vote1112/vote_111_2_00270.htm; 156 Cong. Rec. 22934 (2010), https://www.senate.gov/legislative/LIS/roll_call_votes/vote1112/vote_111_2_00278.htm; David M. Herszenhorn, "Senate Blocks Bill for Young Illegal Immigrants," *New York Times*, December 18, 2010, https://www.nytimes.com/2010/12/19/us/politics/19im mig.html.

6. "Remarks at Univision's 'Es el Momento' Town Hall Meeting and a Question-and-Answer Session," American Presidency Project, UC Santa Barbara, March 28, 2011, https://www.presidency.ucsb.edu/documents/remarks-univisions-es-el-momento-town-hall-meeting-and-question-and-answer-session.

7. Barack Obama, "Remarks by the President on Immigration," White House, June 15, 2012, https://obamawhitehouse.archives.gov/the-press-office/2012/06/15/remarks-president-immigration.

8. Letter from Senator Harry Reid and 19 other Democratic Senators, to President Barack Obama (April 13, 2011), available at https://www.durbin.senate.gov/newsr oom/press-releases/durbin-reid-20-senate-democrats-write-obama-on-current-situation-of-dream-act-students.

9. Barbara E. Armacost, "'Sanctuary' Laws: The New Immigration Federalism," *Michigan State Law Review* 2016, no. 5 (2016): 1197–265.

10. Abby Budiman, "Key Findings about U.S. Immigrants," Pew Research Center, August 20, 2020, https://www.pewresearch.org/fact-tank/2020/08/20/key-findings-about-u-s-immigrants/.

11. Daniel J. Tichenor, "The Congressional Dynamics of Immigration Reform," in *Undecided Nation: Political Gridlock and the Immigration Crisis*, ed. Tony Payan and Erika de la Garza (New York: Springer, 2014), 23–48.

12. "Immigration Reform Measure Dies in House," in *CQ Almanac 1982* (Washington, DC: Congressional Quarterly, 1983), 405–10.

13. "Immigration Reform Dies at Session's End," in *CQ Almanac 1984* (Washington, DC: Congressional Quarterly, 1985), 229–38.

14. "Congress Clears Overhaul of Immigration Law," in *CQ Almanac 1986* (Washington, DC: Congressional Quarterly, 1987), 61–67.

15. David J. Bier, "The Facts about E-Verify: Use Rates, Errors, and Effects on Illegal Employment," Cato Institute, January 31, 2019, https://www.cato.org/blog/facts-about-e-verify-use-rates-errors-effects-illegal-employment.

16. Mark Hugo Lopez et al., "Key Facts about the Changing U.S. Unauthorized Immigrant Population," Pew Research Center, April 13, 2021, https://www.pewresearch.org/fact-tank/2021/04/13/key-facts-about-the-changing-u-s-unauthorized-immigrant-population/.

17. Mark Krikorian, "Downsizing Illegal Immigration: A Strategy of Attrition through Enforcement," Center for Immigration Studies, May 1, 2005, https://cis.org/Report/Downsizing-Illegal-Immigration.

18. Laura Meckler, "Former Speaker Hastert Calls for Immigration Overhaul," *Wall Street Journal*, January 30, 2014, https://www.wsj.com/articles/BL-WB-43243.

19. "Guest Worker, Citizenship Issues Divide GOP and Stymie Overhaul," in *CQ Almanac 2006* (Washington, DC: Congressional Quarterly, 2007), 14-3–14-6.

20. Associated Press, "'Gang of 12' Mulls Over Immigration Bill," *NBC News*, May 24, 2007, https://www.nbcnews.com/id/wbna18842287.

21. Michael Sandler and Jonathan Allen, "Senate Gives Up on Immigration Bill," *CQ TODAY*, June 7, 2007, https://web.archive.org/web/20070705193655/http://public.cq.com/docs/cqt/news110-000002527366.html.

22. Gail Russel Chaddock, "Senate Makes New Try for Immigration Bill," *Christian Science Monitor*, June 21, 2007, https://www.csmonitor.com/2007/0621/p01s01-uspo.html.

23. Maura Reynolds, "Reid Fast-Tracks Revived Immigration Bill," *Los Angeles Times*, June 19, 2007, https://www.latimes.com/archives/la-xpm-2007-jun-19-na-immig19-story.html.

24. Robert Pear and Carl Hulse, "Immigration Bill Fails to Survive Senate Vote," *New York Times*, June 28, 2007, https://www.nytimes.com/2007/06/28/washington/28cnd-immig.html.

25. Quoted in Tichenor, "The Congressional Dynamics of Immigration Reform," 45.

26. Barron, "The DREAM Act," 640–47.

27. Ed O'Keefe, "Senate Approves Comprehensive Immigration Bill," *Washington Post*, June 27, 2013, https://www.washingtonpost.com/politics/senate-poised-to-approve-massive-immigration-bill/2013/06/27/87168096-df32-11e2-b2d4-ea6d8f477a01_story.html.

28. Sarah A. Binder, "Oh 113th Congress Hastert Rule, We Hardly Knew Ye!," Brookings, January 17, 2013, https://www.brookings.edu/blog/up-front/2013/01/17/oh-113th-congress-hastert-rule-we-hardly-knew-ye/; Charles Tiefer, *The Polarized Congress: The Post-Traditional Procedure of Its Current Struggles* (Lanham, MD: University Press of America, 2016), 58–59.

29. Liz Halloran, "House GOP: We Won't Consider Senate Immigration Bill," *NPR*, July 10, 2013, https://www.npr.org/sections/itsallpolitics/2013/07/10/200860744/house-gop-we-wont-consider-senate-immigration-bill.

30. Aaron Blake, "The House Will Not Pass the Senate Immigration Bill. Here's Why," *Washington Post*, July 23, 2013, https://www.washingtonpost.com/news/the-fix/wp/2013/07/23/the-house-will-not-pass-the-senate-immigration-bill-heres-why/.

31. Barack Obama, "Remarks by the President on Border Security and Immigration Reform," White House, June 30, 2014, https://obamawhitehouse.archives.gov/the-press-office/2014/06/30/remarks-president-border-security-and-immigration-reform.

32. *Texas v. United States*, 809 F.3d 134 (C.A. 5th, 2015); 579 US __ (2016).

33. "Judge's Ruling Declaring DACA Illegal and Blocking New Applicants," *CNN*, July 16, 2021, https://www.cnn.com/2021/07/16/politics/daca-ruling-071621/index.html.

34. Russell Berman, "The Great Senate Immigration Debate That Wasn't," *The Atlantic*, February 13, 2018, https://www.theatlantic.com/politics/archive/2018/02/the-great-senate-immigration-debate-that-wasnt/553253/.

35. Dylan Scott, "The Senate Put 4 Immigration Bills Up for a Vote. They All Failed," *Vox*, February 15, 2018, https://www.vox.com/policy-and-politics/2018/2/15/17017682/senate-immigration-daca-bill-vote-failed; C. Lawrence Evans and Wendy J. Schiller, "The U.S. Senate and the Meaning of Dysfunction," in *Congress Reconsidered*, ed. Lawrence C. Dodd et al. (Washington, DC: CQ Press, 2020), 3–32, 4–6.

36. Lindsey McPherson, "At Least 17 Republicans Sign Discharge Petition to Force Votes on DACA Bills," *Roll Call*, May 9, 2018, https://rollcall.com/2018/05/09/at-least-17-republicans-sign-discharge-petition-to-force-votes-on-daca-bills/.

37. Rachael Bade and John Bresnahan, "McCarthy to GOP: DACA Vote Could Cost Us the House," *Politico*, May 16, 2018, https://www.politico.com/story/2018/05/16/republicans-daca-congress-591857.

38. Laurel Harbridge, *Is Bipartisanship Dead?: Policy Agreement and Agenda-Setting in the House of Representatives* (Cambridge: Cambridge University Press, 2015).

39. Thomas Kaplan and Nicholas Fandos, "House Rejects Hard-Line Immigration Bill and Delays Vote on Compromise," *New York Times*, June 21, 2018, https://www.nytimes.com/2018/06/21/us/politics/house-immigration-bills-dreamers-daca-family-separation.html.

40. Ibid.; Thomas Kaplan, "House Rejects Immigration Overhaul despite Trump's Late Plea," *New York Times*, June 27, 2018, https://www.nytimes.com/2018/06/27/us/politics/trump-immigration-house-vote.html; Tara Golshan, "Congress Failed to Do Something on Immigration—Again. Here's Why," *Vox*, July 2, 2018, https://www.vox.com/policy-and-politics/2018/7/2/17509726/congress-fail-immigration-again.

41. William L. Painter and Audrey Singer, "DHS Border Barrier Funding," *Congressional Research Service*, updated January 29, 2020, https://crsreports.congress.gov/product/pdf/R/R45888.

42. Andrew Taylor and Alan Fram, "Congressional Lawmakers Reach Deal on Border Wall Funding," *AP News*, February 11, 2019, https://apnews.com/article/4cffe44a54d541b8bb7ed3a05cb7f056.

43. Donald Trump, "Remarks by President Trump on the National Security and Humanitarian Crisis on Our Southern Border," White House, February 15, 2019,

https://www.whitehouse.gov/briefings-statements/remarks-president-trump-natio
nal-security-humanitariancrisis-southern-border/.

44. H.J. Res. 46, 116th Cong. It passed the House 245–182, 165 Cong. Rec. H2130 (daily ed. February 26, 2019), and the Senate 59–41 165 Cong. Rec. S1882 (daily ed. March 14, 2019).

45. Eliana Johnson and Katie Galioto, "Trump Issues First Veto of His Presidency," *Politico*, March 15, 2019, https://www.politico.com/story/2019/03/15/trump-veto-national-emergency-1223285.

46. The veto override failed in the House 248–181. (Two-thirds is required.) 165 Cong. Rec. H2814 (daily ed. March 26, 2019).

47. Katie Bernard, "Ted Cruz Pushes for El Chapo to Pay for the Wall after Drug Lord's Conviction," *CNN*, February 13, 2019, https://www.cnn.com/2019/02/12/politics/ted-cruz-el-chapo-act-border-wall-drug-lord/index.html.

48. Amy Howe, "Court Allows Border-Wall Construction to Continue," *SCOTUS blog*, July 31, 2020, https://www.scotusblog.com/2020/07/court-allows-border-wall-construction-to-continue/.

49. Nick Niedzwiadek, "Biden Terminating Border Wall Construction Contracts," *Politico*, April 30, 2021, https://www.politico.com/news/2021/04/30/biden-terminates-border-wall-construction-485123.

50. H.R. 3055 and H.R. 3351; Stopping Executive Overreach on Military Appropriations Act, S. 2705; 116th Congress (2019).

51. US Customs and Border Protection, "Border Wall Status—August 7, 2020," press release, August 7, 2020, https://truthout.org/wp-content/uploads/2020/08/CBP-Border-Wall-Status-Paper-as-of-Aug.-7-2020.pdf. This document states that approximately $15 billion was identified for use, of which only around $4.5 billion came from regular congressional appropriations. See also Claire Hansen, "How Much of Trump's Border Wall Was Built?," *U.S. News*, February 7, 2022, https://www.usnews.com/news/politics/articles/2022-02-07/how-much-of-president-donald-trumps-border-wall-was-built.

52. Greg Weiner, *Madison's Metronome: The Constitution, Majority Rule, and the Tempo of American Politics* (Lawrence: University Press of Kansas, 2019), 135.

53. Muzaffar Chishti and Julia Gelatt, "Mounting Backlogs Undermine U.S. Immigration System and Impede Biden Policy Changes," Migration Policy Institute, February 23, 2022, https://www.migrationpolicy.org/article/us-immigration-backlogs-mounting-undermine-biden.

54. Gabriel Poblete and Greg B. Smith, "How Gov. Greg Abbott Exported a Border Crisis to New York City," *Texas Tribune*, August 12, 2022, https://www.texastribune.org/2022/08/12/greg-abbott-eric-adams-migrants-bus/.

55. Sen. Rick Scott (R-FL), "An 11 Point Plan to Rescue America: What Americans Must Do to Save This Country," https://www.politico.com/f/?id=0000017f-1cf5-d281-a7ff-3ffd5f4a0000.

# Chapter 8

1. 166 Cong. Rec. S5387 (daily ed. August 11, 2020).
2. Aaron Ross Coleman, "Cori Bush's Victory Signals the Return of the Protestor-Politician," *Vox*, August 8, 2020, https://www.vox.com/2020/8/8/21358539/cori-bush-victory-lacy-clay-aoc-bernie-sanders-protester-politician.
3. Siobhan Hughes, "How Cori Bush Put Life Story to Work in Eviction Protest at Capitol," *Wall Street Journal*, August 5, 2021, https://www.wsj.com/articles/how-cori-bush-put-life-story-to-work-in-eviction-protest-at-capitol-11628183400.
4. *Alabama Association of Realtors v. United States Department of Health and Human Services*, 141 S. Ct. 2320 (2021), https://www.supremecourt.gov/opinions/20pdf/21a23_ap6c.pdf.
5. For a more detailed version, including additional documentation, see Philip Wallach, "Congress and COVID-19: We Needed Leadership, They Gave Us Cash," American Enterprise Institute, December 2021, from which this chapter is adapted.
6. Jimmy Kolker, "The U.S. Government Was Not Adequately Prepared for Coronavirus at Home or Abroad," *American Diplomacy*, May 2020, https://americandiplomacy.web.unc.edu/2020/05/the-u-s-government-was-not-adequately-prepared-for-coronavirus-at-home-or-abroad/.
7. For a general treatment, see Trust for America's Health, *The Impact of Chronic Underfunding on America's Public Health System: Trends, Risks, and Recommendations, 2020*, April 2020, https://www.tfah.org/wp-content/uploads/2020/04/TFAH2020PublicHealthFunding.pdf.
8. Rebecca Katz, Aurelia Attal-Juncqua, and Julie E. Fischer, "Funding Public Health Emergency Preparedness in the United States," *American Journal of Public Health* 107, no. S2 (2017): S150, https://ajph.aphapublications.org/doi/pdfplus/10.2105/AJPH.2017.303956.
9. Yasmeen Abutaleb and Erica Werner, "HHS Notifies Congress That It May Tap Millions of Additional Dollars for Coronavirus Response," *Washington Post*, February 3, 2020, https://www.washingtonpost.com/health/2020/02/03/hhs-notifies-congress-it-may-tap-millions-additional-dollars-coronavirus-response/.
10. Jongeun You, "Lessons from South Korea's Covid-19 Policy Response," *American Review of Public Administration* 50 (August 2020): 801–8, https://journals.sagepub.com/doi/full/10.1177/0275074020943708; and Seokmin Lee and Tae-Ho Kim, "South Korea's Combating COVID-19 under the Rule of Law," *Verfassungsblog*, April 8, 2021, https://verfassungsblog.de/south-koreas-combating-covid-19-under-the-rule-of-law/.
11. Sayuri Umeda, "South Korea: Parliament Responded Quickly to COVID-19 by Amending Three Acts," Library of Congress, Global Legal Monitor, June 4, 2020, https://www.loc.gov/item/global-legal-monitor/2020-06-04/south-korea-parliament-responded-quickly-to-covid-19-by-amending-three-acts/.
12. 166 Cong. Rec. S519 (daily ed. January 23, 2020).

13. Michael D. Shear et al., "The Lost Month: How a Failure to Test Blinded the U.S. to Covid-19," *New York Times*, March 28, 2020, https://www.nytimes.com/2020/03/28/us/testing-coronavirus-pandemic.html.

14. John Bresnahan and Marianne Levine, "Senate GOP to Begin Talks with Dems on Trillion-Dollar Coronavirus Package," *Politico*, March 19, 2020, https://www.politico.com/news/2020/03/19/senate-negotiates-third-coronavirus-package-137607.

15. See comment of Sen. Patty Murray (D-WA), quoted in Lauren Hirsch and Leslie Josephs, "Coronavirus Stimulus Bill Fails in Key Senate Procedural Vote," CNBC, March 22, 2020, https://www.cnbc.com/2020/03/22/coronavirus-stimulus-congress-struggles-to-reach-a-deal.html.

16. Among Democrats, only Sen. Doug Jones (D-AL) voted with Republicans to take up the bill. 166 Cong. Rec. S1928 (daily ed. March 23, 2020).

17. 166 Cong. Rec. S1935 (daily ed. March 23, 2020).

18. Sen. Dick Durbin (D-IL) explained that the Department of Labor told legislators that instituting a federal payment such that previous earnings would be accounted for would take months, making it impractical to adopt something like Sen. Ben Sasse's (R-NE) amendment. 166 Cong. Rec. S2047 (daily ed. March 25, 2020).

19. 166 Cong. Rec. H1827 (daily ed. March 27, 2020).

20. 166 Cong. Rec. H1864 (daily ed. March 27, 2020). For a narrative account and reactions to Massie, see Quint Forgey, "Both Parties Pile on Massie after Effort to Force Recorded Vote Flops," *Politico*, March 27, 2020, https://www.politico.com/news/2020/03/27/trump-congressman-thomas-massie-coronavirus-vote-151523. Massie easily won his June primary.

21. Jordain Carney, "Senate Passes $484B Coronavirus Relief Package," *The Hill*, April 21, 2020, https://thehill.com/homenews/senate/493959-senate-passes-484b-coronavirus-relief-package.

22. Quoted in Lauren Egan et al., "Senate Passes Massive $2 Trillion Coronavirus Spending Bill," NBC News, March 26, 2020, https://www.nbcnews.com/politics/congress/white-house-senate-reach-deal-massive-2-trillion-coronavirus-spending-n1168136.

23. 166 Cong. Rec. H2024 (daily ed. May 15, 2020).

24. See *McCarthy v. Pelosi*, 480 F. Supp. 3d 28 (D.D.C., 2020); and *McCarthy v. Pelosi*, 5 F.4th 34 (D.C. Cir., 2021).

25. Molly E. Reynolds et al., "Proxy Voting Turns One: The Past, Present, and Future of Remote Voting in the House," Brookings Institution, May 21, 2021, https://www.brookings.edu/blog/fixgov/2021/05/21/proxy-voting-turns-one-the-past-present-and-future-of-remote-voting-in-the-house/.

26. Maggie Haberman, Emily Cochrane, and Jim Tankersley, "Sidestepping Congress, Trump Signs Executive Measures for Pandemic Relief," *New York Times*, September 9, 2021, https://www.nytimes.com/2020/08/08/us/politics/trump-stimulus-bill-coronavirus.html; and Yuval Levin and Adam J. White, "The Return of Pen and Phone Constitutionalism," *National Review*, August 8, 2020, https://www.nationalreview.com/2020/08/the-return-of-pen-and-phone-constitutionalism/.

27. Alan D. Viard, "Payroll Tax Deferral Ends with a Whimper," AEIdeas, January 13, 2021, https://www.aei.org/economics/payroll-tax-deferral-ends-with-a-whimper/.

28. Committee on Ways and Means, "How It Works: Paying the Unemployed through President Trump's Executive Order," August 14, 2020, https://gop-waysandmeans.house.gov/how-it-works-paying-the-unemployed-through-president-trumps-executive-order/.

29. Congressional Budget Office, "Senate Amendment 2137 to H.R. 3684, the Infrastructure Investment and Jobs Act, as Proposed on August 1, 2021," August 9, 2021, 10, https://www.cbo.gov/system/files/2021-08/hr3684_infrastructure.pdf; and Infrastructure Investment and Jobs Act, H.R. 3684, 117th Cong. § 90007 (2021).

30. Emily Berman, "The Roles of the State and Federal Governments in a Pandemic," *Journal of National Security Law & Policy* 11 (2020): 61–81, https://jnslp.com/wp-content/uploads/2020/12/The-Roles-of-the-State-and-Federal-Governments-in-a-Pandemic_2.pdf.

31. For a timeline of this evolution, see Marie Fazio, "How Mask Guidelines Have Evolved," *New York Times*, April 27, 2021, https://www.nytimes.com/2021/04/27/science/face-mask-guidelines-timeline.html.

32. Yasmin Tayag, "Why Are Americans Still—Still!—Wearing Cloth Masks?," *The Atlantic*, October 4, 2021, https://www.theatlantic.com/health/archive/2021/10/why-americans-wear-cloth-masks/620296/.

33. Jon Valant, "School Reopening Plans Linked to Politics Rather Than Public Health," Brookings Institution, July 29, 2020, https://www.brookings.edu/blog/brown-center-chalkboard/2020/07/29/school-reopening-plans-linked-to-politics-rather-than-public-health/.

34. Jim Small, "Ducey: Schools Won't Get COVID Aid Money If They Require Masks," Arizona Mirror, August 17, 2021, https://www.azmirror.com/2021/08/17/ducey-schools-wont-get-covid-aid-money-if-they-require-masks/.

35. Gottlieb, *Uncontrolled Spread*, 212–14.

36. Zeynep Tufekci, "Why Did It Take So Long to Accept the Facts about Covid?," *New York Times*, May 7, 2021, https://www.nytimes.com/2021/05/07/opinion/coronavirus-airborne-transmission.html.

37. Lena H. Sun and Joel Achenbach, "CDC's Credibility Is Eroded by Internal Blunders and External Attacks as Coronavirus Vaccine Campaigns Loom," *Washington Post*, September 28, 2020, https://www.washingtonpost.com/health/2020/09/28/cdc-under-attack/. For a later look, see Jeneen Interlandi, "Can the C.D.C. Be Fixed?," *New York Times Magazine*, June 16, 2021, https://www.nytimes.com/2021/06/16/magazine/cdc-covid-response.html.

38. Viswadha Chander, "CDC Revises Guidance, Says COVID-19 Can Spread Through Virus Lingering in Air," Reuters, October 5, 2020, https://www.reuters.com/article/health-coronavirus-cdc-airborne-int/cdc-revises-guidance-says-covid-19-can-spread-through-virus-lingering-in-air-idUSKBN26Q2UB.

39. Tufekci, "Why Did It Take so Long to Accept the Facts about Covid?"

40. They emphasized the federal government's jurisdiction with reference to the needs of students with special needs, to whom the Individuals with Disabilities Education

Act gives certain guarantees. See Andrew Ujifusa, "Why an Influential Member of Congress Wants a National Investigation into School Closures," *Education Week*, March 15, 2021, https://www.edweek.org/policy-politics/why-an-influential-member-of-congress-wants-a-national-investigation-into-school-closures/2021/03.

41. US testing positivity rates were consistently higher than peer nations', except for the deadly winter 2020–21 period, when they were roughly comparable. See Our World in Data, Coronavirus Data Explorer, https://ourworldindata.org/explorers/coronavirus-data-explorer.

42. Olga Khazan, "The 4 Key Reasons the U.S. Is So Behind on Coronavirus Testing," *The Atlantic*, March 13, 2020, https://www.theatlantic.com/health/archive/2020/03/why-coronavirus-testing-us-so-delayed/607954/.

43. Atul Gawande, "We Can Solve the Coronavirus-Test Mess Now—If We Want To," *New Yorker*, September 2, 2020, https://www.newyorker.com/science/medical-dispatch/we-can-solve-the-coronavirus-test-mess-now-if-we-want-to; Ronald Bailey, "Why the Hell Has the FDA Not Approved Cheap Rapid COVID-19 Self-Tests Yet?," *Reason*, September 9, 2021, https://reason.com/2021/09/09/why-the-hell-has-the-fda-not-approved-cheap-rapid-covid-19-self-tests-yet/.

44. Hannah Norman, "Why At-Home Rapid Covid Tests Cost So Much, Even after Biden's Push for Lower Prices," KHN, September 13, 2021, https://khn.org/news/article/home-rapid-covid-tests-cost-biden-push-to-lower-prices/. Finally, on October 4, 2021, the FDA approved another manufacturer's at-home test and costs came down.

45. Susie Neilson, Andrew Dunn, and Aria Bendix, "Moderna's Groundbreaking Coronavirus Vaccine Was Designed in Just 2 Days," Insider, December 19, 2020, https://www.businessinsider.com/moderna-designed-coronavirus-vaccine-in-2-days-2020-11.

46. BBC, "Covid-19: World's First Human Challenge Trials to Start in UK," February 17, 2021, https://www.bbc.com/news/health-56097088.

47. PREVENT Pandemics Act, S. 3799, 117th Congress (2022); Consolidated Appropriations Act, H.R.2617, 117th Congress (2022), Division FF, Title II.

48. Kathleen Dooling et al., "The Advisory Committee on Immunization Practices' Updated Interim Recommendation for Allocation of COVID-19 Vaccine—United States, December 2020," Centers for Disease Control and Prevention, January 1, 2021, https://www.cdc.gov/mmwr/volumes/69/wr/mm695152e2.htm.

49. Amy Harmon and Danielle Ivory, "How America's Vaccine System Makes People with Health Problems Fight for a Place in Line," *New York Times*, March 9, 2021, https://www.nytimes.com/2021/03/09/us/covid-vaccine-eligible-preexisting-conditions.html.

50. Nambi Ndugga, Samantha Artiga, and Oliva Pham, "How Are States Addressing Racial Equity in COVID-19 Vaccine Efforts?," Kaiser Family Foundation, March 10, 2021, https://www.kff.org/racial-equity-and-health-policy/issue-brief/how-are-states-addressing-racial-equity-in-covid-19-vaccine-efforts/; and Phil Galewitz, "Vermont to Give Minority Residents Vaccine Priority," KHN, April 5, 2021, https://khn.org/news/article/vermont-gives-blacks-and-other-minority-residents-vaccine-priority/.

51. Specifically, they hoped to see an Emergency Use Authorization issued for alternative schedules of second doses for the Pfizer and Moderna vaccines. Six representatives and a senator wrote a letter to reflect that, including Reps. Andy Harris (R-MD), Gregory Murphy (R-NC), Larry Bucshon (R-IN), Paul Gosar (R-AZ), Neal Dunn (R-FL), and Jeff Van Drew (R-NJ) and Sen. Roger Marshall (R-KS). See Andy Harris et al., "Letter to HHS Secretary," March 2, 2021, https://harris.house.gov/sites/harris.house.gov/files/wysiwyg_uploaded/Doc%20Caucus%20Letter%20to%20HHS%20Secretary%20RE%20updated%20vaccine%20data%2003.02.21%20_%20final.pdf.

52. Quotation of Marguerite Roza in Cory Turner, "Schools Are Getting Billions in COVID Relief Money. Here's How They Plan to Spend It," National Public Radio, September 1, 2021, https://www.npr.org/2021/09/01/1033213936/survey-school-superintendents-federal-covid-relief-money-spending.

53. Sam Stein, "Dems Thought Giving Voters Cash Was the Key to Success. So What Happened?," *Politico*, October 11, 2021, https://www.politico.com/news/2021/10/11/democrats-cash-success-covid-relief-515765.

54. Gottlieb, *Uncontrolled Spread*, 235.

# Chapter 9

1. Jonathan Martin, "Manchin Will Seek Re-election but Sends Democrats a Stern Warning," *New York Times*, January 23, 2018, https://www.nytimes.com/2018/01/23/us/politics/manchin-reelection-this-place-sucks.html.

2. William G. Howell and Terry M. Moe, *Relic: How Our Constitution Undermines Effective Government, and Why We Need a More Powerful Presidency* (New York: Basic Books, 2016).

3. For one early example, see Cass Sunstein, *republic.com* (Princeton, NJ: Princeton University Press, 2001).

4. Allison Orr Larsen and Neal Devins, "The Amicus Machine," *Virginia Law Review* 102 (2016): 1901–68.

5. Veronica Stracqualursi, "Newsom Signs California Gun Bill Modeled after Texas Abortion Law," *CNN*, July 22, 2022, https://www.cnn.com/2022/07/22/politics/california-newsom-gun-bill-texas-abortion-law/index.html.

6. Susan Webb Yackee, "Sweet-Talking the Fourth Branch: The Influence of Interest Group Comments on Federal Agency Rulemaking," *Journal of Public Administration Research and Theory* 16, no. 1 (January 1, 2006): 103–24.

7. Lee Drutman, *The Business of America Is Lobbying: How Corporations Became Politicized and Politics Became More Corporate* (New York: Oxford University Press, 2015).

8. Bradford Fitch and Kathy Goldschmidt, "#SocialCongress 2015," Congressional Management Foundation, 2015, http://alliancetoendhunger.org/wp-content/uploads/2018/03/2015-CMF-social-congress.pdf.

9. Maggie Macdonald and Whitney Hua, "Mind the Gap? Negative Tweets & Partisanship in the House of Representatives," *APSA Preprints*, September 9, 2020, https://doi.org/10.33774/apsa-2020-qj6hx.

10. Jon Askonas and Ari Schulman, "Why Speech Platforms Can Never Escape Politics," *National Affairs* 50 (Winter 2022), https://www.nationalaffairs.com/why-speech-platforms-can-never-escape-politics.

11. Rachel Kleinfeld, "The U.S. Shows All the Signs of a Country Spiraling toward Political Violence," *Washington Post*, https://www.washingtonpost.com/outlook/america-political-violence-risk/2020/09/11/be924628-f388-11ea-999c-67ff7bf6a9d2_story.html.

# Chapter 10

1. Bernard Crick, *In Defense of Politics* (London: Weidenfeld & Nicolson, 1992), 73.

2. Stop the Shutdowns Transferring Unnecessary Pain and Inflicting Damage In The coming Years (STUPIDITY) Act, S.198, 116th Cong. (2019).

3. Connoisseurs of legislative procedure may wonder how this could be made self-executing, and perhaps it could not. Instead, it would establish that a motion to proceed to the president's bill would be in order and take precedence over all other business, and perhaps include some mechanism to ensure that neither chamber could duck its responsibility to take up the bill by recess or adjournment.

4. Alayna Treene, "Elizabeth Warren Calls Senate Filibuster Racist," *Axios*, March 18, 2021, https://www.axios.com/elizabeth-warren-senate-filibuster-racist-2a820f54-45d6-4047-bb91-96cdc6c296e8.html.

5. "Majority of Voters Support a Federal Jobs Program," *The Hill*, October 30, 2019, https://thehill.com/hilltv/468236-majority-of-voters-support-a-federal-jobs-guarantee-program; Eduardo Porter, "Should the Feds Guarantee You a Job?," *New York Times*, February 18, 2021, https://www.nytimes.com/2021/02/18/business/economy/job-guarantee.html.

6. William G. Howell and Terry M. Moe, *Relic: How Our Constitution Undermines Effective Government, and Why We Need a More Powerful Presidency* (New York: Basic Books, 2016).

7. Jessica Tollestrup, "Automatic Continuing Resolutions: Background and Overview of Recent Proposals," Congressional Research Service, August 20, 2015, https://sgp.fas.org/crs/misc/R41948.pdf; Erich Warner, "Senate Republicans Hatch Plan to Prevent Future Shutdowns," *Government Executive*, January 14, 2019, https://www.govexec.com/management/2019/01/senate-republicans-hatch-plan-prevent-future-shutdowns/154160/.

8. Clare Foran and Ashley Killough, "Congress Seeks New Ways to Prevent Shutdowns from Happening," *CNN*, January 30, 2019, https://www.cnn.com/2019/01/30/politics/shutdown-prevention-congress/index.html.

9. See Herbert Storing, "Political Parties and the Bureaucracy," in *Toward a More Perfect Union: Writings of Herbert J. Storing*, ed. Joseph M. Bessette (Washington, DC: AEI Press, 1995), 307–26; Christopher J. Bickerton and Carlo Invernizzi Accetti, *Technopopulism: The New Logic of Democratic Politics* (Oxford: Oxford University Press, 2021).

10. For related thoughts, see Matthew B. Crawford, "Defying the Data Priests: On the Threat of Rule by Algorithmic Fiat," *New Atlantis*, Fall 2021, https://www.thenewatlantis.com/publications/defying-the-data-priests.

11. H. L. Mencken, *A Little Book in C Major* (New York: John Lane Company, 1916), 19.

12. "The Project Gutenberg EBook of Tacitus' A Dialogue Concerning Oratory, by Arthur Murphy, Esq.," accessed June 17, 2021, https://www.gutenberg.org/files/15017/15017-h/15017-h.htm#DXXXVII.

13. Melinda N. Ritchie and Hye Young You, "Legislators as Lobbyists," *Legislative Studies Quarterly* 44, no. 1 (2019): 65–95.

14. Alexander C. Furnas, "Legislative Staff Are Spending an Increasing Amount of Time on Constituent Services," *Legbranch.org*, April 11, 2018, https://www.legbranch.org/2018-4-11-legislative-staff-are-spending-an-increasing-amount-of-time-on-constituent-services/.

15. Morris P. Fiorina, "The Case of the Vanishing Marginals: The Bureaucracy Did It," *American Political Science Review* 71, no. 1 (1977): 177–81.

16. Kenneth Lowande, "Who Polices the Administrative State?," *American Political Science Review* 112, no. 4 (November 2018): 874–90.

17. The modern literature on authoritarian legislatures is quite rich; I am especially informed by Rory Truex, *Making Autocracy Work: Representation and Responsiveness in Modern China*, Cambridge Studies in Comparative Politics (Cambridge: Cambridge University Press, 2016); Scott Williamson and Beatriz Magaloni, "Legislatures and Policy Making in Authoritarian Regimes," *Comparative Political Studies* 53, no. 9 (August 1, 2020): 1525–43; and Jennifer Gandhi, Ben Noble, and Milan Svolik, "Legislatures and Legislative Politics without Democracy," *Comparative Political Studies* 53, no. 9 (August 1, 2020): 1359–79.

18. James Madison, "Federalist No. 10," in *The Federalist Papers*, ed. George W. Carey and James McClellan (Indianapolis: Liberty Fund, 2001), 42–48.

19. James A. Morone, *The Democratic Wish: Popular Participation and the Limits of American Government* (New York: Basic Books, 1990), 6.

20. James Burnham, *Congress and the American Tradition* (New York: Henry Regnery Company, 1959), 342–43.

# Chapter 11

1. James Burnham, *Congress and the American Tradition* (New York: Henry Regnery Company, 1959), 321.

2. Edward-Isaac Dovere, "The Next Face of the Democratic Party," *The Atlantic*, August 10, 2021, https://www.theatlantic.com/politics/archive/2021/08/hakeem-jeffries-nancy-pelosi-speaker-house/619695/.

3. See "Rules of the Democratic Caucus, 117th Congress," Adopted January 14, 2021, Rule 34, https://www.dems.gov/download/dem-caucus-rules-117th.

4. Philp Wallach and Kevin R. Kosar, "The Case for a Congressional Regulation Office," *National Affairs* 29 (Fall 2016): 56–68, http://www.nationalaffairs.com/publications/detail/the-case-for-a-congressional-regulation-office.

5. Jeffrey M. Jones, "U.S. Political Party Preferences Shifted Greatly During 2021," Gallup, January 17, 2022, https://news.gallup.com/poll/388781/political-party-preferences-shifted-greatly-during-2021.aspx. More generally, see Morris P. Fiorina, *Unstable Majorities: Polarization, Party Sorting, and Political Stalemate* (Stanford, CA: Hoover Institution Press, 2017).

6. FAANG is an acronym for five of the largest technology companies: Facebook, Apple, Amazon, Netflix, and Google.

7. Steven M. Teles and Robert P. Saldin, "The Future Is Faction," *National Affairs* 45 (Fall 2020), 181–96, 183–84.

8. Ruth Bloch Rubin, *Building the Bloc: Intraparty Organization in the US Congress* (New York: Cambridge University Press, 2017).

9. Teles and Saldin, "The Future Is Faction," 184.

10. Lee Drutman, *Breaking the Two-Party Doom Loop: The Case for Multiparty Democracy in America* (New York: Oxford University Press, 2020).

11. Lee Drutman, Jonathan D. Cohen, Yuval Levin, and Norman J. Ornstein, "The Case for Enlarging the House of Representatives," American Academy of Arts and Sciences, https://www.amacad.org/ourcommonpurpose/enlarging-the-house/section/4.

12. Daniel J. Hopkins, *The Increasingly United States: How and Why American Political Behavior Nationalized* (Chicago: University of Chicago Press, 2018).

13. Michael J. Malbin, "A Neo-Madisonian Perspective on Campaign Finance Reform, Institutions, Pluralism, and Small Donors," *University of Pennsylvania Journal of Constitutional Law* 23 (2021): 907–59.

14. Nick Troiano, "Party Primaries Must Go," *The Atlantic*, March 30, 2021, https://www.theatlantic.com/ideas/archive/2021/03/party-primaries-must-go/618428/.

15. See the excellent discussion in Kevin R. Kosar, "What Is the Role of the Senate's Majority Leader? (with James Wallner)," AEI Understanding Congress Podcast, Episode 17, December 6, 2021, https://www.aei.org/podcast/what-is-the-role-of-the-senates-majority-leader-with-james-wallner/.

16. Mike Gallagher, "How to Salvage Congress," *The Atlantic*, November 13, 2018, https://www.theatlantic.com/ideas/archive/2018/11/gallagher-congress/575689/.

17. Thomas Spulak and George Crawford, "How to Fix Congress in One Step," *Politico*, September 19, 2018, https://www.politico.com/agenda/story/2018/09/19/house-rules-committee-congress-000699/.

18. James Burnham, *Congress and the American Tradition* (New York: Henry Regnery Company, 1959), 347.

19. For example, see David Schoenbrod, *Power without Responsibility: How Congress Abuses the People through Delegation* (New Haven, CT: Yale University Press, 2008); Philip Hamburger, *Is Administrative Law Unlawful?* (Chicago: University of Chicago Press, 2014).

20. Philip A. Wallach, "Losing Hold of the REINS: How Republicans' Attempt to Cut Back on Regulations Has Impeded Congress's Ability to Assert Itself," *Brookings*, May 2, 2019, https://www.brookings.edu/research/losing-hold-of-the-reins/.

21. Burnham, *Congress and the American Tradition*, 278.

22. Alexis de Tocqueville, *Democracy in America*, trans. Harvey C. Mansfield and Delba Winthrop (Chicago: University of Chicago Press, 2000), vol. 1, part 2, chapter 6, 223.

## Postscript

1. E.g., Senate Majority Leader Trent Lott's remarks on the process for a Y2K liability bill in 1999: "I am going to have to take actions to block irrelevant, non-germane amendments that are just part of a political agenda." Congressional Record 106 (April 28, 1999), S4329.

2. Walter Lippmann, *A Preface to Morals* (New York: MacMillan, 1929), 281–82.

# Index